Integrated Chinese

CHENG & TSUI PUBLICATIONS OF RELATED INTEREST

Making Connections: Enhance Your Listening Comprehension in Chinese
(Text & Audio CD Set)
Madeline K. Spring

Simplified Characters   0-88727-366-1
Traditional Characters   0-88727-365-3

Chinese BuilderCards: The Lightning Path to Mastering Vocabulary
Song Jiang

Simplified Characters   0-88727-434-X
Traditional Characters   0-88727-426-9

Cheng & Tsui Chinese-Pinyin-English Dictionary for Learners
Wang Huan, Editor-in-Chief

Paperback   0-88727-316-5

Cheng & Tsui Chinese Character Dictionary
Wang Huidi, Editor-in-Chief

Paperback   0-88727-314-9

Crossing Paths: Living and Learning in China,
An Intermediate Chinese Course
Hong Gang Jin and De Bao Xu, with Der-lin Chao, Yea-fen Chen, and Min Chen

Paperback & Audio CD Set   0-88727-370-X

Shifting Tides: Culture in Contemporary China,
An Intermediate Chinese Course
Hong Gang Jin and De Bao Xu, with Songren Cui, Yea-fen Chen, and Yin Zhang

Paperback & Audio CD Set   0-88727-3726

Pop Chinese: A Cheng & Tsui Handbook of Contemporary Colloquial
Expressions
Yu Feng, Yaohua Shi, Zhijie Jia, Judith M. Amory, and Jie Cai

Paperback   0-88727-424-2

Please visit www.cheng-tsui.com for more information on these and many
other language-learning resources, or visit www.webtech.cheng-tsui.com for
information on web-based and downloadable products.

Integrated Chinese

中文聽説讀寫／中文听说读写

Traditional and Simplified Character Edition

TEXTBOOK

2nd Edition

Yuehua Liu and Tao-chung Yao
Yaohua Shi and Nyan-Ping Bi

CHENG & TSUI COMPANY ▲ Boston

10 09 08 07 06   2 3 4 5 6 7 8 9 10

Published by
Cheng & Tsui Company
25 West Street
Boston, MA 02111-1213 USA
Fax (617) 426-3669
www.cheng-tsui.com
"Bringing Asia to the World"™

Library of Congress Cataloging-in-Publication Data

Integrated Chinese = [Zhong wen ting shuo du xie].
Traditional and simplified character edition. Level 2/Tao-chung Yao ... [et al.].— 2nd ed.
      p. cm. — (C&T Asian language series)
Chinese and English.
Includes index.

ISBN 13: 978-0-88727-480-0
ISBN 10: 0-88727-480-3

1. Chinese language—Textbooks for foreign speakers—English. I. Title: Zhong wen ting shuo du xie. II. Yao, Daozhong. III. Series: C&T Asian languages series.
PL1129.E5I683 2004b
495.1'82421—dc22

                                                  2005047085

The *Integrated Chinese* series includes textbooks, workbooks, character workbooks, audio products, multimedia products, teacher's resources, and more. Visit www.cheng-tsui.com for more information on the other components of *Integrated Chinese*.

Printed in the United States of America

THE INTEGRATED CHINESE SERIES

The *Integrated Chinese* series is a two-year course that includes textbooks, workbooks, character workbooks, audio CDs, CD-ROMs, DVDs, and teacher's resources.

Textbooks introduce Chinese language and culture through a series of dialogues and narratives, with culture notes, language use and grammar explanations, and exercises.

Workbooks follow the format of the textbooks and contain a wide range of integrated activities that teach the four language skills of listening, speaking, reading, and writing.

Character Workbooks help students learn Chinese characters in their correct stroke order. Special emphasis is placed on the radicals that are frequently used to compose Chinese characters.

Audio CDs include the narratives, dialogues and vocabulary presented in the textbooks, as well as pronunciation and listening exercises that correspond to the workbooks.

Teacher's Resources contain answer keys, transcripts of listening exercises, grammar notes, and helpful guidance on using the series in the classroom. Visit www.webtech.cheng-tsui.com to obtain the latest teacher resources.

Multimedia CD-ROMs for Level 1 Part 1 are divided into sections of listening, speaking, reading, and writing, and feature a variety of supplemental interactive games and activities for students to test their skills and get instant feedback.

Workbook DVD shows listening comprehension dialogues from the Level 1 Part 1 Workbook, presented in contemporary settings in color video format.

PUBLISHER'S NOTE

When *Integrated Chinese* was first published in 1997, it set a new standard with its focus on the development and integration of the four language skills (listening, speaking, reading, and writing). Today, to further enrich the learning experience of the many users of *Integrated Chinese* worldwide, the Cheng & Tsui Company is pleased to offer the revised, updated and expanded second edition of *Integrated Chinese*. We would like to thank the many teachers and students who, by offering their valuable insights and suggestions, have helped *Integrated Chinese* evolve and keep pace with the many positive changes in the field of Chinese language instruction. *Integrated Chinese* continues to offer comprehensive language instruction, with many new features.

The Cheng & Tsui Asian Language Series is designed to publish and widely distribute quality language learning materials created by leading instructors from around the world. We welcome readers' comments and suggestions concerning the publications in this series. Please feel free to send feedback to our Editorial Department (e-mail: editor@cheng-tsui.com), or to contact the following members of our Editorial Board.

Professor Shou-hsin Teng, Chief Editor
3 Coach Lane, Amherst, MA 01002

Dana Scott Bourgerie
Asian and Near Eastern Languages
Brigham Young University, Provo, UT 84602

Professor Samuel Cheung
Dept. of Chinese, Chinese University of Hong Kong
Shatin, Hong Kong

Professor Ying-che Li
Dept. of East Asian Languages, University of Hawaii
Honolulu, HI 96822

Professor Timothy Light
Dept. of Comparative Religion, Western Michigan University
Kalamazoo, MI 49008

CONTENTS

Lesson 1: 開學 / 开学   1a

    1. The Dynamic Particle 了

    2. The 是…的… Construction

    3. 除了…以外, 還/还… and 除了…以外, 都…

    4. 再説/再说

    1. 有的…,有的… (some…some…)

    2. 覺得 / 觉得 (to feel)

    3. 不見得 / 不见得 (not necessarily)

    4. 對…有好處 / 对…有好处 (good for…)

Lesson 2: 宿舍   18

    1. Word Order in Chinese (I)

    2. Existential Sentences

    3. 比較 / 比较

    4. (方便) 得很

    5. 那(麼) / 那(么)

    6. 恐怕 (I'm afraid; I think perhaps)

    1. 一般 (generally speaking)

    2. 差不多 (about; roughly)

Lesson 3: 在飯館兒 / 在饭馆儿   38

Lesson 4: 買東西 / 买东西   60

▼▼▼▼▼▼▼▼▼▼▼▼▼▼▼▼▼▼▼▼▼▼▼▼▼▼▼▼▼▼▼▼▼▼▼

Lesson 8: 電視和電影的影響 电视和电影的影响   152

Lesson 9: 旅行   174

Lesson 10: 在郵局 ／ 在邮局   200

▼▼▼▼▼▼▼▼▼▼▼▼▼▼▼▼▼▼▼▼▼▼▼▼▼▼▼▼▼▼▼▼▼▼▼▼▼

Lesson 15: 男女平等   318

▼▼▼▼▼▼▼▼▼▼▼▼▼▼▼▼▼▼▼▼▼▼▼▼▼▼▼▼▼▼▼▼▼

Lesson 20: 環境保護 ／ 环境保护   422

Appendix & Indices

The *Integrated Chinese* series is an acclaimed, best-selling introductory course in Mandarin Chinese. With its holistic, integrated focus on the four language skills of listening, speaking, reading, and writing, it teaches all of the basics that are needed by beginning and intermediate students to function in Chinese. *Integrated Chinese* helps students understand how the Chinese language works syntactically and semantically, and how to use Chinese functionally in real life.

The Chinese title of *Integrated Chinese*, which is simply 中文聽説讀寫 / 中文听说读写 (*Zhōngwén Tīng Shuō Dú Xiě*), reflects our belief that a healthy language program should be a well-balanced one. To ensure that students will be strong in all skills, and because we believe that each of the four skills needs special training, the exercises in the *Integrated Chinese* Workbooks are divided into four sections: listening, speaking, reading, and writing. Within each section, there are two types of exercises, namely, traditional exercises (such as fill-in-the-blank, sentence completion, translation, etc.) to help students build a solid foundation, and communication-oriented exercises to prepare students to face the real world.

How *Integrated Chinese* Has Evolved

Integrated Chinese (IC) began in 1993 as a set of course materials for beginning and intermediate Chinese courses at the East Asian Summer Language Institute's Chinese School, at Indiana University. Since that time, it has become a widely used series of Chinese language textbooks in the United States and beyond. Teachers and students appreciate the fact that IC, with its focus on practical, everyday topics and its numerous and varied exercises, helps learners build a solid foundation in the Chinese language.

What's New in the Second Edition

Thanks to all those who have used *Integrated Chinese* and given us the benefit of their suggestions and comments, we have been able to produce a second edition that includes the following improvements:

▲ **Level 2 offers full text in simplified and traditional characters.** The original Level 2 Textbook and Workbook, although geared toward both traditional- and simplified-character learners, contained sections in which only the traditional characters were given. This was of course problematic for students who were principally interested in learning simplified characters. This difficulty has been resolved in the new edition, as we now provide both traditional and simplified characters throughout both the Textbook and the Workbook. Wherever simplified and traditional character versions of a phrase or sentence fit on the same line, they are separated by a slash (/). Wherever simplified and traditional character versions do not fit on the same line, they appear one after another on separate lines. When only one version is given, the reader is to assume that the traditional and simplified characters are the same. For the **authentic materials** and for some photos that contain Chinese characters, we present them in their original forms to preserve their authenticity. An appendix containing alternate character versions is provided as a learning tool for those interested in reading both forms.

▲ A copy of the **pinyin text** is added at the end of each lesson for easy reference.

▲   Many **examples cited in the Grammar Notes section** have been revised to recycle vocabulary learned in previous levels. When words that have not been taught are introduced, glosses are provided. Grammatically incorrect sentences used in the grammar explanations are marked with an asterisk *.

▲   Typographical errors present in the first edition have been corrected, and the content has been carefully edited to ensure accuracy and minimize errors.

▲   The design has been revised and improved for easier use, and the Textbooks feature two colors.

▲   **New photos** provide the reader with visual interest and relevant cultural information.

▲   The Textbook contains a **new appendix of measure words.** This appendix includes all of the measure words introduced in *Integrated Chinese* as well as some additional, useful measure words.

▲   The original **Chinese-English vocabulary index** has been revised, and an **English-Chinese vocabulary index** has been added to the Textbook.

▲   In the Workbook, there is a **new index of vocabulary words** that are glossed in the workbook exercises.

▲   **The Workbook has been extensively revised.** New and different varieties of exercises have been added. Teachers can choose those that best suit their needs. To help students complete some assignments, visual clues are provided in addition to written instructions. More authentic materials are included. The materials are presented in their original characters to preserve their authenticity.

A Note about Vocabulary Lists

In the vocabulary lists, we indicate the part of speech for each vocabulary item. Four-character phrases, idiomatic expressions, and other phrases that cannot be classified by part of speech are left unmarked.

Vocabulary introduced in *Integrated Chinese*, Level 1, and glossed again in *Integrated Chinese*, Level 2, is marked with an asterisk *. Students who have studied the Level 1 text may refer to the first book if needed.

In the vocabulary lists and pinyin texts, we mark the **tone changes** that sometimes occur when a syllable is juxtaposed with another. But in the indices, we give the base tones for easy viewing.

Basic Organizational Principles

The field of language teaching has increasingly held it self-evident that the ultimate goal of learning a language is to communicate in that language. *Integrated Chinese* is a set of materials that gives students grammatical tools and also prepares them to function in a Chinese language environment. The materials cover two years of instruction, with smooth transitions from one level to the next. They first deal with topics of everyday life and gradually move to more abstract subject matter. The materials are not limited to one method or one approach, but instead they blend several teaching approaches that can produce good results. Here are some of the features of *Integrated Chinese* that distinguish it from other Chinese language textbooks:

▼ ▼

Integrating Pedagogical and Authentic Materials

All of the materials in *Integrated Chinese* are graded. We believe that students can grasp the materials better if they learn simple and easy to control language items before the more difficult or complicated ones. We also believe that students should be taught some authentic materials even in the early stage of their language instruction. Therefore, most of the pedagogical materials are actually simulated authentic materials. Real authentic materials (written by native Chinese speakers for native Chinese speakers) are incorporated in the lessons when appropriate.

Integrating Written Style and Spoken Style

One way to measure a person's Chinese proficiency is to see if she or he can handle the "written style" (書面語/书面语, shūmiànyǔ) with ease. The "written style" language is more formal and literary than the "spoken style" (口語/口语, kǒuyǔ); however, it is also widely used in news broadcasts and formal speeches. In addition to "spoken style" Chinese, basic "written style" expressions are gradually introduced in *Integrated Chinese*, Level 2. Although we try to make the dialogues sound as natural as possible, we have avoided using expressions that are excessively colloquial or clearly reflective of regional usages. Where relevant, we have noted lexical differences between mainland China and Taiwan. In principle, we maintain a course that steers between extreme colloquialism and stilted textbook Chinese, between PRC-inflected and ROC-sounding phraseologies. We think this is the right decision for beginning students.

Integrating Traditional and Simplified Characters

We believe that by the second year of studying Chinese, all students should be taught to read both traditional and simplified characters. Therefore, the text of each lesson in *Integrated Chinese*, Level 2 is shown in both forms, and the vocabulary list in each lesson also contains both forms. Considering that students in a second-year Chinese language class might come from different backgrounds and that some may have learned the traditional form and others the simplified form, students should be allowed to write in either traditional or simplified form. It is important that the learner write in one form only, and not a hybrid of both forms. In the Character Workbook, each of the characters is given a frequency indicator based on the Xiàndài Hànyǔ Pínlǜ Cídiǎn 《現代漢語頻率詞典/现代汉语频率词典》, published in 1986 by the Beijing Language Institute.

Integrating Teaching Approaches

Realizing that there is no single teaching method that is adequate in training a student to be proficient in all four language skills, we employ a variety of teaching methods and approaches in *Integrated Chinese* to maximize the teaching results. In addition to the communicative approach, we also use traditional methods such as grammar-translation and direct method. Users of *Integrated Chinese* appreciate that a major strength of the textbooks is their functional orientation. The focus of each lesson of *Integrated Chinese*, Level 2 is not on discrete grammatical points, but rather, we take a holistic approach to language teaching. Vocabulary, grammar, and discursive strategies are integrated in order to facilitate the learner's ability to function appropriately in different sociolinguistic environments. In short, our aim is not the compilation of a grammar manual but rather the presentation of grammar in a way that will allow learners to use the language in context accurately and appropriately.

Reinforcing Grammar Points Introduced in Integrated Chinese Level 1

Integrated Chinese was conceived and designed as a complete series for beginning and intermediate learners. *Integrated Chinese* Level 2 builds on *Integrated Chinese* Level 1, and the basic grammar introduced in Level 1 is reinforced in Level 2. But rather than simply regurgitate Level 1, we focus on some of the most important and complex grammatical phenomena in Level 2. In many instances, our approach is to zero in on the structures (numbering around 40) that are confusing to non-native learners, e.g., the difference between 了 and 過/过, or between 了 and 是...的. Our treatment of grammar is systematically built and spirals upon the foundation of Level 1. (For instance, there is more analysis on various kinds of complements in Level 2.)

Furthermore, we have added grammar notes on topicalization and cohesion—subjects seldom if ever covered in intermediate level textbooks—to help students achieve greater fluency and proficiency at the discourse level. Users of Level 2 will find that many of the grammatical items are presented in a series—Cohesion (I) and (II), Word Order (I), (II), and (III), for instance. In the revised edition, we have also adjusted the numbering of the structures so that they follow the order of their appearance in the texts.

Online Supplements to Integrated Chinese

Integrated Chinese is not a set of course materials that employs printed volumes only. It is, rather, a network of teaching materials that exist in many forms. Teacher keys, software, and more are posted for *Integrated Chinese* users at www.webtech.cheng-tsui.com, Cheng & Tsui Company's online site for downloadable and web-based resources. Please visit this site often for new offerings.

Other materials are available at the IC website, http://eall.hawaii.edu/yao/icusers/, which was set up by Ted Yao, one of the principal *Integrated Chinese* authors, when the original edition of *Integrated Chinese* was published. Thanks to the generosity of teachers and students who are willing to share their materials with other *Integrated Chinese* users, this website is constantly growing, and has many useful links and resources, such as links to resources that show how to write Chinese characters, provide vocabulary practice, and more.

Acknowledgments

Since publication of the first edition of *Integrated Chinese*, in 1997, many teachers and students have given us helpful comments and suggestions. We cannot list all of these individuals here, but we would like to reiterate our genuine appreciation for their help. We do wish to recognize the following individuals who have made recent contributions to the *Integrated Chinese* revision. We are indebted to Tim Richardson, Jeffrey Hayden, Ying Wang, and Xianmin Liu for field-testing the new edition and sending us their comments and corrections. We would also like to thank Chengzhi Chu for letting us try out his "Chinese TA," a computer program designed for Chinese teachers to create and edit teaching materials. This software saved us many hours of work during the revision. Last, but not least, we want to thank James Dew for his superb, professional editorial job, which enhanced both the content and the style of the new edition. We are also grateful to our editors at Cheng & Tsui, Sandra Korinchak and Kristen Wanner, for their painstaking work throughout the editing and production process. Naturally, the authors assume full responsibility for what appears between the covers of the IC series.

▼ ▼

As much as we would like to eradicate all errors in the new edition, some will undoubtedly remain, so please continue to send your comments and corrections to editor@cheng-tsui.com, and accept our sincere thanks for your help.

▼ ▼

▼ ▼

ABBREVIATIONS FOR GRAMMAR TERMS

abbr	*Abbreviation*
adj	*Adjective*
adv	*Adverb*
av	*Auxiliary verb*
ce	*Common expression*
col	*Colloquialism*
conj	*Conjunction*
excl	*Exclamation*
interj	*Interjection*
m	*Measure word*
n	*Noun*
np	*Noun phrase*
nu	*Numeral*
p	*Particle*
pn	*Proper noun*
pr	*Pronoun*
prefix	*Prefix*
prep	*Preposition*
ono	*Onomatopoeic*
qp	*Question particle*
qpr	*Question pronoun*
qw	*Question word*
suffix	*Suffix*
t	*Time word*
v	*Verb*
vc	*Verb plus complement*
vo	*Verb plus object*

第一課 ▲ 開學

NARRATIVE

　　暑假結束了，學校就要開學了。 學生從各個地方回到了學校。 張天明是一年級的學生，家在波士頓，離這裏很遠。 他是自己一個人坐飛機來的。辦完了註冊手續，他來到了新生宿舍。

DIALOGUE

張天明： 人怎麼這麼多？

柯林： 你是新生嗎？

張天明： 是，我是。 你呢？

柯林： 我是老生，在這兒幫新生搬東西。 你是中國人吧？

張天明： 我祖籍是中國，可是我是在美國出生、在美國長大的。

柯林： 請問，你的中文名字是 ...

張天明： 我姓張，弓長張，也就是一張紙的張，名字是天明，天氣的天，明天的明。

柯林： 我正在學中文，我的中文名字叫柯林。 你手續都辦完了嗎？

第一课 ▲ 开学

NARRATIVE

　　暑假结束了，学校就要开学了。学生从各个地方回到了学校。张天明是一年级的学生，家在波士顿，离这里很远。他是自己一个人坐飞机来的。办完了注册手续，他来到了新生宿舍。

DIALOGUE

张天明：　人怎么这么多？

柯　林：　你是新生吗？

张天明：　是，我是。你呢？

柯　林：　我是老生，在这儿帮新生搬东西。你是中国人吧？

张天明：　我祖籍是中国，可是我是在美国出生、在美国长大的。

柯　林：　请问，你的中文名字是 ...

张天明：　我姓张，弓长张，也就是一张纸的张，名字是天明，天气的天，明天的明。

柯　林：　我正在学中文，我的中文名字叫柯林。你手续都办完了吗？

張天明：　辦完了。你住在哪兒？也住在這兒嗎？

柯林：　　不，這是新生宿舍，我住在校外。

張天明：　住在校內好，還是住在校外好？

柯林：　　有的人喜歡住學校宿舍，覺得方便、安全。有的人喜歡住在校外，
　　　　　覺得省錢。我住在校外，除了為了省錢以外，還為了自由，再說，
　　　　　住在校內也不見得方便。

張天明：　是嗎？那我也搬到校外，好嗎？

柯林：　　你剛來，在學校住對你有好處，可以適應一下大學生活。過些時
　　　　　候如果想搬家，就找我，我幫你找房子。

張天明：　好，謝謝。我離開家的時候，媽媽告訴我："在家靠父母，出門靠
　　　　　朋友。"她說得很有道理。以後請你多幫忙。

柯林：　　沒問題。哎，前邊沒有人了，你可以搬了。我幫你提行李，走吧。

張天明：　好，謝謝。

開學了，學生回到了學校。／开学了，学生回到了学校。

▼ ▼

张天明： 办完了。你住在哪儿？也住在这儿吗？

柯林： 不，这是新生宿舍，我住在校外。

张天明： 住在校内好，还是住在校外好？

柯林： 有的人喜欢住学校宿舍，觉得方便、安全。有的人喜欢住在校外，觉得省钱。我住在校外，除了为了省钱以外，还为了自由，再说，住在校内也不见得方便。

张天明： 是吗？那我也搬到校外，好吗？

柯林： 你刚来，在学校住对你有好处，可以适应一下大学生活。过些时候如果想搬家，就找我，我帮你找房子。

张天明： 好，谢谢。我离开家的时候，妈妈告诉我："在家靠父母，出门靠朋友。"她说得很有道理。以后请你多帮忙。

柯林： 没问题。哎，前边没有人了，你可以搬了。我帮你提行李，走吧。

张天明： 好，谢谢。

张天明是坐飛機來學校的。／张天明是坐飞机来学校的。

VOCABULARY

An asterisk (*) indicates vocabulary that appears in *Integrated Chinese*, Level 1. Parts of speech are indicated for most vocabulary items. Four-character phrases, idiomatic expressions, and other phrases that cannot be categorized by part of speech are left unmarked.

1.	開學	开学	kāi xué	vo	new semester begins; (for a school) to start classes
2.	暑假*		shǔjià	n	summer vacation
3.	結束	结束	jiéshù	v	to end
4.	各*		gè	pr	every; various
5.	年級*	年级	niánjí	n	grade; year
6.	坐*		zuò	v	to sit; to travel by
7.	飛機*	飞机	fēijī	n	airplane
8.	辦*	办	bàn	v	to handle; to do
9.	註冊	注册	zhù cè	vo	to register; to matriculate
10.	手續	手续	shǒuxù	n	procedure
11.	新生		xīnshēng	n	new student
12.	老生		lǎoshēng	n	returning student
13.	搬*		bān	v	to move (objects, or to a new home)
14.	祖籍		zǔjí	n	ancestral home
15.	出生		chūshēng	v	to be born
16.	長大	长大	zhǎng dà	vc	to grow up
17.	弓		gōng	n	bow
18.	長*	长	cháng	adj	long
19.	校外		xiàowài		off campus
20.	校內		xiàonèi		on campus

▼▼▼▼▼▼▼▼▼▼▼▼▼▼▼▼▼▼▼▼▼▼▼▼▼▼▼▼▼▼▼▼▼▼▼▼

21. 方便*　　　　　　　fāngbiàn　　adj　　convenient

住在城裏買東西很方便。／住在城里买东西很方便。

我想問您一個問題, 您現在方便嗎?

我想问您一个问题, 您现在方便吗?

22. 安全　　　　　　　ānquán　　adj/n　　safe; safety

這個地方很安全。／这个地方很安全。

我們宿舍的安全問題很大。／我们宿舍的安全问题很大。

23. 省錢　　省钱　　shěng qián　　vo　　to save money

24. 自由　　　　　　　zìyóu　　adj　　free; unrestricted

25. 再說*　　再说　　zàishuō　　conj　　besides; moreover [see G4]

26. 不見得　　不见得　　bú jiàn de　　　　not necessarily

27. 好處　　好处　　hǎochù　　n　　advantage; benefit

聽錄音對學中文有好處。／听录音对学中文有好处。

坐飛機的好處是很快。／坐飞机的好处是很快。

28. 適應　　适应　　shìyìng　　v　　to adapt; to become accustomed to

我們剛來美國, 對美國的天氣還不適應。

我们刚来美国, 对美国的天气还不适应。

你適應大學的生活了嗎?／你适应大学的生活了吗?

29. 搬家　　　　　　　bān jiā　　vo　　to move (to a different house)

30. 離開　　离开　　lí kāi　　vc　　to leave

31. 靠　　　　　　　　kào　　v　　to depend

一個人應該靠自己, 不應該常常靠別人幫助。

一个人应该靠自己, 不应该常常靠别人帮助。

我不會開車, 去什麼地方都靠你了。

我不会开车, 去什么地方都靠你了。

32. 出門*　　出门　　chū mén　　vo　　to be away from home; to go out

33.	道理		dàoli	n	reason; sense

你說的很有道理。／你说的很有道理。

他這樣做沒有什麼道理。／他这样做没有什么道理。

| 34. | 前邊* | 前边 | qiánbian | | in front |
| 35. | 行李* | | xíngli | n | luggage |

PROPER NOUNS

1.	張天明	张天明	Zhāng Tiānmíng	a masculine name
2.	波士頓	波士顿	Bōshìdùn	Boston
3.	柯林		Kē Lín	Colin

ENLARGED CHARACTERS FOR EASIER VIEWING AND COMPARING

機　　續　　搬　　藉　　離　　邊

机　　续　　搬　　借　　离　　边

Grammar

1. THE DYNAMIC PARTICLE 了

The dynamic particle 了 expresses that an action has occurred or that a state has come into existence. It can appear either after a verb or at the end of a sentence. When 了 appears after a verb, it signals the occurrence of an action. There is usually a time phrase in the sentence.

(1)　昨天晚上我看了一個電影。／昨天晚上我看了一个电影。

    I saw a movie last night.

▼▼▼▼▼▼▼▼▼▼▼▼▼▼▼▼▼▼▼▼▼▼▼▼▼▼▼▼▼▼▼▼▼▼▼▼▼▼

(2) 去年我媽媽去了一次北京, 在那兒住了很長時間。

去年我妈妈去了一次北京, 在那儿住了很长时间。

Last year my mother went to Beijing and stayed there for a long time.

(3) A: 這本書你看了嗎?／这本书你看了吗?

Did you read this book?

B: 我看了。

Yes, I did.

(4) 明天我吃了飯來看你。／明天我吃了饭来看你。

I will come see you tomorrow after dinner.

Notice that 了 is not the equivalent of the past tense. The action can take place in the future as in (4). If there is an object after the verb and 了, the object is usually quantified, as in (1) and the first clause of (2). Under certain circumstances, the object need not be modified in any way. For example:

a. When the object is followed by another 了:

我給小李打了電話了。／我给小李打了电话了。

I called Little Li.

b. When the object is followed by another clause:

張天明買了機票就回家了。／张天明买了机票就回家了。

Zhang Tianming went home right after he bought the plane ticket.

c. When the object refers to a definite person or thing:

昨天我在學校裏看見了王朋。／昨天我在学校里看见了王朋。

Yesterday I saw Wang Peng at school.

When 了 occurs at the end of a sentence, it usually signifies a new situation, some kind of change or the occurrence or realization of an event or state.

(5) 十月了, 天氣慢慢冷了。／十月了, 天气慢慢冷了。

It's October. The weather is gradually turning cold.

(6) 我原來想今天晚上看電影, 可是明天要考試, 所以不看了。

我原来想今天晚上看电影, 可是明天要考试, 所以不看了。

I originally planned to go see a movie tonight, but I have an exam tomorrow, so I won't be going.

(7) A: 你昨天做什麼了? / 你昨天做什么了?

What did you do yesterday?

B: 我搬家了 。

I moved.

Sometimes there isn't a time phrase in the sentence. The time implied is "just now" or "up till now":

(8) A: 你辦註冊手續了嗎? / 你办注册手续了吗?

Did you register?

B: 辦了。 / 办了。

Yes, I did.

A: 等了多長時間? / 等了多长时间?

How long did you wait?

B: 人不多, 只等了五分鐘。 / 人不多, 只等了五分钟。

There weren't many people. I only waited five minutes.

Sometimes there are two verb phrases in a sentence; the first verb phrase is followed by a 了. In that case, the two actions are consecutive.

(9) 他下了飛機就來學校了。 / 他下了飞机就来学校了。

He came to school as soon as he got off the plane.

(10) 我辦了註冊手續就去。 / 我办了注册手续就去。

I'll go as soon as I'm registered.

▼▼▼

In example (9) the time of 來/来 is 下了飛機 / 下了飞机, i.e., right after he disembarked from the plane. In example (10) the time of 去 is 辦了註冊手續 / 办了注册手续, i.e., immediately after registration.

2. THE 是…的… CONSTRUCTION

When both the speaker and the listener know that an action or event has occurred and the speaker wants to draw attention to the time, place, manner, or purpose of the occurrence or to the agent of the action, the 是…的… construction is used. Although we speak of the 是…的… construction, 是 is in fact often optional in such sentences.

(1)   A: 王先生來了嗎? / 王先生来了吗?

Did Mr. Wang come?

   B: 來了。 / 来了。

Yes, he did.

   A: (是)什麼時候來的? / (是)什么时候来的?

When did he come?

   B: (是)昨天晚上來的。 / (是)昨天晚上来的。

Yesterday evening.

   A: (是)跟誰一起來的? / (是)跟谁一起来的?

Whom did he come with?

   B: 是跟他姐姐一起來的。 / 是跟他姐姐一起来的。

With his older sister.

   A: 是坐飛機來的還是開車來的? / 是坐飞机来的还是开车来的?

Did they come by plane or by car?

   B: 開車來的。 / 开车来的。

By car.

(2) 張天明是在波士頓出生的。/ 张天明是在波士顿出生的。

Zhang Tianming was born in Boston.

(The question of birthplace presupposes birth.)

(3) A: 你是大學生嗎? / 你是大学生吗?

Are you an undergrad?

    B: 不, 我是研究生。

No, I am a graduate student.

    A: 你是在哪兒上的大學? / 你是在哪儿上的大学?

Where did you go to college?

    B: 在波士頓大學。/ 在波士顿大学。

Boston University.

To recapitulate, when it is a known fact that an action already took place, to inquire about or explain the time or place of the action one should use 是...的... instead of 了.

3. 除了...以外, 還/还... AND 除了...以外, 都...

除了...以外, 還/还... is an inclusive pattern. The English equivalent is "besides" or "in addition to."

(1) 他除了學中文以外, 還學法文。/ 他除了学中文以外, 还学法文。

(=他學中文, 也學法文。) / (=他学中文, 也学法文。)

Besides Chinese, he's also studying French. (i.e., He's studying both Chinese and French.)

(2) 我們班除了小王以外, 還有小林去過中國。

我们班除了小王以外, 还有小林去过中国。

(=小王和小林都去過中國。) / (=小王和小林都去过中国。)

In our class, besides Little Wang, Little Lin has also been to China.

(Both Little Wang and Little Lin have been to China.)

(3)   昨天張天明除了辦註冊手續以外, 還搬了家。

昨天张天明除了办注册手续以外, 还搬了家。

(=昨天張天明辦註冊手續、搬家。)／(=昨天张天明办注册手续、搬家。)

Besides getting registered, Zhang Tianming also moved yesterday.

(Zhang Tianming registered and moved yesterday.)

除了…以外, 都…, on the other hand, is an exclusive pattern. The English equivalent is "except for":

(1)   除了小柯以外, 我們班的同學都去過中國。

除了小柯以外, 我们班的同学都去过中国。

(=小柯沒去過中國。)／(=小柯没去过中国。)

Except for Little Ke, every student in our class has been to China.

(Little Ke has not been to China.)

(2)   除了看書以外, 晚上什麼事我都願意做。

除了看书以外, 晚上什么事我都愿意做。

(=我晚上不願意看書。)／(=我晚上不愿意看书。)

I'll do anything except read in the evening.

(I don't like to read in the evening.)

4. 再說／再说

再說／再说 is used to provide additional reasons.

(1)   你別走了, 天太晚了, 再說我們要說的事還沒說完呢。

你别走了, 天太晚了, 再说我们要说的事还没说完呢。

Please don't go. It's getting late. Besides, we haven't finished discussing all the things that we need to discuss.

(2)   我不打算學日文, 日文太難, 再說對我的工作也沒有好處。

我不打算学日文, 日文太难, 再说对我的工作也没有好处。

I'm not planning on studying Japanese. Japanese is too difficult. Besides, it isn't helpful for my job.

(3) 她不應該找那樣的人做男朋友, 那個人不太聰明, 再說對她也不好。

她不应该找那样的人做男朋友, 那个人不太聪明, 再说对她也不好。

She shouldn't be dating someone like him. He is not very bright. Besides, he is not very nice to her.

而且 also means "besides" or "in addition." But unlike 再說/再说, it is not used just to explain the reasons for a statement or view. Compare the "not only...but also..." function of 不但...而且... in the following sentences.

(4) 我這個學期不但上英文課, 而且還上中文課。

我这个学期不但上英文课, 而且还上中文课。

Besides English, I'm also taking Chinese this semester.

(5) 我妹妹不但喜歡唱歌, 而且也喜歡跳舞。

我妹妹不但喜欢唱歌, 而且也喜欢跳舞。

My younger sister not only likes to sing but also likes to dance.

搬進宿舍。/搬进宿舍。

▼▼▼

Note: In examples (1), (2), and (3), 再説／再说 is interchangeable with 而且, but in examples (4) and (5) 而且 is not interchangeable with 再説／再说.

Important Words & Phrases

1. 有的…, 有的… (SOME…SOME…)

EXAMPLE:　有的人喜歡住學校宿舍, 覺得方便、安全, 有的人喜歡住校外, 覺得省錢。

　　　　　有的人喜欢住学校宿舍, 觉得方便、安全, 有的人喜欢住校外, 觉得省钱。

(1)　我的同學, 有的走路來上學,_____。

　　　我的同学, 有的走路来上学,_____。

(2)　我買的書,_____,_____。

　　　我买的书,_____,_____。

(3)　張天明的朋友, 有的是_____, 有的是_____。

　　　张天明的朋友, 有的是_____, 有的是_____。

2. 覺得／觉得 (TO FEEL)

EXAMPLE:　有的人喜歡住學校宿舍, 覺得方便、安全, 有的人 喜歡住校外, 覺得省錢。

　　　　　有的人喜欢住学校宿舍, 觉得方便、安全, 有的人 喜欢住校外, 觉得省钱。

(1)　大家都説那個電影好看, 可是我看了以後_____。

　　　大家都说那个电影好看, 可是我看了以后_____。

(2) 很多美國人認為十八歲以後就應該離開家搬到別的地方住,
我＿＿＿＿＿＿＿＿＿＿＿＿＿＿＿＿＿＿。

很多美国人认为十八岁以后就应该离开家搬到别的地方住,
我＿＿＿＿＿＿＿＿＿＿＿＿＿＿＿＿＿＿。

(3) A: 你覺得 "在家靠父母, 出門靠朋友" 這句話有道理嗎?

你觉得 "在家靠父母, 出门靠朋友" 这句话有道理吗?

B: ＿＿＿＿＿＿＿＿＿＿＿＿＿＿＿＿＿＿＿＿＿＿＿＿。

When expressing an opinion, one could use 覺得/觉得, which is less formal than 認為/认为.

3. 不見得 / 不见得 (NOT NECESSARILY)

EXAMPLE: ...再説, 住校內也不見得方便。/ ...再说, 住校内也不见得方便。

(1) 以前大家覺得報上説的都是對的, 可是＿＿＿＿＿＿＿＿＿＿。

以前大家觉得报上说的都是对的, 可是＿＿＿＿＿＿＿＿＿＿。

(2) 波士頓街上車多, 人多, 開車＿＿＿＿＿＿＿＿＿＿。

波士顿街上车多, 人多, 开车＿＿＿＿＿＿＿＿＿＿。

(3) 在中國出生的人, 中文＿＿＿＿＿＿＿＿＿＿。

在中国出生的人, 中文＿＿＿＿＿＿＿＿＿＿。

4. 對...有好處 / 对...有好处 (GOOD FOR...)

EXAMPLE: 你剛來, 在學校住一段時間對你有好處。

你刚来, 在学校住一段时间对你有好处。

(1) 學過外語的人都説多聽錄音＿＿＿＿＿＿＿＿＿＿＿＿＿＿＿＿。

学过外语的人都说多听录音＿＿＿＿＿＿＿＿＿＿＿＿＿＿＿＿。

▼▼

(2) 少喝酒對＿＿＿＿＿＿＿＿＿＿有好處。

少喝酒对＿＿＿＿＿＿＿＿＿＿有好处。

(3) 在中國, 上過大學、會用電腦、會说外语,＿＿＿＿＿＿＿＿＿＿。

在中国, 上过大学、会用电脑、会说外语,＿＿＿＿＿＿＿＿＿＿。

Pinyin Texts

NARRATIVE

Shǔjià jiéshù le, xuéxiào jiù yào kāi xué le. Xuésheng cóng gège dìfāng huídào le xuéxiào. Zhāng Tiānmíng shì yì niánjí de xuésheng, jiā zài Bōshìdùn, lí zhèli hěn yuǎn. Tā shì zìjǐ yí ge rén zuò fēijī lái de. Bàn wán le zhù cè shǒuxù, tā lái dào le xīnshēng sùshè.

DIALOGUE

Zhāng Tiānmíng:	Rén zěnme zhème duō?
Kē Lín:	Nǐ shì xīnshēng ma?
Zhāng Tiānmíng:	Shì, wǒ shì. Nǐ ne?
Kē Lín:	Wǒ shì lǎoshēng, zài zhèr bāng xīnshēng bān dōngxi. Nǐ shì Zhōngguórén ba?
Zhāng Tiānmíng:	Wǒ zǔjí shì Zhōngguó, kěshì wǒ shì zài Měiguó chūshēng, zài Měiguó zhǎng dà de.
Kē Lín:	Qǐng wèn, nǐ de Zhōngwén míngzi shì...
Zhāng Tiānmíng:	Wǒ xìng Zhāng, gōng cháng Zhāng, yě jiùshì yì zhāng zhǐ de zhāng, míngzi shì Tiānmíng, tiānqì de tiān, míngtiān de míng.
Kē Lín:	Wǒ zhèngzài xué Zhōngwén, wǒ de Zhōngwén míngzi jiào Kē Lín. Nǐ shǒuxù dōu bàn wán le ma?
Zhāng Tiānmíng:	Bàn wán le. Nǐ zhù zài nǎr? Yě zhù zài zhèr ma?
Kē Lín:	Bù, zhè shì xīnshēng sùshè, wǒ zhù zài xiàowài.
Zhāng Tiānmíng:	Zhù zài xiàonèi hǎo, háishi zhù zài xiàowài hǎo?
Kē Lín:	Yǒude rén xǐhuan zhù xuéxiào sùshè, juéde fāngbiàn, ānquán. Yǒude rén xǐhuan zhù zài xiàowài, juéde shěng qián. Wǒ zhù zài xiàowài, chúle wèile shěng qián yǐwài, hái wèile zìyóu, zàishuō, zhù zài xiàonèi yě bú jiàn de fāngbiàn.

Zhāng Tiānmíng: Shì ma? Nà wǒ yě bān dào xiàowài, hǎo ma ?

Kē Lín: Nǐ gāng lái, zài xuéxiào zhù duì nǐ yǒu hǎochù, kěyǐ shìyìng yí xià dàxué shēnghuó. Guò xiē shíhou rúguǒ xiǎng bān jiā, jiù zhǎo wǒ, wǒ bāng nǐ zhǎo fángzi.

Zhāng Tiānmíng: Hǎo, xièxie. Wǒ lí kāi jiā de shíhou, māma gàosù wǒ: "zài jiā kào fùmǔ, chū mén kào péngyou." Tā shuō de hěn yǒu dàoli. Yǐhòu qǐng nǐ duō bāng máng.

Kē Lín: Méi wèntí. Ài, qiánbian méiyǒu rén le, nǐ kěyǐ bān le. Wǒ bāng nǐ tí xíngli, zǒu ba.

Zhāng Tiānmíng: Hǎo, xièxie.

Discussion Topic: Arriving on Campus

With the help of the comic strip, recap in Chinese what happened to Zhang Tianming when he first arrived on campus.

第二課 ▲ 宿舍

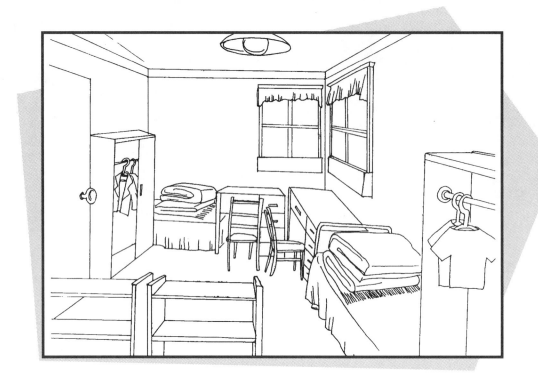

NARRATIVE

　　張天明宿舍的房間不太大,住兩個人。他的同屋叫約翰,是前天從華盛頓來的,對學校已經比較熟悉了。房間裏有一些傢俱。靠窗戶擺著兩張書桌,每張桌子的前邊有一把椅子。書桌的旁邊是床,床上有被子和毯子。床前有兩個衣櫃,櫃子裏掛著一些衣服。門旁邊放著兩個書架,書架還是空的。

DIALOGUE

張天明： 約翰,真熱!房間裏沒有空調嗎?

約翰： 沒有。聽說這棟樓設備比較舊,廁所、浴室也比較小。

張天明： 那住這兒恐怕很不方便吧?

約翰： 不,我來了兩天了,覺得很方便。餐廳就在樓下,餐廳旁邊有一個小商店,賣日用品和文具。教室離這兒不遠,走路差不多五、六分鐘。

第二课 ▲ 宿舍

NARRATIVE

　　张天明宿舍的房间不太大，住两个人。他的同屋叫约翰，是前天从华盛顿来的，对学校已经比较熟悉了。房间里有一些家具。靠窗户摆着两张书桌，每张桌子的前边有一把椅子。书桌的旁边是床，床上有被子和毯子。床前有两个衣柜，柜子里挂着一些衣服。门旁边放着两个书架，书架还是空的。

DIALOGUE

张天明：　约翰，真热！房间里没有空调吗？

约翰：　　没有。听说这栋楼设备比较旧，厕所、浴室也比较小。

张天明：　那住这儿恐怕很不方便吧？

约翰：　　不，我来了两天了，觉得很方便。餐厅就在楼下，餐厅旁边有一个小商店，卖日用品和文具。教室离这儿不远，走路差不多五、六分钟。

張天明：　洗衣服方便嗎？

約翰：　　方便得很。我們這層樓有三台洗衣機和三台烘乾機。

張天明：　這兒吵不吵？

約翰：　　不，這兒離大馬路很遠，很安靜。

張天明：　聽說學校餐廳的飯一般都不太好。這兒的呢？

約翰：　　你猜對了，餐廳的飯真的不怎麼樣。我來這兒以後，剛吃了一天就沒胃口了。

張天明：　真的？那怎麼辦？

約翰：　　你別著急。我聽說附近有很多飯館兒，還有一家中國餐館呢。

張天明：　我覺得美國的中國餐館，好吃的不多。

約翰：　　那也不見得。聽老生說，那家中國餐館的菜很地道。

張天明：　真的嗎？那麼過幾天你帶我去那兒看看，好嗎？

約翰：　　好，沒問題。

Have you seen a squat toilet? Here is one in a college student dorm in China.

▼▼▼▼▼▼▼▼▼▼▼▼▼▼▼▼▼▼▼▼▼▼▼▼▼▼▼▼▼▼▼▼▼▼▼▼

张天明： 洗衣服方便吗？

约翰： 方便得很。我们这层楼有三台洗衣机和三台烘干机。

张天明： 这儿吵不吵？

约翰： 不，这儿离大马路很远，很安静。

张天明： 听说学校餐厅的饭一般都不太好。这儿的呢？

约翰： 你猜对了，餐厅的饭真的不怎么样。我来这儿以后，刚吃了一天就没胃口了。

张天明： 真的？那怎么办？

约翰： 你别着急。我听说附近有很多饭馆儿，还有一家中国餐馆呢。

张天明： 我觉得美国的中国餐馆，好吃的不多。

约翰： 那也不见得。听老生说，那家中国餐馆的菜很地道。

张天明： 真的吗？那么过几天你带我去那儿看看，好吗？

约翰： 好，没问题。

This is a sign found at a staircase in a college dorm in China. Do you know what it means?

(See the Appendix of Alternate Character Versions for traditional characters.)

VOCABULARY

1.	同屋		tóngwū	n	roommate
2.	前天		qiántiān	t	the day before yesterday
3.	熟悉		shúxi	v	to be familiar with

我剛來, 對這兒還不太熟悉。／ 我刚来, 对这儿还不太熟悉。

你不是中學生了, 應該熟悉一下大學老師怎麼上課。

你不是中学生了, 应该熟悉一下大学老师怎么上课。

4.	傢俱*	家具	jiājù	n	furniture
5.	靠		kào	v	to lean against
6.	窗戶		chuānghu	n	window
7.	擺	摆	bǎi	v	to put; to place
8.	床		chuáng	n	bed
9.	被子		bèizi	n	comforter; quilt
10.	毯子		tǎnzi	n	blanket
11.	衣櫃	衣柜	yīguì	n	wardrobe
12.	櫃子	柜子	guìzi	n	cabinet; cupboard
13.	掛*	挂	guà	v	to hang
14.	書架*	书架	shūjià	n	bookshelf
15.	空		kōng	adj	empty
16.	空調	空调	kōngtiáo	n	air-conditioning
17.	棟	栋	dòng	m	measure word for buildings
18.	設備	设备	shèbèi	n	facilities; equipment
19.	舊	旧	jiù	adj	(of things) old
20.	廁所*	厕所	cèsuǒ	n	restroom; toilet

21.	浴室		yùshì	n	bathroom (a room for bathing)
22.	恐怕		kǒngpà	adv	I'm afraid that; I think perhaps; probably [see G6]
23.	餐廳*	餐厅	cāntīng	n	cafeteria
24.	樓下*	楼下	lóuxià		downstairs
25.	商店		shāngdiàn	n	shop
26.	日用品		rìyòngpǐn	n	daily household necessities
27.	文具		wénjù	n	stationery; writing supplies
28.	層	层	céng	m	measure word for floors
29.	台		tái	m	measure word for machines
30.	洗衣機	洗衣机	xǐyījī	n	washing machine
31.	烘乾機	烘干机	hōnggānjī	n	(clothes) dryer
32.	吵*		chǎo	adj	noisy

外邊很吵，我不能看書。／外边很吵，我不能看书。

這兒很安靜，一點也不吵。／这儿很安静，一点也不吵。

| 33. | 馬路 | 马路 | mǎlù | n | road |
| 34. | 安靜* | 安静 | ānjìng | adj | quiet |

我們的宿舍很安靜。／我们的宿舍很安静。

安靜點兒，弟弟在睡覺。／安静点儿，弟弟在睡觉。

35.	一般		yìbān	adv	generally
36.	聽説*	听说	tīngshuō	v	to be told; to hear of
37.	猜對了*	猜对了	cāi duì le	vc	guessed correctly

A: 你猜今天的舞會誰會來？／A: 你猜今天的舞会谁会来？

B: 小張。／B: 小张。

A: 你猜對了。／A: 你猜对了。

38.	胃口		wèikǒu	n	appetite
39.	真的		zhēnde	adv	really; truly
40.	著急	着急	zháo jí	vo	to feel restless or impatient as a result of worrying about something

聽說妹妹病了，我很著急。/听说妹妹病了，我很着急。

別著急，她的病會好的。/别着急，她的病会好的。

| 41. | 餐館 | 餐馆 | cānguǎn | n | restaurant |
| 42. | 地道 | | dìdao | adj | authentic |

他說的北京話很地道。/他说的北京话很地道。

這是地道的中國菜。/这是地道的中国菜。

| 43. | 過幾天 | 过几天 | guò jǐ tiān | | in a few days |
| 44. | 帶* | 帶 | dài | v | to take or bring along |

媽媽常常帶我去公園玩兒。/妈妈常常带我去公园玩儿。

飛機票你帶了嗎? /飞机票你带了吗?

PROPER NOUNS

1.	約翰	约翰	Yuēhàn	John
2.	華盛頓*	华盛顿	Huáshèngdùn	Washington

ENLARGED CHARACTERS FOR EASIER VIEWING AND COMPARING

窗　擺　櫃　舊　餐　廳

窗　摆　柜　旧　餐　厅

請你看看房間裏有幾張床、幾張書桌、幾個書架和幾個衣櫃。
请你看看房间里有几张床、几张书桌、几个书架和几个衣柜。

Grammar

1. WORD ORDER IN CHINESE (I)

In Chinese, if the predicate is a verb, the structure of a sentence can be very complex. How to structure the sentence then becomes an important question. In an isolated sentence the usual word order is: subject-verb-object. For example:

我　買　傢俱了。／我　买　家具了。

I bought (some) furniture.

If the subject or the object is modified by an attributive signifying possession, quantity, etc., the attributive should precede the object modified. In the following sentences, the attributives appear in parentheses.

(1)　(我的)(小)妹妹買了(一張)(很大的)書桌。

　　　(我的)(小)妹妹买了(一张)(很大的)书桌。

(My) (little) sister bought (a) (very big) desk.

(2)   我很喜歡(那家商店賣的)衣服。／我很喜欢(那家商店卖的)衣服。

      I like the clothes (sold in that store) very much.

(3)   這就是(我以前住的)地方。／这就是(我以前住的)地方。

      This is the place (where I used to live).

If there is an adverbial signifying the time, place, co-agent, or manner of an action, it should precede the verb. We could also put the time and place before the subject. In the following sentences the adverbials appear in angle brackets.

(4)   我們<昨天>去了(一個)(很遠的)地方。

      我们<昨天>去了(一个)(很远的)地方。

      <Yesterday> we went to (a) (far-away) place.

(5)   他<在房間裏><慢慢地>走著。

      他<在房间里><慢慢地>走着。

      He was pacing <slowly> <in the room.>

(6)   <明年暑假>我要<跟我的同屋><從學校>開車去南方旅行。

      <明年暑假>我要<跟我的同屋><从学校>开车去南方旅行。

      <Next summer> I'm going to drive <with my roommate> <from school> to the South.

It should be noted that attributives and adverbials always appear before what they modify. However, verbs are often followed by complements indicating the results of the actions. In the following sentences the complements appear in square brackets.

(7)   我<剛才>寫[錯]了(一個)字。

      我<刚才>写[错]了(一个)字。

      I wrote (one) character [wrong] <just now>.

(8)   請你坐[下]。

      请你坐[下]。

      Please sit [down].

The above is a brief description of the basic word order in Chinese. Many factors can affect the word order in Chinese. We will discuss these factors in subsequent lessons.

▼▼

2. EXISTENTIAL SENTENCES

Existential sentences indicate that something exists at a certain place. The word order of an existential sentence is somewhat different from that of the typical Chinese sentence. The structure of existential sentences is as follows: place word + verb + (了/著) / (了/着)+ numerals + noun. For instance, 桌子上放著一本書/ 桌子上放着一本书 (There is a book lying on the desk), 門前有一把椅子 / 门前有一把椅子 (There is a chair in front of the door), 書桌的旁邊是床 / 书桌的旁边是床 (Next to the desk there is a bed). There are three kinds of verbs in existential sentences: 有, 是, and verbs signifying bodily movements.

(1)   教室裏有一些學生。/ 教室里有一些学生。

There are some students in the classroom.

(2)   桌子上是一本書。/ 桌子上是一本书。

On the desk is a book.

(3)   書架上放著三本書。/ 书架上放着三本书。

There are three books on the bookshelf.

(4)   床上坐了一個人。/ 床上坐了一个人。

Someone is sitting on the bed.

Of the three kinds of verbs in existential sentences, 了 or 著/着 is needed only when a verb signifying bodily movement is involved.

When denoting existence, 有 and 是 differ from each other in that 是 suggests that there is only one object at a particular place, unlike 有. Compare:

(5)   桌子上有一本書, 一個本子, 一張報和一些紙。
      桌子上有一本书, 一个本子, 一张报和一些纸。

There's a book, a notebook, a newspaper, and several sheets of paper on the desk.

(6)   A: 你看, 桌子上放著什麼? / 你看, 桌子上放着什么?

           Look, what's on the table?

      B: 桌子上是一瓶可樂。/ 桌子上是一瓶可乐。

           That's a bottle of cola on the table.

(7)   我們學校的前面是一條馬路, 後面是一個公園。

　　　　我们学校的前面是一条马路, 后面是一个公园。

　　　　In front of our school is a road. Behind it is a park.

Existential sentences are used to describe the surroundings of a place or someone's appearance. Examples (1) through (7) describe places. The following are examples of existential sentences that describe people.

(8)   這個時候從前邊走來一個人, 他身上穿著一件白大衣, 手裏拿著一條紅
　　　　毯子。

　　　　这个时候从前边走来一个人, 他身上穿着一件白大衣, 手里拿着一条红
　　　　毯子。

At that moment a man came from the front. He was wearing a white coat and carrying a red blanket in his hand.

(9)   那個男孩子手裏拿著一個小飛機。

　　　　那个男孩子手里拿着一个小飞机。

　　　　That boy is holding a model plane in his hand.

3. 比較 / 比较

The word 比較 / 比较 (relatively, rather) is not the equivalent of the comparative degree in English. It is not used to make explicit comparisons but instead statements whose validity is not predicated upon a specific standard. In other words, 比較 / 比较 cannot be used in "A is more/less than B" type of constructions where the terms of comparison are clearly articulated.

(1)   這把椅子比較貴, 你別買了。

　　　　这把椅子比较贵, 你别买了。

　　　　This chair is rather expensive. Don't buy it.

　　　　(The standard implied here is a rather vague one: the price of this chair exceeds our ability to pay for it, for instance.)

(2)   我比較矮(ǎi), 才五尺四, 不能打籃球。/ 我比较矮(ǎi), 才五尺四, 不能打篮球。

　　　　I am rather short. I'm only 5 feet 4 inches tall. I can't play basketball.

　　　　(Again, the standard for comparison is not explicitly stated. One could take the sentence to mean that the speaker feels ill-equipped in view of the general requirements of the game.)

(3)   今天比較冷, 你多穿點衣服吧。／今天比较冷, 你多穿点衣服吧。

It's rather cold today. You'd better put on more clothes.

(4)   A: 你喜歡吃什麼菜?／你喜欢吃什么菜?

       What kind of food do you like?

  B: 我比較喜歡吃中國菜。／我比较喜欢吃中国菜。

       [Generally speaking,] I prefer Chinese food.

Note that in the following sentences, an asterisk (*) indicates incorrect usage.

(5)   A: 聽說你這兩天不太舒服, 今天覺得怎麼樣?

       听说你这两天不太舒服, 今天觉得怎么样?

       I heard that you were sick the last couple of days. How are you feeling today?

  B: 好一點兒了。／好一点儿了。

       A bit better.

    *比較好。／*比较好。

(6)   我很高, 我哥哥更高。／我很高, 我哥哥更高。

I'm very tall. My older brother is even taller.

    *我很高, 我哥哥比較高。／*我很高, 我哥哥比较高。

Compare:

(7a)   在中國, 北方人一般比較高。／在中国, 北方人一般比较高。

In China, Northerners—generally speaking—are taller.

But,

(7b)   在中國, 北方人一般比南方人高。／在中国, 北方人一般比南方人高。

In China Northerners—generally speaking—are taller *than* Southerners.

*在中國, 北方人一般比較南方人高。

*在中国, 北方人一般比较南方人高。

(8)   A: 這家商店的東西這麼貴, 你怎麼不去別的商店?

           这家商店的东西这么贵, 你怎么不去别的商店?

           This store's merchandise is so expensive. Why don't you go to other stores?

   B: 因為這家商店的東西比較好。／ 因为这家商店的东西比较好。

           It is because its quality is better.

Notice that in his reply B is simply suggesting that the store he likes to patronize is generally speaking superior in terms of the quality of its merchandise. No competitors are mentioned. Therefore, the statement is not a direct comparison.

4. (方便)得很

得很 can be used after adjectives, and also after certain verbs that denote feelings or opinions, to suggest an extreme degree. For instance, 冷得很 suggests a higher degree of coldness than 很冷。

(1)   今天來註冊的新生多得很, 我們明天再註冊吧。

       今天来注册的新生多得很, 我们明天再注册吧。

       There are too many freshmen registering today. Let's do it tomorrow.

(2)   我們的宿舍安靜得很, 大家都很喜歡。

       我们的宿舍安静得很, 大家都很喜欢。

       Our dorms are very quiet. We all like them a lot.

(3)   學校剛開學, 大家都忙得很。／ 学校刚开学, 大家都忙得很。

       School just started. Everyone has been really busy.

(4)   離開家一個多月了, 張天明想家得很。

       离开家一个多月了, 张天明想家得很。

       Zhang Tianming has been away from home for over a month now. He's really homesick.

5. 那(麼) / 那(么)

那(麼) / 那(么) connects two sentences. The second sentence denotes a conclusion or judgment deriving from the preceding sentence. One can simply say 那 instead of 那(麼) /那(么).

(1)   A: 晚上去買洗衣機, 好嗎? / 晚上去买洗衣机, 好吗?

       Shall we go shopping for a washing machine tonight?

       B: 可是今天晚上我沒有空兒。/ 可是今天晚上我没有空儿。

       But I don't have time tonight.

       A: 那(麼)就明天吧。/ 那(么)就明天吧。

       Tomorrow, then.

       B: 好吧。

       O.K.

(2)   A: 媽媽, 我不想當醫生。/ 妈妈, 我不想当医生。

       Mom, I don't want to be a doctor.

       B: 那(麼)學電腦怎麼樣? / 那(么)学电脑怎么样?

       Then how about studying computer science?

       A: 我也沒興趣。/ 我也没兴趣。

       I am not interested in that, either.

       B: 那就什麼都不學,在家裏做飯、洗衣服吧。

            那就什么都不学,在家里做饭、洗衣服吧。

       Then don't study anything. Stay home and cook and do laundry.

       A: 媽, 看您說的! / 妈, 看您说的!

       Mom! "Look at what you're saying!" [an idiomatic expression suggesting reproach]

6. 恐怕 (I'M AFRAID; I THINK PERHAPS)

The adverb 恐怕 is used to express the speaker's assessment of a situation or concern.

(1) 這兒沒空調, 恐怕夏天很熱吧? ／ 这儿没空调, 恐怕夏天很热吧?

There's no air-conditioning here. It's probably very hot in the summer. Is that right?

(2) 下雨了, 恐怕我們不能打球了。 ／ 下雨了, 恐怕我们不能打球了。

It's raining. I'm afraid we can't play ball.

(3) 十一點了, 現在給他打電話恐怕太晚了。

十一点了, 现在给他打电话恐怕太晚了。

It's eleven o'clock. I'm afraid it's too late to call him now.

(4) 窗戶外有一條馬路, 這兒恐怕很吵吧?

窗戶外有一条马路, 这儿恐怕很吵吧?

There's a street outside the window. It must be very noisy here. Is that right?

Note: We do not usually say 我恐怕. For instance, we do not normally say, 我恐怕他不能去. If someone says, 我恐怕不能去了, what he or she really means is, 恐怕我不能去了 (I'm afraid I won't be able to go). We can also say, 他恐怕不能去 meaning 恐怕他不能去了 (I'm afraid he won't be able to go). In other words, in the final example the implied subject is 我, and 他 functions as the topic of the sentence. Also see Lesson 3 Grammar Notes for more on topics.

Important Words & Phrases

1. 一般 (GENERALLY SPEAKING)

EXAMPLE: 我還聽說學校餐廳的飯一般都不太好。

我还听说学校餐厅的饭一般都不太好。

(1) 新生 _____, 差不多都靠老生開車帶他們去買東西。

新生 _____, 差不多都靠老生开车带他们去买东西。

(2) 週末學校宿舍有一點吵, 圖書館比較安靜。

周末学校宿舍有一点吵, 图书馆比较安静。

→ → _____。

▼▼▼▼▼▼▼▼▼▼▼▼▼▼▼▼▼▼▼▼▼▼▼▼▼▼▼▼▼▼▼▼▼▼▼▼

(3) 星期一到星期五, 她都在學校餐廳吃飯,週末常常去飯館。

星期一到星期五, 她都在学校餐厅吃饭,周末常常去饭馆。

→ → _____。

2. 差不多 (ABOUT; ROUGHLY)

EXAMPLE: 教室離這兒不遠, 走路差不多五、六分鐘。

教室离这儿不远, 走路差不多五、六分钟。

(1)　A:　你同屋的書架上一共有幾本書?

你同屋的书架上一共有几本书?

B:　我猜_____。

我猜_____。

(2)　電影兩點開始, 現在差不多_____了,快走吧。

电影两点开始, 现在差不多_____了,快走吧。

(3)　A:　你多長時間給你母親打一次電話?

你多长时间给你母亲打一次电话?

B:　_____。

3. 聽說／听说 (HEAR; HEAR OF)

EXAMPLE:　聽說這棟樓設備比較舊, 廁所、浴室也比較小。

听说这栋楼设备比较旧, 厕所、浴室也比较小。

(1)　A:　過幾天我跟我的日本朋友想去吃日本飯, 學校附近的那家你去過嗎?

过几天我跟我的日本朋友想去吃日本饭, 学校附近的那家你去过吗?

B: 沒去過, 可是＿＿＿＿＿＿＿＿＿＿＿＿＿＿＿＿＿＿＿＿。

　　沒去过, 可是＿＿＿＿＿＿＿＿＿＿＿＿＿＿＿＿＿＿＿＿。

(2) A: 小林怎麼搬到校外去住了? 是不是想省錢?

　　　小林怎么搬到校外去住了? 是不是想省钱?

B: 你猜错了。＿＿＿＿＿＿＿＿＿＿＿＿＿＿＿＿＿＿＿。

　　你猜错了。＿＿＿＿＿＿＿＿＿＿＿＿＿＿＿＿＿＿＿。

(3) A: 我這兩天晚上老睡不好覺, 你說怎麼辦呢?

　　　我这两天晚上老睡不好觉, 你说怎么办呢?

B: ＿＿＿＿＿＿＿＿＿＿＿＿＿＿＿＿＿＿, 對睡覺有幫助。

　　＿＿＿＿＿＿＿＿＿＿＿＿＿＿＿＿＿＿, 对睡觉有帮助。

4. 不怎麼樣/不怎么样 (NOT THAT GREAT; JUST SO-SO)

EXAMPLE: 餐廳的飯真的不怎麼樣。/ 餐厅的饭真的不怎么样。

(1) 這個圖書館不怎麼樣, 書＿＿＿＿＿＿＿＿。

　　这个图书馆不怎么样, 书＿＿＿＿＿＿＿＿。

(2) A: 你覺得這棟樓的設備怎麼樣?

　　　你觉得这栋楼的设备怎么样?

B: ＿＿＿＿＿＿＿＿＿＿＿＿＿＿＿, 又舊又差。

　　＿＿＿＿＿＿＿＿＿＿＿＿＿＿＿, 又旧又差。

(3) A: 你看, 這是我的房間, 你覺得傢俱擺得怎麼樣?

　　　你看, 这是我的房间, 你觉得家具摆得怎么样?

B: ＿＿＿＿＿＿＿＿＿＿＿＿＿＿＿＿＿, 你的床應該＿＿＿＿＿＿＿, 你的書桌

應該＿＿＿＿＿＿＿。

＿＿＿＿＿＿＿＿＿＿＿＿＿＿＿＿＿, 你的床应该＿＿＿＿＿＿＿, 你的书桌

应该＿＿＿＿＿＿＿。

A: 對, 你说的有道理, 我现在就搬。

对, 你说的有道理, 我现在就搬。

Pinyin Texts

NARRATIVE

　　Zhāng Tiānmíng sùshè de fángjiān bú tài dà, zhù liǎng ge rén. Tā de tóngwū jiào Yuēhàn, shì qiántiān cóng Huáshèngdùn lái de, duì xuéxiào yǐjīng bǐjiào shúxi le.

　　Fángjiān li yǒu yìxiē jiājù. Kào chuānghu bǎi zhe liǎng zhāng shūzhuō, měi zhāng zhuōzi de qiánbian yǒu yì bǎ yǐzi. Shūzhuō de pángbiān shì chuáng, chuáng shang yǒu bèizi hé tǎnzi. Chuáng qián yǒu liǎng ge yīguì, guìzi li guà zhe yìxiē yīfu. Mén pángbiān fàng zhe liǎng ge shūjià, shūjià hái shì kōng de.

DIALOGUE

Zhāng Tiānmíng:	Yuēhàn, zhēn rè! Fángjiān li méiyǒu kōngtiáo ma?
Yuēhàn:	Méiyǒu. Tīngshuō zhèdòng lóu shèbèi bǐjiào jiù, cèsuǒ, yùshì yě bǐjiào xiǎo.
Zhāng Tiānmíng:	Nà zhù zhèr kǒngpà hěn bù fāngbiàn ba?
Yuēhàn:	Bù, wǒ lái le liǎng tiān le, juéde hěn fāngbiàn. Cāntīng jiù zài lóuxià, cāntīng pángbiān yǒu yí ge xiǎo shāngdiàn, mài rìyòngpǐn hé wénjù. Jiàoshì lí zhèr bù yuǎn, zǒu lù chà bu duō wǔ, liù fēnzhōng.
Zhāng Tiānmíng:	Xǐ yīfu fāngbiàn ma?
Yuēhàn:	Fāngbiàn de hěn. Wǒmen zhècéng lóu yǒu sān tái xǐyījī hé sān tái hōnggānjī.
Zhāng Tiānmíng:	Zhèr chǎo bu chǎo?
Yuēhàn:	Bù, zhèr lí dà mǎlù hěn yuǎn, hěn ānjìng.
Zhāng Tiānmíng:	Tīngshuō xuéxiào cāntīng de fàn yìbān dōu bú tài hǎo. Zhèr de ne?
Yuēhàn:	Nǐ cāi duì le, cāntīng de fàn zhēnde bù zěnmeyàng. Wǒ lái zhèr yǐhòu, gāng chī le yì tiān jiù méi wèikǒu le.
Zhāng Tiānmíng:	Zhēndē? Nà zěnme bàn?

Yuēhàn: Nǐ bié zháo jí. Wǒ tīngshuō fùjìn yǒu hěn duō fànguǎnr, hái yǒu yì jiā Zhōngguó cānguǎn ne.

Zhāng Tiānmíng: Wǒ juéde Měiguó de Zhōngguó cānguǎn, hǎochī de bù duō.

Yuēhàn: Nà yě bú jiàn de. Tīng lǎoshēng shuō, nàjiā Zhōngguó cānguǎn de cài hěn dìdao.

Zhāng Tiānmíng: Zhēnde ma? Nà guò jǐ tiān nǐ dài wǒ qù nàr kàn kan, hǎo ma?

Yuēhàn: Hǎo, méi wèntí.

Discussion Topic: Dorm Life

Talk in Chinese about the pros and the cons of Zhang Tianming's dorm, with the help of the cartoon.

第三課 ▲ 在飯館兒

NARRATIVE

　　開學已經兩個多星期了,因為太忙,張天明每天只好在學校的餐廳吃飯。很長時間沒吃中國飯了,他很想去中國飯館兒吃一頓。今天是週末,再說功課也不多,他就打了個電話給柯林,問他想不想一起去中國城吃飯。柯林聽了很高興地說,他的女朋友林雪梅正好也想吃中國飯,他讓張天明在宿舍門口等,他開車來接他。一刻鐘以後,柯林的汽車到了。張天明往車裏一看,柯林的女朋友原來是個中國女孩兒,長得很漂亮。十分鐘以後,他們三個人到了柯林常去的一家中國飯館兒。

DIALOGUE

They are entering a Chinese restaurant...

服務員： 柯先生,你好!好久不見了。幾位?

柯林： 小陳,你好。三個人,不吸煙。

服務員： 好,請跟我來。

第三课 ▲ 在饭馆儿

NARRATIVE

开学已经两个多星期了,因为太忙,张天明每天只好在学校的餐厅吃饭。很长时间没吃中国饭了,他很想去中国饭馆儿吃一顿。今天是周末,再说功课也不多,他就打了个电话给柯林,问他想不想一起去中国城吃饭。柯林听了很高兴地说,他的女朋友林雪梅正好也想吃中国饭,他让张天明在宿舍门口等,他开车来接他。一刻钟以后,柯林的汽车到了。张天明往车里一看,柯林的女朋友原来是个中国女孩儿,长得很漂亮。十分钟以后,他们三个人到了柯林常去的一家中国饭馆儿。

DIALOGUE

They are entering a Chinese restaurant...

服务员: 柯先生,你好!好久不见了。几位?

柯林: 小陈,你好。三个人,不吸烟。

服务员: 好,请跟我来。

▼▼▼▼▼▼▼▼▼▼▼▼▼▼▼▼▼▼▼▼▼▼▼▼▼▼▼▼▼▼▼▼

The three of them follow the waitress to their table...

服務員： 這是菜單。

柯林： 謝謝。小張，你想吃點什麼？

張天明： 你是這兒的常客。這個飯館兒什麼菜最拿手？

林雪梅： 這兒魚做得很好，特別是清蒸魚，味道好極了。

柯林： 芥蘭牛肉也不錯，又嫩又香。

林雪梅： 再叫一個湯吧。

柯林： 這兒的菠菜豆腐湯很好，叫一個好不好？

Have you had Peking duck, Běijīng kǎoyā, before? Here is a chef preparing Peking duck for his customers.

▼ ▼

The three of them follow the waitress to their table…

服务员：　这是菜单。

柯林：　　谢谢。小张，你想吃点什么？

张天明：　你是这儿的常客。这个饭馆儿什么菜最拿手？

林雪梅：　这儿鱼做得很好，特别是清蒸鱼，味道好极了。

柯林：　　芥兰牛肉也不错，又嫩又香。

林雪梅：　再叫一个汤吧。

柯林：　　这儿的菠菜豆腐汤很好，叫一个好不好？

In China, while you can order Běijīng kǎoyā in a restaurant, you can also purchase it in a supermarket or at the airport.

張天明： 好，好。再要個什麼？

柯林： 我看再來一個素菜吧。

服務員： 現在可以點菜了嗎？

柯林： 可以了。一個清蒸魚，一個芥蘭牛肉，一個菠菜豆腐湯。今天你們有什麼新鮮的青菜？

服務員： 小白菜怎麼樣？

柯林： 可以。小陳，麻煩跟老闆說少放點鹽，別放味精。

服務員： 好。菜馬上來。

While they are waiting for their dishes...

柯林： 有一個美國記者寫文章說中國菜卡路里多，對健康並沒有好處。你們有什麼看法？

林雪梅： 我認為那個記者的說法太片面。中國菜總的來說，是對身體健康有好處的。也許有的菜油多一些，這就要看你會不會點菜了。我們今天點的菜，除了牛肉以外，都很清淡。

張天明： 我同意小林的看法。柯林，你還沒說你的看法呢。

柯林： 其實，那個記者的看法我也不同意，要不然，今天我就不會帶你們到這兒來。哎，我們的菜來了。

张天明：　好，好。再要个什么？

柯林：　　我看再来一个素菜吧。

服务员：　现在可以点菜了吗？

柯林：　　可以了。一个清蒸鱼，一个芥兰牛肉，一个菠菜豆腐汤。今天你们有什么新鲜的青菜？

服务员：　小白菜怎么样？

柯林：　　可以。小陈，麻烦跟老板说少放点盐，别放味精。

服务员：　好。菜马上来。

While they are waiting for their dishes…

柯林：　　有一个美国记者写文章说中国菜卡路里多，对健康并没有好处。你们有什么看法？

林雪梅：　我认为那个记者的说法太片面。中国菜总的来说，是对身体健康有好处的。也许有的菜油多一些，这就要看你会不会点菜了。我们今天点的菜，除了牛肉以外，都很清淡。

张天明：　我同意小林的看法。柯林，你还没说你的看法呢。

柯林：　　其实，那个记者的看法我也不同意，要不然，今天我就不会带你们到这儿来。哎，我们的菜来了。

VOCABULARY

1. 只好   zhǐhǎo   adv   have to; be forced to

       我没有汽車, 只好坐公共汽車去中國城。

       我没有汽车, 只好坐公共汽车去中国城。

       我的中文書找不到了, 只好再買一本。

       我的中文书找不到了, 只好再买一本。

2. 頓   顿   dùn   m   measure word for meals

3. 週末*   周末   zhōumò   n   weekend

4. 功課*   功课   gōngkè   n   homework

5. 中國城*   中国城   Zhōngguóchéng   n   Chinatown

6. 正好   zhènghǎo   adv   coincidentally

       我今天正好有時間, 我跟你去買衣服吧。

       我今天正好有时间, 我跟你去买衣服吧。

       我去找他的時候, 他正好要出門。 / 我去找他的时候, 他正好要出门。

7. 門口*   门口   ménkǒu   n   doorway; entrance

8. 接*   jiē   v   to pick up (somebody)

9. 一刻鐘*   一刻钟   yí kèzhōng   t   a quarter (of an hour)

10. 原來   原来   yuánlái   adv/adj   as it turns out; formerly; former [see G4]

11. 女孩兒*   女孩儿   nǚháir   n   a girl; a young woman

12. 長得*   长得   zhǎng de   (of a person's physical appearance) to look; to grow to be

       我弟弟長得很高。 / 我弟弟长得很高。

       她長得跟她媽媽差不多。 / 她长得跟她妈妈差不多。

13. 漂亮*   piàoliang   adj   pretty

14. 吸煙   吸烟   xī yān   vo   to smoke

15.	跟		gēn	v	to follow
16.	菜單	菜单	càidān	n	menu
17.	常客		chángkè	n	frequent patron; regular
18.	拿手		náshǒu	adj	good at; adept
19.	清蒸		qīngzhēng	v	to steam (food without heavy sauce)
20.	魚*	鱼	yú	n	fish
21.	味道		wèidao	n	taste; flavor
22.	芥蘭	芥兰	jièlán	n	Chinese broccoli
23.	牛肉*		niúròu	n	beef
24.	嫩		nèn	adj	tender
25.	香		xiāng	adj	fragrant; nice smelling
26.	叫(菜)		jiào (cài)	v	to order (food); to call
27.	湯*	汤	tāng	n	soup
28.	菠菜		bōcài	n	spinach
29.	豆腐		dòufu	n	bean curd; tofu
30.	素菜		sùcài	n	vegetable dishes
31.	點* (菜)	点 (菜)	diǎn (cài)	v	to order (food)
32.	新鮮*	新鲜	xīnxian	adj	fresh
33.	青菜		qīngcài	n	green leafy vegetables
34.	小白菜		xiǎobáicài	n	small Chinese cabbage
35.	麻煩*	麻烦	máfan	v/adj	to trouble; troublesome

做中國菜很麻煩。／做中国菜很麻烦。

麻煩你告訴老師我病了, 不能去上課了。

麻烦你告诉老师我病了, 不能去上课了。

36.	老闆	老板	lǎobǎn	n	boss; owner
37.	少*		shǎo	adv	(of quantity) less [see G7]
38.	鹽	盐	yán	n	salt
39.	味精*		wèijīng	n	MSG (monosodium glutamate)
40.	馬上	马上	mǎshàng	adv	immediately; right away

你的火車是三點的, 你得馬上走。/ 你的火车是三点的, 你得马上走。

你等我一下, 我馬上回來。/ 你等我一下, 我马上回来。

41.	記者	记者	jìzhě	n	reporter
42.	文章		wénzhāng	n	article
43.	卡路里		kǎlùlǐ	n/m	calorie
44.	健康*		jiànkāng	adj/n	healthy; health

我身體很健康。/ 我身体很健康。

他的健康越來越糟糕。

45.	看法		kànfǎ	n	point of view
46.	認為	认为	rènwéi	v	to hold (the opinion that)
47.	説法	说法	shuōfǎ	n	way of saying a thing; statement
48.	片面		piànmiàn	adj	one-sided
49.	總的來説	总的来说	zǒng de lái shuō		generally speaking; on the whole
50.	也許	也许	yěxǔ	adv	perhaps

明年暑假我也許去北京學中文。/ 明年暑假我也许去北京学中文。

他今天沒上課, 也許病了。/ 他今天没上课, 也许病了。

51.	油		yóu	n/adj	oil; oily
52.	會*	会	huì	av	to be good at; to know how to
53.	清淡		qīngdàn	adj	light in flavor

▼▼▼▼▼▼▼▼▼▼▼▼▼▼▼▼▼▼▼▼▼▼▼▼▼▼▼▼▼▼▼▼▼

| 54. | 同意 | | tóngyì | v | to agree |

我同意她的看法。

你的看法我不同意。

| 55. | 其實 | 其实 | qíshí | adv | actually |
| 56. | 要不然* | | yàobùrán | conj | otherwise |

PROPER NOUNS

| 1. | 林雪梅 | | Lín Xuěméi | a feminine name |
| 2. | 小陳 | 小陈 | Xiǎo Chén | "Little" Chen |

ENLARGED CHARACTERS FOR EASIER VIEWING AND COMPARING

蒸　　蘭　　鹽　　總

蒸　　兰　　盐　　总

Jìnzhǐ xī yān.

吸煙＝吸烟＝吸菸

▼▼

Grammar

1. ABOUT "TOPICS" (I)

If someone, something, or some event has already been mentioned, in other words, if it is no longer new information to the interlocutor, then it should appear at the beginning of a sentence. The positioning of known information at the beginning of a sentence is an important characteristic of Chinese.

(1) 其實, 那個記者(對中國菜)的看法我也不同意。

其实, 那个记者(对中国菜)的看法我也不同意。

Actually, that reporter's view (on Chinese food), I don't agree with (it) either.

(2) 他剛才告訴我的那件事我早就聽說了。

他刚才告诉我的那件事我早就听说了。

What he just told me—I had already heard.

(3) 你註冊手續都辦完了嗎? / 你注册手续都办完了吗?

All the registration procedures—have you completed (them)?

(4) 這個餐館魚做得很好。 / 这个餐馆鱼做得很好。

This restaurant's fish dishes are very good.

This type of topic + comment structure differs from the basic Chinese word order introduced in Lesson 2. In example (1), if 那個記者的看法 / 那个记者的看法 were new information, the word order would be, 我給你們介紹一下一個記者對中國菜的看法, 好嗎? / 我给你们介绍一下一个记者对中国菜的看法, 好吗? which would be a typical "subject + verb + object" type of sentence. Similarly, if the "topic" in example (2) were new information, the sentence would read, 他剛才告訴我一件事, 那件事我早就听说了。 / 他刚才告诉我一件事, 那件事我早就听说了。 Notice the difference in structure between the first and second clause. Once it has been mentioned, the object of the first clause 一件事 becomes a specific reference 那件事, and the topic of the second clause. Known information also means information that has already been mentioned or things that are taken for granted, such as eating, sleeping, or students going to classes, doing homework, etc.

▼▼

(5) 這本書你看完了嗎? / 这本书你看完了吗?

Have you finished reading <u>this book</u>?

(6) 功課你做完了嗎? / 功课你做完了吗?

Have you finished <u>your homework</u>?

(7) 飯要慢慢吃, 吃得太快對身體不好。

     饭要慢慢吃, 吃得太快对身体不好。

Eat (more) slowly. Eating too fast is not good for your health.

(8) A: 聽說<u>學校商店的東西</u>學生不能買了, 是真的嗎?

         听说<u>学校商店的东西</u>学生不能买了, 是真的吗?

     I hear that <u>the things in the school store</u> are no longer for sale to students. Is that true?

     B: 誰說的? 那不是真的。/ 谁说的? 那不是真的。

     Who said that? That's not true.

While many Chinese sentences follow a basic word order, "subject + verb + object," similar to English, the topic construction is also an important characteristic of Chinese grammar. It is preferred in certain circumstances, some of which are illustrated here.

2. ADVERBIALS AND 地 (DE)

Some adverbials signify the manner or the accompanying state of an action. The particle 地 (de) is usually required after these adverbials:

(1) 他慢慢地走進了教室。/ 他慢慢地走进了教室。

He slowly walked into the classroom.

(2) 我用力地把桌子搬起來。/ 我用力地把桌子搬起来。

I lifted the table with a great deal of effort.

(3) 看見了我, 妹妹很高興地問: "姐姐, 你跟我玩球, 好嗎?"

     看见了我, 妹妹很高兴地问: "姐姐, 你跟我玩球, 好吗?"

Upon seeing me, my sister very happily asked, "Older sister, play with me, O.K.?"

3. 一 + V

The character 一 plus a verb (usually monosyllabic) suggests the completion of a brief action.

(1)　外面有人叫我, 我開門一看, 原來是送信的。

　　外面有人叫我, 我开门一看, 原来是送信的。

　　There was someone calling my name outside. I opened the door and took a look. It turned out to be the mailman.

(2)　他把書往桌子上一放, 很快地跑了出去。

　　他把书往桌子上一放, 很快地跑了出去。

　　He put down the book on the desk and quickly ran out.

When 一 is used in this way, the following clause denotes the result of the action. 就 serves to link the two actions.

(3)　那個餐館很容易找, 我們一找就找到了。

　　那个餐馆很容易找, 我们一找就找到了。

　　It was very easy to find that restaurant. We found it right away.

(4)　你的聲音我很熟悉, 一聽就知道是你。

　　你的声音我很熟悉, 一听就知道是你。

　　Your voice is familiar to me. The minute I heard your voice, I knew it was you.

(5)　他病了。一看書就頭疼。 / 他病了。一看书就头疼。

　　He's sick. As soon as soon he tries to read, he gets a headache.

(6)　我一吃味精, 就得喝很多水。 / 我一吃味精, 就得喝很多水。

　　I have to drink a lot of water as soon as I eat MSG.

4. 原來 / 原来

原來 / 原来 has two meanings.

A. It is used upon the discovery of new information implying sudden realization. When used in this way, 原來 / 原来 is an adverb.

▼▼▼

(1)　我早就聽説有一個新同屋要來, 原來就是你呀。

　　我早就听说有一个新同屋要来, 原来就是你呀。

　　I heard earlier that a new roommate was coming. So it was you!

(2)　房間裏熱得很, 原來空調壞了。／ 房间里热得很, 原来空调坏了。

　　The room was really hot. It turned out that the air-conditioning was not working.

(3)　我覺得好像在哪兒見過你, 原來你是我的同學的姐姐。

　　我觉得好像在哪儿见过你, 原来你是我的同学的姐姐。

　　I thought that I had seen you somewhere. [I didn't realize that] you're my classmate's older sister.

B. It can be used as an adjective before a noun as in examples (4), (5), and (6), or an adverb before a verb as in examples (7), (8), and (9), meaning "in the past, before a change occurred." Note that in the adjectival use, 原來 ／ 原来 must be followed by 的.

(4)　我的中學老師還是原來的樣子, 一點都沒變。

　　我的中学老师还是原来的样子, 一点都没变。

　　My middle school teacher is still the same as before. He hasn't changed a bit.

(5)　你還住在原來的宿舍嗎? ／ 你还住在原来的宿舍吗?

　　Are you still living in the same dorm as before?

(6)　這棟樓還是原來的樣子, 又小又舊。

　　这栋楼还是原来的样子, 又小又旧。

　　This building is still the same as it used to be—small and old.

(7)　他原來住在學校的宿舍裏, 後來搬到校外去了 。

　　他原来住在学校的宿舍里, 后来搬到校外去了 。

　　He used to live in a dorm on campus, but he later moved off campus.

(8)　她原來吃肉, 現在吃起素來了。／ 她原来吃肉, 现在吃起素来了。

　　She used to eat meat. Now she's a vegetarian.

A menu displayed in a window.

(9)   柯太太原來不喜歡吃豆腐, 後來聽說吃豆腐對身體健康有好處, 慢慢就喜歡吃了。

柯太太原来不喜欢吃豆腐, 后来听说吃豆腐对身体健康有好处, 慢慢就喜欢吃了。

Mrs. Ke didn't used to like tofu. Then she heard that eating tofu was good for you, (so she) gradually started to like eating it.

5. 極了 / 极了

極了 / 极了 is used after adjectives, or after verbs that denote psychological activities to suggest an extreme degree.

(1)   我聽媽媽說暑假帶我去中國旅行,高興極了。

我听妈妈说暑假带我去中国旅行,高兴极了。

When I heard my mother say that she would take me on a trip to China during the summer break, I was really thrilled.

(2)   妹妹說她離開家以後, 想家想極了。/ 妹妹说她离开家以后, 想家想极了。

My younger sister said that she was really homesick after she left home.

(3)　他的衣櫃裏只掛著兩件衣服, 空極了。

　　　他的衣柜里只挂着两件衣服, 空极了。

There are only two pieces of clothing hanging in his closet. It's really, really empty.

(4)　我住的地方離商店很近, 買東西方便極了。

　　　我住的地方离商店很近, 买东西方便极了。

My place is very close to the stores. It's really convenient for shopping.

6. 又 ADJ./VERB, 又 ADJ./VERB

The "又 adj./verb, 又 adj./verb" pattern can be used to indicate two concurrent situations or actions.

(1)　他做的清蒸魚又嫩又好吃。／他做的清蒸鱼又嫩又好吃。

The steamed fish he makes is tender *and* delicious.

(2)　今年夏天天氣真不舒服, 又熱又悶。

　　　今年夏天天气真不舒服, 又热又闷。

This summer's weather was really uncomfortable. It was hot *and* humid.

(3)　孩子們又跑又跳, 玩兒得十分高興。

　　　孩子们又跑又跳, 玩儿得十分高兴。

The kids ran and jumped. They had a great time.

(4)　那個小孩又哭又叫, 我們一點辦法也沒有。

　　　那个小孩又哭又叫, 我们一点办法也没有。

That child cried and fussed. We didn't know what to do.

When two adjectives are used in this way, they must be consistent, i.e., both complimentary or both pejorative. Furthermore, the adjectives must be related in meaning. For instance, when describing people, we often say, "clever and pretty"; "tall and thin"; "short and overweight." And we say the weather is "hot and stuffy" or "cold and humid." When two verbs are involved, the actions denoted must be concurrent. For example, "talk and laugh," "cry and yell," etc.

Note that 也...也..., which is similar in meaning to 又..., 又..., requires a certain kind of context. The adjectives that 也 introduces should have already been mentioned.

▼▼▼▼▼▼▼▼▼▼▼▼▼▼▼▼▼▼▼▼▼▼▼▼▼▼▼▼▼▼▼▼▼▼▼▼▼▼

A: 你幫我找 一個工作好嗎? / 你帮我找 一个工作好吗?

Can you help me find a job?

B: 好啊, 你要找什麼樣的工作? / 好啊, 你要找什么样的工作?

Sure. What kind of job are you looking for?

A: 我要找一個又不累、錢又多的工作。/ 我要找一个又不累、钱又多的工作。

I'd like to find a job that's not too tiring and that also pays a lot of money.

B: 我知道有一個醫院有工作, 也不累, 錢也多, 可是對身體不太好。你想去嗎?

我知道有一个医院有工作, 也不累, 钱也多, 可是对身体不太好。你想去吗?

I know that there is a position at a hospital. It is not too tiring, and it pays well, but it wouldn't be good for your health. Do you want to go (work there)?

A: 不想。

No.

7. 多/少 +V (+NU+M+N)

In imperative sentences, one should say, 多吃一點青菜 / 多吃一点青菜, 少吸一點煙 / 少吸一点烟. We don't say *吃多一點青菜 / 吃多一点青菜, 吸少一點煙 / 吸少一点烟.

Important Words & Phrases

1. 特別是 + N (ESPECIALLY)

EXAMPLE: 這兒魚做得很好, 特別是清蒸魚, 味道好極了。

這兒魚做得很好, 特别是清蒸鱼, 味道好极了。

(1) 王小姐喜歡買東西, 特別是_____。

王小姐喜欢买东西, 特别是_____。

▼▼▼

(2) 小柯不喜歡運動, 特別是_____。

小柯不喜欢运动, 特别是_____。

(3) 李先生覺得中國菜很難做, 特別是_____。

李先生觉得中国菜很难做, 特别是_____。

2. 並/并 + NEG. (NOT REALLY)

EXAMPLE: 有一個美國記者寫文章說中國菜卡路里多, 對健康並沒有好處。

有一个美国记者写文章说中国菜卡路里多, 对健康并没有好处。

(1) 人們都說這兒的天氣好, 可是我來這兒以後覺得_____,
風大, 雨也多。

人们都说这儿的天气好, 可是我来这儿以后觉得_____,
风大, 雨也多。

(2) 大家常說住在校內又安全又方便, 我住了一個學期了, 覺得_____
_____, 下個學期我要搬到校外去。

大家常说住在校内又安全又方便, 我住了一个学期了, 觉得_____
_____, 下个学期我要搬到校外去。

(3) 聽說《好味道》這家中國餐館的菜很地道, 我昨天去那兒叫了三個菜, 發
現_____, 下次不去了。

听说《好味道》这家中国餐馆的菜很地道, 我昨天去那儿叫了三个菜, 发
现_____, 下次不去了。

3. 總的來説 ／ 总的来说 (GENERALLY SPEAKING)

EXAMPLE: 中國菜總的來説, 是對身體健康有好處的。

中国菜总的来说, 是对身体健康有好处的。

▼▼

(1)　總的來說,美國西南部的天氣＿＿＿＿＿＿＿＿＿＿。

　　　总的来说,美国西南部的天气＿＿＿＿＿＿＿＿＿＿。

(2)　A:　王老師,我們家小明中文學得怎麼樣?

　　　　　王老师,我们家小明中文学得怎么样?

　　　B:　林太太,小明除了寫字寫得慢一點兒以外,＿＿＿＿＿＿＿＿＿＿。

　　　　　林太太,小明除了写字写得慢一点儿以外,＿＿＿＿＿＿＿＿＿＿。

(3)　A:　你覺得學校的宿舍怎麼樣?

　　　　　你觉得学校的宿舍怎么样?

　　　B:　雖然設備＿＿＿＿＿＿＿,不過＿＿＿＿＿＿＿＿＿＿＿＿。

　　　　　虽然设备＿＿＿＿＿＿＿,不过＿＿＿＿＿＿＿＿＿＿＿＿。

4. 這(就)要看...(了) / 这(就)要看...了 (IT DEPENDS ON...)

EXAMPLE:　有的菜油是多一些,這就要看你會不會點菜了。

　　　　　　有的菜油是多一些,这就要看你会不会点菜了。

(1)　學生: 明天的考試難不難?

　　　学生: 明天的考试难不难?

　　　老師: 這就要看你＿＿＿＿＿＿＿＿＿＿。

　　　老师: 这就要看你＿＿＿＿＿＿＿＿＿＿。

(2)　A:　這次搬家,你想買多少新傢俱?

　　　　　这次搬家,你想买多少新家具?

　　　B:　＿＿＿＿＿＿＿＿＿＿＿＿＿＿＿＿＿。

(3) A: 學期快結束了，暑假你打算去中國玩嗎？

學期快結束了，暑假你打算去中国玩吗？

B: _____。

5. 其實 ／ 其实 (ACTUALLY)

EXAMPLE: 其實，那個記者的看法我也不同意。

其实，那个记者的看法我也不同意。

(1) 大家都说小張的拿手菜是清蒸魚，_____。

大家都说小张的拿手菜是清蒸鱼，_____。

(2) 同學們都猜柯林的女朋友是從上海來的，_____。

同学们都猜柯林的女朋友是从上海来的，_____。

(3) 很多人都認為住在校外比較省錢，_____。

很多人都认为住在校外比较省钱，_____。

6. (要)不然 (OTHERWISE)

EXAMPLE: 其實，那個記者的看法我也不同意，要不然，今天我就不會帶你們到這兒來。

其实，那个记者的看法我也不同意，要不然，今天我就不会带你们到这儿来。

(1) 這兒的冬天冷得很，得多買幾條被子和毯子，_____。

这儿的冬天冷得很，得多买几条被子和毯子，_____。

(2) 找房子不要找離馬路太近的，_____。

找房子不要找离马路太近的，_____。

(3) 別吃那麼多肉，多吃點青菜，_____。

别吃那么多肉，多吃点青菜，_____。

Pinyin Texts

NARRATIVE

Kāi xué yǐjīng liǎng ge duō xīngqī le, yīnwèi tài máng, Zhāng Tiānmíng měitiān zhǐhǎo zài xuéxiào de cāntīng chī fàn. Hěn cháng shíjiān méi chī Zhōngguó fàn le, tā hěn xiǎng qù Zhōngguó fànguǎnr chī yí dùn. Jīntiān shì zhōumò, zàishuō gōngkè yě bù duō, tā jiù dǎ le ge diànhuà gěi Kē Lín, wèn tā xiǎng bu xiǎng yìqǐ qù Zhōngguóchéng chī fàn. Kē Lín tīng le hěn gāoxīng de shuō, tā de nǚpéngyou Lín Xuěméi zhènghǎo yě xiǎng chī Zhōngguó fàn, tā ràng Zhāng Tiānmíng zài sùshè ménkǒu děng, tā kāi chē lái jiē tā.

Yí kèzhōng yǐhòu, Kē Lín de qìchē dào le. Zhāng Tiānmíng wàng chē li yí kàn, Kē Lín de nǚpéngyou yuánlái shì ge Zhōngguó nǚháir, zhǎng de hěn piàoliang. Shí fēnzhōng yǐhòu, tāmen sān ge rén dào le Kē Lín cháng qù de yì jiā Zhōngguó fànguǎnr.

DIALOGUE

They are entering a Chinese restaurant...

Fúwùyuán:	Kē xiānsheng, nǐ hǎo! Hǎojiǔ bú jiàn le. Jǐ wèi?
Kē Lín:	Xiǎo Chén, nǐ hǎo. Sān ge rén, bù xī yān.
Fúwùyuán:	Hǎo, qǐng gēn wǒ lái.

The three of them follow the waitress to their table...

Fúwùyuán:	Zhè shì càidān.
Kē Lín:	Xièxie. Xiǎo Zhāng, nǐ xiǎng chī diǎn shénme?
Zhāng Tiānmíng:	Nǐ shì zhèr de chángkè. Zhège fànguǎnr shénme cài zuì náshǒu?
Lín Xuěméi:	Zhèr yú zuò de hěn hǎo, tèbié shì qīngzhēngyú, wèidao hǎo jíle.
Kē Lín:	Jièlán niúròu yě búcuò, yòu nèn yòu xiāng.
Lín Xuěméi:	Zài jiào yí ge tāng ba.
Kē Lín:	Zhèr de bōcài dòufu tāng hěn hǎo, jiào yí ge hǎo bu hǎo?
Zhāng Tiānmíng:	Hǎo, hǎo. Zài yào ge shénme?
Kē Lín:	Wǒ kàn zài lái yí ge sùcài ba.
Fúwùyuán:	Xiànzài kěyǐ diǎn cài le ma?
Kē Lín:	Kěyǐ le. Yí ge qīngzhēngyú, yí ge jièlán niúròu, yí ge bōcài dòufu tāng. Jīntiān nǐmen yǒu shénme xīnxian de qīngcài?
Fúwùyuán:	Xiǎobáicài zěnmeyàng?
Kē Lín:	Kěyǐ. Xiǎo Chén, máfan gēn lǎobǎn shuō shǎo fàng diǎn yán, bié fàng wèijīng.
Fúwùyuán:	Hǎo. Cài mǎshàng lái.

▼▼▼▼▼▼▼▼▼▼▼▼▼▼▼▼▼▼▼▼▼▼▼▼▼▼▼▼▼▼▼▼▼▼▼▼

While they are waiting for their dishes...

Kē Lín:　　　　Yǒu yí ge Měiguó jìzhě xiě wénzhāng shuō Zhōngguó cài kǎlùlǐ duō, duì jiànkāng bìng méiyǒu hǎochù. Nǐmen yǒu shénme kànfǎ?

Lín Xuěméi:　　Wǒ rènwéi nàge jìzhě de shuōfǎ tài piànmiàn. Zhōngguó cài zǒng de lái shuō, shì duì shēntǐ jiànkāng yǒu hǎochù de. Yěxǔ yǒude cài yóu duō yìxiē, zhè jiù yào kàn nǐ huì bú huì diǎn cài le. Wǒmen jīntiān diǎn de cài, chúle niúròu yǐwài, dōu hěn qīngdàn.

Zhāng Tiānmíng:　Wǒ tóngyì Xiǎo Lín de kànfǎ. Kē Lín, nǐ hái méi shuō nǐ de kànfǎ ne.

Kē Lín:　　　　Qíshí, nàge jìzhě de kànfǎ wǒ yě bù tóngyì, yàobùrán, jīntiān wǒ jiù bú huì dài nǐmen dào zhèr lái. Ài, wǒmen de cài lái le.

Discussion Topic: Weekend Plans

Look at the following cartoon and describe in Chinese how Zhang Tianming spent his weekend.

第四課 ▲ 買東西

　　從飯館兒出來，張天明想起來應該買一些穿的和用的東西。 他從家裏來的時候，媽媽給他買了幾件衣服，像 T 恤衫、毛衣、牛仔褲等等，可是他覺得無論是樣子還是顏色都不太好，而且也不是名牌。 另外他還需要買洗衣粉、牙膏、香皂、衛生紙等日用品以及喝水的杯子、浴巾什麼的，於是他就請柯林帶他去買東西。 正好林雪梅也想買一些化妝品，他們就一起開車來到附近一家最大的購物中心。

DIALOGUE

柯林： 你要買什麼衣服？

張天明： 我想買一套運動服。

柯林： 這邊兒就是。你看看這一套，樣子、大小、長短、厚薄都合適，而且減價，打八折，價錢不貴。

張天明： 顏色也不錯。 多少錢？什麼牌子的？

第四课 ▲ 买东西

NARRATIVE

　　从饭馆儿出来,张天明想起来应该买一些穿的和用的东西。他从家里来的时候,妈妈给他买了几件衣服,像 T 恤衫、毛衣、牛仔裤等等,可是他觉得无论是样子还是颜色都不太好,而且也不是名牌。另外他还需要买洗衣粉、牙膏、香皂、卫生纸等日用品以及喝水的杯子、浴巾什么的,于是他就请柯林带他去买东西。正好林雪梅也想买一些化妆品,他们就一起开车来到附近一家最大的购物中心。

DIALOGUE

柯林：　　你要买什么衣服?

张天明：　我想买一套运动服。

柯林：　　这边儿就是。你看看这一套,样子、大小、长短、厚薄都合适,而且减价,打八折,价钱不贵。

张天明：　颜色也不错。多少钱?什么牌子的?

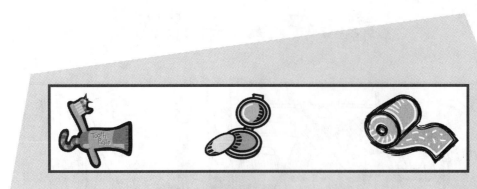

Can you name these items in Chinese?

林雪梅：　四十塊。這個牌子沒聽說過。不過是純棉的。

張天明：　那不行，我想買阿迪達斯的。

柯　林：　那件好像是阿迪達斯的。哎呀，三百多塊，真貴！

張天明：　買東西，我只買好的，名牌的，要不然就不買。因為名牌的衣服質量好。有的衣服便宜是便宜，可是牌子不好，穿一、兩次就不想穿了，只好再買一件。這樣兩件衣服花的錢比買一件名牌的更多。

林雪梅：　我同意小張的看法。

柯　林：　買衣服只圖便宜當然不好，但是也不要太挑剔，非買名牌的不可。我買衣服的標準，第一是穿著舒服，第二是物美價廉，是什麼牌子的，我不在乎。穿衣服是為了自己，也不是為了給別人看。

林雪梅：　我不同意你的看法。

張天明：　對。我也不同意。難道你喜歡看小林穿不好看的衣服嗎？

柯　林：　好，好，好。我不跟你們爭論了。雪梅，我陪你去化妝品那邊看看。

張天明：　你們去吧，我先去付錢，過一會兒去找你們，我還得去買一些日用品。

柯　林：　好吧，我們一會兒見。

How would you say these clothing items in Chinese?

林雪梅： 四十块。这个牌子没听说过。不过是纯棉的。

张天明： 那不行，我想买阿迪达斯的。

柯林： 那件好像是阿迪达斯的。哎呀，三百多块，真贵！

张天明： 买东西，我只买好的，名牌的，要不然就不买。因为名牌的衣服质量好。有的衣服便宜是便宜，可是牌子不好，穿一、两次就不想穿了，只好再买一件。这样两件衣服花的钱比买一件名牌的更多。

林雪梅： 我同意小张的看法。

柯林： 买衣服只图便宜当然不好，但是也不要太挑剔，非买名牌的不可。我买衣服的标准，第一是穿着舒服，第二是物美价廉，是什么牌子的，我不在乎。穿衣服是为了自己，不是为了给别人看。

林雪梅： 我不同意你的看法。

张天明： 对。我也不同意。难道你喜欢看小林穿不好看的衣服吗？

柯林： 好，好，好。我不跟你们争论了。雪梅，我陪你去化妆品那边看看。

张天明： 你们去吧，我先去付钱，过一会儿去找你们，我还得去买一些日用品。

柯林： 好吧，我们一会儿见。

▼▼▼

Zhang Tianming is at the check-out counter...

售貨員：　先生，付現金，還是用信用卡？

張天明：　信用卡。

售貨員：　先生，加上稅一共是三百八十六塊四。

張天明：　這個州的稅怎麼這麼重？百分之八點七五。

售貨員：　是的，請你在這兒簽個字。…這是您的收據，謝謝。

現金

▼▼▼▼▼▼▼▼▼▼▼▼▼▼▼▼▼▼▼▼▼▼▼▼▼▼▼▼▼▼▼▼▼▼▼▼▼▼

Zhang Tianming is at the check-out counter...

售货员：　先生，付现金，还是用信用卡？

张天明：　信用卡。

售货员：　先生，加上税一共是三百八十六块四。

张天明：　这个州的税怎么这么重？百分之八点七五。

售货员：　是的，请你在这儿签个字。…这是您的收据，谢谢。

信用卡和支票 (zhīpiào) / 信用卡和支票 (zhīpiào)

VOCABULARY

1. 想起來*   xiǎng qilai   vc   to realize; to recall

    我走到門口才想起來今天星期六, 不上班。

    我走到门口才想起来今天星期六, 不上班。

    那個新生我見過, 可是想不起來她叫什麼名字。

    那个新生我见过, 可是想不起来她叫什么名字。

2. 穿*   chuān   v   to wear

3. 衣服*   yīfu   n   clothes

4. 像   xiàng   v   such as

5. T恤衫   tīxùshān   n   T-shirt

6. 毛衣   máoyī   n   woolen sweater

7. 牛仔褲   牛仔裤   niúzǎikù   n   cowboy pants; jeans

8. 等等   děng děng   etc.

9. 無論   无论   wúlùn   conj   regardless of...; whether it be...
                                               [see G2]

10. 樣子   样子   yàngzi   n   style

11. 名牌   míngpái   n   famous brand; name brand

12. 需要   xūyào   v/n   to need; need

    你需要什麼樣的書? / 你需要什么样的书?

    我買車是因為工作需要。/ 我买车是因为工作需要。

13. 洗衣粉   xǐyīfěn   n   laundry powder

14. 牙膏   yágāo   n   toothpaste

15. 香皂   xiāngzào   n   scented soap; bath soap; facial soap

16. 衛生紙   卫生纸   wèishēngzhǐ   n   sanitary paper; toilet paper

17. 以及   yǐjí   conj   (formal) and

▼▼▼▼▼▼▼▼▼▼▼▼▼▼▼▼▼▼▼▼▼▼▼▼▼▼▼▼▼▼▼▼▼▼

18.	杯子		bēizi	n	cup; drinking glass
19.	浴巾		yùjīn	n	bath towel
20.	於是	于是	yúshì	conj	so; therefore; thereupon [see G3]
21.	化妝品*	化妆品	huàzhuāngpǐn	n	cosmetic products
22.	購物中心	购物中心	gòuwù zhōngxīn	n	shopping center
23.	套*		tào	m	suite; set
24.	運動服*	运动服	yùndòngfú	n	sportswear; sports clothes
25.	大小*		dàxiǎo	n	size
26.	長短	长短	chángduǎn	n	length
27.	厚薄		hòubó	n	thickness
28.	合適*	合适	héshì	adj	suitable

這件衣服太長, 你穿不合適。／这件衣服太长, 你穿不合适。

這本字典對你學中文很合適。／这本字典对你学中文很合适。

29.	減價*	减价	jiǎn jià	vo	to discount; to be on sale
30.	打折*		dǎ zhé	vo	to discount (from a set or list price)
31.	價錢	价钱	jiàqian	n	price
32.	牌子		páizi	n	brand
33.	純棉 (的)	纯棉 (的)	chúnmián (de)	adj	pure cotton; 100% cotton
34.	行*		xíng	v	(col) will work; will do
35.	好像*		hǎoxiàng	adv	as if; seem to be
36.	哎呀		āiyā	exc	(an exclamation indicating surprise) gosh; oh
37.	質量	质量	zhìliàng	n	quality
38.	圖	图	tú	v	to seek; to pursue

他做事只圖自己高興, 不在乎別人怎麼想。

他做事只图自己高兴, 不在乎别人怎么想。

你這樣努力工作, 圖什麼? / 你这样努力工作, 图什么?

39.	挑剔		tiāoti	adj	picky; fastidious

他買東西很挑剔。/ 他买东西很挑剔。

你不要太挑剔, 這個房間已經很不錯了。

你不要太挑剔, 这个房间已经很不错了。

40.	非...不可		fēi...bù kě		have to be; nothing other than... would do

41.	標準	标准	biāozhǔn	n/adj	criterion; standard

你認為一個好老師的標準是什麼? / 你认为一个好老师的标准是什么?

他説的是標準的北京話。/ 他说的是标准的北京话。

42.	物美價廉	物美价廉	wù měi jià lián		attractive goods at inexpensive prices

43.	在乎		zàihu	v	to mind; to care

他很在乎別人怎麼看他。/ 他很在乎别人怎么看他。

你的車不見了, 你怎麼一點都不在乎?

你的车不见了, 你怎么一点都不在乎?

44.	難道	难道	nándào	adv	(introducing a rhetorical question) Do you mean to say? [see G6]

45.	好看		hǎokàn	adj	nice looking; attractive

46.	爭論	争论	zhēnglùn	v	to argue

47.	陪		péi	v	to accompany; to go with someone

我不太舒服, 你陪我去醫院好嗎? / 我不太舒服, 你陪我去医院好吗?

這個孩子的媽媽出去了, 你陪陪他好嗎?

这个孩子的妈妈出去了, 你陪陪他好吗?

48.	付錢*	付钱	fù qián	vo	to pay (for a purchase)

49.	現金	现金	xiànjīn	n	cash

50.	信用卡*		xìnyòngkǎ	n	credit card

51.	稅		shuì	n	tax
52.	州		zhōu	n	state
53.	百分之		bǎifēn zhī		percent
54.	簽字	签字	qiān zì	vo	to sign one's name
55.	收據	收据	shōujù	n	receipt

PROPER NOUN

阿迪達斯	阿迪达斯	Ādídásī	Adidas

ENLARGED CHARACTERS FOR EASIER VIEWING AND COMPARING

膏	衛	薄	圖	廉	論	據
膏	卫	薄	图	廉	论	据

Grammar

1. THE POSITION OF TIME PHRASES

There are two kinds of time phrases. The first kind signifies points in time, such as today, Monday, 1996, three days ago, or the time when... The second kind has to do with duration of time, such as an hour, three days, or two years. Time phrases that signify points in time are placed at the beginning of a sentence or before the verb, as you already know. In this lesson, we will concentrate on time phrases that have to do with duration of time. These phrases indicate the duration of an action or a state.

(1)   我來了兩天了,覺得很方便。(第二課)

       我来了两天了,觉得很方便。(第二课)

       I have been here for two days. I find it very convenient (to live here). [see L.2]

(2)   開學已經兩個多星期了。(第三課) / 开学已经两个多星期了。(第三课)

School has been in session for more than two weeks now. [see L.3]

(3)   我上個週末洗衣服洗了一個半小時。

我上个周末洗衣服洗了一个半小时。

I spent an hour and a half doing laundry last weekend.

(4)   你昨晚的清蒸魚蒸了多長時間? / 你昨晚的清蒸鱼蒸了多长时间?

How long did you steam the fish last night?

Phrases that signify duration of time are usually placed after the verbs. In this type of sentence, the verbs involved generally have to do with actions that can last, such as 學/学, 做, 寫/写, 走, etc. If there is an object after the verb, one must repeat the verb before stating the duration of the action. See examples (3) and (4). If, however, the actions cannot last by their nature, such as 來/来 come, 結婚 / 结婚 (jié hūn) get married, 畢業 / 毕业 (bì yè) graduate, 死 (sǐ) die, then there is no need to repeat the verbs. See example (1).

If those phrases that normally signify duration of time are preceded by a negative, or if the phrases have to do with the frequency of an action, such as 一天吃三次 eat three times a day, 三天去一次 go every three days, they are placed before the verbs.

(5)   我一個星期沒有看見他了。 / 我一个星期没有看见他了。

I haven't seen him for a week.

(6)   很長時間沒吃中國飯了,他很想去中國飯館吃一頓。(第三課)

很长时间没吃中国饭了,他很想去中国饭馆吃一顿。(第三课)

He hasn't had Chinese food for a long time. He really wants to have a meal in a Chinese restaurant. [see L.3]

(7)   這棟房子你一年得付四次稅。 / 这栋房子你一年得付四次税。

You have to pay taxes on this house four times a year.

2. 無論..., 都... / 无论..., 都...

無論 / 无论 signifies that the result will remain the same under any condition or circumstances. It must be used together with an indefinite interrogative pronoun or an alternative compound.

(1) 明天無論誰請客我都不去。／明天无论谁请客我都不去。

No matter who's paying tomorrow, I'm not going.

(誰／谁 is an indefinite interrogative pronoun meaning *doesn't matter who it is* or *anybody*.)

(2) A: 你想去城裏的哪個購物中心?／你想去城里的哪个购物中心?

Which city shopping center do you want to go to?

B: 城裏無論哪個購物中心我都沒去過, 所以去哪個都可以。
城里无论哪个购物中心我都没去过, 所以去哪个都可以。

I haven't been to any shopping center in town, so going to any one will be fine.

(哪個購物中心／哪个物中心 whichever shopping center is indefinite.)

(3) 我們已經決定明天去買東西, 你無論同意不同意都得跟我們去。
我们已经决定明天去买东西, 你无论同意不同意都得跟我们去。

We've already decided to go shopping tomorrow. Whether you agree or not, you have to go with us.

(同意不同意 is an alternative compound meaning *agree or disagree, it doesn't matter*.)

(4) 他無論在家裏還是在學校, 老是寫文章, 很少看見他玩。
他无论在家里还是在学校, 老是写文章, 很少看见他玩。

Whether he's at home or at school, he's always writing. [You] seldom see him play [relax].

(在家裏還是在學校／在家里还是在学校 is an alternative compound meaning *doesn't matter where*.)

3. 於是／于是

The conjunction 於是／于是 connects two clauses. The second clause usually denotes a new situation or action that is consequent on the situation or action mentioned in the first clause.

(1) 我給他打了很多次電話都沒有人接, 於是就寫了一封信。
我给他打了很多次电话都没有人接, 于是就写了一封信。

I called him many times, but nobody answered, so I wrote him a letter.

▼▼▼

(2) 晚飯後, 他去一家購物中心買運動鞋, 那裏沒有他喜歡的, 於是又開車去了另一家購物中心。

晚饭后, 他去一家购物中心买运动鞋, 那里没有他喜欢的, 于是又开车去了另一家购物中心。

After dinner he went to a shopping center to get a pair of sneakers. That shopping center didn't have what he liked, so he drove to another shopping center.

(3) 原來週末孩子們要上山, 沒想到星期六早上下雨了, 於是他們就不去了。

原来周末孩子们要上山, 没想到星期六早上下雨了, 于是他们就不去了。

The kids were going to go to the mountains over the weekend, but it rained Saturday morning, so they didn't go.

(4) 小明在商店看見一件毛衣, 樣子、顏色他都很喜歡, 於是就買下來了。

小明在商店看见一件毛衣, 样子、颜色他都很喜欢, 于是就买下来了。

Little Ming saw a sweater at the store. He liked the style and the color, so he bought it.

於是 / 于是 differs from 所以 in that with 於是 / 于是 the emphasis is not so much on causal relationship as on sequentiality. It suggests that action A leads to action B or action A gives rise to some kind of change. 於是 / 于是 cannot be substituted with 所以 in the above sentences without the emphasis being shifted from sequentiality to cause and effect. When causal relationship is clearly intended, or when the second clause does not describe an action or a change, 所以 cannot be substituted with 於是 / 于是。

(5) 這次考試, 因為我沒有準備, 所以考得很不好。

这次考试, 因为我没有准备, 所以考得很不好。

I didn't prepare for the exam this time, so I did really badly.

(Lack of preparation is stated as the direct cause of poor performance on the exam.)

(6) 上海人多車多, 所以開車很容易緊張。

上海人多车多, 所以开车很容易紧张。

There are so many people and cars in Shanghai that it is easy to get nervous while you drive. (Crowds and cars lead to nervousness.)

(7)   這兩天他不太舒服, 所以沒有胃口吃東西。

这两天他不太舒服, 所以没有胃口吃东西。

He's been under the weather the past two days, so he has no appetite.
(Bad health results in a loss of appetite.)

名牌運動服／名牌运动服

4. 真

真 is used to convey an affirmative, exclamatory tone of voice. It is used before adjectives and before verbs that express feeling, emotion or opinion.

(1)   好久沒見我妹妹了, 真想去波士頓看她。

好久没见我妹妹了, 真想去波士顿看她。

It's been a long time since I saw my little sister. I would really like to go to Boston to see her.

(2)   今天真冷, 穿三件毛衣都不行。／今天真冷, 穿三件毛衣都不行。

It's really cold today. You could be wearing three sweaters, and you still would be cold.

(3)   這條褲子樣子真好, 我想給哥哥買一條。

这条裤子样子真好, 我想给哥哥买一条。

This pair of pants looks great. I am thinking about getting a pair for my older brother.

(4) 你們老師給的功課真多, 你做了三個鐘頭了還沒做完。

你们老师给的功课真多, 你做了三个钟头了还没做完。

Your teacher really assigned a lot of homework. You've been at it for three hours, and you still haven't finished it.

(5) 這台烘乾機真吵, 你應該買一台新的。

这台烘干机真吵, 你应该买一台新的。

This dryer is really noisy. You should get a new one!

Unlike 很, 十分, and 特別, 真 does not provide new information. It is used to indicate an emphatic tone of voice. Therefore, avoid using 真 in ordinary descriptive sentences, e.g.,

(6) A: 小張, 你聽天氣預報了嗎? 明天的天氣怎麼樣?

小张, 你听天气预报了吗? 明天的天气怎么样?

Little Zhang, did you listen to the weather forecast? What's the weather going to be like tomorrow?

B: 天氣預報說明天的天氣會到二十度(dù), 很冷。

天气预报说明天的天气会到二十度(dù), 很冷。

According to the weather forecast, [the temperature] will be 20 degrees tomorrow. Really cold!

Compared to

*天氣預報說明天的天氣真冷, 會到二十度。

*天气预报说明天的天气真冷, 会到二十度。

真 can sometimes mean truly, honestly. It is often followed by the particle 的.

(7) 這個芥蘭牛肉真的又嫩又香。/ 这个芥兰牛肉真的又嫩又香。

The beef with Chinese broccoli is truly tender and appetizing.
(The speaker is trying to convince the listener.)

(8) A: 學校的宿舍太貴了, 我想搬到校外去住。

学校的宿舍太贵了, 我想搬到校外去住。

It's too expensive to live in the dorm. I plan to move off campus.

B: 校外沒有校內方便, 你真的想搬出去嗎?

校外没有校内方便, 你真的想搬出去吗?

Living off campus is not as convenient as living on campus. Are you serious about moving out?

(The speaker is seeking confirmation.)

5. ADJ./V + 是 + ADJ./V, 可是 ／但是...

This structure is equivalent to "although...(yet)."

(1)　A: 我打算學文學。／我打算学文学。

I plan to study literature.

B: 學文學好是好, 可是將來找工作不太容易。
學文学好是好, 可是将来找工作不太容易。

It *is* good to study literature, but it may not be easy to find a job later.

(2)　A: 這件衣服太貴了, 別買!／这件衣服太贵了, 别买!

This garment is too expensive. Don't buy it.

B: 這件衣服貴是貴, 可是牌子好。／这件衣服贵是贵, 可是牌子好。

It *is* expensive, but it's a good brand.

(3)　A: 張理中先生常常在報上寫文章, 你看不看?
张理中先生常常在报上写文章, 你看不看?

Mr. Zhang Lizhong often writes for newspapers. Do you read his articles?

B: 我看是看, 可是我不太同意他的看法。

I *do*, but I disagree with his views.

(4)　A: 你不吸煙嗎?／你不吸烟吗?

You don't smoke?

B: 我吸是吸, 可是吸得很少。

       我吸是吸, 可是吸得很少。

       I *do* smoke, but very little.

A sale sign in a clothing store.

6. 難道 / 难道

難道 / 难道 is used in rhetorical questions. It lends force to the tone of voice.

(1)   你做菜放那麼多鹽和味精, 難道不在乎自己的健康嗎?

       你做菜放那么多盐和味精, 难道不在乎自己的健康吗?

       You use so much salt and MSG when you cook. Are you telling me that you don't care about your own health?

(2)   他來美國十年了, 難道連一句英文都不會說嗎?

       他来美国十年了, 难道连一句英文都不会说吗?

       Do you mean that he has been in America for ten years ▲ and can't speak even a word of English?

(3) 你已經有八張信用卡了, 難道還想再辦一張?

你已经有八张信用卡了, 难道还想再办一张?

You already have eight credit cards, and now you want to get another one?

(4) 你說這件事不是他做的, 難道是你做的嗎?

你说这件事不是他做的, 难道是你做的吗?

You said that he didn't do it. Are you telling me that you did it?

Note: 難道 / 难道 can be used before or after the subject, but the question takes the 嗎/吗 form as shown in examples (1), (2), and (4). Sometimes the 嗎/吗 can be omitted as in example (3). 難道 / 难道 does not take on other kinds of interrogative forms involving interrogative pronouns or V-not-V constructions. We don't say: *這件事情不是你做的, 難道是誰做的? / 这件事情不是你做的, 难道是谁做的? or *你難道去不去? / 你难道去不去? etc. Note also that rhetorical questions require some kind of context. Therefore, 難道 / 难道 cannot be used out of the blue.

購物中心 / 购物中心

7. REDUPLICATION OF VERBS

Reduplicated verbs are used in imperative sentences to soften the tone of voice.

(1) 我陪你去化妝品那邊看看。/ 我陪你去化妆品那边看看。

I'll go to the cosmetics counter with you.

(2)   你幫我看看這件T恤衫的大小、長短合適不合適。

      你帮我看看这件T恤衫的大小、长短合适不合适。

      Please take a look to see if the size of the T-shirt is all right.

(3)   你跟他說說, 請他明天開車送我去飛機場。

      你跟他说说, 请他明天开车送我去飞机场。

      Please talk to him. Ask him to give me a ride to the airport tomorrow.

一下 has the same effect.

(1)   你看一下我們的空調是不是有問題了?

      你看一下我们的空调是不是有问题了?

      Please see if our air conditioner is broken.

(2)   等一下, 晚飯還沒好。/ 等一下, 晚饭还没好。

      Wait a second. Dinner is not ready yet.

(3)   你們不認識, 我來介紹一下。/ 你们不认识, 我来介绍一下。

      You don't know each other. Let me introduce you.

Important Words & Phrases

1. 另外 (BESIDES)

EXAMPLE: 他要買牙膏, 另外還應該買喝水的杯子。

           他要买牙膏, 另外还应该买喝水的杯子。

(1)   你不舒服, 應該多喝點水,_____。

      你不舒服, 应该多喝点水,_____。

(2)   我住的地方附近有兩個購物中心,_____。

      我住的地方附近有两个购物中心,_____。

(3) 明天考試, 你們要復習生詞語法,＿＿＿＿＿＿＿＿＿＿＿。

   明天考试, 你们要复习生词语法,＿＿＿＿＿＿＿＿＿＿＿。

2. ...什麼的 / ...什么的 (...ETC.)

EXAMPLE: 他還需要買洗衣粉、牙膏、香皂、衛生紙等日品以及喝水的杯子、
         浴巾什麼的。

         他还需要买洗衣粉、牙膏、香皂、卫生纸等日品以及喝水的杯子、
         浴巾什么的。

(1) 媽媽昨天晚上請客, 做了很多菜,＿＿＿＿＿＿＿＿＿＿＿＿＿＿, 都很好吃。

   妈妈昨天晚上请客, 做了很多菜,＿＿＿＿＿＿＿＿＿＿＿＿＿＿, 都很好吃。

(2) 我們這棟宿舍的設備不錯,＿＿＿＿＿＿＿＿＿＿＿＿＿＿＿, 都又好又新。

   我们这栋宿舍的设备不错,＿＿＿＿＿＿＿＿＿＿＿＿＿＿＿, 都又好又新。

(3) 他床上放了很多東西, 有＿＿＿＿＿＿＿＿＿＿＿＿＿＿＿＿。

   他床上放了很多东西, 有＿＿＿＿＿＿＿＿＿＿＿＿＿＿＿＿。

3. 大小、長短 / 长短、厚薄... (SIZE, LENGTH, THICKNESS, ETC.)

EXAMPLE: 你看看這一套, 樣子、大小、長短、厚薄都合適...

         你看看这一套, 样子、大小、长短、厚薄都合适...

(1) 你穿中號的, 這套運動服也是中號的,＿＿＿＿＿＿＿＿＿＿＿。

   你穿中号的, 这套运动服也是中号的,＿＿＿＿＿＿＿＿＿＿＿。

(2) 你寫的文章一共八百字,＿＿＿＿＿＿＿＿＿正好。

   你写的文章一共八百字,＿＿＿＿＿＿＿＿＿正好。

(3) 冬天買衣服, 應該先看＿＿＿＿＿＿＿＿＿, 再看＿＿＿＿＿＿＿＿＿。

   冬天买衣服, 应该先看＿＿＿＿＿＿＿＿＿, 再看＿＿＿＿＿＿＿＿＿。

4. 打折 (DISCOUNT)

EXAMPLE: 減價, 打八折, 價錢不貴。

減价, 打八折, 价钱不贵。

(1) 這個週末很多東西都＿＿＿＿＿＿＿＿＿＿, 我們去買吧。

这个周末很多东西都＿＿＿＿＿＿＿＿＿＿, 我们去买吧。

(2) 這個書架原來八十塊, ＿＿＿＿＿＿＿＿, 現在是五十六塊錢。

这个书架原来八十块, ＿＿＿＿＿＿＿＿, 现在是五十六块钱。

(3) 我買了一張飛機票, ＿＿＿＿＿＿＿＿, 一百二十五塊錢, 原來是二百五十塊錢。

我买了一张飞机票, ＿＿＿＿＿＿＿＿, 一百二十五块钱, 原来是二百五十块钱。

5.非...不可 (INSIST ON)

EXAMPLE: 買衣服只圖便宜當然不好, 但是也不要太挑剔, 非買名牌不可。

买衣服只图便宜当然不好, 但是也不要太挑剔, 非买名牌不可。

(1) 小林吃東西很挑剔, 一般的魚他不吃,＿＿＿＿＿＿＿＿＿＿＿＿＿＿。

小林吃东西很挑剔, 一般的鱼他不吃,＿＿＿＿＿＿＿＿＿＿＿＿＿＿。

(2) 他找房子的標準很高,＿＿＿＿＿＿＿＿＿＿＿＿＿＿＿＿＿。

他找房子的标准很高,＿＿＿＿＿＿＿＿＿＿＿＿＿＿＿＿＿。

(3) 我說那條褲子太貴, 質量也不見得好, 可是她喜歡那個樣子,＿＿＿＿＿＿＿＿＿＿＿。

我说那条裤子太贵, 质量也不见得好, 可是她喜欢那个样子,＿＿＿＿＿＿＿＿＿＿＿。

Pinyin Texts

NARRATIVE

Cóng fànguǎnr chū lái, Zhāng Tiānmíng xiǎng qilai yīnggāi mǎi yìxiē chuān de hé yòng de dōngxi. Tā cóng jiā li lái de shíhou, māma gěi tā mǎi le jǐ jiàn yīfu, xiàng tīxùshān, máoyī, niúzǎikù děng děng, kěshì tā juéde wúlùn shì yàngzi háishi yánsè dōu bú tài hǎo, érqiě yě bú shì míngpái. Lìngwài tā hái xūyào mǎi xǐyīfěn, yágāo, xiāngzào, wèishēngzhǐ děng rìyòngpǐn yǐjí hē shuǐ de bēizi, yùjīn shénme de, yúshì tā jiù qǐng Kē Lín dài tā qù mǎi dōngxi. Zhènghǎo Lín Xuěméi yě xiǎng mǎi yìxiē huàzhuāngpǐn, tāmen jiù yìqǐ kāi chē lái dào fùjìn yì jiā zuì dà de gòuwù zhōngxīn.

DIALOGUE

Kē Lín:	Nǐ yào mǎi shénme yīfu?
Zhāng Tiānmíng:	Wǒ xiǎng mǎi yí tào yùndòngfú.
Kē Lín:	Zhè biānr jiù shì. Nǐ kàn kan zhè yí tào, yàngzi, dàxiǎo, chángduǎn, hòubó dōu héshì, érqiě jiǎn jià, dǎ bā zhé, jiàqian bú guì.
Zhāng Tiānmíng:	Yánsè yě búcuò. Duōshǎo qián? Shénme páizi de?
Lín Xuěméi:	Sìshí kuài. Zhège páizi méi tīngshuō guo. Búguò shì chún mián de.
Zhāng Tiānmíng:	Nà bù xíng, wǒ xiǎng mǎi Ādídásī de.
Kē Lín:	Nà jiàn hǎoxiàng shì Ādídásī de. Āiyā, sān bǎi duō kuài, zhēn guì!
Zhāng Tiānmíng:	Mǎi dōngxi, wǒ zhǐ mǎi hǎo de, míngpái de, yàobùrán jiù bù mǎi. Yīnwèi míngpái de yīfu zhìliàng hǎo. Yǒude yīfu piányi shì piányi, kěshì páizi bù hǎo, chuān yì, liǎng cì jiù bù xiǎng chuān le, zhǐhǎo zài mǎi yí jiàn. Zhè yàng liǎng jiàn yīfu huā de qián bǐ mǎi yí jiàn míngpái de gèng duō.
Lín Xuěméi:	Wǒ tóngyì Xiǎo Zhāng de kànfǎ.
Kē Lín:	Mǎi yīfu zhǐ tú piányi dāngrán bù hǎo, dànshì yě bú yào tài tiāoti, fēi mǎi míngpái de bù kě. Wǒ mǎi yīfu de biāozhǔn, dìyī shì chuān zhe shūfu, dì'èr shì wù měi jià lián, shì shénme páizi de, wǒ bú zàihu. Chuān yīfu shì wèile zìjǐ, bú shì wèile gěi bié rén kàn.
Lín Xuěméi:	Wǒ bù tóngyì nǐ de kànfǎ.
Zhāng Tiānmíng:	Duì. Wǒ yě bù tóngyì. Nándào nǐ xǐhuān kàn Xiǎo Lín chuān bù hǎokàn de yīfu ma?
Kē Lín:	Hǎo, hǎo, hǎo. Wǎ bù gēn nǐmen zhēnglùn le. Xuěméi, wǒ péi nǐ qù huàzhuāngpǐn nàbiān kànkan.
Zhāng Tiānmíng:	Nǐmen qù ba, wǒ xiān qù fù qián, guò yíhuìr qù zhǎo nǐmen, wǒ hái děi qù mǎi yìxiē rìyòngpǐn.
Kē Lín:	Hǎo ba, wǒmen yíhuìr jiàn.

Zhāng Tiānmíng is at the check-out counter...

Shòuhuòyuán: Xiānsheng, fù xiànjīn, háishi yòng xìnyòngkǎ?

Zhāng Tiānmíng: Xìnyòngkǎ.

Shòuhuòyuán: Xiānsheng, jiā shàng shuì yígòng shì sān bǎi bāshí liù kuài sì.

Zhāng Tiānmíng: Zhège zhōu de shuì zěnme zhème zhòng? Bǎifēn zhī bā diǎn qī wǔ.

Shòuhuòyuán: Shìde, qǐng nǐ zài zhèr qiān ge zì...Zhè shì nín de shōujù, xièxie.

Discussion Topic: Shopping

Follow the comic strip and recap in Chinese how Zhang Tianming's shopping went.

第五課 ▲ 選專業

NARRATIVE

　　張天明這個學期選了四門課：東亞史、統計學、美國文學和中文。除了中文以外，其他的課雖然很有意思，也學到了不少東西，只是都得花很多時間準備，有點受不了。因為張天明的父母在家常常說中文，所以一年級的中文課，對他來說，聽和說很容易，就是寫漢字太難，一個字得反復練習才能記住。

　　這個學期已經過了一大半了，馬上又得為下學期註冊了。後天張天明要去見他的指導教授，討論下學期選課的事。他覺得應該找李哲聊聊，聽聽他的想法。

DIALOGUE

張天明：　怎麼樣，下學期的課你選好了嗎？

李哲：　　還沒呢。你呢？

第五课 ▲ 选专业

NARRATIVE

　　张天明这个学期选了四门课：东亚史、统计学、美国文学和中文。除了中文以外，其他的课虽然很有意思，也学到了不少东西，只是都得花很多时间准备，有点受不了。因为张天明的父母在家常常说中文，所以一年级的中文课，对他来说，听和说很容易，就是写汉字太难，一个字得反复练习才能记住。

　　这个学期已经过了一大半了，马上又得为下学期注册了。后天张天明要去见他的指导教授，讨论下学期选课的事。他觉得应该找李哲聊聊，听听他的想法。

DIALOGUE

张天明：　怎么样,下学期的课你选好了吗?

李哲：　　还没呢。你呢?

張天明:　我肯定要選中文，至於另外兩門課選什麼，還不知道。你還得再上幾門課才能畢業？

李哲:　　我還得上三門課。我想拿雙學位，再選一門物理課，另外再選兩門電腦系的課，學分就夠了。

張天明:　你畢業以後打算做什麼呢？

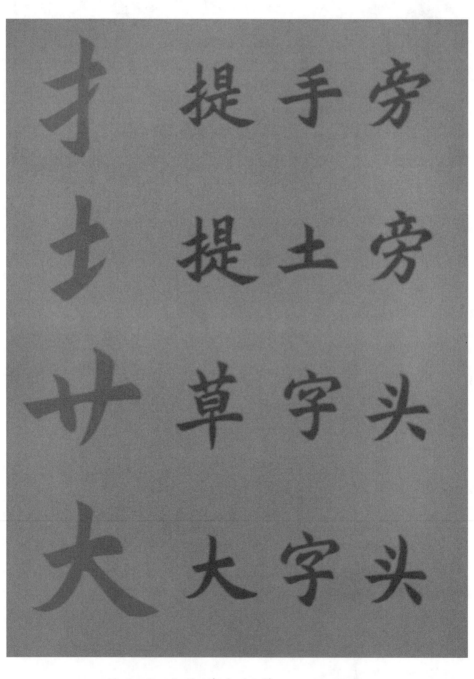

你記住這些漢字部首(bùshǒu)了嗎？

▼▼▼▼▼▼▼▼▼▼▼▼▼▼▼▼▼▼▼▼▼▼▼▼▼▼▼▼▼▼▼▼▼▼▼▼▼

张天明：　我肯定要选中文，至于另外两门课选什么，还不知道。你还得
　　　　　再上几门课才能毕业？

李哲：　　我还得上三门课。我想拿双学位，再选一门物理课，另外再选
　　　　　两门电脑系的课，学分就够了。

张天明：　你毕业以后打算做什么呢？

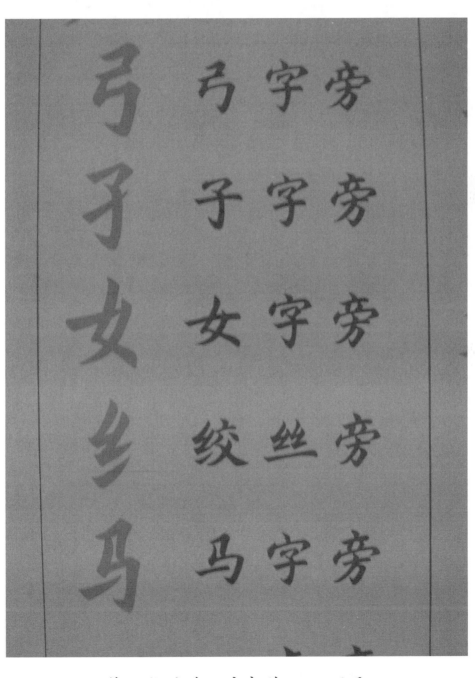

你记住这些汉字部首(bùshǒu)了吗？

李哲： 我想念研究所，要麼是工學院，要麼是管理學院。你想選什麼專業？

張天明： 我想學文學。可是我媽媽說，學文科將來不容易找工作，而且賺錢也少，她讓我念醫學院。但是，我最不願意當醫生，整天跟病人打交道，多沒意思。

李哲： 唉，我的父母跟你的父母差不多。其實，我最喜歡的是哲學，因為我喜歡想問題。西方人一般不太管孩子選什麼專業，比我們自由。

張天明： 你想申請哪些學校？

李哲： 我想申請離家比較近的學校，這樣我就可以搬回家去住，把房租跟飯錢省下來。

張天明： 不過在家裏住太不自由了。

李哲： 是嗎？那我再考慮考慮。

張天明： 也許你可以先找個地方實習一下，有點工作經驗，這樣對你寫履歷有好處，將來申請學校、找工作都可以提一提。

李哲： 我明天去找指導教授的時候，再聽聽他的意見。

張天明： 後天我也要去找指導教授。希望他們能給咱們一些好的建議。

李哲: 我想念研究所，要么是工学院，要么是管理学院。你想选什么专业？

张天明: 我想学文学。可是我妈妈说，学文科将来不容易找工作，而且赚钱也少，她让我念医学院。但是，我最不愿意当医生，整天跟病人打交道，多没意思。

李哲: 唉，我的父母跟你的父母差不多。其实，我最喜欢的是哲学，因为我喜欢想问题。西方人一般不太管孩子选什么专业，比我们自由。

张天明: 你想申请哪些学校？

李哲: 我想申请离家比较近的学校，这样我就可以搬回家去住，把房租跟饭钱省下来。

张天明: 不过在家里住太不自由了。

李哲: 是吗？那我再考虑考虑。

张天明: 也许你可以先找个地方实习一下，有点工作经验，这样对你写履历有好处，将来申请学校、找工作都可以提一提。

李哲: 我明天去找指导教授的时候，再听听他的意见。

张天明: 后天我也要去找指导教授。希望他们能给咱们一些好的建议。

VOCABULARY

1. 選　　選　　xuǎn　　v　　to choose

   你選誰做你的指導教授? / 你选谁做你的指导教授?

2. 專業*　　专业　　zhuānyè　　n　　major; specialization

3. 選課　　选课　　xuǎn kè　　vo　　to select/register for courses

   這個學期我選了三門課。/ 这个学期我选了三门课。

4. 門　　门　　mén　　m　　measure word for (academic) courses

5. 東亞史　　东亚史　　Dōngyàshǐ　　n　　East Asian history

6. 統計學　　统计学　　tǒngjìxué　　n　　statistics

7. 文學　　文学　　wénxué　　n　　literature

8. 其他*　　　　qítā　　pr　　other

9. 準備*　　准备　　zhǔnbèi　　v　　to prepare

10. 學到　　学到　　xué dào　　vc　　to learn; to acquire

11. 受不了　　　　shòu bu liǎo　　vc　　cannot take it

    今天太熱,我真的受不了。/ 今天太热,我真的受不了。

    很久沒吃中國飯了,小張有點兒受不了了。

    很久没吃中国饭了,小张有点儿受不了了。

12. 對...來說　　对...来说　　duì...lái shuō　　　　as to...; so far as...is concerned [see G2]

13. 反復　　反复　　fǎnfù　　adv　　repeatedly

14. 記住　　记住　　jì zhù　　vc　　to remember; to fix in the memory

15. 大半　　　　dàbàn　　nu　　more than half; most

16. 為　　为　　wèi　　prep　　for

17. 後天*　　后天　　hòutiān　　t　　the day after tomorrow

| 18. | 指導教授 | 指导教授 | zhǐdǎo jiàoshòu | n | guiding professor; academic adviser |
| 19. | 討論 | 讨论 | tǎolùn | v | to discuss |

我們正在討論選專業的事。／我们正在讨论选专业的事。

這件事很重要, 你們討論討論吧。／这件事很重要, 你们讨论讨论吧。

20.	聊*		liáo	v	to chat
21.	選好	选好	xuǎn hǎo	vc	to finish choosing
22.	想法		xiǎngfǎ	n	idea; opinion
23.	肯定		kěndìng	adv	definitely
24.	至於	至于	zhìyú	conj	as for; as to [see G3]
25.	畢業	毕业	bì yè	vo	to graduate
26.	雙學位	双学位	shuāng xuéwèi		double degree; double major
27.	物理		wùlǐ	n	physics
28.	電腦*	电脑	diànnǎo	n	computer
29.	系		xì	n	department (of a university)
30.	學分	学分	xuéfēn	n	academic credit
31.	打算		dǎsuàn	v/n	to plan; plan
32.	研究所		yánjiūsuǒ	n	graduate school
33.	要麼...要麼...	要么...要么...	yàome... yàome...	conj	if it's not A, it's B; either... or... [see G4]
34.	工學院	工学院	gōngxuéyuàn	n	school of engineering
35.	管理學院	管理学院	guǎnlǐ xuéyuàn	n	school of management
36.	文科		wénkē	n	humanities
37.	賺錢	赚钱	zhuàn qián	vo	to make money
38.	醫學院	医学院	yīxuéyuàn	n	school of medicine

| 39. | 願意* | 愿意 | yuànyi | av | to want to; to be willing to |

我不願意去圖書館看書,喜歡在家看書。

我不愿意去图书馆看书,喜欢在家看书。

你願意跟我去城裏跳舞嗎? / 你愿意跟我去城里跳舞吗?

| 40. | 當* | 当 | dāng | v | to work as; to be |
| 41. | 整天 | | zhěngtiān | | all day long |

他姐姐很忙, 整天不在家。

你整天打球, 累不累?

42.	病人*		bìngrén	n	sick person; patient
43.	打交道		dǎ jiāodào	vo	to deal with (usually persons)
44.	唉		ài	exc	an exclamation indicating resignation; oh well
45.	哲學	哲学	zhéxué	n	philosophy

跟病人打交道。

46.	西方		Xīfāng	n	the West
47.	孩子*		háizi	n	child
48.	管		guǎn	v	(col) to control, manage; to mind, care about
49.	申請	申请	shēnqǐng	v	to apply (for admission to school; for a job)
50.	這樣*	这样	zhèyàng	pr	in this way
51.	房租*		fángzū	n	rent (for a house or apartment)
52.	飯錢	饭钱	fànqian		money for food
53.	省下來	省下来	shěng xialai	vc	to save (money, time)
54.	不過	不过	búguò	conj	but; however
55.	考慮*	考虑	kǎolǜ	v	to consider; to think over
56.	實習	实习	shíxí	v	to work as an intern
57.	經驗	经验	jīngyàn	n	experience

申請研究所，我沒有經驗。／申请研究所，我没有经验。

有實習經驗對找工作很有幫助。／有实习经验对找工作很有帮助。

| 58. | 履歷 | 履历 | lǚlì | n | curriculum vitae; résumé |
| 59. | 提 | | tí | v | to mention |

哥哥來信時，工作的事一點兒也沒提。

哥哥来信时，工作的事一点儿也没提。

昨天老師上課提到下個星期考試的事了。

昨天老师上课提到下个星期考试的事了。

60.	意見	意见	yìjiàn	n	opinion
61.	咱們	咱们	zánmen	pr	we (including the listener; 我們／我们 does not necessarily include the listener)
62.	建議	建议	jiànyì	v/n	to suggest; suggestion

我建議你學電腦。/ 我建议你学电脑。

我不知道選什麼專業, 你能不能給我提一點兒建議?

我不知道选什么专业, 你能不能给我提一点儿建议?

PROPER NOUN

李哲   Lǐ Zhé   a masculine name

ENLARGED CHARACTERS FOR EASIER VIEWING AND COMPARING

選　專　導　畢　腦　醫　慮　履

选　专　导　毕　脑　医　虑　履

Culture Note ▲

In mainland China, the word 研究所 refers to research institutes, which may or may not be affiliated with universities; the word for graduate school on the mainland is 研究生院. In Taiwan, however, 研究所 can mean either graduate schools or research institutes.

Grammar

1. 只是 / 就是 (IT'S JUST THAT)

只是 or 就是 signifies a turn in thought; it is similar to 不過 / 不过 in usage. It is, however, milder in tone than 但是 and 可是.

(1)   你要搬到校外去住, 我不是不同意, 只是我覺得太早了一點。

你要搬到校外去住, 我不是不同意, 只是我觉得太早了一点。

It's not that I object to your moving off campus. It's just that I feel it's a bit too soon.

(2)   他這個人好是好, 就是身體差一些。

他这个人好是好, 就是身体差一些。

He is a good person, but he's a bit too frail.

(3)　那件毛衣樣子好是好, 只是價錢太貴。

　　那件毛衣样子好是好, 只是价钱太贵。

It's true that the style of the sweater is good, but it's too expensive.

Note: 只是／就是 usually appears in the second clause of a sentence. The first clause is often positive in meaning whereas the second clause modifies the first clause, pointing out a flaw in something that might otherwise be perfect. In this respect 只是 is different from 但是, 可是, and 不過／不过.

她大學畢業了。／她大学毕业了。

2. 對他來說 / 对他来说 (AS FOR HIM)

對他來說 / 对他来说 means *as far as he's concerned*.

(1)   對她來說, 今年最重要的事情是選一個好大學。

     对她来说, 今年最重要的事情是选一个好大学。

     To her, the most important thing this year is to pick a good college.

對他來說 / 对他来说 is different from 認為 / 认为. While 認為 / 认为 may express either the opinion of the speaker or the opinion of the person spoken about, 對他來說 / 对他来说 can only convey the speaker's opinion. See in the following example sentences how the two expressions can be used together.

(2)   (我認為)對他來說, 有工作比沒工作好, 可是他認為工作不好比沒有工作更糟。

     (我认为)对他来说, 有工作比没工作好, 可是他认为工作不好比没有工作更糟。

     [I think that] for him, it's better to have a job than to have no job. However, in his view, having a lousy job is worse than having no job.

(3)   對小王來說, 今年找到工作最重要, 要不然吃飯、住房子都會有問題。

     对小王来说, 今年找到工作最重要, 要不然吃饭、住房子都会有问题。

     As far as Xiao Wang is concerned, the most important thing this year is finding a job. Otherwise both food and housing would become problematic.

(4)   他是中國文學教授, 對他來說, 書是很重要的。

     他是中国文学教授, 对他来说, 书是很重要的。

     He's a professor of Chinese literature. To him, books are very important.

Unlike 對…來說 / 对…来说, 在…看來 / 在…看来 conveys the opinion of the person spoken about. Compare:

(5)   在我看來, 衣服是不是名牌都沒關係, 只要穿著舒服、好看就行。

     在我看来, 衣服是不是名牌都没关系, 只要穿着舒服、好看就行。

     In my view, so long as they are comfortable and look nice, clothes don't have to be name brand.

(6)　在我爸爸看来, 孩子只要學習好就可以了。

　　在我爸爸看来, 孩子只要学习好就可以了。

In my dad's view, so long as a kid studies well, then everything is okay [that's all you need to do].

Note: When stating the opinion of the person spoken about, 在...看來 / 在...看来 is not interchangeable with 對...來說 / 对...来说.

3. 至於 / 至于

至於 / 至于 is used to introduce a new subject that is somehow related to the one mentioned in the preceding discussion, or a different aspect of the issue in question.

(1)　A:　我們明年去旅行, 好嗎? / 我们明年去旅行, 好吗?

Let's take a trip next year. How about it?

　　B:　我們先討論去不去, 至於什麼時候去, 以後再説。

　　　　我们先讨论去不去, 至于什么时候去, 以后再说。

Let's first discuss whether we [want to] go or not. As for when, we'll talk about that later.

(2)　A:　你看這條牛仔褲的大小、樣子、顏色怎麼樣?

　　　　你看这条牛仔裤的大小、样子、颜色怎么样?

What do you think of the size, style, and color of this pair of jeans?

　　B:　這條牛仔褲, 對你來説大小、樣子都合適。至於顏色, 我覺得太難看了。

　　　　这条牛仔裤, 对你来说大小、样子都合适。至于颜色, 我觉得太难看了。

Both the size and style are perfect for you. As for the color, I think it's ugly.

(3)　A:　你跟你太太喜歡吃中國飯還是日本飯?

　　　　你跟你太太喜欢吃中国饭还是日本饭?

Do you and your wife like to eat Chinese or Japanese food?

B: 我喜歡吃中國飯, 至於我太太, 她喜歡吃日本飯。

我喜欢吃中国饭, 至于我太太, 她喜欢吃日本饭。

I like to eat Chinese food. As for my wife, she likes to eat Japanese food.

(4) A: 我想買衣服, 這家商店怎麼樣? / 我想买衣服, 这家商店怎么样?

I would like to buy some clothes. How about this store?

B: 買日用品, 這家商店不錯, 比較便宜。至於買衣服, 還是去大一點的購物中心吧。

买日用品, 这家商店不错, 比较便宜。至于买衣服, 还是去大一点的购物中心吧。

This store is good for [buying] daily necessities. [The prices are] quite cheap [there]. As for clothes, you'd better go to a bigger shopping center.

4. 要麼..., 要麼... / 要么..., 要么... (EITHER...OR...)

要麼..., 要麼... / 要么..., 要么... is a selective conjunction. It is used to mean choosing between two (or occasionally more than two) possibilities or desires.

(1) 你要麼學醫, 要麼學工程, 就是不能學文科。
你要么学医, 要么学工程, 就是不能学文科。
You have to study either medicine or engineering. It can't be the humanities [no matter what you say.]

(2) A: 你説這個週末做什麼? / 你说这个周末做什么?
What do you say we should do this weekend?

B: 要麼聽音樂, 要麼看電影。 / 要么听音乐, 要么看电影。
Either go to a concert or a movie.

A: 今天晚飯想吃點什麼素菜? / 今天晚饭想吃点什么素菜?
What kind of vegetable would you like for dinner tonight?

B: 要麼吃菠菜, 要麼吃芥蘭。 / 要么吃菠菜, 要么吃芥兰。
Either spinach or Chinese broccoli.

電腦教室／电脑教室

5. 另外 (ANOTHER, OTHER, THE OTHER; AND IN ADDITION)

There are two usages of 另外. One of them involves 另外 appearing before a noun acting as a demonstrative pronoun.

(1) 下個學期我打算選三門課。一門電腦, 另外兩門課選什麼, 還不知道。

下个学期我打算选三门课。一门电脑, 另外两门课选什么, 还不知道。

I plan to take three courses next semester. One will be in computer science. As for the other two, I don't know yet.

(2) 這裏有兩個大學, 一個男校, 另外一個是女校, 都很不錯。

这里有两个大学, 一个男校, 另外一个是女校, 都很不错。

There are two colleges here. One is a men's college. The other one is a women's college. Both are quite good.

(3) 他三個妹妹都有工作, 一個是餐館老闆, 另外兩個是大學教授。

他三个妹妹都有工作, 一个是餐馆老板, 另外两个是大学教授。

All three of his younger sisters work. One owns a restaurant. The other two are college professors.

(4) 我的四個中文老師, 三個是從中國大陸來的, 另外一個是從台灣來的。

我的四个中文老师, 三个是从中国大陆来的, 另外一个是从台湾来的。

Of my four Chinese teachers, three are from mainland China. The other one is from Taiwan.

另外 can also be used as an adverb before a verb phrase or as a conjunction at the beginning of a sentence. We have already studied that usage in Lesson 4 under the Important Words & Phrases section. Here are some more examples:

(5) 下個學期我要選一門物理課, 另外再選兩門電腦系的課, 學分就夠了。

下个学期我要选一门物理课, 另外再选两门电脑系的课, 学分就够了。

Next semester I'll take a course in physics, plus two more in the Computer Science department. Then I'll have enough credits.

(6) 在這個州買吃的東西, 除了東西的價錢以外, 另外還得付百分之八的稅。

在这个州买吃的东西, 除了东西的价钱以外, 另外还得付百分之八的税。

To get food in this state, on top of the prices, you also have to pay eight percent in taxes.

(7) 上個週末我買了一些日用品, 另外還買了一些文具。

上个周末我买了一些日用品, 另外还买了一些文具。

Last weekend I bought some daily necessities. I also bought some stationery.

考物理

▼▼▼▼▼▼▼▼▼▼▼▼▼▼▼▼▼▼▼▼▼▼▼▼▼▼▼▼▼▼▼▼▼▼▼▼

6. RESULTATIVE COMPLEMENTS (I)

In Chinese a verb can be followed by an adjective or another verb to indicate the result of the action. We call the second verb or adjective a resultative complement. Resultative complements fall into several categories.

A. Resultative complement elucidating the verb:

(1)　　我搬完家就去購物中心買日用品。(完)

　　　　我搬完家就去购物中心买日用品。(完)

　　　I'll go get some daily necessities in the shopping center after I finish moving.

　　　(完 = the action will have been completed by the time I go out.)

(2)　　一個字得反復練習才能記住。(住) ／ 一个字得反复练习才能记住。(住)

　　　[One has to] repeat a word several times before [one] can remember it.

　　　(住 = fixed; here lodged in memory)

(3)　　下學期的課你選好了嗎?(好) ／ 下学期的课你选好了吗?(好)

　　　Have you finished selecting classes for next semester? (好 = properly, done selecting)

B. Resultative complement indicating a new state or a change on the part of the agent of the action:

(4)　　老師說的我聽懂了。(懂) ／ 老师说的我听懂了。(懂)

　　　I understood what the teacher said. (Now the material is clear to me.)

(5)　　你吃飽了嗎?(飽bǎo) ／ 你吃饱了吗?(饱bǎo)

　　　Are you full? (sated, no longer hungry)

C: Resultative complement indicating a new state or change on the part of the recipient of the action or object:

(6)　　你怎麼把妹妹打哭了?(哭) ／ 你怎么把妹妹打哭了?(哭)

　　　Why did you hit your sister and make her cry? (She is crying now.)

(7)　　他把椅子搬走了。(走) ／ 他把椅子搬走了。(走)

　　　He took away the chair. (The chair is gone.)

(8) 你要把衣服洗乾淨才能去看電影。(乾淨 gānjìng)

你要把衣服洗干净才能去看电影。(干净 gānjìng)

You have to wash the clothes clean [finish the laundry] before you can go watch a movie.

(乾淨 / 干净 = The clothes will be clean after you're done washing them.)

Note: A particular verb can only take certain other verbs or adjectives as its resultative complements. Therefore, it is best to remember each verb together with its resultative complements as if they were one word.

7. 再, 又, AND 還/还 COMPARED

Both 又 and 再 indicate the repetition of an action. 又 is usually used with actions that have already taken place. 再, on the other hand, indicates future recurrences:

(1) 我上星期申請了一個實習工作, 昨天又申請了一個。

我上星期申请了一个实习工作, 昨天又申请了一个。

I applied for an internship last week. I applied for another one yesterday.

(2) 先生, 您剛才點的菜我沒聽清楚, 麻煩您再說一次。

先生, 您刚才点的菜我没听清楚, 麻烦您再说一次。

Sir, I didn't hear what dishes you just ordered very clearly. Could I trouble you to say them again?

Before 是 or certain auxiliary verbs such as 想, 能, 要, 可以, and 會/会, one can only use 又:

(3) 她今天下午又要去見指導教授了。/ 她今天下午又要去见指导教授了。

She's going to see her adviser again this afternoon.

(4) 明天又是星期天了。/ 明天又是星期天了。

Tomorrow will be Sunday again.

還/还 indicates an increase in quantity or amount:

(5) 電腦課我選了一門了, 還得選一門。

电脑课我选了一门了, 还得选一门。

I've already taken one computer class. I have to take one more.

▼▼▼▼▼▼▼▼▼▼▼▼▼▼▼▼▼▼▼▼▼▼▼▼▼▼▼▼▼▼▼▼▼▼▼

(6) 我點了一個清蒸魚，一個豆腐，還點了一個炒青菜。

   我点了一个清蒸鱼，一个豆腐，还点了一个炒青菜。

   I ordered steamed fish, tofu, and stir-fried vegetables.

(7) 昨天我看了一個電影，還去參加了一個朋友的生日晚會。

   昨天我看了一个电影，还去参加了一个朋友的生日晚会。

   Yesterday I saw a movie and attended a friend's birthday party.

Important Words & Phrases

1. 反復／反复 (REPEATEDLY)

反復／反复 often modifies verbs such as 說/说, 念, 寫/写, 記/记, 思考, 討論／讨论, 練習／练习.

EXAMPLE: 一個字得反復練習才能記住。／一个字得反复练习才能记住。

(1) 課文要＿＿＿＿＿＿＿＿＿＿＿＿＿＿，才能念好。

   课文要＿＿＿＿＿＿＿＿＿＿＿＿＿，才能念好。

(2) 小張的父母不同意他選文學做專業。他們＿＿＿＿＿＿＿＿，他都不聽。

   小张的父母不同意他选文学做专业。他们＿＿＿＿＿＿＿，他都不听。

(3) 這個統計問題難極了，同學們＿＿＿＿＿＿＿＿，還是不知道怎麼做，只好去問老師。

   这个统计问题难极了，同学们＿＿＿＿＿＿＿＿，还是不知道怎么做，只好去问老师。

2. 肯定 (DEFINITELY)

EXAMPLE: 我肯定要選電腦和中文。／我肯定要选电脑和中文。

(1) A: 小林會說中文嗎?

   小林会说中文吗?

▼▼

B:　他是在中國出生,在中國長大的,＿＿＿＿＿＿＿＿＿＿＿＿＿＿＿＿＿。

　　他是在中国出生,在中国长大的,＿＿＿＿＿＿＿＿＿＿＿＿＿＿＿＿＿。

(2)　A:　老柯身上穿的那套運動服是名牌嗎?

　　　老柯身上穿的那套运动服是名牌吗?

　　B:　＿＿＿＿＿＿＿＿＿＿＿＿。聽說他是花十塊錢買的。名牌的衣服怎麼會那麼便宜?

　　　＿＿＿＿＿＿＿＿＿＿＿＿。听说他是花十块钱买的。名牌的衣服怎么会那么便宜?

(3)　A:　你姐姐做菜,又不放油,又不放鹽,＿＿＿＿＿＿＿＿＿＿＿＿＿＿＿。

　　　你姐姐做菜,又不放油,又不放盐,＿＿＿＿＿＿＿＿＿＿＿＿＿＿＿。

　　B:　那也不見得。油少、鹽少的菜不一定不好吃。

　　　那也不见得。油少、盐少的菜不一定不好吃。

3. 跟...打交道 (DEAL WITH)

This phrase means to come in contact with certain people or objects because of the nature of one's work.

EXAMPLE:　整天跟病人打交道,多沒意思。

　　　　　整天跟病人打交道,多没意思。

(1)　購物中心的售貨員整天＿＿＿＿＿＿＿＿＿＿＿＿＿＿。

　　购物中心的售货员整天＿＿＿＿＿＿＿＿＿＿＿＿＿＿。

(2)　我媽媽在銀行工作,天天＿＿＿＿＿＿＿＿＿＿＿＿。

　　我妈妈在银行工作,天天＿＿＿＿＿＿＿＿＿＿＿＿。

▼▼▼▼▼▼▼▼▼▼▼▼▼▼▼▼▼▼▼▼▼▼▼▼▼▼▼▼▼▼▼▼▼▼▼▼▼

(3) 我現在在小學教英文, 每天＿＿＿＿＿＿＿＿, 很高興。

我现在在小学教英文, 每天＿＿＿＿＿＿＿＿, 很高兴。

4. 這樣 / 这样 (IN THIS WAY)

EXAMPLE:　我想申請離家比較近的學校, 這樣我就可以搬回家去住。

　　　　　我想申请离家比较近的学校, 这样我就可以搬回家去住。

(1) 學外語得反復聽錄音、念課文,＿＿＿＿＿＿＿＿＿＿＿＿＿＿＿。

学外语得反复听录音、念课文,＿＿＿＿＿＿＿＿＿＿＿＿＿＿＿。

(2) 每次付了錢都應該要收據,＿＿＿＿＿＿＿＿＿＿＿＿＿＿＿。

每次付了钱都应该要收据,＿＿＿＿＿＿＿＿＿＿＿＿＿＿＿。

(3) 買東西應該等商店減價的時候去買,＿＿＿＿＿＿＿＿＿＿＿。

买东西应该等商店减价的时候去买,＿＿＿＿＿＿＿＿＿＿＿。

5. 不過 / 不过 (BUT)

EXAMPLE:　...不過在家裏住太不自由了。 / ...不过在家里住太不自由了。

(1) 一般醫生賺錢都賺得不少,＿＿＿＿＿＿＿＿＿＿＿＿＿＿＿。

一般医生赚钱都赚得不少,＿＿＿＿＿＿＿＿＿＿＿＿＿＿＿。

(2) 學工科又忙又累,＿＿＿＿＿＿＿＿＿＿＿＿＿＿＿。

学工科又忙又累,＿＿＿＿＿＿＿＿＿＿＿＿＿＿＿。

(3) 打折以後買的衣服便宜是便宜, ＿＿＿＿＿＿＿＿＿＿＿＿。

打折以后买的衣服便宜是便宜, ＿＿＿＿＿＿＿＿＿＿＿＿。

Pinyin Texts

NARRATIVE

Zhāng Tiānmíng zhège xuéqī xuǎn le sì mén kè: Dōngyàshǐ, tǒngjìxué, Měiguó wénxué hé Zhōngwén. Chúle Zhōngwén yǐwài, qítā de kè suīrán hěn yǒu yìsi, yě xué dào le bù shǎo dōngxi, zhǐshì dōu děi huā hěn duō shíjiān zhǔnbèi, yǒu diǎn shòu bu liǎo. Yīnwèi Zhāng Tiānmíng de fùmǔ zài jiā chángcháng shuō Zhōngwén, suǒyǐ yì niánjí de Zhōngwén kè, duì tā lái shuō, tīng hé shuō hěn róngyì, jiùshì xiě Hànzì tài nán, yí ge zì děi fǎnfù liànxí cái néng jì zhù.

Zhège xuéqī yǐjīng guò le yí dàbàn le, mǎshàng yòu děi wèi xià xuéqī zhù cè le. Hòutiān Zhāng Tiānmíng yào qù jiàn tā de zhǐdǎo jiàoshòu, tǎolùn xià xuéqī xuǎn kè de shì. Tā juéde yīnggāi zhǎo Lǐ Zhé liáo liao, tīng tīng tā de xiǎngfǎ.

DIALOGUE

Zhāng Tiānmíng:	Zěnmeyàng, xià xuéqī de kè nǐ xuǎn hǎo le ma?
Lǐ Zhé:	Hái méi ne. Nǐ ne?
Zhāng Tiānmíng:	Wǒ kěndìng yào xuǎn Zhōngwén, zhìyú lìngwài liǎng mén kè xuǎn shénme, hái bù zhīdao. Nǐ hái děi zài shàng jǐmén kè cái néng bì yè?
Lǐ Zhé:	Wǒ hái děi shàng sān mén kè. Wǒ xiǎng ná shuāng xuéwèi, zài xuǎn yì mén wùlǐkè, lìngwài zài xuǎn liǎng mén diànnǎoxì de kè, xuéfēn jiù gòu le.
Zhāng Tiānmíng:	Nǐ bì yè yǐhòu dǎsuan zuò shénme ne?
Lǐ Zhé:	Wǒ xiǎng niàn yánjiūsuǒ, yàome shì gōngxuéyuàn, yàome shì guǎnlǐ xuéyuàn. Nǐ xiǎng xuǎn shénme zhuānyè?
Zhāng Tiānmíng:	Wǒ xiǎng xué wénxué. Kěshì wǒ māma shuō, xué wénkē jiānglái bù róngyì zhǎo gōngzuò, érqiě zhuàn qián yě shǎo, tā ràng wǒ niàn yīxuéyuàn. Dànshì, wǒ zuì bú yuànyì dāng yīshēng, zhěngtiān gēn bìngrén dǎ jiāodao, duō méi yìsi.
Lǐ Zhé:	Ài, wǒ de fùmǔ gēn nǐ de fùmǔ chàbuduō. Qíshí, wǒ zuì xǐhuan de shì zhéxué, yīnwèi wǒ xǐhuan xiǎng wèntí. Xīfāng rén yìbān bú tài guǎn háizi xuǎn shénme zhuānyè, bǐ wǒmen zìyóu.
Zhāng Tiānmíng:	Nǐ xiǎng shēnqǐng něi xiē xuéxiào?
Lǐ Zhé:	Wǒ xiǎng shēnqǐng lí jiā bǐjiào jìn de xuéxiào, zhèyàng wǒ jiù kěyǐ bān huí jiā qù zhù, bǎ fángzū gēn fànqian shěng xia lai.
Zhāng Tiānmíng:	Búguò zài jiālǐ zhù tài bú zìyóu le.
Lǐ Zhé:	Shì ma? Nà wǒ zài kǎolǜ kǎolǜ.

Zhāng Tiānmíng: Yěxǔ nǐ kěyǐ xiān zhǎo ge dìfāng shíxí yí xià, yǒu diǎn gōngzuò jīngyàn, zhèyàng duì nǐ xiě lǚlì yǒu hǎochù, jiānglái shēnqǐng xuéxiào, zhǎo gōngzuò dōu kěyǐ tí yì tí.

Lǐ Zhé: Wǒ míngtiān qù zhǎo zhǐdǎo jiàoshòu de shíhòu, zài tīng ting tā de yìjiàn.

Zhāng Tiānmíng: Hòutiān wǒ yě yào qù zhǎo zhǐdǎo jiàoshòu. Xīwàng tāmen néng gěi zánmen yìxiē hǎo de jiànyì.

Discussion Topic: Choosing a Field of Study

With the help of the following pictures, recap the conversation that Li Zhe and Zhang Tianming had on their academic study.

第六課 ▲ 租房子

NARRATIVE

　　開學已經兩個多月了,張天明一直住在學生宿舍裏。小張的房間在二樓,離樓梯很近。每天早上不到六點,就開始有人上下樓梯。晚上,常常到十一、二點,還有人在走廊裏大聲地打招呼或開玩笑,吵得張天明早晚都睡不好覺。住在他隔壁的是安德森。自從上個星期大學籃球比賽開始以後,安德森差不多每天晚上都看球,常常激動得大喊大叫。大學籃球比賽到明年三月才結束,張天明想,這樣下去學習非受影響不可,最好趕緊搬出學校,找個安靜的地方住。

　　他找來一張報紙,翻到廣告欄,看了幾個出租房子的廣告,就打起電話來。

PHONE CONVERSATION I

張天明：　喂,你們有一套房子出租,是嗎?

房東：　　對,有兩間臥室,帶傢俱,有地毯,而且有空調。

第六课 ▲ 租房子

NARRATIVE

开学已经两个多月了,张天明一直住在学生宿舍里。小张的房间在二楼,离楼梯很近。每天早上不到六点,就开始有人上下楼梯。晚上,常常到十一、二点,还有人在走廊里大声地打招呼或开玩笑,吵得张天明早晚都睡不好觉。住在他隔壁的是安德森。自从上个星期大学篮球比赛开始以后,安德森差不多每天晚上都看球,常常激动得大喊大叫。大学篮球比赛到明年三月才结束,张天明想,这样下去学习非受影响不可,最好赶紧搬出学校,找个安静的地方住。

他找来一张报纸,翻到广告栏,看了几个出租房子的广告,就打起电话来。

PHONE CONVERSATION I

张天明:　喂,你们有一套房子出租,是吗?

房东:　　对,有两间卧室,带家具,有地毯,而且有空调。

看報紙找房子。／看报纸找房子。

張天明： 每個月租金是多少？

房　東： 要是租一年的話，每個月四百六十塊。

張天明： 我想你們的房子一定很不錯，不過對我來説，稍微貴了點兒。

房　東： 沒關係，你先找別的地方試試，要是找不到合適的，再來找我。

張天明： 那太好了！多謝！

PHONE CONVERSATION II

張天明： 喂，你好！可以告訴我你們要出租的是什麼樣的房子嗎？

房　東： 不是房子，只是一個房間，帶傢俱，可是沒有空調。

張天明： 在什麼地方？

房　東： 十七街四百二十五號，離體育場很近。 如果你是個球迷的話，住在這兒最理想不過了。

張天明： 不瞞您説，如果我是個球迷的話，就不用搬家了。

打電話租房子。/打电话租房子。

张天明： 每个月租金是多少？

房东： 要是租一年的话，每个月四百六十块。

张天明： 我想你们的房子一定很不错，不过对我来说，稍微贵了点儿。

房东： 没关系，你先找别的地方试试，要是找不到合适的，再来找我。

张天明： 那太好了！多谢！

PHONE CONVERSATION II

张天明： 喂，你好！可以告诉我你们要出租的是什么样的房子吗？

房东： 不是房子，只是一个房间，带家具，可是没有空调。

张天明： 在什么地方？

房东： 十七街四百二十五号，离体育场很近。如果你是个球迷的话，住在这儿最理想不过了。

张天明： 不瞒您说，如果我是个球迷的话，就不用搬家了。

PHONE CONVERSATION III

張天明：　你好！你們的房子租出去了嗎？

房東：　　還沒有，不過已經有好幾個人打過電話了。

張天明：　請問，是什麼樣的房子？

房東：　　是一室一廳的，廚房很大。如果你每天自己做飯的話，住在這兒最合適不過了。

張天明：　租金是多少？

房東：　　每個月三百塊，包水電。

張天明：　是嗎？不算很貴。你們附近有球場嗎？

房東：　　這兒離球場很遠，環境不錯。後面是一片樹林，前面是一條小河，可能對你來說太安靜了吧？

張天明：　我就是要找一個安靜的地方，嗯，就是離學校遠了一點兒。

房東：　　不過這兒交通很方便。

張天明：　好極了。我可以去看看房子嗎？

房東：　　可以，可以。

交通很方便。

PHONE CONVERSATION III

张天明：　你好！你们的房子租出去了吗？

房东：　　还没有，不过已经有好几个人打过电话了。

张天明：　请问，是什么样的房子？

房东：　　是一室一厅的，厨房很大。如果你每天自己做饭的话，住在这儿最合适不过了。

张天明：　租金是多少？

房东：　　每个月三百块，包水电。

张天明：　是吗？不算很贵。你们附近有球场吗？

房东：　　这儿离球场很远，环境不错。后面是一片树林，前面是一条小河，可能对你来说太安静了吧？

张天明：　我就是要找一个安静的地方，嗯，就是离学校远了一点儿。

房东：　　不过这儿交通很方便。

张天明：　好极了。我可以去看看房子吗？

房东：　　可以，可以。

一片樹林／一片树林

VOCABULARY

1.	租*		zū	v	to rent
2.	房子*		fángzi	n	house
3.	一直*		yìzhí	adv	continuously
4.	樓梯	楼梯	lóutī	n	stairway
5.	走廊		zǒuláng	n	hallway
6.	大聲	大声	dàshēng	adv	loudly; "in a big voice"

弟弟睡覺了, 別大聲說話。/ 弟弟睡觉了, 别大声说话。

大聲點兒, 我聽不見。/ 大声点儿, 我听不见。

7.	打招呼		dǎ zhāohu	vo	to greet
8.	或(者)*		huò(zhě)	conj	or
9.	開玩笑	开玩笑	kāi wánxiào	vo	to joke; to joke around
10.	吵		chǎo	v	to disturb; to make noise

你別吵, 慢慢說。/ 你别吵, 慢慢说。

媽媽正在睡覺, 你別把她吵醒了。/ 妈妈正在睡觉, 你别把她吵醒了。

11.	睡不好覺*	睡不好觉	shuì bu hǎo jiào	vc	to not be able to sleep well [see G2]
12.	隔壁		gébì	n	next door
13.	自從	自从	zìcóng	prep	ever since; since
14.	籃球*	篮球	lánqiú	n	basketball
15.	比賽	比赛	bǐsài	n/v	competition; to compete
16.	激動	激动	jīdòng	adj	excited

聽了這個歌, 我很激動。/ 听了这个歌, 我很激动。

她激動地對我說她愛我。/ 她激动地对我说她爱我。

17.	大喊大叫		dà hǎn dà jiào		to yell and shout

▼▼▼▼▼▼▼▼▼▼▼▼▼▼▼▼▼▼▼▼▼▼▼▼▼▼▼▼▼▼▼▼▼

18. 受影響　　受影响　　shòu yǐngxiǎng　vo　to be affected; to be influenced

我選專業不受別人的影響。／我选专业不受别人的影响。

你不會電腦, 工作會受影響嗎? ／你不会电脑, 工作会受影响吗?

19. 趕緊　　赶紧　　gǎnjǐn　adv　in a hurried fashion; right away

你趕緊把功課給老師吧。／你赶紧把功课给老师吧。

飛機快起飛了, 你趕緊去機場吧。／飞机快起飞了, 你赶紧去机场吧。

20. 翻到　　　　　　fān dào　vc　to turn to

21. 廣告欄　　广告栏　　guǎnggào lán　　ad columns; classified ads

22. 出租*　　　　　chūzū　v　to rent out; to let

23. 喂*　　　　　wèi/wéi　exc　(on the phone) hello

24. 套*　　　　　tào　m　a suite of

25. 間　　间　　jiān　m　measure word for rooms

26. 臥室*　　臥室　　wòshì　n　bedroom

27. 帶*　　带　　dài　v　to be equipped with; to come with

28. 地毯　　　　dìtǎn　n　carpet

29. 租金　　　　zūjīn　n　rent money

30. 稍微　　　　shāowēi　adv　a little bit; somewhat

今天比昨天稍微熱點兒。／今天比昨天稍微热点儿。

你稍微走快點兒, 要晚了。／你稍微走快点儿, 要晚了。

31. 試*　　试　　shì　v　to try

32. 找不到*　　　　zhǎo bu dào　vc　to not be able to find

33. 什麼樣　　什么样　　shénmeyàng　pr　what kind

34. 街　　　　jiē　n　street

35. 體育場　　体育场　　tǐyùchǎng　n　sports field

36.	球迷		qiúmí	n	fan (of ball games: basketball, football, etc.)
37.	...的話	...的话	dehuà		if [see G5]
38.	理想		lǐxiǎng	n/adj	ideal

我的理想是在一個好大學當教授。/ 我的理想是在一个好大学当教授。

這個工作不太理想, 我想再找一個新工作。

这个工作不太理想, 我想再找一个新工作。

| 39. | 瞞 | 瞒 | mán | v | to hide the truth from; to obscure |

有什麼事情應該告訴我, 不要瞞我。/ 有什么事情应该告诉我, 不要瞒我。

40.	...室		shì		room (occurs in 教室, 臥室 / 卧室, 浴室, and such fixed expressions as 一室一廳 / 一室一厅)
41.	...廳	厅	tīng		room; living room; an "outer" or more "public" room of a house, such as 客廳 / 客厅, 餐廳 / 餐厅, in contrast to 臥室 / 卧室 and 浴室, the "inner rooms"
42.	廚房*	厨房	chúfáng	n	kitchen
43.	包		bāo	v	to include

這個旅館包早飯。/ 这个旅馆包早饭。

44.	水電*	水电	shuǐ diàn	n	water and electricity
45.	算		suàn	v	to count; to be counted as
46.	球場	球场	qiúchǎng	n	ball court
47.	環境	环境	huánjìng	n	environment; surroundings
48.	後面	后面	hòumian		in the back; back
49.	樹林	树林	shùlín	n	woods
50.	河*		hé	n	river

| 51. | 嗯 | ng | exc | interjection indicating minor regret over an otherwise satisfactory situation |
| 52. | 交通 | jiāotōng | n | transportation |

PROPER NOUN

| 安德森 | Āndésēn | Anderson |

ENLARGED CHARACTERS FOR EASIER VIEWING AND COMPARING

樓　聲　籃　賽　響　欄　微　廚　環　境　樹

楼　声　篮　赛　响　栏　微　厨　环　境　树

報紙上房屋出租的廣告。／报纸上房屋出租的广告。

(See the Appendix of Alternate Character Forms for simplified characters.)

Grammar

1. DESCRIPTIVE COMPLEMENTS WITH 得

Descriptive complements—also known as complements of degree—can be divided into three categories depending on their structure and function:

A. The complement comments on the preceding verb; it describes or indicates the manner of the action.

(1a) 我每個週末都起得很早。／ 我每个周末都起得很早。

I get up very early every weekend. (早 describes 起.)

(2a) 他記漢字記得很快。／他记汉字记得很快。

He memorizes Chinese characters very quickly. (快 describes 記/记.)

(3a)   那個學生每次考試都準備得很好。／那个学生每次考试都准备得很好。

That student is very well prepared for the exams every single time. (好 describes 準備／准备.)

If there is an object after the verb as in example (2a), one must repeat the verb.

To negate this kind of descriptive complement, add 不 before the adjective.

(1b)   我每個週末都起得不早。／我每个周末都起得不早。

I don't get up early every weekend.

(2b)   他記漢字記得不快。／他记汉字记得不快。

He doesn't memorize Chinese characters very quickly.

(3b)   那個學生每次考試都準備得不好。／那个学生每次考试都准备得不好。

That student is not well prepared for the exams.

Notice that in all the examples above the complement is an adjective.

B. The complement describes the mood of the subject or object, which results from the action or state signified by the verb or adjective before the complement. This pattern may be translated "…V with the result that…" or "…so Adj. that…" Unlike in type A, the complement may be a whole clause:

(4)   他聽到老師說明天不考試了, 高興得大喊大叫。

他听到老师说明天不考试了, 高兴得大喊大叫。

When he heard the teacher say that there would be no test tomorrow, he was so happy that he shouted and cheered at the top of his voice.

(大喊大叫 is the result of 高興／高兴; it also describes 他.)

(5)   我同屋身體不太舒服, 病得沒有胃口吃東西。

我同屋身体不太舒服, 病得没有胃口吃东西。

My roommate isn't feeling well. He is so sick that he has no appetite. (沒有胃口吃東西／东西 is the result of 病, but it also describes 我同屋.)

(6)   她累得坐在地上睡起覺來了。／她累得坐在地上睡起觉来了。

She was so tired that she fell asleep sitting on the floor.

(坐在地上睡起覺來了／睡起觉来了 is the result of 累. It also describes 她.)

This kind of complement is descriptive. It is used to describe what has already happened. It cannot be used in the negative. For instance, we do not say *高興得沒大喊大叫 / 高兴得没大喊大叫, or *她累得沒坐在地上. Furthermore, this kind of complement cannot be used in the interrogative form, but can be used with the question 怎麼 / 怎么. For instance, we do not say *他高興得跳起來沒有 / 他高兴得跳起来没有? or *他高興得跳起來了嗎 / 他高兴得跳起来了吗? But we can ask 他高興得怎麼了? / 他高兴得怎么了?

C. The complement indicates degree.

(7)   快過年了, 飛機場裏人多得很。 / 快过年了, 飞机场里人多得很。

      New Year's Day is almost here. There were lots of people at the airport.

This kind of complement of degree also describes what has already happened. It cannot be used in the negative.

2. 睡不好覺/觉

The potential complement takes the form of "V + 得/不 + Adj. + (O)." In this lesson, we have 睡不好覺/觉. 睡覺 / 睡觉 is a VO compound. 覺/觉 is the object of 睡. This is why we have to put 不好 between 睡 and 覺/觉. It is important to be able to distinguish between a solid verb and a VO compound. Pay special attention to disyllabic verbs. Compare:

(1)   工作得了(liǎo) / 工作不了 (liǎo)

      able to work / unable to work

(2)   起得了(liǎo)床 / 起不了(liǎo)床

      able to get out of bed / unable to get out of bed

Note that 工作 is a solid verb whereas 起床 is a VO compound. All VO compounds are indicated as such in the Vocabulary section.

3. ...以後 / ...以后 COMPARED WITH ...的時候 / ...的时候

...以後 / ...以后 is different from ...的時候 / ...的时候. The former means "after (something happens or happened)"; the latter "when (something happens or happened)." Note that in English we frequently use "when" to mean "after." For example, "When John realized his mistake, he apologized" really means, "After John realized his mistake, he apologized." Therefore, this statement must be phrased with "...以後 / ...以后" in Chinese, because the apology came after the realization. Compare:

(1) a.   我看見他的時候, 他正在寫履歷。

           我看见他的时候, 他正在写履历。

           When I saw him, he was writing his résumé.

     b.   我看見他以後, 跟他打了聲招呼。 / 我看见他以后, 跟他打了声招呼。

           After I saw him, I said "hi" to him.

(2) a.   他出門的時候忘了帶錢。 / 他出门的时候忘了带钱。

           When he went out, he forgot to take some money with him.

     b.   他出門以後想起來沒有帶錢。 / 他出门以后想起来没有带钱。

           After he had gone out, he remembered that he hadn't brought any money.

(3) a.   他到飛機場的時候, 接他的朋友還沒來。

           他到飞机场的时候, 接他的朋友还没来。

           When he got to the airport, the friend who was supposed to pick him up was not there
           yet.

     b.   他到了飛機場以後, 給小王打了一個電話。

           他到了飞机场以后, 给小王打了一个电话。

           He called Little Wang after he arrived at the airport.

4. DIRECTIONAL COMPLEMENTS (I)

Verbs of direction can be used as directional complements after other verbs. Verbs of direction include 來/来, 去, 上, 下, 進/进, 出, 回, 過/过, 起, 開/开, 到, and so on. 來/来 and 去 can be combined with other verbs of direction: 上來 / 上来, 上去, 下來 / 下来, 下去, 進來 / 进来, 進去 / 进去, 出來 / 出来, 出去, 回來 / 回来, 回去, 過來 / 过来, 過去 / 过去, 起來 / 起来, 開來 / 开来, 開去/开去, 到...來/来, 到...去, etc. When directional verbs appear after other verbs, we call them directional complements. Directional complements fall into three categories: a. directional complements indicating direction; b. directional complements indicating result; c. directional complements indicating state. In this lesson, we are concerned with the first category. The following complements all indicate direction of movement as a result of an action.

▼▼▼▼▼▼▼▼▼▼▼▼▼▼▼▼▼▼▼▼▼▼▼▼▼▼▼▼▼▼▼▼▼▼▼▼▼▼▼

(1) 你回家去吧。(去)

You'd better go home.

(You'll return home by going in a direction away from the speaker.)

(2) 張天明想最好趕緊搬出學校。(出) / 张天明想最好赶紧搬出学校。(出)

Zhang Tianming thought it was best to move off campus as soon as possible.

(Zhang Tianming would like to move and be out, of or be away from, the school.)

(3) 我明天搬進宿舍。(進) / 我明天搬进宿舍。(进)

I'll move into the dorm tomorrow.

(I'll move and I'll be inside the dorm.)

(4) 請你們拿出一張紙。(出) / 请你们拿出一张纸。(出)

Please take out a sheet of paper.

(You'll take, and the paper will be out.)

(5) 我帶來了一個客人。(來) / 我带来了一个客人。(来)

I brought back a guest.

(I brought, and the guest is here.)

When using a directional complement, pay attention to the position of the object. If the object signifies a place, it can only be placed before 來/来 and 去:

(1) 我九月回北京去。 / 我九月回北京去。

I'm going back to Beijing in September.

(2) 你快一點進房間來。 / 你快一点进房间来。

Come into the room quickly.

When 來/来 and 去 are used as complements, the object denoting a person or thing can be placed either before or after 來/来 or 去. In imperative sentences, the object tends to appear in front of 來/来 or 去.

(3) 請搬一把椅子來。 / 请搬一把椅子来。

Please bring a chair.

(Imperative sentence; verb indicating future action)

If the action has already taken place, then the object tends to appear after 來/来 or 去:

(4)   他從家裏搬來了一把椅子。／他从家里搬来了一把椅子。

He brought a chair from home.

(Completed action)

When 上, 下, 進/进, 出, etc. are used as complements and the object is a place word, then they have to be inserted between the verb and the object.

(1)   上課了, 學生們跑進了教室。／上课了, 学生们跑进了教室。

It was time to begin the class. Students ran into the classroom.

(2)   我們很快走下了飛機。／我们很快走下了飞机。

We got off the airplane quickly.

(3)   請把這些傢俱搬上樓。／请把这些家具搬上楼。

Please move the furniture upstairs.

(4)   字典不能借出圖書館。／字典不能借出图书馆。

Dictionaries cannot be checked out from the library.

When compound complements such as 上來/来, 下去, etc., are involved, and if the object signifies a place, it should be inserted between the compound complements. For example:

(5)   把椅子搬上樓去。／把椅子搬上楼去。

Take the chair upstairs.

(6)   弟弟跳下桌子來了。／弟弟跳下桌子来了。

My younger brother jumped down from the desk.

If the object is an ordinary noun, it can be inserted into compound complements such as 上來/来, 下去, etc. It can also go before or after the complements. For example:

(7)   哥哥買回一個新電腦來。vs. 哥哥買回來一個新電腦。

哥哥买回一个新电脑来。vs. 哥哥买回来一个新电脑。

My older brother bought a new computer.

(8)   剛才從購物中心走出很多人來。vs. 剛才從購物中心走出來很多人。

      刚才从购物中心走出很多人来。vs. 刚才从购物中心走出来很多人。

      A lot of people came out from the shopping center just now.

上, 上來／来, and 上去 all suggest upward movement. However, 上來／来 signifies a movement toward the speaker, whereas 上去 denotes a movement away from the speaker.

(9)   他把椅子搬上樓來了。／他把椅子搬上楼来了。

      He brought the chair upstairs.

      (The speaker is upstairs. The chair is now also upstairs.)

(10) 他把椅子搬下樓去了。／他把椅子搬下楼去了。

      He took the chair downstairs.

      (The speaker is upstairs. The chair is now downstairs.)

The distinction among 下, 下來／来, and 下去, and among 進／进, 進來／进来, and 進去／进去 is the same.

5. (要是／如果)...的話／话 (IF)

(要是／如果)...的話／话 suggests a hypothetical scenario. There must be a follow-up clause to complete the meaning.

(1)   你要是想申請管理學院的話, 一定給我打電話。

      你要是想申请管理学院的话, 一定给我打电话。

      If you are interested in applying to business schools, make sure that you give me a call.

(2)   媽媽如果非讓我學電腦不可的話, 我就不上大學了。

      妈妈如果非让我学电脑不可的话, 我就不上大学了。

      If mother insists that I study computer science, then I'm not going to college.

(3)   報紙文章, 有意思的話, 我就看完, 沒有意思的話, 我看一點就不看了。

      报纸文章, 有意思的话, 我就看完, 没有意思的话, 我看一点就不看了。

      If a newspaper article is interesting, I'll read the whole thing. If not, I'll just read part of it.

6. 最 ADJ. 不過了 / 最 ADJ. 不过了

最 Adj. 不過了 / 最 Adj. 不过了 means "沒有比…更 Adj. 的 (none will surpass)." It is a rather forceful expression, e.g.,

(1)   她過生日, 買花送她最好不過了。/ 她过生日, 买花送她最好不过了。

   Nothing would be a better gift for her birthday than flowers.

(2)   這本書對東亞史的介紹最清楚不過了。

   这本书对东亚史的介绍最清楚不过了。

   This book contains the most lucid introduction to the history of East Asia.

(3)   這個實習工作對物理系的學生來說, 最合適不過了。

   这个实习工作对物理系的学生来说, 最合适不过了。

   No internship is more appropriate for physics majors than this one.

7. CHINESE NUMERICAL SERIES

In Chinese, large numbers precede small ones. That is to say general information comes before specific information. A date, address, list, etc., begins with the most general information and ends with the most specific.

(1)   2009年10月25號 / 2009年10月25号

   October 25, 2009

(2)   中國北京中山路25號1樓2門3號 / 中国北京中山路25号1楼2门3号

   #3, Gate 2, 1st floor, 25 Zhongshan Road, Beijing, China

Important Words & Phrases

1. 一直 (ALL ALONG; CONTINUOUSLY)

EXAMPLE: 開學已經兩個多月了, 張天明一直住在學生宿舍裏。

   开学已经两个多月了, 张天明一直住在学生宿舍里。

▼▼▼▼▼▼▼▼▼▼▼▼▼▼▼▼▼▼▼▼▼▼▼▼▼▼▼▼▼▼▼▼▼▼▼▼

(1) 她搬進新房子後, _____, 房東叫她趕緊付。

她搬进新房子后, _____, 房东叫她赶紧付。

(2) 小林畢業以後, _____, 爸爸媽媽希望他早點搬
出去自己住。

小林毕业以后, _____, 爸爸妈妈希望他早点搬
出去自己住。

(3) 小張有兩條被子, 只用了一條, 另外的一條_____。

小张有两条被子, 只用了一条, 另外的一条_____。

2. 或(者) ("OR," USED IN DECLARATIVE SENTENCES)

(1) A: 今天天氣不錯, 你想做什麼?

今天天气不错, 你想做什么?

B: 去球場打球或(者)去河邊走走都行。

去球场打球或(者)去河边走走都行。

(2) A: 你想喝什麼湯?

你想喝什么汤?

B: 豆腐湯或(者)青菜湯都可以。

豆腐汤或(者)青菜汤都可以。

3. 還是／还是 ("OR," USED IN INTERROGATIVE SENTENCES)

(1) 今天晚上你想先復習物理還是統計學?

今天晚上你想先复习物理还是统计学?

(2) 你想住在體育場旁邊還是樹林後邊?

你想住在体育场旁边还是树林后边?

4. 差不多 (ALMOST)

EXAMPLE: 安德森差不多每天晚上都看球。

安德森差不多每天晚上都看球。

(1) 他今年大學四年級了, ＿＿＿＿＿＿＿＿＿＿＿＿＿＿＿。

他今年大学四年级了, ＿＿＿＿＿＿＿＿＿＿＿＿＿＿＿。

(2) 開學差不多已經有＿＿＿＿＿＿＿＿＿＿＿＿＿＿＿＿＿＿了。

开学差不多已经有＿＿＿＿＿＿＿＿＿＿＿＿＿＿＿＿＿＿了。

(3) A: 你跟那麼多人打招呼, 他們都是你的同學嗎?

你跟那么多人打招呼, 他们都是你的同学吗?

B: ＿＿＿＿＿＿＿＿＿＿＿＿＿＿＿＿＿, 只有一、兩個不是。

＿＿＿＿＿＿＿＿＿＿＿＿＿＿＿＿＿, 只有一、两个不是。

5. 最好 (HAD BETTER; IT'S BEST THAT...)

EXAMPLE: 張天明想, 這樣下去學習非受影響不可, 最好趕緊搬出學校。

张天明想, 这样下去学习非受影响不可, 最好赶紧搬出学校。

(1) 如果你想畢業以後賺大錢的話,＿＿＿＿＿＿＿＿＿＿＿＿＿＿＿。

如果你想毕业以后赚大钱的话,＿＿＿＿＿＿＿＿＿＿＿＿＿＿＿。

(2) 要是你不願意整天跟病人打交道,＿＿＿＿＿＿＿＿＿＿＿＿＿。

要是你不愿意整天跟病人打交道,＿＿＿＿＿＿＿＿＿＿＿＿＿。

(3) 住在馬路旁邊比較吵,＿＿＿＿＿＿＿＿＿＿＿＿＿＿＿＿,那兒比較安靜。

住在马路旁边比较吵,＿＿＿＿＿＿＿＿＿＿＿＿＿＿＿＿,那儿比较安静。

6. 稍微 + ADJ. + 點兒／点儿 (SLIGHTLY)

This expression is often used to indicate that something deviates somewhat from the ideal situation or standard set by the speaker. Note that 稍微 precedes an adjective, which is then followed by (一)點兒／(一),点儿.

EXAMPLE: 我想你們的房子一定很不錯,不過對我來說,稍微貴了點兒。

我想你们的房子一定很不错,不过对我来说,稍微贵了点儿。

(1) 這條褲子便宜是便宜,＿＿＿＿＿＿＿＿＿＿＿＿＿＿＿＿＿＿。

这条裤子便宜是便宜,＿＿＿＿＿＿＿＿＿＿＿＿＿＿＿＿＿＿。

(2) 已經半夜十二點了,現在給他打電話＿＿＿＿＿＿＿＿＿＿＿＿＿＿＿＿。

已经半夜十二点了,现在给他打电话＿＿＿＿＿＿＿＿＿＿＿＿＿＿＿＿。

(3) 請你說話＿＿＿＿＿＿＿＿＿＿＿＿＿＿＿＿＿,別人都睡了。

请你说话＿＿＿＿＿＿＿＿＿＿＿＿＿＿＿＿＿,别人都睡了。

Pinyin Texts

NARRATIVE

     Kāi xué yǐjīng liǎng ge duō yuè le, Zhāng Tiānmíng yìzhí zhù zài xuéshēng sùshè li. Xiǎo Zhāng de fángjiān zài èr lóu, lí lóutī hěn jìn. Měitiān zǎoshang búdào liù diǎn, jiù kāishǐ yǒu rén shàng xià lóutī. Wǎnshang, chángcháng dào shíyī, èr diǎn, hái yǒu rén zài zǒuláng li dàshēng de dǎ zhāohu huò kāi wánxiào, chǎo de Zhāng Tiānmíng zǎowǎn dōu shuì bu hǎo jiào. Zhù zài tā gébì de shì Āndésēn. Zìcóng shàngge xīngqī dàxué lánqiú bǐsài kāishǐ yǐhòu, Āndésēn chàbuduō měitiān wǎnshang dōu kàn qiú, chángcháng jīdòng de dà hǎn dà jiào. Dàxué lánqiú bǐsài dào míngnián sānyuè cái jiéshù, Zhāng Tiānmíng xiǎng, zhèyàng xià qù xuéxí fēi shòu yǐngxiǎng bù kě, zuìhǎo gǎnjǐn bān chū xuéxiào, zhǎo ge ānjìng de dìfāng zhù.

     Tā zhǎo lái yì zhāng bàozhǐ, fān dào guǎnggào lán, kàn le jǐ ge chūzū fángzi de guǎnggào, jiù dǎ qǐ diànhuà lai.

PHONE CONVERSATION I

Zhāng Tiānmíng:	Wèi, nǐmen yǒu yí tào fángzi chūzū, shì ma?
Fángdōng:	Duì, yǒu liǎng jiān wòshì, dài jiājù, yǒu dìtǎn, érqiě yǒu kōngtiáo.
Zhāng Tiānmíng:	Měige yuè zūjīn shì duōshao?
Fángdōng:	Yàoshì zū yì nián de huà, měige yuè sì bǎi liù shí kuài.
Zhāng Tiānmíng:	Wǒ xiǎng nǐmen de fángzi yídìng hěn búcuò, búguò duì wǒ lái shuō, shāowēi guì le diǎnr.
Fángdōng:	Méi guānxi, nǐ xiān zhǎo bié de dìfāng shì shi, yàoshì zhǎo bu dào héshì de, zài lái zhǎo wǒ.
Zhāng Tiānmíng:	Nà tài hǎo le! Duō xiè!

PHONE CONVERSATION II

Zhāng Tiānmíng:	Wèi, nǐ hǎo! Kěyǐ gàosù wǒ nǐmen yào chūzū de shì shénmeyàng de fángzi ma?
Fángdōng:	Bú shì fángzi, zhǐshì yí ge fángjiān, dài jiājù, kěshì méiyǒu kōngtiáo.
Zhāng Tiānmíng:	Zài shénme dìfāng?
Fángdōng:	Shíqī jiē sì bǎi èrshí wǔ hào, lí tǐyùchǎng hěn jìn. Rúguǒ nǐ shì ge qiúmí de huà, zhù zài zhèr zuì lǐxiǎng bú guò le.
Zhāng Tiānmíng:	Bù mán nín shuō, rúguǒ wǒ shì ge qiúmí de huà, jiù bú yòng bān jiā le.

PHONE CONVERSATION III

Zhāng Tiānmíng:	Nǐ hǎo! Nǐmen de fángzi zū chuqu le ma?
Fángdōng:	Hái méiyǒu, búguò yǐjīng yǒu hǎo jǐ ge rén dǎ guo diànhuà le.
Zhāng Tiānmíng:	Qǐng wèn, shì shénmeyàng de fángzi?
Fángdōng:	Shì yíshì yìtīng de, chúfáng hěn dà. Rúguǒ nǐ měitiān zìjǐ zuò fàn de huà, zhù zài zhèr zuì héshì bú guò le.
Zhāng Tiānmíng:	Zūjīn shì duōshao?
Fángdōng:	Měi ge yuè sān bǎi kuài, bāo shuǐ diàn.
Zhāng Tiānmíng:	Shì ma? Bú suàn hěn guì. Nǐmen fùjìn yǒu qiúchǎng ma?
Fángdōng:	Zhèr lí qiúchǎng hěn yuǎn, huánjìng búcuò. Hòumian shì yí piàn shùlín, qiánmian shì yì tiáo xiǎo hé, kěnéng duì nǐ lái shuō tài ānjìng le ba?
Zhāng Tiānmíng:	Wǒ jiùshì yào zhǎo yí ge ānjìng de dìfang. Ng, jiùshì lí xuéxiào yuǎn le yì diǎnr.

Fángdōng: Búguò zhèr jiāotōng hěn fāngbiàn.

Zhāng Tiānmíng: Hǎo jíle. Wǒ kěyǐ qù kàn kan fángzi ma?

Fángdōng: Kěyǐ, kěyǐ.

Discussion Topic: Apartment Hunting

With the help of the comic, cite the advantages and disadvantages of the three places that Zhang Tianming inquired about.

第七課 ▲ 男朋友

　　前幾天張天明給他妹妹天華打電話，在電話裏，天華聽起來好像有什麼心事。張天明問了她好幾次，天華才說，她跟男朋友鬧翻了。她還說等心情好一些以後，再把詳細情況告訴天明。

　　天華的男朋友湯姆是張天明的高中同學，湯姆經常到天明家去玩兒，天華就是這樣認識湯姆的。湯姆人很好，性格十分開朗，學習也不錯，就是脾氣有點兒急躁。在興趣上，他跟天華不太一樣。湯姆是個球迷，電視裏一有體育節目，他就非看不可；天華是個戲迷，一有新戲就去看。她喜歡古典音樂，湯姆喜歡搖滾樂。雖然兩個人興趣不同，可是交往了一年多以後，他們相處得越來越好。張天明想來想去想不出他們為什麼鬧翻了。是因為

第七课 ▲ 男朋友

NARRATIVE

前几天张天明给他妹妹天华打电话，在电话里，天华听起来好像有什么心事。张天明问了她好几次，天华才说，她跟男朋友闹翻了。她还说等心情好一些以后，再把详细情况告诉天明。

天华的男朋友汤姆是张天明的高中同学，汤姆经常到天明家去玩儿，天华就是这样认识汤姆的。汤姆人很好，性格十分开朗，学习也不错，就是脾气有点儿急躁。在兴趣上，他跟天华不太一样。汤姆是个球迷，电视里一有体育节目，他就非看不可；天华是个戏迷，一有新戏就去看。她喜欢古典音乐，汤姆喜欢摇滚乐。虽然两个人兴趣不同，可是交往了一年多以后，他们相处得越来越好。张天明想来想去想不出他们为什么闹翻了。是因为文化背景不同嗎？還是湯姆有了新的女朋友？正好今天晚上有空，張天明就給妹妹打了一個電話。

PHONE CONVERSATION

張天明：   喂？

張天華：   噢，哥哥，是你啊。

張天明：   你怎麼樣？

張天華：   好多了。

張天明：   你跟湯姆怎麼了？

張天華：   他最近老喝醉酒。

▼▼▼▼▼▼▼▼▼▼▼▼▼▼▼▼▼▼▼▼▼▼▼▼▼▼▼▼▼▼▼▼▼▼▼▼▼

文化背景不同吗？还是汤姆有了新的女朋友？正好今天晚上有空，张天明就给妹妹打了一个电话。

PHONE CONVERSATION

张天明： 喂？

张天华： 噢，哥哥，是你啊。

张天明： 你怎么样？

张天华： 好多了。

张天明： 你跟汤姆怎么了？

张天华： 他最近老喝醉酒。

張天明： 醉得很厲害嗎？

張天華： 嗯。 兩個星期以來，這已經是第四次了。 有一次，他醉得把屋裏的鏡子都打破了，還對我說了很多難聽的話。 我真想跟他吹了。

張天明： 難怪你心情不好，原來是湯姆喝酒的事。 我知道湯姆喜歡喝酒，可是從來沒見到他喝醉過。 要不要我給他打個電話，跟他說說？

張天華： 我想你最好別管。 我們吵架以後，他好像挺後悔的。 你跟麗莎怎麼樣？

張天明： 挺好的。 對了，這個週末我們放三天假，想去你那兒看看你們。 這兒真把我們憋死了。

張天華： 那太好了。 我們學校校園很美，附近有很多餐館兒、 酒吧，還有不少電影院。 有一家正在演幾部中國電影。

張天明： 你看了嗎？

張天華： 我看了一部，很不錯，另外兩部還沒看。 等你們來了一起去看。

張天明： 好，等我們見面以後，再好好談談。

張天華： 好吧，來以前打個電話。

張天明： 好，再見。

张天明： 醉得很厉害吗？

张天华： 嗯。两个星期以来，这已经是第四次了。有一次，他醉得把屋里的镜子都打破了，还对我说了很多难听的话。我真想跟他吹了。

张天明： 难怪你心情不好，原来是汤姆喝酒的事。我知道汤姆喜欢喝酒，可是从来没见到他喝醉过。要不要我给他打个电话，跟他说说？

张天华： 我想你最好别管。我们吵架以后，他好像挺后悔的。你跟丽莎怎么样？

张天明： 挺好的。对了，这个周末我们放三天假，想去你那儿看看你们。这儿真把我们憋死了。

张天华： 那太好了。我们学校校园很美，附近有很多餐馆儿、酒吧，还有不少电影院。有一家正在演几部中国电影。

张天明： 你看了吗？

张天华： 我看了一部，很不错，另外两部还没看。等你们来了一起去看。

张天明： 好，等我们见面以后，再好好谈谈。

张天华： 好吧，来以前打个电话。

张天明： 好，再见。

VOCABULARY

1. 心事   xīnshì   n   something weighing on one's mind

2. 鬧翻   鬧翻   nào fān   vc   to have a falling out (with somebody)

3. 心情   xīnqíng   n   mood

4. 詳細   詳细   xiángxì   adj   detailed; in detail

   請你寫一個詳細的報告。/ 请你写一个详细的报告。

   那件事剛才他說得很詳細。/ 那件事刚才他说得很详细。

5. 情況   情况   qíngkuàng   n   situation

   他最近的健康情況怎麼樣? / 他最近的健康情况怎么样?

   你把學生情況說給我聽聽。/ 你把学生情况说给我听听。

6. 高中   gāozhōng   n   senior high school

7. 經常   经常   jīngcháng   adv   frequently

8. 性格   xìnggé   n   personality; disposition

9. 十分   shífēn   adv   very

10. 開朗   开朗   kāilǎng   adj   outgoing and cheerful

11. 脾氣   脾气   píqi   n   temper; temperament

12. 急躁   jízào   adj   impetuous; impatient

13. 興趣   兴趣   xìngqu   n   hobbies

14. 體育   体育   tǐyù   n   physical education; sports

15. 節目   节目   jiémù   n   (TV, radio) program

16. 戲迷   戏迷   xìmí   n   theater buff

17. 戲   戏   xì   n   play; drama

18. 古典音樂   古典音乐   gǔdiǎn yīnyuè   classical music

19. 搖滾樂   摇滚乐   yáogǔnyuè   n   rock 'n' roll music

▼▼

20. 不同   bùtóng   adj/n   different; difference

中文和日文的語法很不同。/ 中文和日文的语法很不同。

"天" 和 "夫" 有什麼不同? / "天" 和 "夫" 有什么不同?

21. 交往   jiāowǎng   v   to socialize; to have dealings with

他們兩個人交往很久了。/ 他们两个人交往很久了。

這個人不好, 你別跟他交往。/ 这个人不好, 你别跟他交往。

22. 相處   相处   xiāngchǔ   v   to get along; to interact

他很好相處, 跟大家的關係不錯。/ 他很好相处, 跟大家的关系不错。

我跟她相處一年多了, 從來沒跟她吵過架。

我跟她相处一年多了, 从来没跟她吵过架。

23. 文化*   wénhuà   n   culture

24. 背景   bèijǐng   n   background

他一點中文背景都沒有, 可是中文學得很好。

他一点中文背景都没有, 可是中文学得很好。

請你把他的政治背景介紹一下。/ 请你把他的政治背景介绍一下。

25. 有空*   yǒu kòng   vo   to have free time

26. 噢   ō   exc   oh

27. 喝醉酒   hē zuì jiǔ   vc   to get drunk

28. 醉   zuì   adj   drunk

29. 屬害   厉害   lìhai   adj   terrible; severe

他病得很屬害。/ 他病得很厉害。

這個人很屬害, 你跟他相處要小心一點。

这个人很厉害, 你跟他相处要小心一点。

30. 以來   以来   yǐlái   n   since

31. 屋裏   屋里   wūli   inside the room

32.	鏡子	镜子	jìngzi	n	mirror
33.	打破		dǎ pò	vc	to break into pieces
34.	難聽	难听	nántīng	adj	ugly to listen to
35.	吹		chuī	v	(col) to break up; (lit) to blow
36.	難怪	难怪	nánguài	adv	no wonder
37.	從來	从来	cónglái	adv	ever (usually followed by a negative)

我上課從來沒晚過。/ 我上课从来没晚过。

他從來不喜歡抽煙喝酒。/ 他从来不喜欢抽烟喝酒。

38.	吵架		chǎo jià	vo	to quarrel
39.	挺		tǐng	adv	(col) quite; rather
40.	後悔	后悔	hòuhuǐ	v	to regret

我很後悔昨天沒去上課。/ 我很后悔昨天没去上课。

跟他分手是好事,不必後悔。/ 跟他分手是好事,不必后悔。

41.	放假*		fàng jià	vo	to have a holiday/vacation; to have a day off
42.	憋死		biē sǐ	vc	to suffocate; to feel stifled
43.	校園	校园	xiàoyuán	n	campus
44.	酒吧		jiǔbā	n	bar
45.	電影院	电影院	diànyǐngyuàn	n	cinema; movie theater
46.	演*		yǎn	v	(of plays or movies) to show
47.	部		bù	m	measure word (for movies, multivolume books, etc.)
48.	等*		děng	v	to wait
49.	見面	见面	jiàn miàn	vo	to meet; to get together

你們在哪兒見面?/ 你们在哪儿见面?

我從來沒跟他見過面,不認識他。/ 我从来没跟他见过面,不认识他。

| 50. | 談* | 谈 | tán | v | to talk; to discuss |

他們倆相處得不錯。／他们俩相处得不错。

PROPER NOUNS

1.	天華	天华	Tiānhuá	a unisex name (in this lesson, the name of Zhang Tianming's younger sister)
2.	湯姆*	汤姆	Tāngmǔ	Tom
3.	麗莎	丽莎	Lìshā	Lisa

ENLARGED CHARACTERS FOR EASIER VIEWING AND COMPARING

脾	戲	噢	屬	裏	鏡	憋
脾	戏	噢	厉	里	镜	憋

Grammar

1. 才

才 can link two clauses and indicate that the action described in the first clause is a necessary condition for the action in the second clause. In other words, the second action will not or cannot occur until the action in the first clause has occurred. 才 in this usage can be translated "only then" or "not until." So in the sentence, 張天明問了好幾次, 妹妹才告訴他 / 张天明问了好几次, 妹妹才告诉他..., 張天明問了好幾次 / 张天明问了好几次 is the condition for 妹妹告訴他 / 妹妹告诉他.

(1) 你先給我錢, 我才能給你東西。/ 你先给我钱, 我才能给你东西。

Give me the money first. Then I'll give you the stuff.

(2) 你得註完冊, 才能搬進宿舍。/ 你得注完册, 才能搬进宿舍。

You have to finish registering before you can move into the dorm.

(3) 爸爸對我說: "你今年能畢業, 我才給你錢去中國旅行。"

爸爸对我说: "你今年能毕业, 我才给你钱去中国旅行。"

My dad said to me, "Unless you graduate this year, I won't give you any money to take a trip to China."

2. (先)..., 再...

The (先)...,再... pattern can be translated as "(first)..., then...". Like 才, 再 can link two clauses, the first of which occurs before the second. However, 再 indicates that the action described in the first clause is a desired condition for the action in the second clause. In other words, the speaker would like to postpone the second action until the first action has occurred.

(1) 老師, 我今天想先不考試, 準備好了以後再考, 可以嗎?

老师, 我今天想先不考试, 准备好了以后再考, 可以吗?

Teacher, I don't feel like taking the exam today. Can I take it when I'm ready?

(2)   A: 咱們今年夏天去台灣旅行好嗎? / 咱们今年夏天去台湾旅行好吗?

          Can we travel to Taiwan this summer?

    B: 我今年不想去, 畢業以後再去。 / 我今年不想去, 毕业以后再去。

          I don't feel like going this year. [I want to wait] until after I graduate.

(3)   你先進電影院去吧。我等我們班那個影迷來了以後再進去。

       你先进电影院去吧。我等我们班那个影迷来了以后再进去。

       Why don't you go into the movie theater first? I'll go in when that movie buff from our class gets here.

Compare:

(4a)   他寫完功課才能吃飯。 / 他写完功课才能吃饭。

       He can't eat until he finishes his homework.

       (He may not eat now.)

(4b)   他寫完功課再吃飯。 / 他写完功课再吃饭。

       He'll finish his homework first and then he will eat.

       (He doesn't want to eat now.)

Note that modal verbs like 能 cannot be used after 再.

3. (在)...上

...上 can be used after abstract nouns. It means "in terms of"; for instance, "in terms of character, interest, study, work," etc.

(1)   在興趣上, 湯姆跟天華不太一樣。 / 在兴趣上, 汤姆跟天华不太一样。

       In terms of interests, Tom and Tianhua are not quite the same.

(2)   小林在文學上比小張知道的多, 可是在哲學上, 小張比小林知道的多多了。

       小林在文学上比小张知道的多, 可是在哲学上, 小张比小林知道的多多了。

Little Lin knows more about literature than Little Zhang does. But when it comes to philosophy, Little Zhang is much more knowledgeable than Little Lin.

(3)   在性格上, 她以前的男朋友比現在的男朋友好多了。

       在性格上, 她以前的男朋友比现在的男朋友好多了。

In terms of personality, her old boyfriend was much better than her current boyfriend.

他脾氣不好。 / 他脾气不好。

4. V來V去 / V来V去

V來V去 / V来V去 signifies a repetitive action, e.g., 走來走去 / 走来走去 (walk back and forth), 飛來飛去 / 飞来飞去 (fly here and there), 想來想去 / 想来想去 (think again and again), 說來說去 / 说来说去 (say again and again), 討論來討論去 / 讨论来讨论去 (discuss again and again), 研究來研究去 / 研究来研究去 (consider [research] again and again).

(1)   你別老在房間裏走來走去, 大家都睡覺了。

       你别老在房间里走来走去, 大家都睡觉了。

Don't pace back and forth in the room. Everybody has gone to bed.

(2)   這個問題我們討論來討論去, 最後還是沒有結果。

       这个问题我们讨论来讨论去, 最后还是没有结果。

We discussed this issue again and again. In the end we still couldn't come to any conclusion.

(3)   媽媽叫我學物理, 我想來想去還是選了統計。

       妈妈叫我学物理, 我想来想去还是选了统计。

My mother wanted me to study physics. After going back and forth over it (in my mind), I decided to study statistics.

5. DIRECTIONAL COMPLEMENTS (II): INDICATING RESULT

Directional complements that indicate result are similar to resultative complements, although not all directional complements indicate result.

(1) 先生, 加上稅一共是三百八十六塊四。(加上, 第四課)

先生, 加上税一共是三百八十六块四。(加上, 第四课)

Sir, with tax, it's $386.40. [see L.4]

(2) 其他的課…也學到了不少東西。(學到, 第五課)

其他的课…也学到了不少东西。(学到, 第五课)

From the other classes, (he) also learned a lot. [see L.5]

(3) 把房租跟飯錢省下來。(省下來, 第五課)

把房租跟饭钱省下来。(省下来, 第五课)

Save money [by not paying] room and board. [see L.5]

Note: Every directional complement indicating result is different. Some can have several different meanings. Although we can explain the meaning of each directional complement, it is better to treat the complement and its preceding verb as one word. We will list them as such in the vocabulary sections.

6. V + 出(來/来): INDICATING RESULT

As a complement, 出來 / 出来 signifies emergence from a state of non-existence to existence or obscurity to clarity. 想出來一個辦法 / 想出来一个办法 suggests a process of transformation from the absence of ideas to the coming forth of a particular method through the act of thinking. 聽出來他的話的意思 / 听出来他的话的意思 means "he didn't express himself directly, but the listener understood what he was really trying to say."

In this lesson, we have the following sentence:

張天明想來想去想不出他們為什麼鬧翻了。

张天明想来想去想不出他们为什么闹翻了。

Zhang Tianming racked his brain over it, but couldn't figure out why they had had a falling out.

When used with verbs such as 看, 聽/听, 吃, or 想, the pattern V + 出(來/来) signifies that a situation can be figured out through either direct experience or cognitive deliberation. Thus, 看出

(來/来) means "tell by looking," 聽出(來) / 听出(来) "tell by listening," and 吃出(來/来) "tell by eating." Similarly, 想出(來/来) means "figuring out something through reasoning." When the object is explicitly stated, the word 來/来 can be left out. However, when the construction occurs at the end of a sentence, 來/来 cannot be omitted.

(1) 我想出(來)一個好辦法。/ 我想出(来)一个好办法。

       I came up with a good idea.

(2) 從電話裏我聽出(來)是姐姐的聲音。

       从电话里我听出(来)是姐姐的声音。

       I recognized my sister's voice on the phone.

The negative form of this pattern is V + 不出(來/来) or 没V + 出(來/来), e.g., 看不出(來/来) (can't tell by looking), 沒看出(來/来) (couldn't tell by looking).

(3) 這兩本書有什麼不同, 我沒看出來。/ 这两本书有什么不同, 我没看出来。

       I couldn't see any difference between these two books.

7. 以後 / 以后 AND 以來 / 以来

以後 / 以后 means "from a certain point in the past" or "a certain time from now," e.g.,

(1) 她跟我吵架以後, 我就不喜歡她了。

       她跟我吵架以后, 我就不喜欢她了。

       After she fought with me, I began to dislike her.

(2) 2005年我們住在一個宿舍, 2006年以後我搬走了。

       2005年我们住在一个宿舍, 2006年以后我搬走了。

       In 2005 we lived in the same dormitory. After 2006 I moved away.

(3) 你一個星期以後再來。/ 你一个星期以后再来。

       Come again in one week.

以來 / 以来 means "from a certain point in the past up to now."

(1) 2005年以來, 我沒有搬過家。/ 2005年以来, 我没有搬过家。

       I haven't moved since 2005.

▼▼▼▼▼▼▼▼▼▼▼▼▼▼▼▼▼▼▼▼▼▼▼▼▼▼▼▼▼▼▼▼▼

(2)　自從我認識她以來, 沒有看見她哭過。

自从我认识她以来, 没有看见她哭过。

Ever since I became acquainted with her, I've never seen her cry.

(3)　他們交往以來, 一直相處得很好。／他们交往以来, 一直相处得很好。

Since they started socializing, they have been getting along very well.

(4)　三天以來, 他一直在考試。／三天以来, 他一直在考试。

He's been taking exams for three days.

Compare the following sentences:

上大學以後, 我們一直沒有見過她。

上大学以后, 我们一直没有见过她。

Ever since we started college, we haven't seen her.

Or: After we started college, we never saw her.

(Depending on the context, the speaker can be describing either the present or the past.)

上大學以來, 我一直沒有見過她。／上大学以来, 我一直没有见过她。

Since I started going to college, I haven't seen her.

(The speaker is still in college.)

Important Words & Phrases

1. 聽起來好像／听起来好像 (SOUND AS IF)

EXAMPLE:　天華聽起來好像有什麼心事。

天华听起来好像有什么心事。

(1)　小王兩個月都沒跟他的指導教授見面了,＿＿＿＿＿＿。

小王两个月都没跟他的指导教授见面了,＿＿＿＿＿＿。

(2) 這本書書店的老闆給我介紹了,＿＿＿＿＿＿＿,我想買一本。

這本书书店的老板给我介绍了,＿＿＿＿＿＿＿,我想买一本。

(3) A: 高小姐是從哪兒來的?

高小姐是从哪儿来的?

B: 我也不知道,不過我跟她聊過一次天,＿＿＿＿＿＿＿＿＿＿＿＿。

我也不知道,不过我跟她聊过一次天,＿＿＿＿＿＿＿＿＿＿＿＿。

2. 電視裏 / 电视里 (ON TELEVISION)

EXAMPLE: 電視裏一有體育節目,他就非看不可。

电视里一有体育节目,他就非看不可。

(1) 週末電視裏的節目,都＿＿＿＿＿＿＿＿＿＿＿＿＿＿＿。

周末电视里的节目,都＿＿＿＿＿＿＿＿＿＿＿＿＿＿＿。

(2) 今天電視裏＿＿＿＿＿＿＿＿＿＿＿＿＿＿＿＿＿＿?

今天电视里＿＿＿＿＿＿＿＿＿＿＿＿＿＿＿＿＿＿?

Note: 電視上 means "on the TV set."

3. 跟...一樣 / 跟...一样 (THE SAME AS...)

EXAMPLE: 在興趣上他跟天華不太一樣...

在兴趣上他跟天华不太一样...

(1) A: 天華跟湯姆的文化背景一樣嗎?

天华跟汤姆的文化背景一样吗?

B: ＿＿＿＿＿＿＿＿＿＿＿＿＿＿＿＿＿＿＿＿＿。

▼▼▼▼▼▼▼▼▼▼▼▼▼▼▼▼▼▼▼▼▼▼▼▼▼▼▼▼▼▼▼▼▼▼▼▼

(2) A: 小王的脾氣有點兒急躁, 那他弟弟呢?

小王的脾气有点儿急躁, 那他弟弟呢?

B: _____。。

(3) A: 我買衣服的標準是樣子漂亮, 質量好, 至於價錢多少, 我不在乎。你呢?

我买衣服的标准是样子漂亮, 质量好, 至于价钱多少, 我不在乎。你呢?

B: _____, 我的標準是_____。

_____, 我的标准是_____。

4. 越來越 (MORE AND MORE)

(1) A: 你女兒學音樂學得怎麼樣了?

你女儿学音乐学得怎么样了?

B: 不瞞你説,_____。

不瞞你说,_____。

(2) 他打籃球打得_____,球迷_____。

他打籃球打得_____,球迷_____。

(3) 自從當了醫生以後, 她_____。

自从当了医生以后, 她_____。

5. 難怪 / 难怪 (NO WONDER)

EXAMPLE: 難怪你心情不好!

难怪你心情不好!

(1) 難怪他＿＿＿＿＿＿＿＿＿＿＿＿＿＿＿＿, 原來他從來不看報紙!

　　　难怪他＿＿＿＿＿＿＿＿＿＿＿＿＿＿＿＿, 原来他从来不看报纸!

(2) 難怪他不申請上研究所, 原來＿＿＿＿＿＿＿＿＿＿＿＿＿＿＿。

　　　难怪他不申请上研究所, 原来＿＿＿＿＿＿＿＿＿＿＿＿＿＿＿。

(3) 難怪這兩天他睡不好覺, 原來＿＿＿＿＿＿＿＿＿＿＿＿＿＿＿。

　　　难怪这两天他睡不好觉, 原来＿＿＿＿＿＿＿＿＿＿＿＿＿＿＿。

6. 見面 / 见面 (MEET)

EXAMPLE:　等我們見面以後, 再好好談談。

　　　　　等我们见面以后, 再好好谈谈。

(1) A:　你跟小張見過面嗎?

　　　　你跟小张见过面吗?

　　B:　＿＿＿＿＿＿＿＿＿＿＿＿＿＿＿＿＿, 我們認識。

　　　　＿＿＿＿＿＿＿＿＿＿＿＿＿＿＿＿＿, 我们认识。

(2) A:　明天你跟他＿＿＿＿＿＿＿＿＿＿＿＿＿?

　　　　明天你跟他＿＿＿＿＿＿＿＿＿＿＿＿＿?

　　B:　我們在購物中心門口見面。

　　　　我们在购物中心门口见面。

(3) A:　你跟老師說好＿＿＿＿＿＿＿＿＿＿＿＿?

　　　　你跟老师说好＿＿＿＿＿＿＿＿＿＿＿＿?

　　B:　我跟老師下午兩點鐘見面。

　　　　我跟老师下午两点钟见面。

▼▼

Pinyin Texts

NARRATIVE

Qián jǐ tiān Zhāng Tiānmíng gěi tā mèimei Tiānhuá dǎ diànhuà, zài diànhuà li, Tiānhuá tīng qilai hǎoxiàng yǒu shénme xīnshì. Zhāng Tiānmíng wèn le tā hǎo jǐ cì, Tiānhuá cái shuō, tā gēn nánpéngyou nào fān le. Tā hái shuō děng xīnqíng hǎo yìxiē yǐhòu, zài bǎ xiángxì qíngkuàng gàosù Tiānmíng.

Tiānhuá de nánpéngyou Tāngmǔ shì Zhāng Tiānmíng de gāozhōng tóngxué, Tāngmǔ jīngcháng dào Tiānmíng jiā qù wánr, Tiānhuá jiùshì zhèyàng rènshi Tāngmǔ de. Tāngmǔ rén hěn hǎo, xìnggé shífēn kāilǎng, xuéxí yě búcuò, jiùshì píqi yǒu diǎnr jízào. Zài xìngqu shàng, tā gēn Tiānhuá bú tài yíyàng. Tāngmǔ shì ge qiúmí, diànshì li yì yǒu tǐyù jiémù, tā jiù fēi kàn bù kě; Tiānhuá shì ge xìmí, yì yǒu xīn xì jiù qù kàn. Tā xǐhuan gǔdiǎn yīnyuè, Tāngmǔ xǐhuan yáogǔnyuè. Suīrán liǎng ge rén xìngqu bùtóng, kěshì jiāowǎng le yì nián duō yǐhòu, tāmen xiāngchǔ de yuè lái yuè hǎo. Zhāng Tiānmíng xiǎng lái xiǎng qù xiǎng bu chū tāmen wèi shénme nào fān le. Shì yīnwèi wénhuà bèijǐng bùtóng ma? Háishi Tāngmǔ yǒu le xīn de nǚpéngyou? Zhènghǎo jīntiān wǎnshang yǒu kòng, Zhāng Tiānmíng jiù gěi mèimei dǎ le yí ge diànhuà.

PHONE CONVERSATION

Zhāng Tiānmíng:	Wèi?
Zhāng Tiānhuá:	Ō, gēge, shì nǐ a.
Zhāng Tiānmíng:	Nǐ zěnmeyàng?
Zhāng Tiānhuá:	Hǎo duō le.
Zhāng Tiānmíng:	Nǐ gēn Tāngmǔ zěnme le?
Zhāng Tiānhuá:	Tā zuìjìn lǎo hē zuì jiǔ.
Zhāng Tiānmíng:	Zuì de hěn lìhai ma?
Zhāng Tiānhuá:	Ng. Liǎng ge xīngqī yǐlái, zhè yǐjīng shì dì sì cì le. Yǒu yí cì, tā zuì de bǎ wū li de jìngzi dōu dǎ pò le, hái duì wǒ shuō le hěn duō nántīng de huà. Wǒ zhēn xiǎng gēn tā chuī le.
Zhāng Tiānmíng:	Nánguài nǐ xīnqíng bù hǎo, yuánlái shì Tāngmǔ hē jiǔ de shì. Wǒ zhīdao Tāngmǔ xǐhuan hē jiǔ, kěshì cónglái méi jiàn dào tā hē zuì guo. Yào bu yào wǒ gěi tā dǎ ge diànhuà, gēn tā shuō shuo?
Zhāng Tiānhuá:	Wǒ xiǎng nǐ zuìhǎo bié guǎn. Wǒmen chǎo jià yǐhòu, tā hǎoxiàng tǐng hòuhuǐ de. Nǐ gēn Lìshā zěnmeyàng?
Zhāng Tiānmíng:	Tǐng hǎo de. Duì le, zhège zhōumò wǒmen fàng sān tiān jià, xiǎng qù nǐ nàr kàn kan nǐmen. Zhèr zhēn bǎ wǒmen biē sǐ le.
Zhāng Tiānhuá:	Nà tài hǎo le. Wǒmen xuéxiào xiàoyuán hěn měi, fùjìn yǒu hěn duō cānguǎnr, jiǔbā, hái yǒu bù shǎo diànyǐngyuàn. Yǒu yì jiā zhèngzài yǎn jǐ bù Zhōngguó diànyǐng.

Zhāng Tiānmíng: Nǐ kàn le ma?

Zhāng Tiānhuá: Wǒ kàn le yí bù, hěn búcuò, lìngwài liǎng bù hái méi kàn. Děng nǐmen lái le yìqǐ qù kàn.

Zhāng Tiānmíng: Hǎo, děng wǒmen jiàn miàn yǐhòu, zài hǎohāo tán tan.

Zhāng Tiānhuá: Hǎo ba, lái yǐqián dǎ ge diànhuà.

Zhāng Tiānmíng: Hǎo, zàijiàn.

Discussion Topic: Dating

Look at the pictures and talk in Chinese about the ups and downs of Tianhua and Tom's relationship.

第八課 ▲ 電視和電影的影響

　　張天明的女朋友麗莎很喜歡看電影,新電影一上演,她就去看。這個學期她選了一門電影課,得看很多電影,張天明有空也陪她一起看。

　　學校附近有兩、三家電影院,演的都是商業片。學校禮堂幾乎每天晚上都演電影,演的多半是藝術片,偶爾也有紀錄片。今天上午麗莎來電話說,晚上想去看一部外國電影。張天明閒著沒事,坐在沙發上一邊看電視,一邊等他的女朋友。八頻道正在播一條新聞說,MTV 的卡通片對兒童的影響很不好,引起了很多家長的反對。據說加州有一個小男孩看了 MTV 的卡通片以後,模仿片裏的人物玩火柴,引起了一場火災,把他的妹妹燒死了。張天明看到這兒,他的女朋友走了進來。

DIALOGUE

張天明:　你聽說了嗎?加州的一個小男孩看了 MTV 以後玩火,結果不小
　　　　　心把他的妹妹燒死了。

第八课 ▲ 电视和电影的影响

NARRATIVE

　　张天明的女朋友丽莎很喜欢看电影，新电影一上演，她就去看。这个学期她选了一门电影课，得看很多电影，张天明有空也陪她一起看。

　　学校附近有两、三家电影院，演的都是商业片。学校礼堂几乎每天晚上都演电影，演的多半是艺术片，偶尔也有纪录片。今天上午丽莎来电话说，晚上想去看一部外国电影。张天明闲着没事，坐在沙发上一边看电视，一边等他的女朋友。八频道正在播一条新闻说，MTV 的卡通片对儿童的影响很不好，引起了很多家长的反对。据说加州有一个小男孩看了 MTV 的卡通片以后，模仿片里的人物玩火柴，引起了一场火灾，把他的妹妹烧死了。张天明看到这儿，他的女朋友走了进来。

DIALOGUE

张天明：　你听说了吗？加州的一个小男孩看了 MTV 以后玩火，结果不小心把他的妹妹烧死了。

麗莎： 真的？唉，電視裏老播些亂七八糟的東西，小孩兒能學好嗎？

張天明： 這也不見得是電視的影響。大人不好好教育孩子，反而怪電視！電視裏也有不少好的節目啊，像《芝蔴街》什麼的，為什麼不學？

麗莎： 像那樣的節目有幾個？小孩兒學壞容易，學好難哪！就是大人也難免會受電視電影的影響。你沒聽說有個女的向她男朋友的女兒開槍。她說她以為她男朋友的女兒是他的另一個女朋友，還說她開槍是因為受了一部電影的影響！

張天明： 她完全是找藉口。她是個大人，不是孩子，難道可以對自己的行為不負責任嗎？

麗莎： 你剛才不是說小孩兒不見得會受電視的影響嗎？你這不是自相矛盾嗎？

張天明： 我並沒有自相矛盾。好了，好了，我不跟你爭論了，我們還是去看電影吧。

麗莎： 電影不演了，有人威脅要炸禮堂。我敢說，這肯定是什麼人從哪個電影裏學來的。

張天明： 你是在開玩笑吧？

The heading of a TV listing from a Chinese newspaper.

(See the Alternate Character Appendix for traditional characters.)

丽莎：　　真的？唉，电视里老播些乱七八糟的东西，小孩儿能学好吗？

张天明：　这也不见得是电视的影响。大人不好好教育孩子，反而怪电视！电视里也有不少好的节目啊，像《芝麻街》什么的，为什么不学？

丽莎：　　像那样的节目有几个？小孩儿学坏容易，学好难哪！就是大人也难免会受电视电影的影响。你没听说有个女的向她男朋友的女儿开枪。她说她以为她男朋友的女儿是他的另一个女朋友，还说她开枪是因为受了一部电影的影响！

张天明：　她完全是找借口。她是个大人，不是孩子，难道可以对自己的行为不负责任吗？

丽莎：　　你刚才不是说小孩儿不见得会受电视的影响吗？你这不是自相矛盾吗？

张天明：　我并没有自相矛盾。好了，好了，我不跟你争论了，我们还是去看电影吧。

丽莎：　　电影不演了，有人威胁要炸礼堂。我敢说，这肯定是什么人从哪个电影里学来的。

张天明：　你是在开玩笑吧？

明日好节目

6:02	京城健身潮	BTV-1
7:40	健康生活	BTV-7
7:51	连续剧：小丈夫(11—14)	江苏电视台
8:35	剧场：军人机密(32、33)	河北电视台
9:00	连续剧：醉拳(22—24)	福建电视台
9:00	动画片：迷你宠物星	BTV-10
9:30	连续剧：说出你的爱(15、16)	山西电视台
11:55	体育新闻	BTV-6

Part of a TV listing in a Chinese newspaper.

(See the Appendix of Alternate Character Versions for traditional characters.)

VOCABULARY

1. 影響*   影响   yǐngxiǎng   n/v   influence; to influence

   每天花很多時間看電視,會影響孩子的學習。

   每天花很多时间看电视,会影响孩子的学习。

   這件事對我有很大的影響。/ 这件事对我有很大的影响。

2. 上演   shàngyǎn   v   (of plays or movies) to show

3. 商業片   商业片   shāngyèpiàn   n   commercial film

4. ...片   piàn   film

5. 禮堂   礼堂   lǐtáng   n   auditorium

6. 幾乎   几乎   jīhū   adv   almost

7. 多半   duōbàn   adv   mostly

8. 藝術片   艺术片   yìshùpiàn   n   art film

9. 偶爾   偶尔   ǒu'ěr   adv   occasionally

10. 紀錄片   纪录片   jìlùpiàn   n   documentary film

11. 閑著沒事   闲着没事   xián zhe méi shì   idle with nothing to do

12. 沙發*   沙发   shāfā   n   sofa

13. 頻道   频道   píndào   n   TV channel

14. 播   bō   v   to broadcast

15. 新聞   新闻   xīnwén   n   news

16. 卡通   kǎtōng   n   cartoon

17. 兒童   儿童   értóng   n   (formal) children

   兒童節 / 儿童节; 兒童用品 / 儿童用品

   這個節目不適合兒童看。/ 这个节目不适合儿童看。

   我們應該關心兒童的成長。/ 我们应该关心儿童的成长。

▼ ▼

18.	引起		yǐnqǐ	v	to give rise to; to arouse; to provoke
19.	家長	家长	jiāzhǎng	n	parent; head of a family

冬冬的媽媽到學校去參加家長會了。

冬冬的妈妈到学校去参加家长会了。

學校請學生家長來學校和老師見面。

学校请学生家长来学校和老师见面。

20.	反對	反对	fǎnduì	v	to oppose

我爸爸反對我搬到校外去住。／我爸爸反对我搬到校外去住。

21.	據說	据说	jùshuō	v	it is said that; allegedly
22.	小男孩*		xiǎo nánhái	n	a little boy
23.	模仿		mófǎng	v	to imitate

他很喜歡模仿別人說話。／他很喜欢模仿别人说话。

24.	人物		rénwù	n	character in a play, story, etc.
25.	火柴		huǒchái	n	match
26.	火災	火灾	huǒzāi	n	fire (disaster)
27.	燒死	烧死	shāo sǐ	vc	to burn to death
28.	火		huǒ	n	fire
29.	結果	结果	jiéguǒ	conj/n	as a result; result

那個孩子常常看不好的電視，結果學壞了。

那个孩子常常看不好的电视，结果学坏了。

他申請學校還沒有結果。／他申请学校还没有结果。

30.	亂七八糟	乱七八糟	luàn qī bā zāo		messy; messed up
31.	大人		dàren	n	adult
32.	教育		jiàoyù	v/n	to educate; education

家長應該好好教育孩子。／家长应该好好教育孩子。

從這件事情上我受到很大教育。／从这件事情上我受到很大教育。

33.	反而		fǎn'ér	adv	on the contrary [see G3]
34.	怪		guài	v	to blame

你們別怪他，他沒有錯。／你们别怪他，他没有错。

這個人做錯了事常常喜歡怪別人。／这个人做错了事常常喜欢怪别人。

35.	那樣	那样	nàyàng	pr	that manner; that kind
36.	小孩兒	小孩儿	xiǎoháir	n	child
37.	難免	难免	nánmiǎn	adv	inevitably; hard to avoid [see G5]
38.	向		xiàng	prep	toward
39.	開槍	开枪	kāi qiāng	vo	to fire a gun
40.	以為*	以为	yǐwéi	v	to think erroneously
41.	另*		lìng	pr	the other; another
42.	完全		wánquán	adv	completely

老師說的話我完全聽不懂。／老师说的话我完全听不懂。

這件事不能完全怪他。／这件事不能完全怪他。

43.	找藉口	找借口	zhǎo jièkǒu	vo	to look for an excuse
44.	行為	行为	xíngwéi	n	behavior
45.	負責任	负责任	fù zérèn	vo	to take responsibility

他這個人做事很負責任。／他这个人做事很负责任。

父母應該對自己的孩子負責任。／父母应该对自己的孩子负责任。

46.	自相矛盾		zìxiāng máodùn		to contradict oneself; self-contradictory
47.	威脅	威胁	wēixié	v/n	to threaten; threat

那個人用槍威脅他，可是他不怕。／那个人用枪威胁他，可是他不怕。

那個人很厲害，對我們是一個很大的威脅。

那个人很厉害，对我们是一个很大的威胁。

▼▼▼▼▼▼▼▼▼▼▼▼▼▼▼▼▼▼▼▼▼▼▼▼▼▼▼

48.	炸		zhà	v	to bomb
49.	敢		gǎn	v	to dare

外面太黑，我不敢出去。

這件事我不敢告訴爸爸。／这件事我不敢告诉爸爸。

PROPER NOUNS

1.	加州*		Jiāzhōu	(abbr.) the state of California
2.	芝蔴街	芝麻街	Zhīmajiē	Sesame Street (TV program)

ENLARGED CHARACTERS FOR EASIER VIEWING AND COMPARING

禮	藝	爾	亂	威	脅
礼	艺	尔	乱	威	胁

Notes

▲**1**▲ Another word for 頻道 ／ 频道 is 台. One can also say 第五台 instead of 第五頻道 ／ 第五频道.

▲**2**▲ "Cartoon" can be either 卡通 or 動畫 ／ 动画 in Chinese. 卡通 is the transliteration of its English counterpart. 動畫 ／ 动画 literally means "moving picture," that is, animation.

小孩會受電視節目的影響嗎？／小孩会受电视节目的影响吗？

▼▼

Grammar

1. DISTINGUISHING AMONG 的, 地, 得 (ALL PRONOUNCED *DE*)

A. When the particle *de* links an attributive to the noun or noun phrase that it modifies, it is written "的."

(1)   我的專業是統計學, 妹妹的專業是文學。

我的专业是统计学, 妹妹的专业是文学。

My major is statistics. My sister's major is literature.

(2)   王朋的建議不錯。 / 王朋的建议不错。

Wang Peng's suggestion is not bad.

(3)   小張買的衣服不太好看。

小张买的衣服不太好看。

The clothes that Little Zhang buys do not look very good.

(4)   我喜歡跟性格開朗的人交朋友。 / 我喜欢跟性格开朗的人交朋友。

I like making friends with people who are outgoing and cheerful.

B. When the particle *de* links an adverbial (or adjectival) modifier to the verb or verb phrase that it modifies, it is written "地." Note that while this rule is strictly followed in mainland China, in Taiwan the character 的 is used in this context more often than 地.

(1)   老師慢慢地走進教室來。 / 老师慢慢地走进教室来。

The teacher slowly walked into the classroom.

(2)   孩子們很快地跑了出去。 / 孩子们很快地跑了出去。

The kids quickly ran out.

(3)   學生們正在努力地學習中文。 / 学生们正在努力地学习中文。

The students are diligently studying Chinese.

C. 得 pronounced as *de*, is a complement marker. It is used after verbs or adjectives. 得 is generally followed by an adjective, a verb phrase, or an adverb.

▼ ▼

(1)　我和同屋一直相處得很好。／我和同屋一直相处得很好。

　　　I've been getting along with my roommate very well.

(2)　李明知道自己能上一個名牌大學以後, 高興得睡不著覺。

　　　李明知道自己能上一个名牌大学以后, 高兴得睡不着觉。

　　　When Li Ming heard that he got into a famous college, he was too excited to sleep.

(3)　我跟女朋友吵架以後, 後悔得很。／我跟女朋友吵架以后, 后悔得很。

　　　I was very regretful after I had a fight with my girlfriend.

2. 一邊…, 一邊… ／ 一边…, 一边…

一邊…, 一邊… ／ 一边…,一边… is used to describe two simultaneous actions—although in reality very often the first action starts before the second one.

(1)　我喜歡一邊吃飯一邊看電視。／我喜欢一边吃饭一边看电视。

　　　I like to watch TV while I'm eating.

(2)　他一邊聽古典音樂一邊給他家人寫信。

　　　他一边听古典音乐一边给他家人写信。

　　　He listened to classical music while writing to his family.

(3)　你不要一邊走路一邊看書。／你不要一边走路一边看书。

　　　Don't read and walk at the same time.

3. 反而

反而 expresses a turn or twist. The second clause signifies something that is diametrically opposite to the speaker's expectation.

(1)　難的字他都會寫, 容易的字他反而不會寫。

　　　难的字他都会写, 容易的字他反而不会写。

　　　He can write difficult characters, but not simple ones!

(2)   他怎麼了? 這次考試考得很好, 好像反而不高興了。

他怎么了? 这次考试考得很好, 好像反而不高兴了。

What's wrong with him? He did really well on this exam, but he seemed unhappy [for some strange reason].

(3)   他每天都是第一個來, 今天有這麼重要的事, 反而來晚了。

他每天都是第一个来, 今天有这么重要的事, 反而来晚了。

He is always the first one to get here every day, but today when we had such an important thing [to attend to], he was late.

Note: 反而 is an adverb. If there is a subject in the second clause, 反而 should appear after the subject. Because 反而 signifies a shift in thought, there must be some context preceding it. In other words, one cannot use 反而 out of the blue.

4. 就是..., 也... (EVEN IF... STILL...)

The conjunction 就是...,也... expresses supposition. There are two usages:

A. The two clauses or phrases refer to two related things. The first clause or phrase signifies a hypothesis; the second clause or phrase indicates that the hypothesis will not in any way change the result.

(1)   A: 外邊很黑, 他要是不來, 你就不要去看電影了。

外边很黑, 他要是不来, 你就不要去看电影了。

It's dark out there. If he doesn't show up, then don't go to the movie.

B: 我不怕, 他就是不來, 我一個人也要去。

我不怕, 他就是不来, 我一个人也要去。

I'm not afraid. Even if he doesn't come, I'll go by myself.

(2)   A: 明天要是天氣不好, 我們還去聽音樂會嗎?

明天要是天气不好, 我们还去听音乐会吗?

If the weather is bad tomorrow, are we still going to the concert?

B: 票已經買了, 就是天氣不好, 也要去。

票已经买了, 就是天气不好, 也要去。

We've got tickets. We'll go even if the weather is bad.

The hypothesis described in the first clause is often extreme. For example:

(3) 你就是給我一百萬塊錢, 我也不跟你結婚。

你就是给我一百万块钱, 我也不跟你结婚。

Even if you gave me a million dollars, I still wouldn't marry you.

就是... can be followed by a noun. What appears after 也... is the predicate of the noun.

(4) 我餓得很, 誰有吃的, 就是一小塊糖也可以。

我饿得很, 谁有吃的, 就是一小块糖也可以。

I'm starved to death. Who has something to eat, even if it is just a small piece of candy?

(5) 別説是你, 就是指導教授我也不怕。

别说是你, 就是指导教授我也不怕。

Even my adviser wouldn't be able to intimidate me, let alone you.

(6) 這兒很暖和, 就是冬天也不用穿毛衣。

这儿很暖和, 就是冬天也不用穿毛衣。

It's very warm here. You don't need to wear a sweater, even in the winter.

B. The two clauses or phrases refer to the same thing. The second clause or phrase signifies a cautious, measured guess.

(1) A: 這個音樂會聽説很不錯, 現在還有票嗎?

这个音乐会听说很不错, 现在还有票吗?

I hear this is going to be a good concert. Are there still tickets available?

B: 我想, 就是有也不多了。／ 我想, 就是有也不多了。

I don't think there are many left, if any.

(2)   明天的討論會我可能去不了,就是去也會很晚。

明天的讨论会我可能去不了,就是去也会很晚。

I probably won't make it to tomorrow's symposium. Even if I could make it, I'd be very late.

5. 難免 / 难免

難免 / 难免 literally means "difficult to avoid," suggesting a predictable response to a given situation or scenario. As an adjective, 難免 / 难免 means "unavoidable" or "inevitable." As an adverb, it means "inevitably."

(1)   兒童難免會受電視的影響。/ 儿童难免会受电视的影响。

It's inevitable that children will be influenced by TV.

(2)   第一次教課, 緊張總是難免的。/ 第一次教课, 紧张总是难免的。

It's inevitable that [you will] get nervous when [you] teach for the first time.

(3)   你在同學面前說難聽的話, 難免讓他們不高興。

你在同学面前说难听的话, 难免让他们不高兴。

You used [such] foul language in front of your classmates. No wonder [they] were upset.

(4)   就是兩個好朋友, 有時也難免意見不同。

就是两个好朋友, 有时也难免意见不同。

Even between two good friends, disagreements are unavoidable.

6. 反問句 / 反问句 (RHETORICAL QUESTIONS)

Sometimes a sentence is in the form of a question, but it does not require an answer. This type of question is used to emphasize a point.

(1)   這麼簡單的道理, 難道你都不懂嗎?

这么简单的道理, 难道你都不懂吗?

Such a simple principle! You don't understand it?

(You should be able to understand it.)

▼ ▼

(2)　A:　小明, 你剛才拿我的東西了吧? ／ 小明, 你刚才拿我的东西了吧?

　　　　Little Ming, did you take my stuff just now?

　　B:　誰拿你的東西了? 你別亂説。 ／ 谁拿你的东西了? 你别乱说。

　　　　Who would take your stuff? Don't talk nonsense.

　　　　(I didn't take your stuff.)

(3)　這麼貴的衣服, 我怎麼買得起呢? ／ 这么贵的衣服, 我怎么买得起呢?

　　These clothes are so expensive. How can I afford them?

　　(I can't afford them.)

(4)　電視裏老播些亂七八糟的東西, 小孩能學好嗎?

　　电视里老播些乱七八糟的东西, 小孩能学好吗?

　　There's nothing but junk on TV. How can kids learn to be good by example?

　　(They can't.)

(5)　我每天去工作得換三次車, 你说麻煩不麻煩?

　　我每天去工作得换三次车, 你说麻烦不麻烦?

　　I have to change buses three times when I go to work every day. Isn't that a chore?

　　(It is a chore.)

(6)　你说我應該給你錢, 我是你爸爸還是你媽媽?

　　你说我应该给你钱, 我是你爸爸还是你妈妈?

　　You said I should give you money. Am I your mother or your father?

　　(I'm neither.)

From these examples it is clear that rhetorical questions in the form of affirmative sentences are negative in implication; rhetorical questions in the form of negative sentences are affirmative in implication. Rhetorical questions are much more emphatic than non-rhetorical questions.

7. COHESION (I)

When we speak or write, we do so not in isolated sentences; rather, we string sentences together using a variety of cohesive devices. In Chinese these devices can be quite complex. One common way to ensure cohesion is to omit unnecessary nouns or pronouns.

(1) a.   學校禮堂幾乎每天晚上都演電影。

學校礼堂几乎每天晚上都演电影。

There's a film at the school auditorium almost every evening.

b.   學校禮堂演的多半是藝術片。／学校礼堂演的多半是艺术片。

Most of the films shown at the school auditorium are art films.

c.   學校禮堂偶爾也有紀錄片。／学校礼堂偶尔也有纪录片。

Occasionally, there's a documentary at the school auditorium.

To connect the sentences, we must delete the common subject, 學校禮堂／学校礼堂 from the subsequent clauses:

學校禮堂幾乎每天晚上都演電影, 演的多半是藝術片, 偶爾也有紀錄片。

学校礼堂几乎每天晚上都演电影, 演的多半是艺术片, 偶尔也有纪录片。

There's a film at the school auditorium almost every evening. Most are art films. Occasionally, there's a documentary.

Another example:

(2) a.   張天明閑著沒事。／张天明闲着没事。

Zhang Tianming didn't have anything to do.

b.   張天明坐在沙發上看電視。／张天明坐在沙发上看电视。

Zhang Tianming sat on the sofa watching TV.

c.   張天明等他的女朋友。／张天明等他的女朋友。

Zhang Tianming was waiting for his girlfriend.

To connect these three sentences, we delete 張天明／张天明 from the second and third clauses:

張天明閑著沒事, 一邊坐在沙發上看電視, 一邊等他的女朋友。

张天明闲着没事, 一边坐在沙发上看电视, 一边等他的女朋友。

Zhang Tianming didn't have anything to do. [He] sat on the sofa watching TV and waiting for his girlfriend.

Still another example:

(3) 她是個大人, (她)不是孩子, (她)難道可以對自己的行為不負責任嗎?

她是个大人, (她)不是孩子, (她)难道可以对自己的行为不负责任吗?

She's a grownup, not a kid. How could [she] not take responsibility for her behavior?

When the subject of the first clause is a noun, generally speaking, the tendency is to replace the noun with a pronoun. In the following sentences the words in parentheses are those omitted in connected discourse:

(4) 你沒聽説有個女的向她(女的)男朋友的女兒開槍, 她(女的)説她(女的)以為她(女的)男朋友的女兒是他(男朋友)的另一個女朋友, (女的)還説她(女的)開槍是因為受了一部電影的影響。

你没听说有个女的向她(女的)男朋友的女儿开枪, 她(女的)说她(女的)以为她(女的)男朋友的女儿是他(男朋友)的另一个女朋友, (女的)还说她(女的)开枪是因为受了一部电影的影响。

Didn't you hear that there was a woman who shot at her boyfriend's daughter? She said that she thought that her boyfriend's daughter was another girlfriend. She also said that the reason that she fired (at her boyfriend's daughter) was she had been influenced by a film (that she had seen).

Important Words & Phrases

1. 幾乎 ／ 几乎 (ALMOST)

EXAMPLE: 學校禮堂幾乎每天晚上都演電影。

学校礼堂几乎每天晚上都演电影。

(1) 他是個球迷, 幾乎每個週末_____。

他是个球迷, 几乎每个周末_____。

(2) 小林跟他隔壁的同學相處得非常不好,_____。

小林跟他隔壁的同学相处得非常不好,_____。

▼▼

(3)　他＿＿＿＿＿＿＿＿＿＿＿＿＿＿＿＿＿＿＿＿，幾乎天天都去酒吧喝酒。

　　　他＿＿＿＿＿＿＿＿＿＿＿＿＿＿＿＿＿＿＿＿，几乎天天都去酒吧喝酒。

Note: 幾乎 / 几乎 is more formal than 差不多 when acting as an adverbial.

2. 偶爾 / 偶尔 (OCCASIONALLY)

EXAMPLE:　學校禮堂…演的多半是藝術片，偶爾也有紀錄片。

　　　　　学校礼堂…演的多半是艺术片，偶尔也有纪录片。

(1)　我一般自己做飯，＿＿＿＿＿＿＿＿＿＿＿＿＿＿＿＿＿＿。

　　　我一般自己做饭，＿＿＿＿＿＿＿＿＿＿＿＿＿＿＿＿＿＿。

(2)　他喜歡聽搖滾樂，不過＿＿＿＿＿＿＿＿＿＿＿＿＿＿＿＿。

　　　他喜欢听摇滚乐，不过＿＿＿＿＿＿＿＿＿＿＿＿＿＿＿＿。

(3)　她一般都在自己的房間看書，偶爾＿＿＿＿＿＿＿＿＿＿＿＿。

　　　她一般都在自己的房间看书，偶尔＿＿＿＿＿＿＿＿＿＿＿＿。

3. 多半 (LIT. "MORE THAN HALF," USED BEFORE VERBS)

EXAMPLE:　學校禮堂…演的多半是藝術片，偶爾也有紀錄片。

　　　　　学校礼堂…演的多半是艺术片，偶尔也有纪录片。

(1)　張教授寫的文章我多半＿＿＿＿＿＿＿＿＿＿＿＿＿＿＿。

　　　张教授写的文章我多半＿＿＿＿＿＿＿＿＿＿＿＿＿＿＿。

(2)　現在放假了，他多半＿＿＿＿＿＿＿＿＿＿＿＿＿，你去找他吧。

　　　现在放假了，他多半＿＿＿＿＿＿＿＿＿＿＿＿＿，你去找他吧。

(3)　小孩多半愛看＿＿＿＿＿＿＿＿＿＿＿＿＿＿＿，不喜歡看新聞。

　　　小孩多半爱看＿＿＿＿＿＿＿＿＿＿＿＿＿＿＿，不喜欢看新闻。

▼▼▼▼▼▼▼▼▼▼▼▼▼▼▼▼▼▼▼▼▼▼▼▼▼▼

多半 cannot appear before nouns:

*多半的学生不喜欢住在家里。／*多半的学生不喜欢住在家里。

The correct way to say this is:

多數學生不喜歡住在家裏。／ 多数学生不喜欢住在家里。

4. 引起...反對 ／ 火災 ／ 興趣 ／ 爭論 ／ 討論
引起...反对 ／ 火灾 ／ 兴趣 ／ 争论 ／ 讨论

(PROVOKE/GIVE RISE TO...OPPOSITION/FIRE/INTEREST/
DISPUTE/DISCUSSION)

EXAMPLE: 加州的一個小男孩玩火柴引起了一場火災。

加州的一个小男孩玩火柴引起了一场火灾。

(1) 學校認為為了安全, 一年級新生都應該住在校內。這個建議_____
_____。

学校认为为了安全, 一年级新生都应该住在校内。这个建议_____
_____。

(2) 這本書寫得好, 圖也畫得漂亮, 引起孩子們很大的_____
_____。

这本书写得好, 图也画得漂亮, 引起孩子们很大的_____
_____。

(3) 大大購物中心的老闆打算在河邊再開一家商店,_____
_____。有的人覺得對環境不好, 有的人認為對找工作很有幫助。

大大购物中心的老板打算在河边再开一家商店,_____
_____。有的人觉得对环境不好, 有的人认为对找工作很有帮助。

5. THE ADVERB 老 (COLLOQ. "ALWAYS")

EXAMPLE: 電視裏老播些亂七八糟的東西。

電視里老播些乱七八糟的东西。

(1) 他老買些＿＿＿＿＿＿＿＿＿＿＿＿＿＿＿＿＿＿＿＿＿＿東西。

他老买些＿＿＿＿＿＿＿＿＿＿＿＿＿＿＿＿＿＿＿＿＿＿东西。

(2) 別老喝酒,＿＿＿＿＿＿＿＿＿＿＿＿＿＿＿＿＿＿＿＿＿！

(3) 你怎麼＿＿＿＿＿＿＿＿＿＿＿＿＿＿＿＿＿＿? 難道你不洗衣服嗎?

你怎么＿＿＿＿＿＿＿＿＿＿＿＿＿＿＿＿＿＿? 难道你不洗衣服吗?

6. 還是...(吧) / 还是...(吧) (HAD BETTER)

EXAMPLE: 好了, 好了, 我不跟你爭論了, 我們還是去看電影吧。

好了, 好了, 我不跟你争论了, 我们还是去看电影吧。

(1) 買衣服得看樣子、大小、顏色合適不合適, 你怎麼讓別人幫你買呢?

＿＿＿＿＿＿＿＿＿＿＿＿＿＿＿＿＿＿＿＿＿＿＿＿＿。

买衣服得看样子、大小、颜色合适不合适, 你怎么让别人帮你买呢?

＿＿＿＿＿＿＿＿＿＿＿＿＿＿＿＿＿＿＿＿＿＿＿＿＿。

(2) 這個問題比較難, 我做不出來,＿＿＿＿＿＿＿＿＿＿＿＿＿＿＿＿。

这个问题比较难, 我做不出来,＿＿＿＿＿＿＿＿＿＿＿＿＿＿＿＿。

(3) 明天是她二十歲的生日, 我們＿＿＿＿＿＿＿＿＿, 要不然她會生氣的。

明天是她二十岁的生日, 我们＿＿＿＿＿＿＿＿＿, 要不然她会生气的。

Pinyin Texts

NARRATIVE

Zhāng Tiānmíng de nǚpéngyou Lìshā hěn xǐhuan kàn diànyǐng, xīn diànyǐng yí shàngyǎn, tā jiù qù kàn. Zhège xuéqī tā xuǎn le yì mén diànyǐng kè, děi kàn hěn duō diànyǐng, Zhāng Tiānmíng yǒu kòng yě péi tā yìqǐ kàn.

Xuéxiào fùjìn yǒu liǎng, sān jiā diànyǐngyuàn, yǎn de dōu shì shāngyèpiàn. Xuéxiào lǐtáng jīhū měitiān wǎnshang dōu yǎn diànyǐng, yǎn de duōbàn shì yìshùpiàn, ǒu'ěr yě yǒu jìlùpiàn. Jīntiān shàngwǔ Lìshā lái diànhuà shuō, wǎnshang xiǎng qù kàn yí bù wàiguó diànyǐng. Zhāng Tiānmíng xián zhe méi shì, zuò zài shāfā shang yìbiān kàn diànshì, yìbiān děng tā de nǚpéngyou. Bā píndào zhèngzài bō yì tiáo xīnwén shuō, MTV de kǎtōngpiàn duì értóng de yǐngxiǎng hěn bù hǎo, yǐnqǐ le hěn duō jiāzhǎng de fǎnduì. Jùshuō Jiāzhōu yǒu yí ge xiǎonánhái kàn le MTV de kǎtōngpiàn yǐhòu, mófǎng piàn li de rénwù wán huǒchái, yǐnqǐ le yì chǎng huǒzāi, bǎ tā de mèimei shāo sǐ le. Zhāng Tiānmíng kàn dào zhèr, tā de nǚpéngyou zǒu le jìn lái.

DIALOGUE

Zhāng Tiānmíng: Nǐ tīngshuō le ma? Jiāzhōu de yí ge xiǎonánhái kàn le MTV yǐhòu wán huǒ, jiéguǒ bù xiǎoxīn bǎ tā de mèimei shāo sǐ le.

Lìshā: Zhēndē? Ài, diànshì li lǎo bō xiē luàn qī bā zāo de dōngxi, xiǎohái'r néng xué hǎo ma?

Zhāng Tiānmíng: Zhè yě bú jiàn de shì diànshì de yǐngxiǎng. Dàren bù hǎohāo jiàoyù háizi, fǎn'ér guài diànshì! Diànshì lǐ yě yǒu bù shǎo hǎode jiémù a, xiàng 《Zhīmajiē》 shénme de, wèishénme bù xué?

Lìshā: Xiàng nàyàng de jiémù yǒu jǐ ge? Xiǎohái'r xué huài róngyì, xué hǎo nán na! Jiùshì dàren yě nánmiǎn huì shòu diànshì diànyǐng de yǐngxiǎng. Nǐ méi tīngshuō yǒu ge nǚ de xiàng tā nánpéngyou de nǚ'ér kāi qiāng. Tā shuō tā yǐwéi tā nánpéngyou de nǚ'ér shì tā de lìng yí ge nǚpéngyou, hái shuō tā kāi qiāng shì yīnwèi shòu le yí bù diànyǐng de yǐngxiǎng!

Zhāng Tiānmíng: Tā wánquán shì zhǎo jièkǒu. Tā shì ge dàren, bú shì háizi, nándào kěyǐ duì zìjǐ de xíngwéi bú fù zérèn ma?

Lìshā: Nǐ gāngcái bú shì shuō xiǎohái'r bú jiàn de huì shòu diànshì de yǐngxiǎng ma? Nǐ zhè bú shì zìxiāng máodùn ma?

Zhāng Tiānmíng: Wǒ bìng méiyǒu zìxiāng máodùn. Hǎo le, hǎo le, wǒ bù gēn nǐ zhēnglùn le, wǒmen háishi qù kàn diànyǐng ba.

Lìshā: Diànyǐng bù yǎn le, yǒu rén wēixié yào zhà lǐtáng. Wǒ gǎn shuō, zhè kěndìng shì shénme rén cóng nǎge diànyǐng li xué lái de.

Zhāng Tiānmíng: Nǐ shì zài kāi wánxiào ba?

Discussion Topic: Television and the Movies

What did Tianming and Lisa plan for the evening? What did they end up doing?

明 日

中央电视台 CCTV

● 中央电视台—1
6:00 走近科学
9:24 连续剧:西游记（缩编版）（22–24）
12:38 今日说法

● 中央电视台—新闻频道
6:30 媒体广场
11:00 整点新闻
12:00 新闻30分

● 中央电视台—2
9:00 中国证券
9:48 健康之路
10:43 广告经济信息中心特别节目
12:00 全球资讯榜

● 中央电视台—3
7:45 文化访谈录
8:20 中国音乐电视
9:05 剧场:东北一家人（38–40）
11:55 曲苑杂坛
12:30 快乐驿站
12:45 曲苑杂坛

● 中央电视台—4
7:10 探索·发现
8:00 新闻60分
9:00 连续剧:表演系的故事（8）
10:15 动画城
11:10 走遍中国

● 中央电视台—5
6:00 健身房
9:00 早安中国
10:00 实况录像:2005年焦作U17乒乓球挑战赛

● 中央电视台—6
6:51 故事片:东归英雄传
8:36 故事片:神女峰的迷雾
12:59 纪录片长廊:饮食文化:世界蛋糕纵览:澳门

● 中央电视台—7
7:30 科技博览
8:30 动画城
9:19 智慧树
11:30 人与自然
12:30 致富经

● 中央电视台—8
6:00 每日佳艺（佳艺剧场）:隐秘的激情（第二部）（20）（哥伦比亚）
7:46 连续剧:再见阿郎（55–58）
11:38 连续剧:闲人马大姐（133、134）
12:51 魅力100分:武装特警（5、6）

● 中央电视台—10
7:55 教科文行动之科学发现篇
9:35 走近科学
10:05 教科文行动
11:05 科技之光
12:05 地图上的故事
12:15 希望·英语杂志

● 中央电视台—11
6:00 九州大戏台
7:35 名段欣赏
8:45 九州大戏台（地方版）:越剧:灰阑记（周燕萍、郑曼丽、李宝赢主演）
12:05 跟我学
12:40 名段欣赏

● 中央电视台–12
8:15 大家看法
8:35 道德观察
9:00 第一线
10:25 法治视界
12:00 中国法治报道
12:30 大家看法

● 中央电视台–少儿频道
6:00 中国动画
8:00 中国动画
9:20 （首播）中国动画
10:00 动漫世界
10:30 快乐体验
11:00 中国动画
12:00 中国动画
12:30 新闻袋袋裤

● 中央电视台–（音乐频道）
10:21 CCTV·音乐厅（214）
12:40 影视留声机（214）

北京电视台 BTV

● 北京电视台—1
8:02 世界报道（早间版）
8:40 今日话题
10:50 纪录

11:30 身边
11:58 世界报道

● 北京电视台—2
7:40 连续剧:杨门虎将（24、25）
9:45 天天影视圈
10:55 每日文化播报
11:35 留声机
12:10 电影直通车——小人国

● 北京电视台—3
7:43 世纪之约
8:41 连续剧：仙剑奇侠传（22–24）
11:22 科技全方位（1249）
12:00 法治进行时（1782）
12:37 印象

● 北京电视台—4
6:07 连续剧:大马帮（21、22）
8:00 连续剧：谷穗黄了（28–30）
11:00 连续剧:浴血男儿（16、17）

● 北京电视台–5
8:20 首都经济报道
9:57 连续剧:巡城御史鬼难缠（14、15）
12:30 首都经济报道

● 北京电视台—6
6:02 棋道经纬
7:35 BTV赛场2004/2005WNBA
11:15 京城健身潮
12:20 足球报道

● 北京电视台—7
9:10 时尚装苑
10:07 快乐生活一点通
11:30 生活广角
12:40 健康生活

● 北京电视台–8
7:27 七色光
11:00 黄金五分钟
12:00 开心一刻
12:35 连续剧：苦菜花（13–15）

● 北京电视台–9
9:05 连续剧：少年包青天（二）（37–39）
12:00 系列片
12:30 都市阳光

● 北京电视台–10

Part of a TV listing in a Chinese newspaper.

(See the Appendix of Alternate Character Versions for traditional characters.)

第九課 ▲ 旅行

NARRATIVE

　　快放假了,這幾天張天明一直在考慮假期的旅行計劃。 張天明的父母是五十年代從中國南京移民來美國的。 張天明自己是在美國出生,在美國長大的,從來沒去過中國。 他的父母曾經多次讓他去中國大陸看看,特別是去南京看看。 張天明自己也確實想去看看爸爸媽媽出生的地方。 可是他覺得除非麗莎跟他一起去,否則,一個人旅行有什麼意思? 這天晚飯後,張天明和麗莎一邊散步,一邊談起了旅行的事。

DIALOGUE

張天明: 就要放假了,你說我們該去哪兒玩兒?

麗莎: 哪兒好玩兒就去哪兒。

張天明: 以前咱們不是去東岸就是去西岸,都快玩兒膩了。 這次咱們去遠一點的地方怎麼樣? 出國旅行!

麗莎: 出國? 好啊。 去墨西哥!

第九课 ▲ 旅行

NARRATIVE

　　快放假了，这几天张天明一直在考虑假期的旅行计划。张天明的父母是五十年代从中国南京移民来美国的。张天明自己是在美国出生，在美国长大的，从来没去过中国。他的父母曾经多次让他去中国大陆看看，特别是去南京看看。张天明自己也确实想去看看爸爸妈妈出生的地方。可是他觉得除非丽莎跟他一起去，否则，一个人旅行有什么意思？这天晚饭后，张天明和丽莎一边散步，一边谈起了旅行的事。

DIALOGUE

张天明： 就要放假了，你说我们该去哪儿玩儿？

丽莎： 哪儿好玩儿就去哪儿。

张天明： 以前咱们不是去东岸就是去西岸，都快玩儿腻了。这次咱们去远一点的地方怎么样？出国旅行！

丽莎： 出国？好啊。去墨西哥！

張天明：　墨西哥太近，還有，聽說一打開電視，節目有一半都是在美國演過的。

麗莎：　你說的這些都是藉口。要是不去墨西哥，那你說咱們去哪兒？

張天明：　去中國好嗎？我真的很想去南京看看，當然還有北京、上海。

麗莎：　難怪這幾天你老看中國地圖！可是我聽說夏天南京熱得很，像個大火爐一樣。

張天明：　其實沒那麼可怕，我父母的老家就在南京。我有一個姑媽住在那兒，我應該去看看她。我要是今年不去南京，就得等到畢業以後了。

麗莎：　好吧，既然你這麼想去，我就陪你去一趟吧。你現在就給旅行社打電話訂機票吧。

介紹旅遊的書 / 介绍旅游的书

张天明： 墨西哥太近，还有，听说一打开电视，节目有一半都是在美国演过的。

丽莎： 你说的这些都是借口。要是不去墨西哥，那你说咱们去哪儿？

张天明： 去中国好吗？我真的很想去南京看看，当然还有北京、上海。

丽莎： 难怪这几天你老看中国地图！可是我听说夏天南京热得很，像个大火炉一样。

张天明： 其实没那么可怕，我父母的老家就在南京。我有一个姑妈住在那儿，我应该去看看她。我要是今年不去南京，就得等到毕业以后了。

丽莎： 好吧，既然你这么想去，我就陪你去一趟吧。你现在就给旅行社打电话订机票吧。

全国主要城市今日天气

城市	天气	温度	城市	天气	温度
哈尔滨	晴	20–26℃	济南	雷阵雨	22–30℃
长春	多云	20–27℃	郑州	雷阵雨	24–30℃
沈阳	多云	21–29℃	合肥	中雨	25–32℃
天津	雷阵雨	22–30℃	南京	雷阵雨	25–33℃
呼和浩特	多云	18–28℃	上海	多云	30–37℃
乌鲁木齐	多云	20–31℃	武汉	大雨	26–31℃
西宁	晴	13–31℃	长沙	雷阵雨	26–35℃
银川	晴	21–32℃	南昌	多云	28–36℃
兰州	晴	20–31℃	杭州	多云	28–37℃
西安	多云	26–34℃	福州	多云	27–37℃
拉萨	阴	15–24℃	南宁	阵雨	27–34℃
成都	多云	23–31℃	海口	多云	27–35℃
重庆	阵雨	25–33℃	广州	晴	27–36℃
贵阳	雷阵雨	20–28℃	台北	多云	24–36℃
昆明	小雨	18–26℃	香港	晴	28–32℃
太原	雷阵雨	20–28℃	澳门	晴	28–34℃
石家庄	中雨	22–29℃			

報上的天氣預報／报上的天气预报

南京熱嗎？／南京热吗？

(See the Appendix of Alternate Character Versions for traditional characters.)

A half-hour later...

張天明： 我已經打過電話了，沒有從紐約直飛南京的飛機。 一條路線是從芝加哥到上海，再從上海坐火車到南京，是東方航空公司；另一條是先到香港，然後從香港飛南京，是韓國航空公司。 我們得商量商量走哪條路線好。

麗莎： 走香港！我們可以順便去看看斯蒂夫。 他在香港做生意，可以讓他開車到機場接我們，當我們的導遊。

張天明： 你總是忘不了你那個斯蒂夫！

麗莎： 別吃醋，我跟他只不過是一般的朋友。

張天明： 我知道。 我只是怕時間來不及。

麗莎： 我們可以在南京少待兩天，那麼熱的地方。 對了，我還得去郵局辦護照呢，聽說一般要等兩個禮拜。

張天明： 咱們還得辦簽證。 這麼多事情，得趕快辦。

麗莎： 我馬上去照相。

張天明： 好，我也去打聽打聽中國領事館的電話和地址。

旅行社的機票廣告 / 旅行社的机票广告

(See the Appendix of Alternate Character Versions for traditional characters.)

A half-hour later...

张天明：　我已经打过电话了，没有从纽约直飞南京的飞机。一条路线是从芝加哥到上海，再从上海坐火车到南京，是东方航空公司；另一条是先到香港，然后从香港飞南京，是韩国航空公司。我们得商量商量走哪条路线好。

丽莎：　　走香港！我们可以顺便去看看斯蒂夫。他在香港做生意，可以让他开车到机场接我们，当我们的导游。

张天明：　你总是忘不了你那个斯蒂夫！

丽莎：　　别吃醋，我跟他只不过是一般的朋友。

张天明：　我知道。我只是怕时间来不及。

丽莎：　　我们可以在南京少待两天，那么热的地方。对了，我还得去邮局办护照呢，听说一般要等两个礼拜。

张天明：　咱们还得办签证。这么多事情，得赶快办。

丽莎：　　我马上去照相。

张天明：　好，我也去打听打听中国领事馆的电话和地址。

香　港	5300/ 5600	馬尼拉	9600
	6600/ 7500	吉隆坡	9200
澳　門	5900/ 6400	檳　城	9200
深　圳	9300	漢　城	9000/10000
上　海	13300/13000	東　京	11000/11300
	14200/14600	大　阪	9100/11400
廈　門	10600/11800	美　西	23000
	11900	洛杉磯	20000/21000
福　州	11800/12400		25700
杭　州	13400/14700	舊金山	20000
寧　波	14700	紐　約	25000
北　京	16900/18200	溫哥華	22000
曼　谷	5800/ 7300	歐　洲	24500/25500
新加坡	9200/11000	澳　洲	22000

▲以上報價均為現金價(不含各地機場稅、兵險費、安檢費、燃料費)
★代辦出國手續、各國簽證、各國訂房、各航空公司自由行、半自助旅遊，專業人員為您作最精緻的安排！

這家旅行社除了可以幫忙買機票以外，還有什麼別的服務？
这家旅行社除了可以帮忙买机票以外，还有什么别的服务？

(See the Appendix of Alternate Character Forms for simplified characters.)

VOCABULARY

1.	假期		jiàqī	n	vacation; "vacation period"
2.	年代		niándài	n	decade, as in 五十年代, "the (decade of the) fifties"
3.	移民		yímín	v/n	to emigrate or immigrate; immigrant
4.	曾經	曾经	céngjīng	adv	(indicating that something happened before) once
5.	大陸	大陆	dàlù	n	mainland; continent
6.	確實	确实	quèshí	adv	indeed; in truth
7.	除非		chúfēi	conj	unless; only if [see G3]
8.	否則	否则	fǒuzé	conj	otherwise [see G3]

我必須再學一門外語, 否則畢不了業。

我必须再学一门外语, 否则毕不了业。

明天的會議你一定要來, 否則會影響你的工作。

明天的会议你一定要来, 否则会影响你的工作。

9.	散步		sàn bù	vo	to take a walk

我們去公園散散步吧。 / 我们去公园散散步吧。

他每天吃了晚飯就去散步。 / 他每天吃了晚饭就去散步。

10.	該	该	gāi	av	should; 應該 / 应该
11.	東岸	东岸	dōng'àn	n	east coast; east shore
12.	西岸		xī'àn	n	west coast; west shore
13.	V+膩(了)	V+腻(了)	V+nì (le)	vc	(col) to be bored with doing something; to be sick of doing something

這道菜我天天吃, 都吃膩了。 / 这道菜我天天吃, 都吃腻了。

這種電影太多了, 我看膩了。 / 这种电影太多了, 我看腻了。

14.	出國	出国	chū guó	vo	to go abroad

| 15. | 火爐 | 火炉 | huǒlú | n | furnace |
| 16. | 可怕 | | kěpà | adj | terrible |

那個地方壞人很多, 很可怕。／那个地方坏人很多, 很可怕。

剛才他講了一個可怕的故事。／刚才他讲了一个可怕的故事。

17.	姑媽	姑妈	gūmā	n	aunt (father's sister)
18.	既然		jìrán	conj	since; now that
19.	趟		tàng	m	measure word (for trips)
20.	旅行社*		lǚxíngshè	n	travel agency
21.	訂*	订	dìng	v	to reserve; to book

給飯館打電話訂位子。／给饭馆打电话订位子。

22.	機票*	机票	jīpiào	n	plane ticket
23.	直飛*	直飞	zhí fēi		to fly directly
24.	路線	路线	lùxiàn	n	route
25.	火車	火车	huǒchē	n	train
26.	東方	东方	dōngfāng	n	east; the Orient
27.	航空公司*		hángkōng gōngsī		airline
28.	公司*		gōngsī	n	company
29.	然後*	然后	ránhòu	adv	then; after that; next
30.	商量		shāngliang	v	to discuss; to negotiate

你們商量一下明天旅行的路線。／你们商量一下明天旅行的路线。

你提出來的事我們正在商量。／你提出来的事我们正在商量。

31.	順便	顺便	shùnbiàn	adv	in passing; on the way; conveniently
32.	做生意		zuò shēngyi	vo	to do business
33.	機場*	机场	jīchǎng	n	airport
34.	導遊*	导游	dǎoyóu	n	tour guide

| 35. | 忘不了 | | wàng bu liǎo | vc | cannot forget; unable to forget |
| 36. | 吃醋 | | chī cù | vo | (col) to be jealous (because of rivalry in love); (lit) to eat vinegar |

我們老闆的太太最愛吃醋。／我们老板的太太最爱吃醋。

他跟那個女孩只是一般的朋友, 你不要吃醋。

他跟那个女孩只是一般的朋友, 你不要吃醋。

37.	不過*	不过	búguò	adv	no more than; just; only
38.	怕*		pà	v	to be afraid
39.	來不及*	来不及	lái bu jí	vc	there's not enough time (for)
40.	待		dāi	v	to stay
41.	郵局*	邮局	yóujú	n	post office
42.	護照*	护照	hùzhào	n	passport
43.	禮拜	礼拜	lǐbài	n	week
44.	簽證*	签证	qiānzhèng	n	visa
45.	趕快*	赶快	gǎnkuài	adv	quickly

趕快走, 快上課了。／赶快走, 快上课了。

他病了, 趕快帶他去醫院吧。／他病了, 赶快带他去医院吧。

| 46. | 照相 | | zhào xiàng | vo | to have a picture taken; to take a picture |
| 47. | 打聽 | 打听 | dǎtīng | v | to ask about; to inquire about |

你去打聽一下, 這附近有沒有中國飯館。

你去打听一下, 这附近有没有中国饭馆。

剛才我去打聽了, 明天放假, 圖書館不開。

刚才我去打听了, 明天放假, 图书馆不开。

| 48. | 領事館 | 领事馆 | lǐngshìguǎn | n | consulate |
| 49. | 地址 | | dìzhǐ | n | address |

▼▼▼▼▼▼▼▼▼▼▼▼▼▼▼▼▼▼▼▼▼▼▼▼▼▼▼▼▼▼▼▼▼▼▼▼

PROPER NOUNS

1.	南京		Nánjīng	Nanjing
2.	墨西哥		Mòxīgē	Mexico
3.	芝加哥*		Zhījiāgē	Chicago
4.	香港*		Xiānggǎng	Hong Kong
5.	韓國*	韩国	Hánguó	(South) Korea
6.	斯蒂夫		Sīdìfū	Steve

ENLARGED CHARACTERS FOR EASIER VIEWING AND COMPARING

確	膩	爐	護	證
确	腻	炉	护	证

Culture Notes ▲

1 ▿ Because of their hot and humid weather, Nánjīng, Chóngqìng, Wǔhàn, and Nánchāng are commonly known as the "Four Furnaces" of China.

2 ▿ North Korea is called 朝鮮 / 朝鲜 Cháoxiǎn in mainland China, and 北韓 / 北韩 in Taiwan.

Grammar

1. 過/过 (INDICATING EXPERIENCE)

To indicate that someone has had the experience of doing something, we use the dynamic particle 過/过. It differs from 了 in two ways.

A. 了 is descriptive in nature and is used to describe the occurrence of an action.

(1) 聽說你去年去了一趟中國, 在那兒住了三個月, 請給我們一些建議, 去哪兒旅行最好。

听说你去年去了一趟中国, 在那儿住了三个月, 请给我们一些建议, 去哪
儿旅行最好。

We heard that you went to China last year and stayed there for three months. Please give us some tips on the best places to go.

(2) 第二天早上, 我很早就起來了, 起床後就去體育場跑步。

第二天早上, 我很早就起来了, 起床后就去体育场跑步。

The following morning I got up really early. After I got up, I went jogging at the athletic field.

(3) 客人們進來以後, 找到了自己的位子, 坐了下來。

客人们进来以后, 找到了自己的位子, 坐了下来。

The guests walked in, found their seats, and sat down.

There isn't an explicit time phrase in example (3), because it is part of an extended narrative in which the temporal background has already been stated or is implicitly understood.

過/过 is explanatory in nature. It is used to explain the rationale behind an action mentioned in a separate clause.

(1) (以前)我們在一起學過英文, 我知道他英文很好。

(以前)我们在一起学过英文, 我知道他英文很好。

(因為我們在一起學過英文, 所以我知道他英文很好。)

(因为我们在一起学过英文, 所以我知道他英文很好。)

We used to study English together. That's why I know his English is very good.

(Because we studied English together, I know his English is very good.)

(2) A: 你去過中國, 請給我們一些建議, 去哪兒旅行最好。

你去过中国, 请给我们一些建议, 去哪儿旅行最好。

You've been to China. Give us some tips on the best places to go.

(因為你去過中國, 所以請給我們一些建議, 去哪兒旅行最好。)

(因为你去过中国, 所以请给我们一些建议, 去哪儿旅行最好。)

(Because you've been to China, you can give us some tips on the best places to go.)

B:　誰説我去過中國? 對不起, 我不能給你們什麼建議。

　　誰说我去过中国? 对不起, 我不能给你们什么建议。

　　Who says I've been to China? I'm sorry. I can't offer you any suggestions.

(3)　他學過好幾年中文, 都能看中國電影了。

　　他学过好几年中文, 都能看中国电影了。

　　He's been studying Chinese for several years. He can even understand Chinese movies.

　　(因為他學過好幾年中文, 所以都能看中國電影了。)

　　(因为他学过好几年中文, 所以都能看中国电影了。)

　　(Because he's been studying Chinese for several years, he can understand Chinese movies.)

In the above sentences the clauses containing 過/过 all serve as explanatory background to the following clauses. 過/过 indicates the effect of a past action on the present.

B. 了 generally requires a specific time phrase. 過/过 does not. When we use 過/过, the time implied is often rather vague: "before," or "in the past." Only when we want to be more precise do we use a time phrase. Note that when 過/过 is used in the experiential sense, it usually cannot be followed by 了.

A:　我聽説你沒去過別的國家, 是真的嗎?

　　我听说你没去过别的国家, 是真的吗?

　　I heard that you have never been abroad. Is that true?

B:　誰説的? 我去年去過日本。/ 谁说的? 我去年去过日本。

　　Who said that? I went to Japan last year.

2. 過/过 (INDICATING COMPLETION)

過/过 can also indicate completion as in 我已經打過電話了 / 我打过电话了 (I've called.) More examples:

(1)　你叫我看的那本書我看過了, 很不錯。

　　你叫我看的那本书我看过了, 很不错。

　　I've read that book that you asked me to read [that you recommended]. It's not bad.

(2)　A: 我們一起去註冊, 好嗎? / 我们一起去注册, 好吗?

Let's go to register together, O.K.?

　　B: 我已經註過冊了。/ 我已经注过册了。

I've registered already.

(3)　A: 你在我們這兒吃飯吧。/ 你在我们这儿吃饭吧。

Why don't you eat with us?

　　B: 不, 我吃過了。/ 不, 我吃过了。

Oh no, I've already eaten.

Note: Verbs that can be used with 過/过 in this way have to do with actions that are known or familiar to the speaker, such as 看(那本書 / 那本书) in example (1), 註冊 / 注册 in example (2), and 吃(飯/饭)in example (3). 過/过 in this usage is interchangeable with 了. One could also put 了 after 過/过.

3. 除非

除非 is a conjunction. It introduces a precondition. There is usually a second clause containing 才 or 否則 / 否则. In some cases both 才 and 否則 / 否则 occur in subsequent clauses.

(1)　衣服除非是名牌他才買。/ 衣服除非是名牌他才买。

He only buys brand name clothes. (Unless the clothes are brand name, he won't buy them.)

(2)　A: 你想租這套公寓嗎? / 你想租这套公寓吗?

Do you want to rent this apartment?

　　B: 除非你給我找一個同屋, 房租便宜一點, 我才會租, 否則我不租。
　　　 除非你给我找一个同屋, 房租便宜一点, 我才会租, 否则我不租。

Only if you find me a roommate and lower the rent. Otherwise I won't rent it.

(3)　A: 今天去看電影好不好? / 今天去看电影好不好?

Shall we go to a movie today?

　　B: 除非看外國電影我才去。/ 除非看外国电影我才去。

I'll only go if [we're] going to see a foreign movie.

否則／否则 can be interchanged with (要)不然.

(1)   A: 今天去看電影好不好?／今天去看电影好不好?

           Shall we go to a movie today?

    B: 除非看外國電影, 我才去, 否則(要不然)我就不去。
        除非看外国电影, 我才去, 否则(要不然)我就不去。

           I'll go only if it's a foreign movie. Otherwise, I'm not going.

Often the middle clause with 才 can be omitted.

(2)   A: 明天我的生日晚會她會來嗎?／明天我的生日晚会她会来吗?

           Do you think she'll come to my birthday party tomorrow evening?

    B: 除非你自己去請她, 否則(要不然)她不會來。
        除非你自己去请她, 否则(要不然)她不会来。

           She won't come unless you ask her in person.

(3)   除非天氣特別好, 否則(要不然)我是不會出去散步的。
     除非天气特别好, 否则(要不然)我是不会出去散步的。

     I won't go out for a walk unless the weather is exceptionally good.

With 除非, the conclusion can also be stated before the precondition.

(1)   今年夏天我不想出去旅行, 除非我女朋友跟我一起去。

     I don't feel like traveling this summer — unless my girlfriend goes with me.

(2)   明天我們一定去打籃球, 除非下大雨。
     明天我们一定去打篮球, 除非下大雨。

     We'll definitely go play basketball tomorrow, unless it pours.

(3)   他一般十點鐘就睡了, 除非第二天有考試。
     他一般十点钟就睡了, 除非第二天有考试。

     Usually he's asleep by ten unless there's an exam the next day.

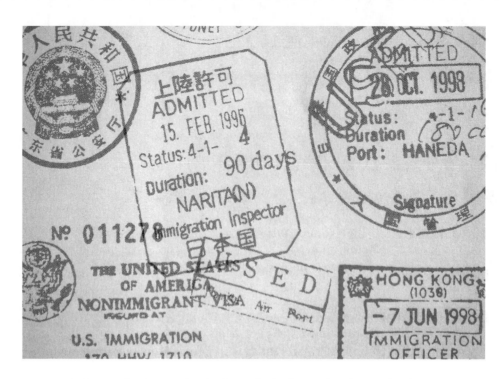

這個人去過哪些地方？/ 这个人去过哪些地方？

4. 哪兒..., 哪兒... / 哪儿..., 哪儿... (INTERROGATIVE PRONOUNS)

Interrogative pronouns such as 哪兒 / 哪儿, 什麼 / 什么, 怎麼 / 怎么, 誰/谁 can be used for non-interrogative purposes. The same interrogative pronoun appears in both clauses, and refers to the same indefinite person, thing, time, or place.

(1)   哪兒好玩, 我去哪兒。/ 哪儿好玩, 我去哪儿。

I'll go wherever is fun.

(2)   A: 咱們點菜吧。你想吃什麼？/ 咱们点菜吧。你想吃什么？

Let's order. What would you like to eat?

B: 什麼都可以, 你喜歡吃什麼, 我就吃什麼。
什么都可以, 你喜欢吃什么, 我就吃什么。

Anything will do. I'll eat whatever you like to eat.

(3)   很奇怪, 她姐姐喜歡看什麼電影, 她也喜歡看什麼電影。
很奇怪, 她姐姐喜欢看什么电影, 她也喜欢看什么电影。

It's odd. She likes whatever movies her sister likes.

(4) 你什麼時候有時間, 什麼時候來找我。

你什么时候有时间, 什么时候来找我。

Come look for me whenever you have time.

(5) 這個問題, 誰會請誰回答。／这个问题, 谁会请谁回答。

Whoever knows the answer to this question can answer.

(6) A: 咱們怎麼走?／咱们怎么走?

Which way shall we go?

B: 怎麼近怎麼走。／怎么近怎么走。

Whichever way is nearest.

When interrogative pronouns are used in this way, their positions remain unchanged from normal affirmative sentences. For instance, in (2) 你喜歡吃什麼, 我就吃什麼 ／ 你喜欢吃什么, 我就吃什么, 什麼 ／ 什么 is the object. Therefore, it stays in the normal position of the object—after the verb. In (4), 你什麼時候有時間, 什麼時候來 ／ 你什么时候有时间, 什么时候来, 什麼時候 ／ 什么时候 is an adverbial. Therefore, it stays in the normal position of the adverbial—before the verb. In this lesson we have 哪兒好玩兒就去哪兒 ／ 哪儿好玩儿就去哪儿. The word 哪兒 ／ 哪儿 appears at the beginning of the first clause as its subject and appears after the verb in the second clause as its object.

5. 既然..., 就...

既然 introduces a fact or circumstance which is the cause of the condition indicated in the second clause. Conversely, the second clause expresses a conclusion that is derived from the fact or circumstance mentioned in the first clause.

(1) A: 老師, 這本書我看過了。／老师, 这本书我看过了。

Teacher, I've read this book.

B: 既然你看過了, 那麼就不必再看了。

既然你看过了, 那么就不必再看了。

In that case, you don't have to read it again.

(2) A: 我很不喜歡這兒的天氣。／我很不喜歡這兒的天氣。

I really don't like the weather here.

B: 既然你不喜歡這兒的天氣, 就應該搬家。

既然你不喜欢这儿的天气, 就应该搬家。

Well, if you don't like the weather here, you should move elsewhere.

(3) 既然你不想住在校外, 咱們就住學校宿舍吧。

既然你不想住在校外, 咱们就住学校宿舍吧。

Since you don't want to move off campus, let's stay in the dorms.

Notice that 既然 introduces a fact or circumstance that is already known. In this respect, it differs from 因為 ／ 因为. Compare:

(4) A: 為什麼中國人一家只能生一個孩子?

为什么中国人一家只能生一个孩子?

Why must each Chinese family only have one child?

B: 因為中國的人口太多了, 所以不得不這麼做。

因为中国的人口太多了, 所以不得不这么做。

It is because there are too many people in China. There is no other way [choice].

B: *既然中國的人口太多了, 所以不得不這麼做。

*既然中国的人口太多了, 所以不得不这么做。

(5) A: 老師, 我有一點不舒服。／老师, 我有一点不舒服。

Teacher, I don't feel well.

B: 既然你不舒服, 就回去休息 (xiūxi) 吧。

既然你不舒服, 就回去休息 (xiūxi) 吧。

In that case [since you're not feeling well], go home and rest.

B: *因為你不舒服, 就回去休息吧。／*因为你不舒服, 就回去休息吧。

6. 然後 / 然后

然後 / 然后 is used to describe two consecutive actions. They are usually future actions, but they also can be past actions.

(1) 你們先復習這一課的語法, 然後預習下一課的生詞。

你们先复习这一课的语法, 然后预习下一课的生词。

Review this lesson's grammar first. Then study the following lesson's vocabulary.

(2) 在這個學校, 你得先念碩士(shuòshì), 然後才能念博士(bóshì)。

在这个学校, 你得先念硕士(shuòshì), 然后才能念博士(bóshì)。

At this school, you have to get a master's degree before you can go on to the Ph.D. program.

(3) 昨天他們先去看了一場電影, 然後去一家中國餐館吃了一頓飯, 很晚才回家。

昨天他们先去看了一场电影, 然后去一家中国餐馆吃了一顿饭, 很晚才回家。

Yesterday they first saw a movie and then went to a Chinese restaurant. They got home very late.

然後 / 然后 is different from 後來 / 后来:

A: 後來 / 后来 can only be used to refer to past actions.

B: When 然後 / 然后 is used in reference to the past, it connects two concrete actions or events. Furthermore, they must be consecutive actions or events. This restriction does not apply to 後來 / 后来. Compare:

(4) 他們交往了一年多, 後來就結婚了。/ 他们交往了一年多, 后来就结婚了。

They dated for more than a year and then got married.

*他們交往了一年多, 然後就結婚了。/ *他们交往了一年多, 然后就结婚了。

(5) 我們學了兩年日文, 後來就不學了。/ 我们学了两年日文, 后来就不学了。

We studied Japanese for two years. Then we quit.

*我們學了兩年日文, 然後就不學了。/ *我们学了两年日文, 然后就不学了。

7. WORD ORDER IN CHINESE (II)

Chinese word order follows the chronological principle. For instance,

(1)   我還得去郵局辦護照呢。/ 我还得去邮局办护照呢。

I have to go to the post office to get my passport.

(One has to get to the office first before one can get one's passport.)

(2)   一條路線是從芝加哥到上海, 再從上海坐火車到南京。

一条路线是从芝加哥到上海, 再从上海坐火车到南京。

One route is from Chicago to Shanghai and then from Shanghai to Nanjing by train.

(You have to be in Chicago first before you can go on to the next destination, Shanghai; you have to be in Shanghai first before you can board the train to Nanjing.)

(3)   他在香港做生意, 可以讓他開車到機場接我們。

他在香港做生意, 可以让他开车到机场接我们。

He does business in Hong Kong. We could ask him drive to the airport to pick us up.

(He has to drive to the airport first before he can pick us up.)

Remember this important principle.

Important Words & Phrases

1. 從來不/沒
从来不/沒 (NEVER)

EXAMPLE: 張天明自己是在美國出生, 在美國長大的, 從來沒去過中國。

張天明自己是在美国出生, 在美国长大的, 从来没去过中国。

(1)   這家電影院只演商業片,_____。

这家电影院只演商业片,_____。

▼▼▼▼▼▼▼▼▼▼▼▼▼▼▼▼▼▼▼▼▼▼▼▼▼▼▼▼▼▼▼▼

(2) 我弟弟性格開朗, 很容易相處, 從來＿＿＿＿＿＿＿＿＿＿＿＿＿＿＿。

　　我弟弟性格开朗, 很容易相处, 从来＿＿＿＿＿＿＿＿＿＿＿＿＿＿＿。

(3) 小林聽説墨西哥飯味道不錯, 可是＿＿＿＿＿＿＿＿＿＿＿＿＿＿。

　　小林听说墨西哥饭味道不错, 可是＿＿＿＿＿＿＿＿＿＿＿＿＿＿。

2. 曾(經) / 曾(经) ("AT ONE TIME IN THE PAST"; INDICATING PAST ACTION)

EXAMPLE: 他的父母親曾經去過很多國家, 可以給你一些建議。

　　　　 他的父母亲曾经去过很多国家, 可以给你一些建议。

(1) A: 你會説日文嗎? / 你会说日文吗?

　　 B: ＿＿＿＿＿＿＿＿＿＿＿＿＿＿＿＿＿＿＿, 可是我差不多都忘了。

　　　　＿＿＿＿＿＿＿＿＿＿＿＿＿＿＿＿＿, 可是我差不多都忘了。

(2) 我們可以叫柯林介紹一下波士頓, 他＿＿＿＿＿＿＿＿＿＿＿＿＿。

　　我们可以叫柯林介绍一下波士顿, 他＿＿＿＿＿＿＿＿＿＿＿＿＿。

(3) A: 那個人對我説了很多難聽的話, 還用槍威脅我。

　　　 那个人对我说了很多难听的话, 还用枪威胁我。

　　 B: 你最好別跟他打交道, 聽説他＿＿＿＿＿＿＿＿＿＿＿＿。

　　　 你最好别跟他打交道, 听说他＿＿＿＿＿＿＿＿＿＿＿＿。

3. 就要…了 (ALMOST; INDICATING AN IMMINENT ACTION OR STATE)

EXAMPLE: 就要放假了, 你説我們該去哪兒玩兒?

　　　　 就要放假了, 你说我们该去哪儿玩儿?

(1) _____, 你的護照和簽證辦好了嗎?

_____, 你的护照和签证办好了吗?

(2) _____, 你怎麼還不準備一下?

_____, 你怎么还不准备一下?

(3) _____, 小王的指導教授建議他
再選兩門電腦課。

_____, 小王的指导教授建议他
再选两门电脑课。

4. 不是…, 就是… (IF IT'S NOT A, IT'S B; EITHER A OR B)

EXAMPLE: 以前咱們不是去東岸就是去西岸。

以前咱们不是去东岸就是去西岸。

(1) 這個學期我很忙, 不是在圖書館_____, 就是在
電腦房_____。

这个学期我很忙, 不是在图书馆_____, 就是在
电脑房_____。

(2) 現在租房子很不容易,_____, _____,
麻煩得很。

现在租房子很不容易,_____, _____,
麻烦得很。

(3) 張天明只買_____, 不是阿迪達斯的就是
耐克(Nàikè: Nike)的。

张天明只买_____, 不是阿迪达斯的就是
耐克(Nàikè: Nike)的。

▼▼▼▼▼▼▼▼▼▼▼▼▼▼▼▼▼▼▼▼▼▼▼▼▼▼▼▼▼▼▼▼▼▼▼▼▼

5. 像…一樣 / 像…一样 (LIKE A...; RESEMBLING)

EXAMPLE:　夏天南京熱得很, 像個大火爐一樣。

　　　　　夏天南京热得很, 像个大火炉一样。

(1)　無論什麼事他都管, 像＿＿＿＿＿＿＿＿＿＿＿一樣。

　　　无论什么事他都管, 像＿＿＿＿＿＿＿＿＿＿＿一样。

(2)　他們的校園, 又大又漂亮, 像＿＿＿＿＿＿＿＿＿＿＿一樣。

　　　他们的校园, 又大又漂亮, 像＿＿＿＿＿＿＿＿＿＿＿一样。

(3)　那個人很喜歡看卡通, 像＿＿＿＿＿＿＿＿＿＿＿一樣。

　　　那个人很喜欢看卡通, 像＿＿＿＿＿＿＿＿＿＿＿一样。

6. 順便 / 顺便 (IN PASSING)

EXAMPLE:　我們可以順便去看看斯蒂夫。

　　　　　我们可以顺便去看看斯蒂夫。

(1)　你看電視新聞的時候, 順便幫我＿＿＿＿＿＿＿,
　　　好嗎?

　　　你看电视新闻的时候, 顺便帮我＿＿＿＿＿＿＿,
　　　好吗?

(2)　你需要衛生紙、香皂嗎? 我正好要去買日用品, 可以＿＿＿＿＿＿＿＿。

　　　你需要卫生纸、香皂吗? 我正好要去买日用品, 可以＿＿＿＿＿＿＿＿。

(3)　我弟弟住在波士頓, 你暑假去玩的時候, 麻煩你＿＿＿＿＿＿＿＿。

　　　我弟弟住在波士顿, 你暑假去玩的时候, 麻烦你＿＿＿＿＿＿＿＿。

▼▼▼▼▼▼▼▼▼▼▼▼▼▼▼▼▼▼▼▼▼▼▼▼▼▼▼▼

7. 趕快／赶快 (HURRY UP)

EXAMPLE: 這麼多事情, 得趕快去辦。

這麼多事情, 得趕快去辦。

这么多事情, 得赶快去办。

(1) 這本書今天得還, 圖書館就要關門了, 你＿＿＿＿＿＿＿＿＿吧。

这本书今天得还, 图书馆就要关门了, 你＿＿＿＿＿＿＿＿＿吧。

(2) 他病得這麼屬害, 你＿＿＿＿＿＿＿＿＿＿吧。

他病得这么厉害, 你＿＿＿＿＿＿＿＿＿＿吧。

(3) 下個星期你就要出國旅行去了, ＿＿＿＿＿＿＿＿吧。

下个星期你就要出国旅行去了, ＿＿＿＿＿＿＿＿吧。

Pinyin Texts

NARRATIVE

Kuài fàng jià le, zhè jǐ tiān Zhāng Tiānmíng yìzhí zài kǎolǜ jiàqī de lǚxíng jìhuà. Zhāng Tiānmíng de fùmǔ shì wǔshí niándài cóng Zhōngguó Nánjīng yímín lái Měiguó de. Zhāng Tiānmíng zìjǐ shì zài Měiguó chūshēng, zài Měiguó zhǎngdà de, cónglái méi qù guò Zhōngguó. Tā de fùmǔ céngjīng duōcì ràng tā qù Zhōngguó dàlù kàn kan, tèbié shì qù Nánjīng kàn kan.

Zhāng Tiānmíng zìjǐ yě quèshí xiǎng qù kàn kan bàba māma chūshēng de dìfang. Kěshì tā juéde chúfēi Lìshā gēn tā yìqǐ qù, fǒuzé, yí ge rén lǚxíng yǒu shénme yìsi? Zhètiān wǎnfàn hòu, Zhāng Tiānmíng hé Lìshā yìbiān sàn bù, yìbiān tán qǐ le lǚxíng de shì.

DIALOGUE

Zhāng Tiānmíng: Jiùyào fàng jià le, nǐ shuō wǒmen gāi qù nǎr wánr?

Lìshā: Nǎr hǎowánr jiù qù nǎr.

Zhāng Tiānmíng: Yǐqián zánmen búshì qù Dong'an jiùshì qù Xī'ān, dōu kuài wánr nì le. Zhècì zánmen qù yuǎn yìdiǎn de dìfang zěnmeyàng? Chū guó lǚxíng!

Lìshā: Chū guó? Hǎo a. Qù Mòxīgē!

▼ ▼

Zhāng Tiānmíng:	Mòxīgē tài jìn, háiyǒu, tīngshuō yì dǎ kāi diànshì, jiémù yǒu yíbàn dōu shì zài Měiguó yǎn guò de.
Lìshā:	Nǐ shuō de zhèxiē dōu shì jièkǒu. Yàoshì bú qù Mòxīgē, nà nǐ shuō zánmen qù nǎr?
Zhāng Tiānmíng:	Qù Zhōngguó hǎo ma? Wǒ zhēnde hěn xiǎng qù Nánjīng kàn kan, dāngrán hái yǒu Běijīng, Shànghǎi.
Lìshā:	Nánguài zhè jǐ tiān nǐ lǎo kàn Zhōngguó dìtú! Kěshì wǒ tīngshuō xiàtiān Nánjīng rè de hěn, xiàng ge dà huǒlú yíyàng.
Zhāng Tiānmíng:	Qíshí méi nàme kěpà, wǒ fùmǔ de lǎojiā jiù zài Nánjīng. Wǒ yǒu yí ge gūmā zhù zài nàr, wǒ yīnggāi qù kàn kan tā. Wǒ yàoshi jīnnián bú qù Nánjīng, jiù děi děng dào bì yè yǐhòu le.
Lìshā:	Hǎo ba, jìrán nǐ zhème xiǎng qù, wǒ jiù péi nǐ qù yí tàng ba. Nǐ xiànzài jiù gěi lǚxíngshè dǎ diànhuà dìng jīpiào ba.

A half-hour later…

Zhāng Tiānmíng:	Wǒ yǐjīng dǎ guò diànhuà le, méiyǒu cóng Niǔyuē zhífēi Nánjīng de fēijī. Yì tiáo lùxiàn shì cóng Zhījiāgē dào Shànghǎi, zài cóng Shànghǎi zuò huǒchē dào Nánjīng, shì Dōngfāng Hángkōng Gōngsī; lìng yì tiáo shì xiān dào Xiānggǎng, ránhòu cóng Xiānggǎng fēi Nánjīng, shì Hánguó Hángkōng Gōngsī. Wǒmen děi shāngliang shāngliang zǒu nǎtiáo lùxiàn hǎo.
Lìshā:	Zǒu Xiānggǎng! Wǒmen kěyǐ shùnbiàn qù kàn kan Sīdìfū. Tā zài Xiānggǎng zuò shēngyi, kěyǐ ràng tā kāi chē dào jīchǎng jiē wǒmen, dāng wǒmen de dǎoyóu.
Zhāng Tiānmíng:	Nǐ zǒngshì wàng bu liǎo nǐ nàge Sīdìfū!
Lìshā:	Bié chī cù, wǒ gēn tā zhǐ búguò shì yìbān de péngyou.
Zhāng Tiānmíng:	Wǒ zhīdao. Wǒ zhǐshì pà shíjiān lái bu jí.
Lìshā:	Wǒmen kěyǐ zài Nánjīng shǎo dāi liǎng tiān, nàme rè de dìfāng. Duìle, wǒ hái děi qù yóujú bàn hùzhào ne, tīngshuō yìbān yào děng liǎng ge lǐbài.
Zhāng Tiānmíng:	Zánmen hái děi bàn qiānzhèng. Zhème duō shìqing, děi gǎnkuài bàn.
Lìshā:	Wǒ mǎshàng qù zhào xiàng.
Zhāng Tiānmíng:	Hǎo, wǒ yě qù dǎtīng dǎtīng Zhōngguó lǐngshìguǎn de diànhuà hé dìzhǐ.

Discussion Topic: Making Travel Arrangements

Recap how Zhang Tianming and Lisa planned their trip to China.

第十課 ▲ 在郵局

在南京

NARRATIVE I

　　星期六下午張天明和麗莎去逛街,他們走著走著來到了中山路。 他們看見馬路對面的一棟大樓上寫著"郵電局"三個大字。 很多人進進出出,張天明和麗莎很好奇,就走了過去。

DIALOGUE I

張天明: 奇怪,星期六下午郵局還辦公?

麗莎: 這跟美國的郵局不一樣。

張天明: 麗莎,我正好可以買一些明信片跟郵票,給美國的朋友寫信。

麗莎: 對。 那邊好像可以打長途電話,我去給你母親和我母親打電話,告訴她們我們一路上都很順利,請她們放心。

第十课 ▲ 在邮局

在南京

NARRATIVE I

　　星期六下午张天明和丽莎去逛街，他们走着走着来到了中山路。 他们看见马路对面的一栋大楼上写着"邮电局"三个大字。很多人进进出出，张天明和丽莎很好奇，就走了过去。

DIALOGUE I

张天明：　奇怪，星期六下午邮局还办公？

丽莎：　　这跟美国的邮局不一样。

张天明：　丽莎，我正好可以买一些明信片跟邮票，给美国的朋友写信。

丽莎：　　对。 那边好像可以打长途电话，我去给你母亲和我母亲打电话，告诉她们我们一路上都很顺利，请她们放心。

Twenty minutes later...

張天明: 我把東西都買好了,你呢?電話打通了嗎?

麗莎: 對,都打通了。排隊打電話的人真多,等了半天才輪到我。

張天明: 趁你打電話的時候,我寫了三張明信片,寄給李哲、柯林和我妹妹。信筒在門口。我現在就把明信片寄了。你等我一下...

麗莎: 咱們還應該買些郵簡,在去西安的路上,我可以寫幾張寄給我的大學同學和斯蒂夫。

張天明: 又是斯蒂夫。為了他,我們特地去了香港,沒想到他卻跑到台北去了。對了,我們還應該給西安拍個電報,把我們的日程告訴那邊的旅行社。

麗莎: 今天真的來對了,一下子辦了這麼多事。你趕快去拍電報,我去買郵簡。

Twenty minutes later…

张天明：　我把东西都买好了，你呢？电话打通了吗？

丽莎：　　对，都打通了。排队打电话的人真多，等了半天才轮到我。

张天明：　趁你打电话的时候，我写了三张明信片，寄给李哲、柯林和我妹妹。信筒在门口。我现在就把明信片寄了。你等我一下…

丽莎：　　咱们还应该买些邮简，在去西安的路上，我可以写几张寄给我的大学同学和斯蒂夫。

张天明：　又是斯蒂夫。为了他，我们特地去了香港，没想到他却跑到台北去了。对了，我们还应该给西安拍个电报，把我们的日程告诉那边的旅行社。

丽莎：　　今天真的来对了，一下子办了这么多事。你赶快去拍电报，我去买邮简。

在台北

NARRATIVE II

斯蒂夫從香港到台北出差,買了些台灣特產,想寄給麗莎。

DIALOGUE II

斯蒂夫：　小姐,我要把這個包裹寄到美國。

櫃台：　　好的,你要寄空運,海運,還是陸空聯運?

斯蒂夫：　哪個快,哪個便宜,就寄哪個。

櫃台：　　那就寄航空掛號吧,又快又安全,就是貴一點。裏邊是什麼東西?

斯蒂夫：　台灣特產和糖果、餅乾什麼的。

櫃台：　　我幫你稱稱。不太重,四百二十塊台幣。

斯蒂夫：　好。萬一東西寄丟了,怎麼辦?

櫃台：　　航空掛號一向安全可靠,不會有什麼問題的。給你這張收據,
　　　　　有問題可以打電話來問。

▼▼▼▼▼▼▼▼▼▼▼▼▼▼▼▼▼▼▼▼▼▼▼▼▼▼▼▼▼▼▼▼▼▼▼▼

在台北

NARRATIVE II

斯蒂夫从香港到台北出差，买了些台湾特产，想寄给丽莎。

DIALOGUE II

斯蒂夫：　小姐，我要把这个包裹寄到美国。

柜台：　　好的，你要寄空运，海运，还是陆空联运？

斯蒂夫：　哪个快，哪个便宜，就寄哪个。

柜台：　　那就寄航空挂号吧，又快又安全，就是贵一点。里边是什么东西？

斯蒂夫：　台湾特产和糖果、饼干什么的。

柜台：　　我帮你称称。不太重，四百二十块台币。

斯蒂夫：　好。万一东西寄丢了，怎么办？

柜台：　　航空挂号一向安全可靠，不会有什么问题的。给你这张收据，有问题可以打电话来问。

VOCABULARY

1. 郵局*   邮局   yóujú   n   post office

2. 逛街   guàng jiē   vo   to go window shopping; to stroll (in the city)

3. 對面*   对面   duìmiàn   n   opposite; the other side

    郵局在商店的對面。／邮局在商店的对面。

    對面的大樓是一個醫院。／对面的大楼是一个医院。

4. 大樓   大楼   dàlóu   n   tall building

5. 郵電局   邮电局   yóudiànjú   n   post and telecommunications office

6. 好奇   hàoqí   adj   curious

    他對什麼事情都很好奇。／他对什么事情都很好奇。

    孩子差不多都有好奇心。

7. …過去   …过去   …guò qu   (v)c   …toward

8. 奇怪   qíguài   adj   strange; unfamiliar

    他今天怎麼沒來上課？我覺得很奇怪。

    他今天怎么没来上课？我觉得很奇怪。

    學校最近常常有些奇怪的事。／学校最近常常有些奇怪的事。

9. 辦公   办公   bàn gōng   vo   to work (in an office); open for business

10. 明信片*   míngxìnpiàn   n   postcard

11. 郵票*   邮票   yóupiào   n   stamp

12. 長途*   长途   chángtú   adj   long distance

    昨天他打了很多長途電話。／昨天他打了很多长途电话。

    長途旅行以後，他很累。／长途旅行以后，他很累。

13. 母親*   母亲   mǔqin   n   mother

14. 路上*   lùshang   n   on the way

在回宿舍的路上, 他碰到了一個老朋友。

在回宿舍的路上, 他碰到了一个老朋友。

這次出國旅行, 一路上都很順利。／这次出国旅行, 一路上都很顺利。

15.	順利	顺利	shùnlì	adj	without a hitch; smooth
16.	放心		fàng xīn	vo	to relax; to rest assured

你放心吧, 他的病很快就會好的。／你放心吧, 他的病很快就会好的。

媽媽給他打了電話, 他好幾天不回電話, 媽媽很不放心。

妈妈给他打了电话, 他好几天不回电话, 妈妈很不放心。

17.	打通		dǎ tōng	vc	to go through; to make a successful connection (on the telephone)
18.	排隊	排队	pái duì	vo	to stand in line; to line up
19.	輪到	轮到	lún dào	vc	to become the turn of

我排隊排了很久才輪到我。／我排队排了很久才轮到我。

輪到你了, 快進去吧。／轮到你了, 快进去吧。

20.	趁		chèn	prep	to take advantage of (an opportunity or situation)
21.	寄*		jì	v	to send by mail
22.	郵簡	邮简	yóujiǎn	n	aerogram
23.	信筒		xìntǒng	n	street mailbox for posting mail
24.	特地		tèdì	adv	specially
25.	卻	却	què	conj	however
26.	一下子		yíxiàzi		at one go; in a short while

弟弟的書丟了, 我幫他找, 一下子就找到了。

弟弟的书丢了, 我帮他找, 一下子就找到了。

老師說的話, 他下了課, 一下子就忘了。

老师说的话, 他下了课, 一下子就忘了。

27. 拍　　　　　　　　　　pāi　　　　v　　to send (a telegram); to pat

　　　　拍電報 / 拍电报

28. 電報　　　电报　　　diànbào　　n　　telegram

29. 日程*　　　　　　　ríchéng　　　n　　schedule; itinerary

　　　　這是開會的日程, 你看看。/ 这是开会的日程, 你看看。

　　　　旅行的日程定下來了。/ 旅行的日程定下来了。

30. 來對了　　　来对了　　lái duì le　　vc　　(it was a) right (decision) to come

31. 出差　　　　　　　　chū chāi　　vo　　to go on a business trip

　　　　我明天要去韓國出差。/ 我明天要去韩国出差。

　　　　出差的人常常會覺得還是家裏最舒服。

　　　　出差的人常常会觉得还是家里最舒服。

32. 特產　　　特产　　　tèchǎn　　　n　　unique local product

　　　　你們家鄉有什麼特產? / 你们家乡有什么特产?

　　　　他給你帶來一些上海特產。/ 他给你带来一些上海特产。

33. 包裹　　　　　　　　bāoguǒ　　n　　parcel

34. 空運　　　空运　　　kōngyùn　　v　　transport by air

35. 海運　　　海运　　　hǎiyùn　　　v　　transport by sea

36. 陸空聯運　陆空联运　lù kōng liányùn　　　land-air linked transport

37. 掛號*　　　挂号　　　guà hào　　vo　　to register (mail)

38. 糖果　　　　　　　　tángguǒ　　n　　candies

39. 餅乾　　　饼干　　　bǐnggān　　n　　cookies; crackers

40. 稱*　　　　称　　　　chēng　　　v　　to weigh

41. 台幣　　　台币　　　Táibì　　　n　　Taiwan currency

42. 萬一　　　万一　　　wànyī　　　adv　　in case; in the highly unlikely event that...

43. 寄丟了　　　　　　　jì diū le　　vc　　to get lost in the mail

44.	一向		yíxiàng	adv	consistently; always (in the past) [see G6]
45.	可靠		kěkào	adj	reliable

他是一個可靠的人。／他是一个可靠的人。

他這個人很可靠。／他这个人很可靠。

PROPER NOUNS

1.	中山路	Zhōngshān lù	Zhongshan Road
2.	西安	Xī'ān	Xi'an, famous historic city in western China

SUPPLEMENTARY VOCABULARY

1.	手機	手机	shǒujī	n	cell phone
2.	電話卡	电话卡	diànhuàkǎ	n	phone card
3.	電子郵件	电子邮件	diànzǐ yóujiàn	n	email

ENLARGED CHARACTERS FOR EASIER VIEWING AND COMPARING

輪	簡	裹	聯	幣
轮	简	裹	联	币

Notes

▲1▲ Post office is "郵局／邮局" in Taiwan and in mainland China. Sometimes you may hear people refer to it as "郵電局／邮电局" (post and telephone/telegram bureau) in mainland China, but telephone and telegram services are now separated from postal services. Hence the new name, 郵政／邮政 (yóuzhèng: postal administration), is often seen on the building of the post office, as shown in the images here.

▼▼▼▼▼▼▼▼▼▼▼▼▼▼▼▼▼▼▼▼▼▼▼▼▼▼▼▼▼▼

▲**2**▲ As China modernizes its communications systems, email (diànzǐ yóujiàn 電子郵件 / 电子邮件), long distance phone calls, and fax (chuánzhēn 傳真 / 传真) have replaced telegrams.

明信片

Grammar

1. V著V著... / V着V着...

V著V著... / V着V着... must be followed by a second verb phrase. It signifies that while the action denoted in the phrase of V著V著... / V着V着... is going on, a second action happens as an unintended result or by surprise. There is often a 就 before the second verb.

(1)　媽媽走了以後, 那個孩子哭著哭著就睡著了。

　　妈妈走了以后, 那个孩子哭着哭着就睡着了。

After his mother left, the child cried and cried and fell asleep.

(2) 我第一次來這個城市, 開車出去, 開著開著就迷路了。

我第一次来这个城市, 开车出去, 开着开着就迷路了。

The first time I came to this city, I was driving around and got lost.

(3) 弟弟躺在床上想下午剛看的卡通片, 想著想著笑了起來。

弟弟躺在床上想下午刚看的卡通片, 想着想着笑了起来。

Lying in bed and thinking about the cartoon he just saw in the afternoon, my younger brother burst out laughing.

2. RESULTATIVE COMPLEMENTS (II)

A verb or adjective can be followed by another adjective or verb. When the second verb or adjective signifies the result of the first verb or adjective, it is called a resultative complement. We have learned several kinds of resultative complements as you recall.

A. The complement clarifies the action or state.

(1) 寫完了 ／ 写完了

finish writing

(2) 睡著了 ／ 睡着了

fall asleep

B. The complement clarifies the subject.

(1) 他喝醉了。

He got himself drunk. (He drank—he was drunk.)

(2) 我聽懂了。／ 我听懂了。

I listened and understood. (I listened—I understood.)

(3) 書放在桌子上。／ 书放在桌子上。

The book was put on the desk. (The book was lying on the desk as a result of the action.)

(4) 信寄給哥哥。／ 信寄给哥哥。

The letter was sent to [my] older brother. (He now has the letter.)

(5)   我走到購物中心。／ 我走到购物中心。

I walked to the shopping center. (I'm now at the shopping center.)

C. The complement clarifies the object.

(1)   妹妹打破了鏡子。／ 妹妹打破了镜子。

[My] sister broke the mirror. (The mirror is now broken.)

(2)   我寄丟了明信片。

I lost the postcard in the mail. (The postcard was lost.)

(3)   弟弟寫錯了一個字。／ 弟弟写错了一个字。

[My] brother wrote a character incorrectly. (The character was wrong.)

(4)   哥哥洗乾淨(gānjìng)衣服。／ 哥哥洗干净(gānjìng)衣服。

[My] brother washed the clothes until they were clean. (The clothes are now clean.)

D. Some complements that appear after adjectives or verbs that denote emotional responses indicate an extreme degree.

(1)   電影好極了。／ 电影好极了。

The film was extremely good.

(2)   那個孩子餓壞了。／ 那个孩子饿坏了。

That kid was starving.

(3)   我們高興極了。／ 我们高兴极了。

We're extremely happy.

(4)   老師急死了。／ 老师急死了。

The teacher is worried sick.

Note: Because many resultative complements are closely related to the preceding verbs or adjectives, they are mutually selective. In other words, their combination is not unrestricted. One must remember which complement can be used after which verb or adjective, or which verb or adjective can take which complement. In other words, one must learn resultative complements the way one learns new words—by memorizing them.

▼▼▼▼▼▼▼▼▼▼▼▼▼▼▼▼▼▼▼▼▼▼▼▼▼▼▼▼▼▼▼▼▼▼▼▼▼▼

3. THE 把 STRUCTURE

If one wants to say that someone causes something or some other person to undergo a change, or somehow affects that thing or person through an action, one needs to use the 把 structure.

(1)   弟弟把我新買的杯子打破了。／弟弟把我新买的杯子打破了。

     [My] younger brother broke my new cup.

     (My younger brother's behavior resulted in my broken cup.)

(2)   考試的時候, 我把 "人" 字寫成了 "入" 字。

     考试的时候, 我把 "人" 字写成了 "入" 字。

     I wrote "人" incorrectly as "入" on the exam.

     (My writing resulted in a wrong character.)

The subject can be inanimate.

(3)   大風把那朵(duǒ)花吹下來了。／大风把那朵(duǒ)花吹下来了。

     The gusty wind blew that flower to the ground.

(4)   昨天的剩菜把我的肚子吃壞了。／昨天的剩菜把我的肚子吃坏了。

     The leftovers from yesterday gave me stomach trouble.

     (The leftovers that I ate upset my stomach.)

(5)   請把這封信拿給老師。／请把这封信拿给老师。

     Please give this letter to the teacher.

     (Your giving will cause the letter to be in the teacher's possession.)

When using the 把 structure, one should pay attention to the following:

A. The noun after 把 is generally specific and known information. When the focus is on the effect of the action on the object rather than the action itself, then the 把 structure is called for.

B. There have to be some other words or phrases after the verbs. Usually, it is a complement as in examples (1), (2), (3), and (4), or an indirect object as in example (5). Or it can be 了, which suggests disappearance or loss as in example (6).

(6)   我把明天的電影票丟了。／我把明天的电影票丢了。

     I lost tomorrow's movie tickets.

C. The subject in the 把 structure is indispensable. It indicates the originator of the action or the agent responsible for the result of the action, as in example (4). However, when the subject is known to the listener, it may not be explicitly stated, as in example (7).

(7)   忙了一天, 没有吃饭, 真把我饿死了。

     忙了一天, 没有吃饭, 真把我饿死了。

       I've been busy all day. I haven't had anything to eat, and I'm starving.

As you see, the subject is implied or understood rather than clearly stated.

D. If there is a specific addressee, if there is a complement after the verb such as 在, 給/给, 到, and if the object is known information, then the 把 structure is called for.

(8)   请你把杯子拿给我。 / 请你把杯子拿给我。

       Please hand me the glass.

     *请你拿杯子给我。 / *请你拿杯子给我。

(9)   把照片挂在墙上。 / 把照片挂在墙上。

       Hang the picture on the wall.

     *挂照片在墙上。 / *挂照片在墙上。

(10)   把包裹送到邮局。 / 把包裹送到邮局。

       Take the parcel to the post office.

     *送包裹到邮局。 / *送包裹到邮局。

Notice also that all these sentences imply a specific addressee even though the addressee may not be clearly stated; see examples (9) and (10). Examples (8), (9), and (10) are all imperative sentences or commands.

4. ATTRIBUTIVES AND 的

Here are some simple rules governing the use of 的 between attributives and nouns.

A. Nouns modifying nouns

If the relationship between the nouns is one of possession, then 的 must be used.

媽媽的衣服 ／ 妈妈的衣服 (mother's clothes)

老師的筆 ／ 老师的笔 (teacher's pen)

學校的名字 ／ 学校的名字 (name of the school)

商店的東西 ／ 商店的东西 (store's goods)

If the relationship between the nouns is not possessive, but rather one of modification, then 的 is not needed.

中文老師 ／ 中文老师 (teacher of Chinese)

體育節目 ／ 体育节目 (sports program)

兒童用品 ／ 儿童用品 (daily necessities for children)

電影藝術 ／ 电影艺术 (film art)

汽車廣告 ／ 汽车广告 (auto ads)

Modification can indicate profession, quality, and material, etc. It is different from possession. Compare:

中國的城市一定在中國。／ 中国的城市一定在中国。

China's cities by definition are in China. (possession)

中國城不在中國。／ 中国城不在中国。

Chinatowns are not in China. (modification)

B. Adjectives modifying nouns

Generally, 的 is not needed after monosyllabic adjectives.

紅花 / 红花 (red flower)

小桌子 (small table)

白紙 / 白纸 (piece of white paper)

新書 / 新书 (new book)

舊報紙 / 旧报纸 (old newspaper)

的 is usually required after disyllabic adjectives.

漂亮的衣服 (beautiful clothes)

可愛的孩子 / 可爱的孩子 (adorable kid)

重要的事情 (important matter)

聰明的學生 / 聪明的学生 (intelligent student)

的 is not used in familiar adjectival nominal phrases.

客氣話 /客气话 (polite or modest language)

重要人物 (important person)

新鮮水果 / 新鲜水果 (fresh fruit)

的 is required after adjectival phrases.

很小的桌子 (very small table)

非常新的房子 (brand new house)

大大的眼睛 (big eyes)

深藍色的襯衫 / 深蓝色的衬衫 (dark blue shirt)

C. Pronouns modifying nouns

的 is required to indicate possession.

我的書 ／ 我的书 (my book)

他們的問題 ／ 他们的问题 (their problem/question)

你的事情 (your matter)

我們的朋友 ／ 我们的朋友 (our friend)

你們的時間 ／ 你们的时间 (your time)

If the nouns indicate familial relations or official affiliation, 的 can be omitted:

我媽媽 ／ 我妈妈

他女朋友

我同學 ／ 我同学

我們學校 ／ 我们学校

你家

D. 的 is generally required if the modifier is a verb, verb phrase, or a subject-predicate phrase.

吃的東西 ／ 吃的东西 (edible things)

買的書 ／ 买的书 (purchased book)

寫信用的紙 ／ 写信用的纸 (paper for writing letters)

剛照的照片 ／ 刚照的照片 (recently taken photograph)

打破的鏡子 ／ 打破的镜子 (broken mirror)

我看的書 ／ 我看的书 (book I'm reading)

你說的事情 ／ 你说的事情 (thing you're saying)

姑媽穿的衣服 ／ 姑妈穿的衣服 (clothes my aunt wears)

教授給的功課 / 教授给的功课 (homework assigned by the professor)

朋友來的信 / 朋友来的信 (letter from a friend)

E. 的 does not enter into the noun phrase constructions Nu + M + N.

一本書 / 一本书 (book)

兩雙鞋 /两双鞋 (two pairs of shoes)

三件衣服 (three pieces of clothing)

四棟大樓 /四栋大楼 (four tall buildings)

五張照片 /五张照片 (five photos)

六把椅子 (six chairs)

Set phrases that have become part of familiar vocabulary do not require 的.

拿手菜 (specialty dishes)

知識份子 /知识份子 (intellectual)

清蒸魚 /清蒸鱼 (steamed fish)

指導教授 /指导教授 (advising professor)

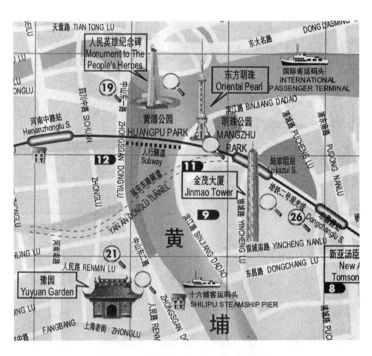

A map of an area in Shanghai.

(See the Appendix of Alternate Character Versions for traditional characters.)

5. 一 + MEASURE WORD + NOUN

When 一 + Measure Word + Noun is positioned as an object, the "一" can be and is often dropped in informal Chinese. One example seen in this lesson is 買了(一)些台灣特產/买了(一)些台湾特产. Other examples are: 買本書/买本书, 寫了封信/写了封信, and 喝了杯茶.

6. 一向 AND 一直

一向 often indicates an incessant action or a consistent state from the past up to the present. It is usually followed by a word that denotes habit or predilection.

(1)　我姐姐一向不喜歡看電影。／我姐姐一向不喜欢看电影。

　　　My sister has never liked going to the movies.

(2)　她做菜一向不放味精。／她做菜一向不放味精。

　　　She never uses any MSG when she cooks.

(3)　她的男朋友一向不吸煙、不喝酒。／她的男朋友一向不吸烟、不喝酒。

　　　Her boyfriend never smokes or drinks.

(4)　他跟朋友一向相處得不錯, 很少有矛盾。

　　　他跟朋友一向相处得不错, 很少有矛盾。

　　　He always gets along well with his friends. He seldom gets into any conflict [with them].

一直 is used to suggest an incessant action or a consistent state within a specific time frame. The implied time period is usually shorter than 一向.

(1)　我到中國後, 一直沒有給家裏打電話, 所以媽媽很不放心。

　　　我到中国后, 一直没有给家里打电话, 所以妈妈很不放心。

　　　I hadn't called home after I arrived in China. My mother was very worried.

(2)　上個星期她一直生病, 沒來上課。／上个星期她一直生病, 没来上课。

　　　Last week she was sick all week and didn't go to school.

(3)　這件事過去我一直不知道, 前兩天老師才告訴我。

　　　这件事过去我一直不知道, 前两天老师才告诉我。

　　　I didn't know about this for some time. The teacher didn't tell me till a couple of days ago.

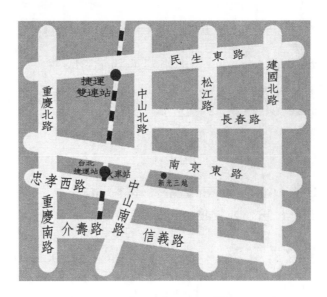

Major roads in the city of Taipei.

(See the Appendix of Alternate Character Forms for simplified characters.)

(4)   上大學後, 我一直住在學校宿舍裏, 從來沒有想過租房子的事。

上大学后, 我一直住在学校宿舍里, 从来没有想过租房子的事。

I've been staying in the dorm since I first got into college. I've never thought about renting an apartment.

Important Words & Phrases

1. 輪到 / 轮到 (IT'S SOMEONE'S TURN)

EXAMPLE: 排隊打電話的人真多, 我等了半天才輪到我。

排队打电话的人真多, 我等了半天才轮到我。

(1)   上次我生日你請我吃飯, 這次＿＿＿＿＿＿＿＿＿＿＿＿＿＿。

上次我生日你请我吃饭, 这次＿＿＿＿＿＿＿＿＿＿＿＿＿＿。

(2)   買票的人太多, 票太少, 等輪到我的時候,＿＿＿＿＿＿＿＿＿＿＿＿＿。

买票的人太多, 票太少, 等轮到我的时候,＿＿＿＿＿＿＿＿＿＿＿＿＿。

(3)   去年北京辦了全中國的大學籃球比賽, 今年＿＿＿＿＿＿＿＿＿＿＿。

去年北京办了全中国的大学篮球比赛, 今年＿＿＿＿＿＿＿＿＿＿＿。

▼▼▼▼▼▼▼▼▼▼▼▼▼▼▼▼▼▼▼▼▼▼▼▼▼▼▼▼▼▼▼▼▼▼▼

2. 趁 (TO TAKE ADVANTAGE OF THE FACT THAT...)

EXAMPLE: 趁你打電話的時候, 我寫了三張明信片。

　　　　　趁你打电话的时候, 我写了三张明信片。

(1)   A: 快放假了, 假期裏你打算做什麼?

　　　　　快放假了, 假期里你打算做什么?

　　　B: 我這個學期物理學得不理想。＿＿＿＿＿＿＿, 我打算好好復習一下。

　　　　　我这个学期物理学得不理想。＿＿＿＿＿＿＿, 我打算好好复习一下。

(2)   A: 從上大學以來, 我不是學習就是打工賺錢。沒有時間認識新朋友。我
　　　　　只好等畢業以後再交朋友了。

　　　　　从上大学以来, 我不是学习就是打工赚钱。没有时间认识新朋友。我
　　　　　只好等毕业以后再交朋友了。

　　　B: 那你就錯了。畢業以後更沒時間, 你最好＿＿＿＿＿＿＿＿, 多跟不
　　　　　同的人交往。

　　　　　那你就错了。毕业以后更没时间, 你最好＿＿＿＿＿＿＿＿, 多跟不
　　　　　同的人交往。

(3)   A: 老張, 你曾經去過墨西哥, 你覺得八月去那兒旅行合適嗎?

　　　　　老张, 你曾经去过墨西哥, 你觉得八月去那儿旅行合适吗?

　　　B: 不合適, 不合適, 墨西哥八月太熱了, 你還是＿＿＿＿＿＿＿＿吧。

　　　　　不合适, 不合适, 墨西哥八月太热了, 你还是＿＿＿＿＿＿＿＿吧。

3. 特地 (SPECIALLY; FOR A SPECIAL PURPOSE)

EXAMPLE: 為了他, 我們特地去了香港, 沒想到他卻跑到台北去了。

　　　　　为了他, 我们特地去了香港, 没想到他却跑到台北去了。

(1) 小王聽説老師病了,＿＿＿＿＿＿＿＿＿＿＿＿＿＿＿＿＿＿＿＿。

小王听说老师病了,＿＿＿＿＿＿＿＿＿＿＿＿＿＿＿＿＿＿＿＿。

(2) 我們知道你喜歡吃清蒸魚,＿＿＿＿＿＿＿＿＿＿＿＿＿＿＿＿。

我们知道你喜欢吃清蒸鱼,＿＿＿＿＿＿＿＿＿＿＿＿＿＿＿＿。

(3) 她的男朋友特地從加州坐飛機來看她, 她卻＿＿＿＿＿＿＿＿＿＿＿＿＿＿。

她的男朋友特地从加州坐飞机来看她, 她却＿＿＿＿＿＿＿＿＿＿＿＿＿＿。

4. 卻/却 (HOWEVER)

EXAMPLE: 為了他, 我們特地去了香港, 沒想到他卻跑到台北去了。

為了他, 我们特地去了香港, 没想到他却跑到台北去了。

(1) 她不讓她的孩子吸煙,＿＿＿＿＿＿＿＿＿＿＿＿＿＿＿＿＿＿。

她不让她的孩子吸烟,＿＿＿＿＿＿＿＿＿＿＿＿＿＿＿＿＿＿。

(2) 郵局告訴我寄掛號, 安全可靠。可是我上個星期用掛號寄的包裹＿＿＿＿＿＿
＿＿＿＿＿＿＿＿＿＿＿。

邮局告诉我寄挂号, 安全可靠。可是我上个星期用挂号寄的包裹＿＿＿＿＿＿
＿＿＿＿＿＿＿＿＿＿＿。

(3) 航空公司老説他們的服務越來越好, 我＿＿＿＿＿＿＿＿＿＿＿＿＿＿＿＿。

航空公司老说他们的服务越来越好, 我＿＿＿＿＿＿＿＿＿＿＿＿＿＿＿＿。

5. 萬一 / 万一 (IN CASE)

EXAMPLE: 萬一東西寄丟了, 怎麼辦? / 万一东西寄丢了, 怎么办?

(1) 外邊很冷。還是多穿件毛衣吧!＿＿＿＿＿＿＿＿＿＿＿＿＿, 怎麼辦?

外边很冷。还是多穿件毛衣吧!＿＿＿＿＿＿＿＿＿＿＿＿＿, 怎么办?

▼▼▼▼▼▼▼▼▼▼▼▼▼▼▼▼▼▼▼▼▼▼▼▼▼▼▼▼▼▼▼▼▼▼

(2)   買東西應該拿收據,＿＿＿＿＿＿＿＿＿＿＿還可以換。

       买东西应该拿收据,＿＿＿＿＿＿＿＿＿＿＿还可以换。

(3)   你把我的電話寫下來,＿＿＿＿＿＿＿＿＿＿＿＿, 你可以給我打電話。

       你把我的电话写下来,＿＿＿＿＿＿＿＿＿＿＿＿, 你可以给我打电话。

Pinyin Texts

Zài Nánjīng

NARRATIVE I

Xīngqīliù xiàwǔ Zhāng Tiānmíng hé Lìshā qù guàng jiē, tāmen zǒu zhe zǒu zhe lái dào le Zhōngshānlù. Tāmen kàn jiàn mǎlù duìmiàn de yí dòng dàlóu shang xiě zhe "yóudiànjú" sān ge dà zì. Hěn duō rén jìn jìn chū chū, Zhāng Tiānmíng hé Lìshā hěn hàoqí, jiù zǒu le guòqu.

DIALOGUE I

Zhāng Tiānmíng:	Qíguài, xīngqīliù xiàwǔ yóujú hái bàn gōng?
Lìshā:	Zhè gēn Měiguó de yóujú bù yíyàng.
Zhāng Tiānmíng:	Lìshā, wǒ zhènghǎo kěyǐ mǎi yìxiē míngxìnpiàn gēn yóupiào, gěi Měiguó de péngyou xiě xìn.
Lìshā:	Duì. Nàbiān hǎoxiàng kěyǐ dǎ chángtú diànhuà, wǒ qù gěi nǐ mǔqīn hé wǒ mǔqīn dǎ diànhuà, gàosù tāmen wǒmen yí lùshang dōu hěn shùnlì, qǐng tāmen fàng xīn.

Twenty minutes later...

Zhāng Tiānmíng:	Wǒ bǎ dōngxi dōu mǎi hǎo le, nǐ ne? Diànhuà dǎ tōng le ma?
Lìshā:	Duì, dōu dǎ tōng le. Pái duì dǎ diànhuà de rén zhēn duō, děng le bàntiān cái lún dào wǒ.
Zhāng Tiānmíng:	Chèn nǐ dǎ diànhuà de shíhou, wǒ xiě le sān zhāng míngxìnpiàn, jì gěi Lǐ Zhé, Kē Lín hé wǒ mèimei. Xìntǒng zài ménkǒu. Wǒ xiànzài jiù bǎ míngxìnpiàn jì le. Nǐ děng wǒ yíxià...
Lìshā:	Zánmen hái yīnggāi mǎi xiē yóujiǎn, zài qù Xī'ān de lùshang, wǒ kěyǐ xiě jǐ zhāng jì gěi wǒ de dàxué tóngxué hé Sīdìfū.
Zhāng Tiānmíng:	Yòu shì Sīdìfū. Wèile tā, wǒmen tèdì qù le Xiānggǎng, méi xiǎng dào tā què pǎo dào Táiběi qù le. Duì le, wǒmen hái yīnggāi gěi Xī'ān pāi ge diànbào, bǎ wǒmen de rìchéng gàosù nàbiān de lǚxíngshè.

Lìshā: Jīntiān zhēnde lái duì le, yíxiàzi bàn le zhème duō shì. Nǐ gǎnkuài qù pāi diànbào, wǒ qù mǎi yóujiǎn.

Zài Táiběi

NARRATIVE II

Sīdìfū cóng Xiānggǎng dào Táiběi chū chāi, mǎi le xiē Táiwān tèchǎn, xiǎng jì gěi Lìshā.

DIALOGUE II

Sīdìfū: Xiǎojie, wǒ yào bǎ zhè ge bāoguǒ jì dào Měiguó.

Guìtái: Hǎode, nǐ yào jì kōngyùn, hǎiyùn, háishi lù kōng liányùn?

Sīdìfū: Nǎ ge kuài, nǎ ge piányi, jiù jì nǎ ge.

Guìtái: Nà jiù jì hángkōng guà hào ba, yòu kuài yòu ānquán, jiùshì guì yìdiǎn. Lǐbiān shì shénme dōngxi?

Sīdìfū: Táiwān tèchǎn hé tángguǒ, bǐnggān shénme de.

Guìtái: Wǒ bāng nǐ chēng cheng. Bú tài zhòng, sì bǎi èrshí kuài Táibì.

Sīdìfū: Hǎo. Wànyī dōngxi jì diū le, zěnmebàn?

Guìtái: Hángkōng guà hào yíxiàng ānquán kěkào, bú huì yǒu shénme wèntí de. Gěi nǐ zhèzhāng shōujù, yǒu wèntí kěyǐ dǎ diànhuà lái wèn.

Discussion Topic: Going to the Post Office

What did Tianming and Lisa accomplish in the post office?

Lesson 10: 在郵局／在邮局

第十一課 ▲ 一封信

爸爸、媽媽：

　　你們好！我們到南京已經快一個星期了。幾天來，我們遊覽了南京的許多名勝古蹟，南京比我想像的好得多。我小的時候就從你們那兒聽到不少南京的故事，可是到現在才真的看到了南京！

　　我們到南京的第二天，表弟就陪我們去了夫子廟，我們是坐公共汽車去的。那天是星期天，汽車上的人真多。到了夫子廟，我們好不容易才從車上擠下來。夫子廟那兒真是人山人海。我以前老聽說中國人口多，可是想像不出多到什麼程度，到了夫子廟才體會到什麼叫"擠"。不過我們很喜歡那裏的建築，夫子廟的遊客所以那麼多，可能正是因為那裏的建築別具風格吧。夫子廟旁邊就是秦淮河，聽說秦淮河以前很漂亮，可是現在我看不出那條窄窄的小河有什麼吸引人的地方。也許它當年是妙齡少女，現在已經人老珠黃了吧。我跟麗莎這麼說以後，她狠狠地瞪了我一眼。

　　前幾天我們去了玄武湖公園，在湖上划了船，還去了古城牆。不過給我們印象最深的還是中山陵。我不說你們也知道，中山陵就是孫中山先生的

中山陵

第十一课 ▲ 一封信

A LETTER

爸爸、妈妈：

　　你们好！我们到南京已经快一个星期了。几天来，我们游览了南京的许多名胜古迹，南京比我想像的好得多。我小的时候就从你们那儿听到不少南京的故事，可是到现在才真的看到了南京！

　　我们到南京的第二天，表弟就陪我们去了夫子庙，我们是坐公共汽车去的。那天是星期天，汽车上的人真多。到了夫子庙，我们好不容易才从车上挤下来。夫子庙那儿真是人山人海。我以前老听说中国人口多，可是想像不出多到什么程度，到了夫子庙才体会到什么叫"挤"。不过我们很喜欢那里的建筑，夫子庙的游客所以那么多，可能正是因为那里的建筑别具风格吧。夫子庙旁边就是秦淮河，听说秦淮河以前很漂亮，可是现在我看不出那条窄窄的小河有什么吸引人的地方。也许它当年是妙龄少女，现在已经人老珠黄了吧。我跟丽莎这么说以后，她狠狠地瞪了我一眼。

　　前几天我们去了玄武湖公园，在湖上划了船，还去了古城墙。不过给我们印象最深的还是中山陵。我不说你们也知道，中山陵就是孙中山先生的

一片樹海／一片树海

陵墓。 陵墓在山上，從中山陵向下看，是一片樹海，非常壯觀。 麗莎特別喜歡這個地方，在山上待了很長時間，我再三催她下山，她都不肯走。 最後她總算戀戀不捨地跟我下了山。 我們等公共汽車的時候，她突然對我說："天明，咱們死後也葬到這兒吧。" 我聽了，忍不住哈哈大笑起來。 我說"你以為誰死後都可以葬到這兒嗎？你知道孫中山是一位偉大的大人物啊！"沒想到麗莎一本正經地問我："你怎麼知道我們幾十年以後不會成為大人物呢？" 我一想，她的話也有點道理，就說："好，我們就這麼說定了：我們倆以後就葬在中山陵旁邊的山上，我的墓碑上寫'南京的兒子張天明'，你的墓碑上寫'南京的媳婦麗莎'。" 媽媽，別生氣，我們在開玩笑。 明天我們就要去西安了，告訴你們一個小秘密。 麗莎說，她今天不洗澡了，明天要到楊貴妃洗澡的華清池裏好好洗一洗。 不過，我們回美國以後你們千萬別跟她提洗澡的事，要不然她又要跟我瞪眼睛了！

　　姑媽在叫我們吃飯呢。 好吧，到了西安再給你們寫信。

　　　　敬祝

安好！

　　　　　　　　　　兒
　　　　　　　　　　天明
　　　　　　　　　　六月五日

陵墓。陵墓在山上，从中山陵向下看，是一片树海，非常壮观。丽莎特别喜欢这个地方，在山上待了很长时间，我再三催她下山，她都不肯走。最后她总算恋恋不舍地跟我下了山。我们等公共汽车的时候，她突然对我说："天明，咱们死后也葬到这儿吧。"我听了，忍不住哈哈大笑起来。我说："你以为谁死后都可以葬到这儿吗？你知道孙中山是一位伟大的大人物啊！"没想到丽莎一本正经地问我："你怎么知道我们几十年以后不会成为大人物呢？"我一想，她的话也有点道理，就说："好，我们就这么说定了：我们俩以后就葬在中山陵旁边的山上，我的墓碑上写'南京的儿子张天明'，你的墓碑上写'南京的媳妇丽莎'。"妈妈，别生气，我们在开玩笑。明天我们就要去西安了，告诉你们一个小秘密。丽莎说，她今天不洗澡了，明天要到杨贵妃洗澡的华清池里好好洗一洗。不过，我们回美国以后你们千万别跟她提洗澡的事，要不然她又要跟我瞪眼睛了！

　　姑妈在叫我们吃饭呢。好吧，到了西安再给你们写信。

　　　　敬祝

安好！

　　　　　　　　　　儿
　　　　　　　　　　天明
　　　　　　　　　　　六月五日

VOCABULARY

1.	遊覽	游览	yóulǎn v	to go sight-seeing
2.	許多	许多	xǔduō	很多; many; a lot
3.	名勝古蹟	名胜古迹	míngshèng gǔjì	famous scenic spots and ancient historic sites

名勝古蹟 / 名胜古迹

4.	想像		xiǎngxiàng v	to imagine; to visualize

波士頓的冬天比我想像的更冷。/ 波士顿的冬天比我想像的更冷。

你想像不出這兒的風景多麼美。/ 你想像不出这儿的风景多么美。

5.	故事		gùshi n	story
6.	表弟*		biǎodì n	(younger male) cousin (of different surname, i.e., on mother's side of the family)
7.	擠下來	挤下来	jǐ xialai vc	to squeeze one's way down; to push one's way off

8. 人山人海　　　　rén shān rén hǎi　　　　huge crowds of people

9. 人口*　　　　rénkǒu　　　n　　　population

10. 程度　　　　chéngdù　　　n　　　degree; extent

他的中文差不多是三年級的程度。/ 他的中文差不多是三年级的程度。

波士頓冬天冷到什麼程度? / 波士顿冬天冷到什么程度?

11. 體會到　　体会到　　tǐhuì dào　　vc　　to learn from experience; to realize

離開了家才體會到爸爸媽媽對我們的關心。

离开了家才体会到爸爸妈妈对我们的关心。

工作以後才體會到還是當學生好。/ 工作以后才体会到还是当学生好。

12. 擠　　　挤　　ji　　adj/v　　crowded; to squeeze, press, push against

13. 建築　　　建筑　　jiànzhù　　n/v　　architecture; to build

14. 遊客　　　游客　　yóukè　　n　　tourist

15. 別具風格　別具风格　bié jù fēnggé　　to have a distinctive style

16. 窄　　　　zhǎi　　adj　　narrow

建築別具風格 / 建筑别具风格

17. 吸引   xīyǐn   v   to attract

中山陵每年都吸引很多的遊客。/ 中山陵每年都吸引很多的游客。

這本書很吸引人。/ 这本书很吸引人。

18. 當年   当年   dāngnián   in those years; at that time

想起當年我們的大學生活, 現在還很激動。

想起当年我们的大学生活, 现在还很激动。

老師還是當年的樣子。/ 老师还是当年的样子。

19. 妙齡   妙龄   miàolíng   adj   (of young girls) the wonderful age

20. 少女   shàonǚ   n   young girl

21. 人老珠黃   人老珠黄   rén lǎo zhū huáng   (metaphor) women grow old and pearls turn yellow; not as beautiful as before

22. 狠狠地   hěnhěn de   adv   vigorously; with a great deal of intensity

23. 瞪   dèng   v   to glower at

24. 湖   hú   n   lake

25. 划船   huá chuán   vo   to row/paddle a boat

26. 古城牆   古城墙   gǔ chéngqiáng   ancient city wall

27. 印象*   yìnxiàng   n   impression

我對那個女孩兒印象很好。/ 我对那个女孩儿印象很好。

我在那個城市只待了一天, 印象已經不深了。

我在那个城市只待了一天, 印象已经不深了。

28. 深   shēn   adj   deep

29. 陵墓   língmù   n   mausoleum; tomb

30. 海*   hǎi   n   ocean

31. 壯觀   壯观   zhuàngguān   adj   (of buildings, monuments, scenery etc.) grand

長城很壯觀。/ 长城很壮观。

32. 再三   zàisān   adv   over and over again [see G5]

▼▼▼▼▼▼▼▼▼▼▼▼▼▼▼▼▼▼▼▼▼▼▼▼▼▼▼▼▼▼▼▼▼▼▼▼▼▼

壮觀的長城／壮观的长城

33.	催		cuī	v	to hurry; to urge
34.	肯		kěn	av	to be willing to
35.	總算	总算	zǒngsuàn	adv	finally; in the end
36.	戀戀不捨	恋恋不舍	liànliàn bù shě		(to leave) reluctantly

我們戀戀不捨地離開了家鄉。／我们恋恋不舍地离开了家乡。

離開家鄉的時候，我們都有些戀戀不捨。

离开家乡的时候，我们都有些恋恋不舍。

| 37. | 突然 | | tūrán | adv | suddenly |

突然門開了，一個人跑了進來。／突然门开了，一个人跑了进来。

電話突然響了起來。／电话突然响了起来。

38.	死*		sǐ	v	to die
39.	葬		zàng	v	to bury (a person)
40.	忍不住		rěn bu zhù	vc	unable to bear; can't help but
41.	哈哈大笑		hāhā dà xiào		to laugh heartily

▼▼▼▼▼▼▼▼▼▼▼▼▼▼▼▼▼▼▼▼▼▼▼▼▼▼▼▼▼▼▼▼

| 42. | 偉大 | 伟大 | wěidà | adj | great; mighty |

什麼人最偉大? / 什么人最伟大?

歷史上有哪些偉大人物? / 历史上有哪些伟大人物?

43.	大人物		dà rénwù		important person
44.	一本正經	一本正经	yì běn zhèngjīng		in all seriousness
45.	說定	说定	shuō dìng	vc	to agree on; to settle
46.	墓碑	墓碑	mùbēi	n	tombstone
47.	媳婦	媳妇	xífù	n	daughter-in-law; wife
48.	生氣	生气	shēng qì	vo	be angry

學生沒復習課文, 老師很生氣。 / 学生没复习课文, 老师很生气。

他一生氣就又喊又叫。 / 他一生气就又喊又叫。

| 49. | 秘密 | | mìmì | n/adj | secret |

這是我們兩個人的秘密。 / 这是我们两个人的秘密。

他們倆秘密地談了很長時間。 / 他们俩秘密地谈了很长时间。

50.	洗澡*		xǐ zǎo	vo	to bathe; to take a bath/shower
51.	千萬	千万	qiānwàn	adv	be sure to
52.	敬祝		jìngzhù	v	to wish respectfully
53.	安好		ānhǎo	adj	to be safe and sound

PROPER NOUNS

1.	夫子廟	夫子庙	Fūzǐ Miào	The Temple of Confucius
2.	秦淮河		Qínhuái Hé	The Qinhuai River
3.	玄武湖		Xuánwǔ Hú	Lake Xuanwu, a scenic lake in Nanjing
4.	中山陵		Zhōngshān Líng	Sun Yat-sen's Mausoleum
5.	孫中山	孙中山	Sūn Zhōngshān	Sun Yat-sen, founding father of modern China
6.	楊貴妃	杨贵妃	Yáng Guìfēi	Imperial Concubine Yang
7.	華清池	华清池	Huáqīng Chí	Huaqing Springs, a famous hot spring outside Xi'an

▼▼▼▼▼▼▼▼▼▼▼▼▼▼▼▼▼▼▼▼▼▼▼▼▼▼▼▼▼▼▼▼▼▼▼▼

ENLARGED CHARACTERS FOR EASIER VIEWING AND COMPARING

覽　齡　牆　陵　墓　觀　戀　葬　萬
览　龄　墙　陵　墓　观　恋　葬　万

Note

楊貴妃／杨贵妃 was a concubine of 唐玄宗 (Táng Xuánzōng: Emperor Xuanzong of the Tang dynasty). They famously renedezvoused at the hot springs of Huaqing.

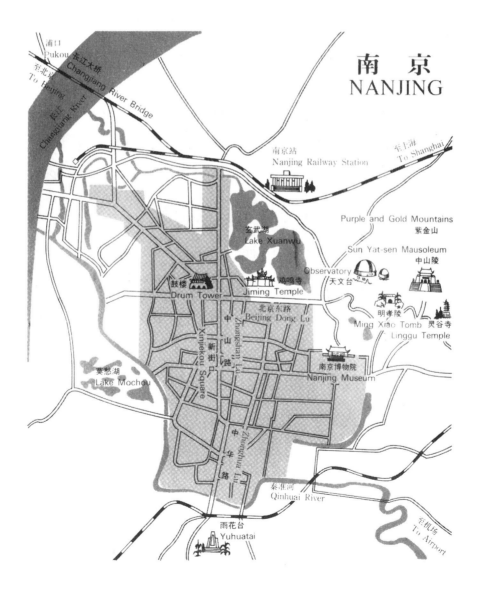

This is a map of Nanjing. Can you locate on it the scenic spots that are mentioned in the letter?

(See the Appendix of Alternate Character Versions for traditional characters.)

Grammar

1. 幾天來 / 几天来

The word 來/来 in 幾天來 / 几天来 means the same thing as 以來 / 以来. It also denotes continuation from a certain point in time in the past to the present, but it is used after phrases that suggest duration of time: 三年來 / 三年来 (from three years ago up to the present), 一年來 / 一年来 (from one year ago to the present), and 五個月來 / 五个月来 (from five months ago to the present). It cannot be preceded by 自 or 自從 / 自从; *自從五月來 / 自从五月来 is incorrect. But we can say, 自從五月以來 / 自从五月以来. Neither can 來/来 be used after phrases other than those that suggest duration of time, e.g., we don't say, *認識他來 / 认识他来, or *放假來 / 放假来, but we can say, 認識他以來 / 认识他以来, and 放假以來 / 放假以来. Also see Lesson 7 on 以來 / 以来.

2. 才 AND 就 COMPARED

The adverb 才 is used to suggest that an action occurred later or more slowly than expected. 就 is the opposite. It suggests that an action occurred sooner or more quickly than expected.

(1)   八點上課, 她八點一刻才到教室。/ 八点上课, 她八点一刻才到教室。

    The class began at eight o'clock. She didn't get to the classroom till eight fifteen.

    八點上課, 她七點半就到教室了。/ 八点上课, 她七点半就到教室了。

    The class began at eight. She came (as early as) seven thirty.

(2)   我現在有事, 過一個鐘頭才能去商店買東西。
    我现在有事, 过一个钟头才能去商店买东西。

    I am busy right now. I won't be able to go to the store for another hour.

    我現在沒事, 現在就可以去。/ 我现在没事, 现在就可以去。

    I am free now. I can go right away.

(3)   他念了六年才大學畢業。/ 他念了六年才大学毕业。

    He didn't graduate till after six years at college.

她念了三年半就大學畢業了。／她念了三年半就大学毕业了。

She graduated from college after just three and a half years.

Note: When using 就, if the action already took place, there should be a 了 at the end of the sentence.

3. 好(不)容易

Both 好不容易 and 好容易 mean 很不容易 (with a lot of difficulty).

(1) 　這個電影票很難買, 我好容易(好不容易)才買到一張。

　　這个电影票很难买, 我好容易(好不容易)才买到一张。

　　It was really hard to get tickets for this movie. I went to a lot of trouble to get one.

(2) 　今天的功課真多, 我好不容易(好容易)才做完。

　　今天的功课真多, 我好不容易(好容易)才做完。

　　There was so much homework today. It took me forever to get it done.

(3) 　這個生詞昨天我好容易(好不容易)才記住了, 可是今天又忘了。

　　这个生词昨天我好容易(好不容易)才记住了, 可是今天又忘了。

　　I finally managed to remember this new word yesterday, but I forgot it again today.

4. ...所以..., 是因為... / ...所以..., 是因为...
(THE REASON IS THAT)

This pattern occurs most often in formal Chinese. Notice that "...所以..., 是因為... /...所以..., 是因为..." reverses the order of the more familiar "因為 / 因为...所以...." The two differ in meaning as well. "...所以..., 是因為... / ...所以..., 是因为..." is used to state a reason whereas "因為 / 因为...所以..." denotes a cause-and-effect relationship.

(1) 　夫子廟的遊客所以那麼多, 可能正是因為那裏的建築別具風格吧。

　　夫子庙的游客所以那么多, 可能正是因为那里的建筑别具风格吧。

　　The reason there are so many tourists at the Confucian Temple is probably that its architecture is unique in style.

(2)   我所以不同意孩子看這個電視節目, 是因為對他們沒有好處。

      我所以不同意孩子看这个电视节目, 是因为对他们没有好处。

      The reason I object to children watching this TV program is that it's not good for them.

Compare:

(3a)   他所以上醫學院, 是因為醫生賺的錢多。

      他所以上医学院, 是因为医生赚的钱多。

      The reason he went/is going to medical school was/is that doctors have high incomes.

(3b)   因為醫生收入高, 所以他上醫學院。

      因为医生收入高, 所以他上医学院。

      Because doctors have high incomes, he went/is going to medical school.

5. THE PREPOSITIONS 跟, 向, AND 對/对 COMPARED

跟, 向, and 對/对 all have several meanings, which overlap but also differ from one another.

A. 對/对 and 向 indicate the direction of an action whereas 跟 signifies the target of the action. The three prepositions are sometimes interchangeable.

(1a)   我在走廊裏看見他的時候, 他<u>跟</u>我笑了笑。

      我在走廊里看见他的时候, 他<u>跟</u>我笑了笑。

      When I saw him in the hallway, he gave me a smile.

      (我 is the object of 笑.)

(1b)   我在走廊裏看見他的時候, 他<u>對</u>我笑了笑。

      我在走廊里看见他的时候, 他<u>对</u>我笑了笑。

(1c)   我在走廊裏看見他的時候, 他<u>向</u>我笑了笑。

      我在走廊里看见他的时候, 他<u>向</u>我笑了笑。

(2a)   在中國, 在路上見到一個認識的人, <u>跟</u>他點點頭就可以了, 不必說什麼。

      在中国, 在路上见到一个认识的人, <u>跟</u>他点点头就可以了, 不必说什么。

In China when you run into an acquaintance, you only have to give him a nod. You don't have to say anything.

(2b)　在中國, 在路上見到一個認識的人, 對他點點頭就可以了, 不必説什麼。

　　　在中国, 在路上见到一个认识的人, 对他点点头就可以了, 不必说什么。

(2c)　在中國, 在路上見到一個認識的人, 向他點點頭就可以了, 不必説什麼。

　　　在中国, 在路上见到一个认识的人, 向他点点头就可以了, 不必说什么。

(3a)　我把我的想法跟他説了説, 他沒説什麼。

　　　我把我的想法跟他说了说, 他没说什么。

　　　I told him my idea. He didn't say anything.

(3b)　我把我的想法對他説了説, 他沒説什麼。

　　　我把我的想法对他说了说, 他没说什么。

(3c)　我把我的想法向他説了説, 他沒説什麼。

　　　我把我的想法向他说了说, 他没说什么。

B. Both 跟 and 向 also suggest "from someone or some place."

(4a)　剛才我跟一個同學借了一本書, 那本書很有意思。

　　　刚才我跟一个同学借了一本书, 那本书很有意思。

　　　I just borrowed a book from a classmate. It's really an interesting book.

(4b)　剛才我向一個同學借了一本書, 那本書很有意思。

　　　刚才我向一个同学借了一本书, 那本书很有意思。

(5a)　我跟你打聽一件事, 不知道你知道不知道。

　　　我跟你打听一件事, 不知道你知道不知道。

　　　I'd like to ask you something [get some information from you]. I don't know if you would know [the answer].

(5b) 我<u>向</u>你打聽一件事, 不知道你知道不知道。

我<u>向</u>你打听一件事, 不知道你知道不知道。

Note: 對/对 cannot be used in this way. Therefore, these three prepositions sometimes have dissimilar meanings and are not always interchangeable.

6. 再三

再三 means to do something "again and again." The actions involved usually have to do with speaking and thinking, e.g., 告訴 / 告诉, 考慮 / 考虑, 打聽 / 打听, 說明 / 说明 (clarify), 解釋 / 解释(jiěshì: explain), 囑咐 / 嘱咐(zhǔfù: exhort, tell), 表示(biǎoshì: express; indicate). Note that all these verbs are disyllabic.

(1) 我再三向他說明我給他打電話只是想聊聊天, 沒有別的事, 可是他不相信。

我再三向他说明我给他打电话只是想聊聊天, 没有别的事, 可是他不相信。

I told him again and again that I was just calling to chat with him; there was no other reason, but he wouldn't believe me.

(2) 那個導遊幫了我很多忙, 我再三向他表示感謝 (gǎnxiè)。

那个导游帮了我很多忙, 我再三向他表示感谢 (gǎnxiè)。

That tour guide helped me a great deal. I thanked him repeatedly.

(3) 我離開家的時候, 媽媽再三告訴我要小心身體, 要常常打電話回家。

我离开家的时候, 妈妈再三告诉我要小心身体, 要常常打电话回家。

When I left home, my mother told me again and again to take care of myself and call home often.

(4) 爸爸讓我考醫學院, 我考慮再三, 選了統計學。

爸爸让我考医学院, 我考虑再三, 选了统计学。

Dad wanted me to go to medical school. After a lot of thinking, I chose statistics.

窄不窄？

Important Words & Phrases

1. 快...了 (SOON; BEFORE LONG)

EXAMPLE: 我們到南京已經快一個星期了。

我們到南京已经快一个星期了。

(1)   楊先生和楊太太整天不是吵架就是打架 (fistfight),＿＿＿＿＿＿＿＿＿＿。

杨先生和杨太太整天不是吵架就是打架,＿＿＿＿＿＿＿＿＿＿＿。

(2)   A: 小姐, 七月去南京的機票還有嗎?

小姐, 七月去南京的机票还有吗?

B: _____。暑假去中國出差、旅行的人多,你要趕緊訂票。

_____。暑假去中国出差、旅行的人多,你要赶紧订票。

(3) A: 媽媽, 廁所人那麼多, 我們排隊排那麼久了, 我快受不了了。

妈妈, 厕所人那么多, 我们排队排那么久了, 我快受不了了。

B: 小麗, 別急,_____, 再等一下。

小丽, 别急,_____, 再等一下。

2. 催 (URGE)

EXAMPLE: 我再三催她下山, 她都不肯走。

(1) 電影七點鐘開演, 現在已經六點三刻了, 我催大家_____。

电影七点钟开演, 现在已经六点三刻了, 我催大家_____。

(2) 弟弟上廁所時喜歡在裏邊看書, 所以時間特別長, 每天早上媽媽都

_____。

弟弟上厕所时喜欢在里边看书, 所以时间特别长, 每天早上妈妈都

_____。

(3) 你太太化妝已經化了一個多鐘頭了。我們快來不及了。麻煩你_____

_____。

你太太化妆已经化了一个多钟头了。我们快来不及了。麻烦你_____

_____。

3. 忍不住 (CANNOT HELP DOING SOMETHING)

EXAMPLE: 我聽了, 忍不住哈哈大笑起來。

我听了, 忍不住哈哈大笑起来。

(1)　妹妹看見電影裏的小狗被打死了, 忍不住＿＿＿＿＿＿起來。

　　妹妹看见电影里的小狗被打死了, 忍不住＿＿＿＿＿＿起来。

(2)　妹妹想讓弟弟著急, 不讓我告訴弟弟他的女朋友來電話的事, 可是我看見
　　弟弟著急的樣子, 就＿＿＿＿＿＿＿＿了他。

　　妹妹想让弟弟着急, 不让我告诉弟弟他的女朋友来电话的事, 可是我看见
　　弟弟着急的样子, 就＿＿＿＿＿＿＿＿了他。

(3)　在飯館, 有一個人對服務員很不客氣, 老闆＿＿＿＿＿＿＿了起來。

　　在饭馆, 有一个人对服务员很不客气, 老板＿＿＿＿＿＿＿了起来。

4. 千萬／千万 (BE SURE TO)

EXAMPLE:　你千萬別跟她提洗澡的事。／你千万别跟她提洗澡的事。

(1)　我聽説他跟他的女朋友鬧翻了, 你＿＿＿＿＿＿＿＿＿＿＿＿。

　　我听说他跟他的女朋友闹翻了, 你＿＿＿＿＿＿＿＿＿＿＿＿。

(2)　千萬別讓小孩玩火柴, 很容易＿＿＿＿＿＿＿＿＿＿＿。

　　千万别让小孩玩火柴, 很容易＿＿＿＿＿＿＿＿＿＿＿。

(3)　明天是你姑媽的生日,＿＿＿＿＿＿＿＿＿＿＿＿。

　　明天是你姑妈的生日,＿＿＿＿＿＿＿＿＿＿＿＿。

Pinyin Texts

A LETTER

Bàba, māma:

　　Nǐmen hǎo! Wǒmen dào Nánjīng yǐjīng kuài yí ge xīngqī le. Jǐ tiān lái, wǒmen yóulǎn le Nánjīng de xǔduō míngshèng gǔjì, Nánjīng bǐ wǒ xiǎngxiàng de hǎo de duō. Wǒ xiǎo de shíhou jiù cóng nǐmen nàr tīng dào bù shǎo Nánjīng de gùshi, kěshì dào xiànzài cái zhēnde kàn dào le Nánjīng!

Wǒmen dào Nánjīng de dì'èr tiān, biǎodì jiù péi wǒmen qù le Fūzǐ Miào, wǒmen shì zuò gōnggòng qìchē qù de. Nàtiān shì xīngqītiān, qìchē shang de rén zhēn duō. Dào le Fūzǐ Miào, wǒmen hǎobù róngyì cái cóng chē shang jǐ xià lái. Fūzǐ Miào nàr zhēn shì rén shān rén hǎi. Wǒ yǐqián lǎo tīngshuō Zhōngguó rénkǒu duō, kěshì xiǎngxiàng bu chū duō dào shénme chéngdù, dào le Fūzǐ Miào cái tǐhuì dào shénme jiào "jǐ". Búguò wǒmen hěn xǐhuan nàlǐ de jiànzhù, Fūzǐ Miào de yóukè suǒyǐ nàme duō, kěnéng zhèngshì yīnwèi nàlǐ de jiànzhù bié jù fēnggé ba. Fūzǐ Miào pángbiān jiùshì Qínhuái Hé, tīngshuō Qínhuái Hé yǐqián hěn piàoliang, kěshì xiànzài wǒ kàn bu chū nàtiáo zhǎizhǎi de xiǎo hé yǒu shénme xīyǐn rén de dìfang. Yěxǔ tā dāngnián shì miàolíng shàonǚ, xiànzài yǐjīng rén lǎo zhū huáng le ba. Wǒ gēn Lìshā zhème shuō yǐhòu, tā hěnhěn de dèng le wǒ yì yǎn.

Qián jǐ tiān wǒmen qù le Xuánwǔ Hú Gōngyuán, zài hú shang huá le chuán, hái qù le gǔ chéngqiáng. Búguò gěi wǒmen yìnxiàng zuì shēn de háishi Zhōngshān Líng. Wǒ bù shuō nǐmen yě zhīdao, Zhōngshān Líng jiùshì Sūn Zhōngshān xiānsheng de língmù. Língmù zài shān shang, cóng Zhōngshān Líng xiàng xià kàn, shì yí piàn shùhǎi, fēicháng zhuàngguān. Lìshā tèbié xǐhuan zhège dìfang, zài shān shang dāi le hěn cháng shíjiān, wǒ zàisān cuī tā xià shān, tā dōu bù kěn zǒu. Zuìhòu tā zǒngsuàn liàn liàn bù shě de gēn wǒ xià le shān. Wǒmen děng gōnggòng qìchē de shíhou, tā tūrán duì wǒ shuō: "Tiānmíng, zánmen sǐ hòu yě zàng dào zhèr ba." Wǒ tīng le, rěn bu zhù hāhā dà xiào qilai. Wǒ shuō: "nǐ yǐwéi shéi sǐ hòu dōu kěyǐ zàng dào zhèr ma? Nǐ zhīdao Sūn Zhōngshān shì yí wèi wěidà de dà rénwù a!" Méi xiǎng dào Lìshā yì běn zhèngjīng de wèn wǒ: "Nǐ zěnme zhīdao wǒmen jǐ shí nián yǐhòu bú huì chéngwéi dà rénwù ne?" Wǒ yì xiǎng, tā de huà yě yǒu diǎnr dàoli, jiù shuō: "Hǎo, wǒmen jiù zhème shuō dìng le: wǒmen liǎ yǐhòu jiù zàng zài Zhōngshān Líng pángbiān de shān shang, wǒ de mùbēi shang xiě 'Nánjīng de érzi Zhāng Tiānmíng', nǐ de mùbēi shang xiě 'Nánjīng de xífù Lìshā'." Māma, bié shēngqì, wǒmen zài kāi wánxiào. Míngtiān wǒmen jiùyào qù Xī'ān le, gàosù nǐmen yí ge xiǎo mìmì. Lìshā shuō, tā jīntiān bù xǐ zǎo le, míngtiān yào dào Yáng Guìfēi xǐ zǎo de Huáqīng Chí li hǎohāo xǐ yì xǐ. Búguò, wǒmen huí Měiguó yǐhòu nǐmen qiānwàn bié gēn tā tí xǐ zǎo de shì, yàobùrán tā yòu yào gēn wǒ dèng yǎnjing le!

Gūmā zài jiào wǒmen chī fàn ne. Hǎo ba, dào le Xī'ān zài gěi nǐmen xiě xìn.

Jìngzhù

Ānhǎo!

Ér

Tiānmíng

Liù yuè wǔ rì

Discussion Topic: Travelogue

Look at the four pictures and repeat the comments that Tianming made about each place.

第十二課 ▲ 中國的節日

NARRATIVE

　　今天是端午節。早晨起床後,姑媽給張天明和麗莎每人一個很漂亮的小東西。姑媽說那是荷包,戴在身上就不會生病了。不過姑媽笑著說,這只是過去的一種風俗習慣,戴著玩兒,不一定有什麼特別的用處。

　　中午,他們和姑媽一家人吃飯,因為是過節,所以菜特別豐盛。除了雞、鴨、魚、肉以外,還有幾盤在美國根本吃不到的青菜。最後姑媽又端上一大盤粽子。

DIALOGUE

麗莎:　　這是什麼?

表哥:　　這是粽子,是端午節特別要吃的東西。

張天明:　表哥,為什麼粽子是端午節特別要吃的東西?

第十二课 ▲ 中国的节日

NARRATIVE

　　今天是端午节。早晨起床后，姑妈给张天明和丽莎每人一个很漂亮的小东西。姑妈说那是荷包，戴在身上就不会生病了。不过姑妈笑着说，这只是过去的一种风俗习惯，戴着玩儿，不一定有什么特别的用处。

　　中午，他们和姑妈一家人吃饭，因为是过节，所以菜特别丰盛。除了鸡、鸭、鱼、肉以外，还有几盘在美国根本吃不到的青菜。最后姑妈又端上一大盘粽子。

DIALOGUE

丽莎：　　这是什么？

表哥：　　这是粽子，是端午节特别要吃的东西。

张天明：　表哥，为什么粽子是端午节特别要吃的东西？

表哥：　　　這裏邊有一個故事。兩千多年前，楚國有一個大官叫屈原。他看出來秦國雖然表面上對楚國不錯，可是實際上早晚要來打楚國，所以就建議楚國國王要早一點做準備。可是楚國國王不但不聽屈原的話，反而把他趕到南方去了。屈原因為憂國憂民，最後投江自殺了。

張天明：　　屈原還是一位大詩人吧？我上中文學校的時候，好像聽我們的老師說過。

表哥：　　　對，他是中國最偉大的詩人之一。他寫的詩表現了他的愛國精神。

麗莎：　　　那粽子跟屈原有什麼關係呢？

表哥：　　　為了祭祀屈原，老百姓把米放在竹筒裏，然後投到江裏。這就是後來的粽子。

麗莎：　　　我聽說端午節還常常賽龍舟，跟屈原有關係嗎？

姑媽：　　　有啊。那象徵當時人們爭先恐後地去救屈原呀。

麗莎：　　　真是個動人的故事！

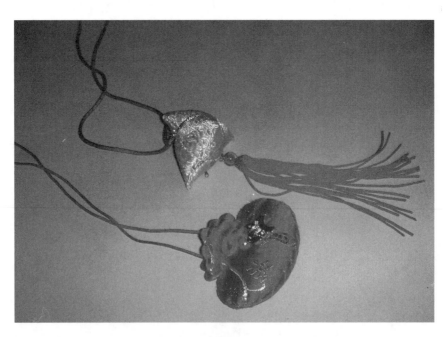

荷包

▼▼▼▼▼▼▼▼▼▼▼▼▼▼▼▼▼▼▼▼▼▼▼▼▼▼▼▼▼▼▼▼▼▼▼▼

表哥：　　这里边有一个故事。两千多年前，楚国有一个大官叫屈原。他看出来秦国虽然表面上对楚国不错，可是实际上早晚要来打楚国，所以就建议楚国国王要早一点做准备。可是楚国国王不但不听屈原的话，反而把他赶到南方去了。屈原因为忧国忧民，最后投江自杀了。

张天明：　屈原还是一位大诗人吧？我上中文学校的时候，好像听我们的老师说过。

表哥：　　对，他是中国最伟大的诗人之一。他写的诗表现了他的爱国精神。

丽莎：　　那粽子跟屈原有什么关系呢？

表哥：　　为了祭祀屈原，老百姓把米放在竹筒里，然后投到江里。这就是后来的粽子。

丽莎：　　我听说端午节还常常赛龙舟，跟屈原有关系吗？

姑妈：　　有啊。那象征当时人们争先恐后地去救屈原呀。

丽莎：　　真是个动人的故事！

粽子

READING

　　中國傳統的節日很多,除了端午節以外,最重要的節日還有春節(中國新年)、中秋節、和元宵節。

　　春節是中國最大的節日。 過春節的時候,人們要放鞭炮,到親朋好友家拜年,大人要給小孩兒壓歲錢。

　　元宵節也叫燈節,是農曆的正月(一月)十五,那一天家家吃元宵,有的地方人們會做各種各樣好看的燈掛在門口,晚上人們都上街看燈。

　　中秋節是農曆的八月十五,那一天月亮最圓、最亮。 中秋節是一家人團圓的日子,在外面工作的人,儘可能回家過節。晚上,一家人常常坐在院子裏,一邊吃著象徵著團圓的月餅,一邊賞月。

門口掛著燈籠 (dēnglong) ╱ 门口挂着灯笼 (dēnglong)

READING

中国传统的节日很多，除了端午节以外，最重要的节日还有春节（中国新年）、中秋节、和元宵节。

春节是中国最大的节日。过春节的时候，人们要放鞭炮，到亲朋好友家拜年，大人要给小孩儿压岁钱。

元宵节也叫灯节，是农历的正月（一月）十五，那一天家家吃元宵，有的地方人们会做各种各样好看的灯挂在门口，晚上人们都上街看灯。

中秋节是农历的八月十五，那一天月亮最圆、最亮。中秋节是一家人团圆的日子，在外面工作的人，尽可能回家过节。晚上，一家人常常坐在院子里，一边吃着象征着团圆的月饼，一边赏月。

月餅／月饼

VOCABULARY

1.	節日	节日	jiérì	n	festival; holiday
2.	早晨		zǎochen	t	early morning
3.	荷包		hébāo	n	embroidered pouch; pouch; purse
4.	戴		dài	v	to wear (jewelry, hat, watch, glasses, etc.)

戴手錶 / 戴手表, 戴首飾 / 戴首饰, 戴帽子

5.	身上		shēnshang		on the body
6.	風俗	风俗	fēngsú	n	folk customs
7.	習慣*	习惯	xíguàn	n/v	usual practice; to be accustomed to

你知道中國人過春節有什麼習慣嗎? / 你知道中国人过春节有什么习惯吗?

我來這個地方已經兩年了, 還是不習慣這裏的天氣。

我来这个地方已经两年了, 还是不习惯这里的天气。

8.	用處	用处	yòngchu	n	use
9.	過節	过节	guò jié	vo	to celebrate a festival or a holiday
10.	豐盛	丰盛	fēngshèng	adj	sumptuous (meal)
11.	雞	鸡	jī	n	chicken
12.	鴨	鸭	yā	n	duck
13.	盤*	盘	pán	m	plate; platter
14.	根本		gēnběn	adv	fundamentally; (often used in the negative form) not at all

那個女孩我根本不認識, 可是媽媽讓她做我女朋友。

那个女孩我根本不认识, 可是妈妈让她做我女朋友。

這筆生意根本沒希望, 不要再談下去了。

这笔生意根本没希望, 不要再谈下去了。

15.	端		duān	v	to carry or hold something level with both hands

16.	粽子		zòngzi	n	a kind of dumpling wrapped in bamboo leaves eaten during the Dragon Boat Festival
17.	大官		dà guān	n	high-ranking official
18.	表面上		biǎomiàn shang	adv	on the surface
19.	實際上	实际上	shíjì shang	adv	actually; in fact; in reality
20.	早晚		zǎowǎn	adv	sooner or later

你不好好學習,早晚會後悔。／你不好好学习,早晚会后悔。

別著急,他早晚會來。／别着急,他早晚会来。

21.	國王	国王	guówáng	n	king
22.	趕	赶	gǎn	v	to drive away
23.	南方		nánfāng	n	the south
24.	憂國憂民	忧国忧民	yōu guó yōu mín		concerned about one's country and one's people
25.	投江		tóu jiāng	vo	to jump into the river
26.	自殺	自杀	zìshā	v	to commit suicide
27.	詩人	诗人	shīrén	n	poet
28.	...之一		...zhīyī		one of...
29.	詩	诗	shī	n	poem; poetry
30.	表現	表现	biǎoxiàn	v	to display; to manifest
31.	愛國	爱国	àiguó	adj	patriotic
32.	精神		jīngshén	n	spirit
33.	祭祀		jìsì	v	to offer sacrifices to
34.	老百姓		lǎobǎixìng	n	"old hundred names"; ordinary folks; common people
35.	米		mǐ	n	(uncooked) rice

36.	竹筒		zhútǒng	n	bamboo tube
37.	投		tóu	v	to throw
38.	江		jiāng	n	river
39.	賽	赛	sài	v	to race; to compete
40.	龍舟	龙舟	lóngzhōu	n	dragon boat
41.	象徵	象征	xiàngzhēng	v/n	to symbolize; symbol
42.	當時	当时	dāngshí	t	at that time; of that time
43.	人們	人们	rénmen	n	people
44.	爭先恐後	争先恐后	zhēng xiān kǒng hòu		to strive to be the first and fear to lag behind; to vie with one another
45.	救		jiù	v	to save (life)
46.	動人	动人	dòngrén	adj	moving; touching
47.	傳統	传统	chuántǒng	adj/n	traditional; tradition

我很喜歡中國的傳統文化。／我很喜欢中国的传统文化。

尊敬老師是中國人的傳統。／尊敬老师是中国人的传统。

48.	鞭炮		biānpào	n	firecracker; a long string of small firecrackers
49.	親朋好友	亲朋好友	qīn péng hǎo yǒu		good friends and dear relatives
50.	拜年		bài nián	vo	to pay a New Year call; to wish someone a happy New Year
51.	壓歲錢	压岁钱	yāsuìqián	n	money given to children as a lunar New Year gift
52.	農曆	农历	nónglì	n	"agricultural" calendar; lunar calendar
53.	正月		zhēngyuè	n	the first month of the lunar calendar
54.	元宵		yuánxiāo	n	night of the fifteenth of the first lunar month; sweet dumplings made of glutinous rice, eaten on this date

▼▼▼▼▼▼▼▼▼▼▼▼▼▼▼▼▼▼▼▼▼▼▼▼▼▼▼▼▼▼▼▼▼▼▼▼

55.	各種各樣	各种各样	gè zhǒng gè yang		various kinds of
56.	燈	灯	dēng	n	lantern; lamp
57.	上街		shàng jiē	vo	to go into the streets
58.	月亮		yuèliang	n	the moon
59.	圓	圆	yuán	adj	round
60.	亮		liàng	adj	bright
61.	團圓	团圆	tuányuán	v	to reunite as a family
62.	日子		rìzi	n	day; time; life
63.	外面		wàimian		outside
64.	儘可能	尽可能	jǐnkěnéng	adv	try one's best
65.	院子		yuànzi	n	courtyard
66.	月餅	月饼	yuèbǐng	n	moon cake
67.	賞月	赏月	shǎng yuè	vo	to admire the full moon

PROPER NOUNS

1.	端午節	端午节	Duānwǔ Jié	the Dragon Boat Festival
2.	楚國	楚国	Chǔguó	the State of Chu (740-330 BCE)
3.	屈原		Qū Yuán	Qu Yuan (343-290 BCE)
4.	秦國	秦国	Qínguó	the State of Qin (879-221 BCE)
5.	春節	春节	Chūn Jié	the Spring Festival (Chinese New Year)
6.	中秋節	中秋节	Zhōngqiū Jié	the Mid-Autumn Festival
7.	元宵節	元宵节	Yuánxiāo Jié	the Lantern Festival
8.	燈節	灯节	Dēng Jié	the Lantern Festival

ENLARGED CHARACTERS FOR EASIER VIEWING AND COMPARING

戴	豐	雞	鴨	憂	龍	徵	鞭	壓	歲	團	圓
戴	丰	鸡	鸭	忧	龙	征	鞭	压	岁	团	圆

壓歲錢 / 压岁钱

Note

雞/鸡, 鴨/鸭, 魚/鱼, and 肉 are often said or written together as one word 雞鴨魚肉 / 鸡鸭鱼肉 to describe how varied and sumptuous the food is. It is illustrative or general rather than specific. When written separately or said with pauses in between, 雞、鴨、魚、肉 / 鸡、鸭、鱼、肉 refer specifically to four kinds of food: chicken, duck, fish, and meat. 肉, unless specified, refers to pork.

Traditional Chinese Festivals ▲

春節(農曆正月初一) / 春节(农历正月初一)

Spring Festival (Chinese New Year) (first day of the first lunar month)

▼▼▼▼▼▼▼▼▼▼▼▼▼▼▼▼▼▼▼▼▼▼▼▼▼▼▼▼▼▼▼▼▼▼▼▼▼▼

元宵節(農曆正月十五) / 元宵节(农历正月十五)

Lantern Festival (fifteenth day of the first lunar month)

端午節(農曆五月初五) / 端午节(农历五月初五)

Dragon Boat Festival (fifteenth day of the fifth lunar month)

中秋節(農曆八月十五) / 中秋节(农历八月十五)

Mid-Autumn Festival (fifteenth day of the eighth lunar month)

美國吃不到的青菜 / 美国吃不到的青菜

Grammar

1. 戴著玩 / 戴着玩

Phrases like 戴著玩 / 戴着玩 are made up of two parts. The first part consists of a verb plus 著/着. The second part is a verb phrase. The second part indicates the purpose of the action. For instance, in 戴著玩 / 戴着玩 from this lesson, 玩 is the purpose of 戴著(荷包) / 戴着(荷包). More examples follow.

(1)   你別生氣, 他是跟你說著玩兒的。 / 你别生气, 他是跟你说着玩儿的。

Don't get mad. He's saying this to tease you.

(2)   媽媽: 你怎麼剛吃完飯, 又在吃? / 妈妈: 你怎么刚吃完饭, 又在吃?

Mother: You just ate. How come you're eating again?

女兒: 您看, 這是餅乾, 我吃著玩兒。 / 女儿: 您看, 这是饼干, 我吃着玩儿。

Daughter: Look, Mom, this is just a cookie. I'm eating it for fun [I'm just snacking].

(3)   他最近正忙著找工作, 沒有時間給你打電話。

他最近正忙着找工作, 没有时间给你打电话。

He's been busy lately looking for a job. He doesn't have the time to call you.

(4)   我到老師的辦公室的時候, 她正急著回家, 因為聽說孩子病了。

我到老师的办公室的时候, 她正急着回家, 因为听说孩子病了。

When I went to the teacher's office, she was in a hurry to go home because she heard that her child was sick.

2. THE INDEFINITE USE OF THE INTERROGATIVE PRONOUN 什麼 / 什么

The interrogative pronoun 什麼 / 什么 can refer to an indefinite person or thing.

(1)   A: 你為什麼問我這個問題? / 你为什么问我这个问题?

Why did you ask me this question?

B: 沒什麼, 我只是問問。 / 没什么, 我只是问问。

No reason. I was just asking.

(2)   別念了, 這本書沒什麼意思。 / 别念了, 这本书没什么意思。

Don't read it anymore. This book is not that interesting.

(3)   A: 你馬上就要畢業了, 有什麼打算? / 你马上就要毕业了, 有什么打算?

You're graduating soon. Do you have any particular plans?

B: 我還沒有什麼打算。 / 我还没有什么打算。

No, I don't have any particular plans yet.

In the above sentences 什麼 / 什么 is followed by a noun. The meaning of the sentence would not be affected if one left out 什麼 / 什么, but with it the tone of voice is more moderate. This kind of usage is not limited to 什麼 / 什么. Notice that there is no noun after it or its equivalent in the following examples.

(4)　　我餓了, 想吃點什麼。／我饿了, 想吃点什么。

I'm hungry. I'd like to eat something.

(5)　　今天下午沒事, 我想找誰聊聊。／今天下午没事, 我想找谁聊聊。

I've nothing to do this afternoon. I'd like to find someone to chat with.

(6)　　今年夏天我想去哪兒旅行幾天。／今年夏天我想去哪儿旅行几天。

This summer I'd like to take a trip somewhere for a few days.

3. POTENTIAL COMPLEMENTS

One can insert 得 or 不 between a verb and its resultative or directional complement to indicate if one has the ability to carry out an action, or if circumstances permit the realization of an objective.

(1a)　今天的功課太多了, 我做不完。／今天的功课太多了, 我做不完。

There is so much homework today that I can't finish it.

(I don't have the ability or the time to finish the homework.)

(2a)　這是誰的聲音? 我怎麼聽不出來?／这是谁的声音? 我怎么听不出来?

Whose voice is this? How come I can't tell?

(I don't have the ability to tell.)

(3a)　這個房間太小, 擺不下三張床。／这个房间太小, 摆不下三张床。

This room is too small. There isn't room for three beds.

(The room doesn't have the capacity.)

(4a)　A:　老師說的話, 你聽得懂聽不懂?／老师说的话, 你听得懂听不懂?

Do you understand what the teacher says?

　　　B:　我聽得懂。／我听得懂。

Yes, I do.

It should be noted that potential complements often appear in their negative form to indicate that one doesn't have the ability to realize an objective or that circumstances do not permit the realization of such an objective. Furthermore, very often this meaning can only be expressed through the negative form of potential complements rather than 不能 + V + resultative complement / directional complement.

(1b)   *今天的功課太多了, 我不能做完。/ *今天的功课太多了, 我不能做完。

(2b)   *這是誰的聲音? 我怎麼不能聽出來?

       *这是谁的声音? 我怎么不能听出来?

(3b)   *這個房間太小, 不能擺下三張床。/ *这个房间太小, 不能摆下三张床。

In interrogative sentences one can use either the affirmative or the negative form. When answering affirmatively a question containing a positive potential complement, use the positive form of the potential complement.

(4b)   A: 老師說的話, 你聽得懂嗎? / 老师说的话, 你听得懂吗?

           Do you understand what the teacher says?

     B: 聽得懂。/ 听得懂。

           Yes, I do.

Less natural:

       我能聽懂。/ 我能听懂。

Here, since the question is 聽得懂嗎 / 听得懂吗? one tends to echo the same structure, so 能聽懂 / 能听懂 is less likely and less natural.

Sometimes the pattern "不能 + V + resultative complement/directional complement" differs from its corresponding potential complement in meaning.

(5)   你給我的飯太多了, 我吃不完。/ 你给我的饭太多了, 我吃不完。

     You gave me too much food. I can't eat it all.

     (I don't have the ability to finish all the food.)

(6)   飯你不能吃完, 給你哥哥留一點。/ 饭你不能吃完, 给你哥哥留一点。

     You may not eat all the food. You have to leave some for your brother.

     (You are not allowed to eat all the food.)

Pay special attention to potential complements as they are an important means of expression in Chinese.

4. NU + M + N CONSTRUCTION AND 大/小

Adjectives such as 大 and 小 can be inserted between measure words and nouns, e.g., 一小杯茶 (a small cup of tea), 一滿(mǎn)杯酒 ／ 一满(mǎn)杯酒 (a full cup of wine), 兩大盤菜 ／ 两大盘菜 (two big plates of dishes), etc.

5. COHESION (II): CONNECTING NARRATIVE SENTENCES

The kinds of cohesive devices used to connect narrative sentences differ from those used to connect explanatory sentences. Here are some of the cohesive devices frequently used to link narrative sentences.

a. time expressions, e.g., 今天, 1998年, 星期五, 後來 ／ 后来, 然後 ／ 然后, 這時候／这时候, 以後 ／ 以后, 突然, 馬上 ／ 马上, etc.

b. place expressions, e.g., 在那兒 ／ 在那儿, 房間裏 ／ 房间里, 前面, 街上, etc.

c. connectives, e.g., 因為...所以 ／ 因为...所以, 不但...而且..., 就, 也, etc.

In Lesson 8 we learned that when one combines sentences, one sometimes needs to replace nouns with pronouns or omit nouns or pronouns. Let's see how the following sentences can be combined into a paragraph:

a.　張天明今天早上十點起床。／ 张天明今天早上十点起床。

　　Zhang Tianming got up at ten o'clock this morning.

b.　張天明十點半吃早飯。／ 张天明十点半吃早饭。

　　Zhang Tianming had breakfast at ten thirty.

c.　十點四十分給麗莎打電話, 約她逛街。

　　十点四十分给丽莎打电话, 约她逛街。

　　At 10:40 [he] called Lisa and asked her to go shopping.

d.　十一點張天明開車去接麗莎了。／ 十一点张天明开车去接丽莎了。

　　At eleven o'clock Zhang Tianming went to pick up Lisa in his car.

e.　幾分鐘以後張天明和麗莎到了購物中心。

　　几分钟以后张天明和丽莎到了购物中心。

　　Several minutes later Zhang Tianming and Lisa arrived at the shopping center.

f.   張天明和麗莎在購物中心買了很多東西。

張天明和丽莎在购物中心买了很多东西。

Zhang Tianming and Lisa bought a lot of things at the shopping center.

g.   張天明和麗莎在購物中心的一家中國飯館吃午飯了。

張天明和丽莎在购物中心的一家中国饭馆吃午饭了。

Zhang Tianming and Lisa had lunch at a Chinese restaurant at the shopping center.

h.   張天明和麗莎下午三點回到了家。

張天明和丽莎下午三点回到了家。

Zhang Tianming and Lisa got back home at 3:00 PM.

→ →張天明今天早上十點起床, <u>十點半</u>吃早飯。<u>十分鐘以後</u>就給麗莎打電話, 約她逛街。<u>然後</u>他開車去接麗莎。<u>幾分鐘以後</u>他們<u>就</u>到了購物中心, <u>在那兒</u>他們買了很多東西, 還在一家中國飯館吃了午飯。<u>下午三點</u>回到了家。

→ →張天明今天早上十点起床, <u>十点半</u>吃早饭。<u>十分钟以后</u>就给丽莎打电话, 约她逛街。<u>然后</u>他开车去接丽莎。<u>几分钟以后</u>他们<u>就</u>到了购物中心, <u>在那儿</u>他们买了很多东西, 还在一家中国饭馆吃了午饭。<u>下午三点</u>回到了家。

→ → Zhang Tianming got up at 10:00 this morning. At 10:30 he had breakfast. Ten minutes later [he] called Lisa and asked her to go shopping. Then he went to pick up Lisa in his car. Several minutes later they arrived at the shopping center. There they bought a lot of things. They also had lunch at a Chinese restaurant. At 3:00 PM they got back home.

Important Words & Phrases

1. 表面上 (ON THE SURFACE)

EXAMPLE: 他看出來秦國雖然表面上對楚國不錯, 可是實際上早晚要來打楚國。

他看出来秦国虽然表面上对楚国不错, 可是实际上早晚要来打楚国。

▼▼

(1) 他這個人不可靠, 表面上＿＿＿＿＿＿, 可是實際上一點都不想幫你。

　　他这个人不可靠, 表面上＿＿＿＿＿＿, 可是实际上一点都不想帮你。

(2) 這個人＿＿＿＿＿＿＿看起來很屬害,＿＿＿＿＿＿＿人很好。

　　这个人＿＿＿＿＿＿＿看起来很厉害,＿＿＿＿＿＿＿人很好。

2. 好像 (SEEM LIKE; SEEM AS IF)

EXAMPLE:　我上中文學校的時候, 好像聽我們的老師説過。

　　　　　我上中文学校的时候, 好像听我们的老师说过。

(1) 老王跟他女朋友兩個人最近都不説話,＿＿＿＿＿＿＿＿＿＿＿＿。

　　老王跟他女朋友两个人最近都不说话,＿＿＿＿＿＿＿＿＿＿＿＿。

(2) 張教授今天很不舒服,＿＿＿＿＿＿＿＿＿＿＿＿。

　　张教授今天很不舒服,＿＿＿＿＿＿＿＿＿＿＿＿。

(3) 王先生: 我來介紹一下, 這是張先生, 這是李小姐。

　　王先生: 我来介绍一下, 这是张先生, 这是李小姐。

　　張先生: 你好, 李小姐! 哎, 我們＿＿＿＿＿＿＿＿＿＿＿＿。

　　张先生: 你好, 李小姐! 哎, 我们＿＿＿＿＿＿＿＿＿＿＿＿。

　　李小姐: 你好, 對不起, 我不記得我們見過面。

　　李小姐: 你好, 对不起, 我不记得我们见过面。

Note: 女兒長得很像爸爸／女儿长得很像爸爸 cannot be said as 女兒長得好像爸爸／女儿长得好像爸爸.

3. 跟...有關係 / 跟...有关系 (HAVE TO DO WITH)

EXAMPLE:　我聽説端午節還常常賽龍舟, 跟屈原有關係嗎?

　　　　　我听说端午节还常常赛龙舟, 跟屈原有关系吗?

(1)　這件事情＿＿＿＿＿＿＿＿＿＿＿＿, 你不必管。

　　　这件事情＿＿＿＿＿＿＿＿＿＿＿＿, 你不必管。

(2)　A:　這個地方的建築窗戶都特別小。

　　　　　这个地方的建筑窗户都特别小。

　　　B:　＿＿＿＿＿＿＿＿＿＿＿＿。這兒無論春夏秋冬, 風都特別大。

　　　　　＿＿＿＿＿＿＿＿＿＿＿＿。这儿无论春夏秋冬, 风都特别大。

　　　A:　原來是這樣啊!

　　　　　原来是这样啊!

(3)　A:　你身體為什麼這麼健康?

　　　　　你身体为什么这么健康?

　　　B:　我身體很好, ＿＿＿＿＿＿＿＿＿＿＿＿＿＿＿＿。

　　　　　我身体很好, ＿＿＿＿＿＿＿＿＿＿＿＿＿＿＿＿。

4. 各種各樣 / 各种各样 (VARIOUS KINDS OF)

EXAMPLE:　有的地方人們會做各種各樣好看的燈掛在門口。

　　　　　有的地方人们会做各种各样好看的灯挂在门口。

(1)　上課的時候, 學生問的＿＿＿＿＿＿＿＿＿＿, 老師都回答得很清楚。

　　　上课的时候, 学生问的＿＿＿＿＿＿＿＿＿＿, 老师都回答得很清楚。

▼▼▼▼▼▼▼▼▼▼▼▼▼▼▼▼▼▼▼▼▼▼▼▼▼▼▼▼▼▼▼

(2) 購物中心裏有＿＿＿＿＿＿＿＿＿＿＿＿＿＿, 你想買什麼, 就買什麼。

　　购物中心里有＿＿＿＿＿＿＿＿＿＿＿＿＿＿, 你想买什么, 就买什么。

(3) 每年春節, 媽媽都準備＿＿＿＿＿＿＿＿＿＿＿＿, 豐盛極了。

　　每年春节, 妈妈都准备＿＿＿＿＿＿＿＿＿＿＿＿, 丰盛极了。

5. ...之一 (ONE OF THE...)

EXAMPLE:　屈原是中國最偉大的詩人之一。

　　　　　屈原是中国最伟大的诗人之一。

(1) 中山陵是南京＿＿＿＿＿＿＿＿＿＿＿＿＿＿＿＿＿＿。

(2) 那家飯館的清蒸魚是他們＿＿＿＿＿＿＿＿＿＿＿＿＿＿。

　　那家饭馆的清蒸鱼是他们＿＿＿＿＿＿＿＿＿＿＿＿＿＿。

(3) 《芝蔴街》是小孩＿＿＿＿＿＿＿＿＿＿＿＿＿＿＿＿。

　　《芝麻街》是小孩＿＿＿＿＿＿＿＿＿＿＿＿＿＿＿＿。

6. 儘可能/尽可能 (TRY ONE'S BEST)

EXAMPLE:　中秋節是一家人團圓的日子, 在外面工作的人, 儘可能回家過節。

　　　　　中秋节是一家人团圆的日子, 在外面工作的人, 尽可能回家过节。

(1) 明天考試, 我今天晚上＿＿＿＿＿＿＿＿＿＿＿＿＿＿＿＿。

　　明天考试, 我今天晚上＿＿＿＿＿＿＿＿＿＿＿＿＿＿＿＿。

(2) 醫生說你吃得太油, 希望你＿＿＿＿＿＿＿＿＿＿＿＿＿＿＿。

　　医生说你吃得太油, 希望你＿＿＿＿＿＿＿＿＿＿＿＿＿＿＿。

(3) 出去旅行的時候,＿＿＿＿＿＿＿＿＿＿＿＿＿＿＿＿＿。

　　出去旅行的时候,＿＿＿＿＿＿＿＿＿＿＿＿＿＿＿＿＿。

Pinyin Texts

NARRATIVE

Jīntiān shì Duānwǔ Jié. Zǎochen qǐ chuáng hòu, gūmā gěi Zhāng Tiānmíng hé Lìshā měirén yí ge hěn piàoliang de xiǎo dōngxi. Gūmā shuō nà shì hébāo, dài zài shēnshang jiù bú huì shēngbìng le. Búguò gūmā xiào zhe shuō, zhè zhǐshì guòqù de yìzhǒng fēngsú xíguàn, dài zhe wánr, bù yídìng yǒu shénme tèbié de yòngchu.

Zhōngwǔ, tāmen hé gūmā yì jiā rén chī fàn, yīnwèi shì guò jié, suǒyǐ cài tèbié fēngshèng. Chúle jī, yā, yú, ròu yǐwài, hái yǒu jǐ pán zài Měiguó gēnběn chī bu dào de qīngcài. Zuìhòu gūmā yòu duān shang yí dà pán zòngzi.

DIALOGUE

Lìshā:	Zhè shì shénme?
Biǎogē:	Zhè shì zòngzi, shì Duānwǔ Jié tèbié yào chī de dōngxi.
Zhāng Tiānmíng:	Biǎogē, wèi shénme zòngzi shì Duānwǔ Jié tèbié yào chī de dōngxi?
Biǎogē:	Zhè lǐbiān yǒu yí ge gùshi. Liǎng qiān duō nián qián, Chǔguó yǒu yí ge dà guān jiào Qū Yuán. Tā kàn chulai Qínguó suīrán biǎomiàn shang duì Chǔguó búcuò, kěshì shíjì shang zǎowǎn yào lái dǎ Chǔguó, suǒyǐ jiù jiànyì Chǔguó guówáng yào zǎo yìdiǎn zuò zhǔnbèi. Kěshì Chǔguó guówáng búdàn bù tīng Qū Yuán de huà, fǎn'ér bǎ tā gǎn dào nánfāng qù le. Qū Yuán yīnwèi yōu guó yōu mín, zuìhòu tóu jiāng zì shā le.
Zhāng Tiānmíng:	Qū Yuán hái shì yí wèi dà shīrén ba? Wǒ shàng Zhōngwén xuéxiào de shíhou, hǎoxiàng tīng wǒmen de lǎoshī shuō guò.
Biǎogē:	Duì, tā shì Zhōngguó zuì wěidà de shīrén zhīyī. Tā xiě de shī biǎoxiàn le tā de ài guó jīngshén.
Lìshā:	Nà zòngzi gēn Qū Yuán yǒu shénme guānxì ne?
Biǎogē:	Wèile jìsì Qū Yuán, lǎobǎixìng bǎ mǐ fàng zài zhútǒng li, ránhòu tóu dào jiāng lǐ. Zhè jiùshì hòulái de zòngzi.
Lìshā:	Wǒ tīngshuō Duānwǔ Jié hái chángcháng sài lóngzhōu, gēn Qū Yuán yǒu guānxi ma?
Gūmā:	Yǒu a. Nà xiàngzhēng dāngshí rénmen zhēng xiān kǒng hòu de qù jiù Qū Yuán ya.
Lìshā:	Zhēn shì ge dòngrén de gùshi!

READING

Zhōngguó chuántǒng de jiérì hěn duō, chúle Duānwǔ Jié yǐwài, zuì zhòngyào de jiérì hái yǒu Chūn Jié (Zhōngguó xīnnián), Zhōngqiū Jié, hé Yuánxiāo Jié.

Chūn Jié shì Zhōngguó zuì dà de jiérì. Guò Chūn Jié de shíhou, rénmen yào fàng biānpào, dào qīn péng hǎoyǒu jiā bài nián, dàren yào gěi xiǎoháir yāsuìqián.

Yuánxiāo Jié yě jiào Dēng Jié, shì nónglì de zhēngyuè (yīyuè) shí wǔ, nà yì tiān jiā jiā chī yuánxiāo, yǒude dìfang rénmen huì zuò gè zhǒng gè yàng hǎokàn de dēng guà zài ménkǒu, wǎnshang rénmen dōu shàng jiē kàn dēng.

Zhōngqiū Jié shì nónglì de bāyuè shí wǔ, nà yì tiān yuèliang zuì yuán, zuì liàng. Zhōngqiū Jié shì yì jiā rén tuányuán de rìzi, zài wàimian gōngzuò de rén, jǐnkěnéng huí jiā guò jié. Wǎnshang, yì jiā rén chángcháng zuò zài yuànzi li, yìbiān chī zhe xiàngzhēng zhe tuányuán de yuèbǐng, yìbiān shǎng yuè.

Discussion Topic: The Dragon Boat Festival

Use the pictures as a guide to retell the story of Qu Yuan in Chinese.

第十三課 ▲ 談體育

💿
NARRATIVE

　　張天明搬出學生宿舍已經好幾個月了。他一個人住在校外比住在校內安靜多了,有很多時間做功課。可是有的時候一個人也會覺得寂寞。這天晚上張天明做完了功課,閑著沒事,就給安德森打了一個電話。

DIALOGUE

張天明： 喂,安德森嗎?

安德森： 對,我是安德森。請問您是 ...

張天明： 怎麼,你連我的聲音都聽不出來了?

安德森： 啊,天明,是你!看今天晚上的球賽了嗎?

張天明： 球賽?今天晚上我根本沒看電視。

安德森： 怎麼,連這麼重要的籃球比賽你都不看。

張天明： 誰跟誰比賽?

安德森： 咱們學校跟密西根。

第十三课　▲　谈体育

NARRATIVE

张天明搬出学生宿舍已经好几个月了。他一个人住在校外比住在校内安静多了，有很多时间做功课。可是有的时候一个人也会觉得寂寞。这天晚上张天明做完了功课，闲着没事，就给安德森打了一个电话。

DIALOGUE

张天明：　喂，安德森吗？

安德森：　对，我是安德森。请问您是 ...

张天明：　怎么，你连我的声音都听不出来了？

安德森：　啊，天明，是你！看今天晚上的球赛了吗？

张天明：　球赛？今天晚上我根本没看电视。

安德森：　怎么，连这么重要的篮球比赛你都不看。

张天明：　谁跟谁比赛？

安德森：　咱们学校跟密西根。

張天明： 結果怎麼樣？

安德森： 唉，咱們輸了。

張天明： 又輸了？太讓人失望了。

安德森： 可不是，密西根隊個個身強體壯，特別是他們的五號，速度快極了⋯

張天明： 我聽說咱們隊的速度也不慢呀，而且我們的教練的經驗比他們的豐富多了。

安德森： 是啊。本來咱們一直領先，可是後來人家把比分慢慢地追上來了。最緊張的是最後二十秒鐘，比分是八十比八十。這時候他們的五號又進一球，球剛一進籃，時間就到了。八十二比八十，人家贏了。

張天明： 輸一次也沒什麼，反正不是決賽。

安德森： 這倒也是。其實，咱們隊打得還是不錯的，就是比賽經驗沒有他們多。打得最好的是咱們的三號，他得了三十分。

張天明： 誰是三號？

安德森： 你連三號都不知道？就是女孩子都喜歡的那位"帥哥"。

張天明： 哦，我想起來了。下次再有精彩的比賽，別忘了告訴我。

安德森： 好！

張天明： 再見。

READING

　　上個星期，張天明收到表哥從南京寄來的一封信，信中提到中國體育運動的情況。八十年代以來，中國的體育運動有了很大的發展，中國運動員在奧林匹克運動會上拿到了很多金牌和銀牌，不少人還打破了世界記錄。很多中國人為此感到很驕傲，覺得這是整個國家的光榮。每當中國運動員在國際比賽中取得好成績時，就有成千上萬的人上街慶祝。表哥談到這些事情张天明：　结果怎么样？

安德森：　唉，咱们输了。

张天明：　又输了？太让人失望了。

安德森：　可不是，密西根队个个身强体壮，特别是他们的五号，速度快极了……

张天明：　我听说咱们队的速度也不慢呀，而且我们的教练的经验比他们的丰富多了。

安德森：　是啊。本来咱们一直领先，可是后来人家把比分慢慢地追上来了。最紧张的是最后二十秒钟，比分是八十比八十。这时候他们的五号又进一球，球刚一进篮，时间就到了。八十二比八十，人家赢了。

张天明：　输一次也没什么，反正不是决赛。

安德森：　这倒也是。其实，咱们队打得还是不错的，就是比赛经验没有他们多。打得最好的是咱们的三号，他得了三十分。

张天明：　谁是三号？

安德森：　你连三号都不知道？就是女孩子都喜欢的那位"帅哥"。

张天明：　哦，我想起来了。下次再有精彩的比赛，别忘了告诉我。

安德森：　好！

张天明：　再见。

READING

　　上个星期，张天明收到表哥从南京寄来的一封信，信中提到中国体育运动的情况。八十年代以来，中国的体育运动有了很大的发展，中国运动员在奥林匹克运动会上拿到了很多金牌和银牌，不少人还打破了世界记录。很多中国人为此感到很骄傲，觉得这是整个国家的光荣。每当中国运动员在国际比赛中取得好成绩时，就有成千上万的人上街庆祝。表哥谈到这些事情時很激動。可是張天明認為，人們所以參加體育運動，是因為運動有益於身體健康，不是為了給國家爭榮譽。而且因為贏了一兩塊金牌就上街慶祝，實在沒有必要。

时很激动。可是张天明认为，人们所以参加体育运动，是因为运动有益于身体健康，不是为了给国家争荣誉。而且因为赢了一两块金牌就上街庆祝，实在没有必要。

VOCABULARY

1. 寂寞   jìmò   adj   lonely

   他一個朋友都沒有, 常常覺得很寂寞。

   他一个朋友都没有, 常常觉得很寂寞。

   你寂寞的時候做什麼? / 你寂寞的时候做什么?

2. 聲音   声音   shēngyīn   n   voice; sound

3. 球賽   球赛   qiúsài   n   ball game (match)

4. 重要*   zhòngyào   adj   important

   想贏球, 找一個好教練很重要。/ 想赢球, 找一个好教练很重要。

   我今天有重要的事要做。

5. 結果   结果   jiéguǒ   adv/n as a result; result

6. 輸   输   shū   v   to lose (a competition)

7. 失望   shīwàng   v/adj disappointed

   他對這場球賽的結果很失望。/ 他对这场球赛的结果很失望。

   他對一件事感到很失望的時候會大喊大叫。

   他对一件事感到很失望的时候会大喊大叫。

   妹妹失望地说: "他今天來不了了。"

   妹妹失望地说: "他今天来不了了。"

8. 可不是   kě bú shì   Isn't that the truth?

9. 隊   队   duì   n   team

10. 身強體壯   身强体壮   shēn qiáng tǐ zhuàng   (of a person) strong; sturdy

11. 身體*   身体   shēntǐ   n   body

12. 強壯   强壮   qiángzhuàng   adj   strong

13. 速度   sùdù   n   speed

14. 教練   教练   jiàoliàn   n   coach

▼▼▼▼▼▼▼▼▼▼▼▼▼▼▼▼▼▼▼▼▼▼▼▼▼▼▼

| 15. | 豐富 | 丰富 | fēngfù | adj | abundant |

經驗豐富, 商品豐富, 節目豐富 ／ 经验丰富, 商品丰富, 节目丰富

16.	本來	本来	běnlái	adv	at first; originally
17.	領先	领先	lǐngxiān	v	(in ball games) to lead
18.	人家		rénjia	pr	others; they
19.	比分		bǐfēn	n	score (of a basketball match, etc.)
20.	追		zhuī	v	to catch up; to chase; to pursue
21.	緊張*	紧张	jǐnzhāng	adj	tense; nervous

聽到這件事他很緊張。／ 听到这件事他很紧张。

比賽太緊張的時候, 我常常不敢看下去。

比赛太紧张的时候, 我常常不敢看下去。

22.	秒鐘	秒钟	miǎozhōng	n	second (of time)
23.	籃	篮	lán	n	basket
24.	贏	赢	yíng	v	to win (a prize, a game, etc.)
25.	反正		fǎnzhèng	conj	anyway [see G3]
26.	決賽	决赛	juésài	n	final match
27.	倒也是		dào yě shì		That's true (indicating concession)
28.	得		dé	v	to get
29.	帥哥	帅哥	shuàigē	n	(col) handsome young guy
30.	精彩		jīngcǎi	adj	spectacular; exciting

奧林匹克運動會的比賽都很精彩。／ 奥林匹克运动会的比赛都很精彩。

明天有場精彩的籃球決賽。／ 明天有场精彩的篮球决赛。

31.	表哥*		biǎogē	n	(elder male) cousin
32.	封*		fēng	m	measure word for letters
33.	發展	发展	fāzhǎn	n/v	development; to develop
34.	運動員	运动员	yùndòngyuán	n	athlete

35.	運動會	运动会	yùndònghuì	n	sports meet
36.	金牌		jīnpái	n	gold medal
37.	銀牌	银牌	yínpái	n	silver medal
38.	世界記錄	世界记录	shìjiè jìlù		world record
39.	為此	为此	wèi cǐ		for this; of this
40.	感到		gǎn dào	vc	to feel

他的父母為他找到一個好工作感到很高興。

他的父母为他找到一个好工作感到很高兴。

學習了一天, 我感到很累。/ 学习了一天, 我感到很累。

41.	驕傲	骄傲	jiāo'ào	adj	proud
42.	整個	整个	zhěnggè		entire
43.	國家	国家	guójiā	n	country
44.	光榮	光荣	guāngróng	n/adj	glory; glorious
45.	每當...時	每当...时	měi dāng...shí		whenever
46.	國際*	国际	guójì	adj	international
47.	取得		qǔdé	v	to obtain

去中國以後, 他中文取得了很大的進步。

去中国以后, 他中文取得了很大的进步。

由於他很努力, 所以學習取得了好成績。

由于他很努力, 所以学习取得了好成绩。

48.	成績	成绩	chéngjì	n	achievement
49.	成千上萬	成千上万	chéng qiān shàng wàn		tens of thousands [see G4]
50.	慶祝*	庆祝	qìngzhù	v	to celebrate
51.	參加*	参加	cānjiā	v	to attend; to take part in
52.	有益於	有益于	yǒuyì yú	vc	to be good for [see G5]
53.	爭	争	zhēng	v	to fight for; to strive for; to compete for

54.	榮譽	荣誉	róngyù	n	honor
55.	實在	实在	shízài	adv	indeed; really
56.	必要		bìyào	n/adj	necessity; necessary

PROPER NOUNS

| 1. | 密西根 | | Mìxīgēn | Michigan |
| 2. | 奧林匹克 | | Aòlínpǐkè | Olympics |

ENLARGED CHARACTERS FOR EASIER VIEWING AND COMPARING

| 竅 | 聲 | 輸 | 籃 | 贏 | 驕 | 慶 | 譽 |
| 窍 | 声 | 输 | 篮 | 赢 | 骄 | 庆 | 誉 |

Note

體育／体育 (physical education) and 運動／运动 (exercises) are often combined to form 體育運動／体育运动, meaning sports and physical activity in general.

Grammar

1. 連...也/都...
连...也/都...

連...也/都... ／ 连...也/都... introduces an extreme example illustrating the conclusion denoted in the following clause.

(1)   A: 他會說中文嗎? ／ 他会说中文吗?

Can he speak Chinese?

    B: 中文他連聽都沒聽過, 怎麼會說呢?

中文他连听都没听过, 怎么会说呢?

He's never even heard Chinese spoken. How could he speak it?

(2)　我連這個人的名字都沒聽説過, 怎麼會認識他呢?

　　我连这个人的名字都没听说过, 怎么会认识他呢?

I've never even heard of his name. How would I know him?

(3)　我姐姐會很多種語言, 連越南話都會。

　　我姐姐会很多种语言, 连越南话都会。

My older sister knows many languages. [She] even knows Vietnamese.

(4)　這兒天氣很冷, 連夏天都得穿毛衣。

　　这儿天气很冷, 连夏天都得穿毛衣。

The weather is really cold here. Even in the summer [you] have to wear a sweater.

In example (1) the speaker implies that 聽過中文 / 听过中文 is the minimum condition for the ability to speak Chinese; from that, one can draw the conclusion that the person cannot possibly speak Chinese. In example (3) one can deduce from the fact that the speaker's sister knows Vietnamese, one of the most difficult languages to learn, that she could be proficient in many foreign languages. In example (4) one can conclude that the weather here is very cold based upon the fact that many people wear sweaters even in the summer.

2. 一球 IN 進一球 / 进一球

進一球 / 进一球 means "make a goal" at a sports game. Here 一球 is short for 一個球 / 一个球. In colloquial Chinese, 一 plus a measure word often becomes 一 (second tone). The measure word is inaudible but implied.

3. 反正

The adverb 反正 has two meanings.

A. It can emphasize that the result or conclusion will not change under any circumstances. The word literally means "the reverse and obverse (side)," i.e., "regardless," "no matter what." 反正 generally appears in the second clause.

(1)　這間房子你想住就住, 反正我不住。

　　这间房子你想住就住, 反正我不住。

If you want to move into this house, go ahead. Either way I am not going to live here.

(2)　那個電影, 你們誰想看誰看, 反正我不看。

　　那个电影, 你们谁想看谁看, 反正我不看。

Whoever wants to see that film, go ahead. I am not going (to see it).

▼▼▼▼▼▼▼▼▼▼▼▼▼▼▼▼▼▼▼▼▼▼▼▼▼▼▼▼▼▼▼▼▼

(3)　無論你信不信, 反正我不信。／无论你信不信, 反正我不信。

Believe it or don't believe it. I don't.

B. 反正 can also explain a situation or offer a reason. The situation or reason is often already known or obvious.

(1)　圖書館反正也不遠, 咱們走著去吧。

图书馆反正也不远, 咱们走着去吧。

Anyway, the library is not far away. Let's walk.

(2)　你別復習第十課了, 反正也不會考。／你别复习第十课了, 反正也不会考。

Don't bother to review Lesson 10. It won't be on the exam anyway.

(3)　我送你回去吧, 反正我開車。／我送你回去吧, 反正我开车。

Let me take you home. I'm driving anyway.

In this lesson we are learning the second usage.

4. (成千)上(萬) ／ (成千)上(万)

上 here means "reach."

(1)　上百個中學生參加了這次考試。／上百个中学生参加了这次考试。

As many as a hundred high school students took part in the examination.

(2)　這件毛衣上千塊錢, 我怎麼買得起?

这件毛衣上千块钱, 我怎么买得起?

This sweater costs [as much as] a thousand dollars. How can I afford it?

(3)　他賺的錢都上百萬了, 還說不多?

他赚的钱都上百万了, 还说不多?

He made [as much as] a million dollars. [How can you] say that's not a lot [of money]?

(4)　這場決賽有成千上萬的人排隊買票。

这场决赛有成千上万的人排队买票。

There are thousands of people lining up to get tickets for the final game.

成千上萬的人在球場看球賽 / 成千上万的人在球场看球赛

5. (有益)於 / (有益)于

The preposition 於/于 is generally used in written language. It often appears after a verb. In the phrase 有益於 / 有益于, 於/于 is equivalent to 對(於) / 对(于). 體育運動有益於身體健康 / 体育运动有益于身体健康 is the same as 體育運動對身體健康有益 / 体育运动对身体健康有益. Notice the difference in word order.

(1) 少吃鹽, 少吃糖, 有益於健康。 / 少吃盐, 少吃糖, 有益于健康。

Eating less salt and less sugar is good for one's health.

(2) 多聽別人意見, 有益於與(yǔ)人相處。

多听别人意见, 有益于与(yǔ)人相处。

Listening to others more helps [you] get along with people.

(3)   多聽錄音, 有益於中文學習。／多听录音,有益于中文学习。

   Listening to recordings more helps [you] learn Chinese.

6. MAKING COMPARISONS

There are several ways to make comparisons in Chinese:

A. When the comparison results in two things being identical, we can use the following pattern:

<u>A 跟/和 B</u>一樣 (+ Adj.)

(1)   這本書跟那本書的價錢一樣。／这本书和跟那本书的价钱一样。

   The price of this book is the same as that one.

(2)   A: 我愛吃中國飯, 你為什麼請我吃日本飯?

      我爱吃中国饭, 你为什么请我吃日本饭?

      I love Chinese food. Why are you treating me to Japanese food?

      B: 因為我覺得日本飯和中國飯一樣好吃。

      因为我觉得日本饭和中国饭一样好吃。

      Because I think Japanese food is (just) as delicious as Chinese food.

(3)   A: 你認為電視和電影哪個對青少年的影響大?

      你认为电视和电影哪个对青少年的影响大?

      Which of the two do you think has a greater impact on teenagers—TV or film?

      B: 我認為電視跟電影對青少年的影響一樣大。

      我认为电视跟电影对青少年的影响一样大。

      I think TV and film have the same impact on young people.

B. When the two things being compared are not identical, we can use one of the following forms of comparison:

a. <u>A 比 B + Adj.</u> (+ 得多 / numeral + noun / 一點兒 / 一点儿 / 多了)

(1)   打籃球比跑步有意思。／打篮球比跑步有意思。

   Playing basketball is more fun than jogging.

(2)   決賽比一般的比賽緊張得多。/ 決赛比一般的比赛紧张得多。

The final game is much more nerve-racking than ordinary games.

(3)   去日本的飛機票比去中國的便宜五十美元。

去日本的飞机票比去中国的便宜五十美元。

The airfare to Japan is fifty dollars cheaper than the airfare to China.

Note that 很 cannot be placed before the adjective.

(4)   *我比你很聰明。/ *我比你很聪明。

(5)   *美國比中國人口很少。/ *美国比中国人口很少。

If there is a phrase denoting degree or quantity, it must be placed after the adjective, as 得多 in example (2) and 五十美元 in example (3). More examples:

(6)   中國人口比美國人口多得多。/ 中国人口比美国人口多得多。

The population of China is much bigger than that of the United States.

(7)   今年比去年熱多了。/ 今年比去年热多了。

It's much hotter this year than last year.

(8)   小張的男朋友只比她高一點。/ 小张的男朋友只比她高一点。

Little Zhang's boyfriend is just a bit taller than she is.

b. A 沒有 B + Adj.

(1)   日文語法沒有中文語法好學。/ 日文语法没有中文语法好学。

Japanese grammar is not as easy to learn as Chinese grammar.

(2)   今天沒有昨天那麼冷。/ 今天没有昨天那么冷。

Today is not as cold as yesterday.

(3)   在中國, 過新年沒有過農曆春節那麼熱鬧 (rènao)。

在中国, 过新年没有过农历春节那么热闹 (rènao)。

In China, New Year's is not as festive as the Spring Festival.

▼▼▼▼▼▼▼▼▼▼▼▼▼▼▼▼▼▼▼▼▼▼▼▼▼▼▼▼▼▼▼▼▼▼▼▼▼

One seldom uses 沒有 with the adjectives 小, 短, 壞/坏, 細/细 (thin), 醜/丑 (chǒu: ugly), and 難看／难看, but rather with their more positive opposites, 大, 長/长, 好, 粗 (cū: thick), 漂亮, and 好看. But if we add the word 那麼／那么 before the adjective, then this restriction no longer applies.

When making comparisons between A and B, the structures or phrases used tend to echo each other. Some identical components of A and B can be omitted as long as the meaning of the sentence remains intact. The sentences A(1), B-a(3), and B-b(1) above are some examples.

c. A 不如 B + Adj. (See Lesson 16.)

7. WRITTEN STYLE

There are substantial differences between written Chinese and spoken colloquial Chinese. The former is characterized by

a. Longer sentences and more modifiers such as attributives and adverbials.

b. Vestiges of classical Chinese, e.g., 於/于 as in 有益於／有益于, and 此 as in 為此／为此. Compare: 有益於健康／有益于健康 (written style) and 對健康有好處／对健康有好处 (spoken style); 為此／为此 (written style) and 因為這個／因为这个 (spoken style).

c. More connectives. Notice the following underlined words:

　　每當中國運動員在國際比賽中取得好成績時, 就有成千上萬的人上街慶祝。表哥談到這些事情時很激動。<u>可是</u>張天明認為, 人們<u>所以</u>參加體育運動, <u>是因為</u>運動有益於身體健康, <u>不是為了</u>給國家爭榮譽。<u>而且因為</u>贏了一兩塊金牌就上街慶祝, 實在沒有必要。

　　每当中国运动员在国际比赛中取得好成绩时, 就有成千上万的人上街庆祝。表哥谈到这些事情时很激动。<u>可是</u>张天明认为, 人们<u>所以</u>参加体育运动, <u>是因为</u>运动有益于身体健康, <u>不是为了</u>给国家争荣誉。<u>而且因为</u>赢了一两块金牌就上街庆祝, 实在没有必要。

d. Function words that tend to be monosyllabic. On the other hand, verbs and nouns that are monosyllabic in spoken Chinese are sometimes disyllabic in written Chinese.

SPOKEN STYLE	WRITTEN STYLE	PARTS OF SPEECH	ENGLISH
曾經 / 曾经	曾	adv	once
已經 / 已经	已	adv	already
因為 / 因为	因	connective	because
學 / 学	學習 / 学习	v	to study
生	出生	v	to be born
偷 (tōu)	偷竊 / 偷窃 (tōuqiè)	v	to steal

（美東時間）

31日(周四)戰績

亞特蘭大勝猶他 105:98
華府勝波士頓 114:69
沙加緬度勝波特蘭 100:72

籃球比賽的成績　誰贏了?誰輸了? / 篮球比赛的成绩　谁赢了?谁输了?

(See the Appendix of Alternate Character Forms for simplified characters.)

8. COHESION (III): LINKING NARRATIVE SENTENCES

Here is a comprehensive exercise on how to link narrative sentences. First, see if you can read the following sentences.

1.　鄭國有個人想買一雙鞋。/ 郑国有个人想买一双鞋。

   A man from the state of Zheng wanted to buy a pair of shoes.

Note: Zhèngguó is the state of Zheng, a small state that existed during the Spring and Autumn period, 770–476 BCE.

2.　他在家裏拿一根繩子 (shéngzi: string) 比著自己的腳 (jiǎo: feet) 量 (liáng: to measure) 了尺寸 (chǐcùn: size)。

   他在家里拿一根绳子 (shéngzi: string) 比着自己的脚 (jiǎo: feet) 量 (liáng: to measure) 了尺寸 (chǐcùn: size)。

   He took the measurements of his feet with a piece of string at home.

3. 他高高興興地到集市 (jíshì: market) 上去了。

   他高高兴兴地到集市 (jíshì: market) 上去了。

   He went to the market cheerfully.

4. 他找到了賣鞋的地方。／他找到了卖鞋的地方。

   He found the place where shoes were sold.

5. 他挑了一雙鞋。／他挑了一双鞋。

   He chose a pair.

6. 他想比比合適不合適。／他想比比合适不合适。

   He wanted to try them on for size.

7. 他摸 (mō: to feel, to find) 身上。

   He felt over himself [to try and locate the measurements].

8. 他知道忘了帶來量好的尺寸。／他知道忘了带来量好的尺寸。

   He discovered that he had forgotten to take the measurements with him.

9. 他很著急。／他很着急。

   He panicked.

10. 他心想：“自己真是太粗心 (cūxīn: careless)了，白 (in vain) 跑了一趟。”

    He said to himself, "That was really careless of me. I came here for nothing."

11. 他急急忙忙跑回家去拿。

    He immediately rushed home to get (the measurements).

12. 他回到集市來，天已經很晚。／他回到集市来，天已经很晚。

    When he got back to the market, it was already dark.

13. 賣鞋的早就走了。／卖鞋的早就走了。

    The shoe-seller had already left.

14. 他沒有買成鞋。/ 他没有买成鞋。

He wasn't able to buy the shoes.

15. 別人知道了這件事。/ 别人知道了这件事。

People heard about this.

16. 別人問他: "你給自己買鞋, 你在腳上試試不就可以了嗎?"

別人问他: "你给自己买鞋, 你在脚上试试不就可以了吗?"

People asked him, "You were getting shoes for yourself. Why didn't you just try them on?"

17. 你怎麼還要跑回去拿尺寸呢? / 你怎么还要跑回去拿尺寸呢?

"Why did you have to go home to get the measurements?"

18. 他回答说: "我只相信 (xiāngxìn: to trust; to believe) 量好的尺寸, 我不相信自己的腳。"

他回答说: "我只相信 (xiāngxìn: to trust; to believe) 量好的尺寸, 我不相信自己的脚。"

He replied, "I only believe in the measurements that I took. I don't believe my feet."

This is a well-known Chinese parable. The cohesive devices involved in turning the above sentences into a continuous narrative are rather complex. We will take three steps in order to achieve cohesion. We will begin by adding the following connectives:

1) 古時候 / 古时候 (in ancient times); 先, 然後 /先, 然后; ...時候 / ...时候; 已經 /已经; 早; ...以後 / ...以后

2) 在集市上 (at the marketplace)

3) 可是, 才, 於是 /于是, 就, 就

This is what we get:

(Traditional Characters)

古時候, 鄭國有個人想買一雙鞋。他先在家裏拿一根繩子比著自己的腳量了尺寸, 然後他就高高興興地到集市上去了。

　　<u>在集市上</u>，他找到了賣鞋的地方。他挑了一雙鞋，他想比比合適不合適。<u>可是</u>他一摸身上，他<u>才</u>知道忘了帶來量好的尺寸。他很著急。他心想："自己真是太粗心了，白跑了一趟。"<u>於是</u>他急急忙忙跑回家去拿。

　　<u>他回到集市來的時候</u>，天已經很晚了，賣鞋的早<u>就</u>走了。他沒有買成鞋。<u>別人知道了這件事以後</u>，別人<u>就</u>問他："你給自己買鞋，你在腳上試試不就可以了嗎？你怎麼還要跑回去拿尺寸呢？"

　　他回答说："因為我只相信量好的尺寸，我不相信自己的腳。"

(Simplified Characters)

　　<u>古时候</u>，郑国有个人想买一双鞋。他<u>先</u>在家里拿一根绳子比着自己的脚量了尺寸，<u>然后他就</u>高高兴兴地到集市上去了。

　　<u>在集市上</u>，他找到了卖鞋的地方。他挑了一双鞋，他想比比合适不合适。<u>可是</u>他一摸身上，他<u>才</u>知道忘了带来量好的尺寸。他很着急。他心想："自己真是太粗心了，白跑了一趟。"<u>于是</u>他急急忙忙跑回家去拿。

　　<u>他回到集市来的时候</u>，天已经很晚了，卖鞋的早<u>就</u>走了。他没有买成鞋。<u>别人知道了这件事以后</u>，别人<u>就</u>问他："你给自己买鞋，你在脚上试试不就可以了吗？你怎么还要跑回去拿尺寸呢？"

　　他回答说："因为我只相信量好的尺寸，我不相信自己的脚。"

We will now omit superfluous nouns and pronouns. The ▲ symbol indicates the places where nouns and pronouns have been omitted. See Lesson 8 Cohesion I.

(Traditional Characters)

　　<u>古時候</u>，鄭國有個人想買一雙鞋。他<u>先</u>在家裏拿一根繩子比著自己的腳量了尺寸，<u>然後</u>▲<u>就</u>高高興興地到集市上去了。

　　<u>在集市上</u>，他找到了賣鞋的地方，▲挑了一雙鞋，▲想比比合適不合適。<u>可是</u>▲一摸身上，▲<u>才</u>知道忘了帶來量好的尺寸。他很著急，▲心想："自己真是太粗心了，白跑了一趟。"<u>於是</u>▲急急忙忙跑回家去拿。

他回到集市來的時候，天已經很晚了，賣鞋的早就走了。 他沒有買成鞋。別人知道了這件事以後，▲就問他："你給自己買鞋，▲在腳上試試不就可以了嗎？▲怎麼還要跑回去拿尺寸呢？"

他回答説："因為我只相信量好的尺寸，▲不相信自己的腳。"

(Simplified Characters)

古时候，郑国有个人想买一双鞋。他先在家里拿一根绳子比着自己的脚量了尺寸，然后▲就高高兴兴地到集市上去了。

在集市上，他找到了卖鞋的地方，▲挑了一双鞋，▲想比比合适不合适。可是▲一摸身上，▲才知道忘了带来量好的尺寸。 他很着急，▲心想："自己真是太粗心了，白跑了一趟。" 于是▲急急忙忙跑回家去拿。

他回到集市来的时候，天已经很晚了，卖鞋的早就走了。 他没有买成鞋。别人知道了这件事以后，▲就问他："你给自己买鞋，▲在脚上试试不就可以了吗？▲怎么还要跑回去拿尺寸呢？"

他回答说："因为我只相信量好的尺寸，▲不相信自己的脚。"

Let us now readjust the word order. For instance, we can put known information at the front—in other words, treat it as a topic, and put new information in the position of the object. In the above parable, when the word 尺寸 first appears, it is new information. Therefore, it appears as the object of the clause 量了尺寸. When it makes its second appearance, instead of 忘了帶量好的尺寸 / 忘了带量好的尺寸, it is far more idiomatic to use the 把 structure and say, 忘了把量好的尺寸帶來了 / 忘了把量好的尺寸带来了. Likewise, when the word 鞋 appears for the first time, it is new information. Therefore, it appears as the object of the clause 想買一雙鞋 / 想买一双鞋. When it reappears, it becomes the topic of the clause 他的鞋沒買成 / 他的鞋没买成, since it is now known information.

You may wonder why 這件事 / 这件事, also known information, appears as the object 別人都知道了這件事 / 别人都知道了这件事? That is because, like 這件事 / 这件事, 別人, the agent of the action, is also known information. Therefore, it can be used as the subject of the clause. Notice that we are also looking at the beginning of a new paragraph, and a change in point of view. The narrative focus shifts from what happens to the character to others' reaction. If we do not want to shift the point of view, we can change this sentence to 這件事別人知道了 / 这件事别人知道了.

Here is another version of the story after adding the appropriate cohesive devices, deleting all the superfluous nouns and pronouns, and readjusting the word order:

鄭人買履 (Zhèngrén mǎi lǚ) [lǚ: (literary) shoes]

古時侯，鄭國有個人想買一雙鞋。他先在家裏拿一根繩子比著自己的腳量了尺寸，就高高興興地到集市上去了。

在集市上他找到了賣鞋的地方，他挑了一雙鞋，想比比合適不合適。往身上一摸，才知道忘了把良好的尺寸帶來了。他很著急，心想："自己真是太粗心了，白跑了一趟。"於是他急急忙忙跑回家去拿。可是等回到集市來的時侯，天已經很晚，賣鞋的早就走了。他的鞋沒有買成。別人知道了這件事以後，就問他："你給你自己買鞋，在腳上試試不就可以了嗎？怎麼還要跑回去拿尺寸呢？"他回答說："我只相信量好的尺寸，不相信自己的腳。"

郑人买履 (Zhèngrén mǎi lǚ) [lǚ: (literary) shoes]

古时侯，郑国有个人想买一双鞋。他先在家里拿一根绳子比着自己的脚量了尺寸，就高高兴兴地到集市上去了。

在集市上他找到了卖鞋的地方，他挑了一双鞋，想比比合适不合适。往身上一摸，才知道忘了把良好的尺寸带来了。他很着急，心想："自己真是太粗心了，白跑了一趟。"于是他急急忙忙跑回家去拿。可是等回到集市来的时侯，天已经很晚，卖鞋的早就走了。他的鞋没有买成。别人知道了这件事以后，就问他："你给你自己买鞋，在脚上试试不就可以了吗？怎么还要跑回去拿尺寸呢？"他回答说："我只相信量好的尺寸，不相信自己的脚。"

```
衛 視 體 育
02-273430 **
0700 2004美國網球公開賽
1030 FIM世界摩托車錦標賽
1200 SAMSUNG國家盃馬術賽
1300 2004年雅典奧運會
2300 2004美國網球公開賽
0500 FIM世界摩托車錦標賽
```

這是一個體育頻道。請問，幾點播奧林匹克運動會的比賽？
这是一个体育频道。请问，几点播奥林匹克运动会的比赛？

(See the Appendix of Alternate Character Forms for simplified characters.)

Important Words & Phrases

1. 本來 / 本来 (ORIGINALLY; AT FIRST)

EXAMPLE:　本來咱們一直領先。/ 本来咱们一直领先。

(1)　他＿＿＿＿＿＿＿＿＿＿，經常生病，後來他經常運動，現在身體好多了。

　　他＿＿＿＿＿＿＿＿＿＿，经常生病，后来他经常运动，现在身体好多了。

(2)　張天明本來想去加州上大學，後來決定＿＿＿＿＿＿＿＿＿＿＿了。

　　张天明本来想去加州上大学，后来决定＿＿＿＿＿＿＿＿＿＿＿了。

(3)　柯林本來想夏天去台灣學中文，後來＿＿＿＿＿＿＿＿＿＿＿了。

　　柯林本来想夏天去台湾学中文，后来＿＿＿＿＿＿＿＿＿＿＿了。

(4)　＿＿＿＿＿＿＿＿＿＿，後來上商學院了。

　　＿＿＿＿＿＿＿＿＿＿，后来上商学院了。

2. 倒也是 (THAT IS TRUE; YOU'RE RIGHT ABOUT THAT)

EXAMPLE:　張天明: 輸一次也沒什麼，反正不是決賽。

　　　　　张天明: 输一次也没什么，反正不是决赛。

　　　　　安德森: 這倒也是。/ 这倒也是。

(1)　A:　我的錢包丟了，裏邊有現金還有信用卡。急死我了。

　　　　我的钱包丢了，里边有现金还有信用卡。急死我了。

　　B:　你別著急，先打電話給信用卡公司。

　　　　你别着急，先打电话给信用卡公司。

　　A:　＿＿＿＿＿＿＿＿＿＿＿＿＿＿＿。

　　　　＿＿＿＿＿＿＿＿＿＿＿＿＿＿＿。

▼▼▼▼▼▼▼▼▼▼▼▼▼▼▼▼▼▼▼▼▼▼▼▼▼▼▼▼▼▼▼▼▼▼▼

(2)　A:　我反對他們兩個交往, 文化背景太不一樣了。

　　　　我反对他们两个交往, 文化背景太不一样了。

　　B:　別急, 他們剛認識,＿＿＿＿＿＿＿＿＿＿＿＿＿＿＿。(男女朋友)

　　　　别急, 他们刚认识,＿＿＿＿＿＿＿＿＿＿＿＿＿＿＿。(男女朋友)

　　A:　這倒也是。／ 这倒也是。

(3)　A:　我真不喜歡小明的女朋友。

　　　　我真不喜欢小明的女朋友。

　　B:　＿＿＿＿＿＿＿＿＿＿＿＿＿＿＿＿＿, 跟你沒關係。(他喜歡)

　　　　＿＿＿＿＿＿＿＿＿＿＿＿＿＿＿＿＿, 跟你没关系。(他喜欢)

　　A:　倒也是。／ 倒也是。

3. 還是...的, 就是... ／ 还是...的, 就是 (...IT'S JUST)

EXAMPLE:　A:　這兒的天氣不錯吧? ／ 这儿的天气不错吧?

　　　　　B:　這兒天氣還是挺好的, 就是風大。

　　　　　　　这儿天气还是挺好的, 就是风大。

(1)　小張的男朋友人還是不錯的, 就是＿＿＿＿＿＿＿＿＿＿＿。(脾氣)

　　　小张的男朋友人还是不错的, 就是＿＿＿＿＿＿＿＿＿＿＿。(脾气)

(2)　當醫生賺的錢還是挺多的, 就是＿＿＿＿＿＿＿＿＿＿。(忙)

　　　当医生赚的钱还是挺多的, 就是＿＿＿＿＿＿＿＿＿＿。(忙)

(3)　這個學校的老師和設備還是不錯的, 就是＿＿＿＿＿＿＿＿＿＿。(學費)

　　　这个学校的老师和设备还是不错的, 就是＿＿＿＿＿＿＿＿＿＿。(学费)

4.每當...時／的時候, 就...
每当...时／的时候, 就... (WHENEVER)

EXAMPLE: 每當中國運動員在國際比賽中取得好成績時, 就有成千上萬的人上街慶祝。

每当中国运动员在国际比赛中取得好成绩时, 就有成千上万的人上街庆祝。

(1) 每當過年過節的時候, 他＿＿＿＿＿＿＿＿＿＿＿＿＿＿＿＿。(想家)

每当过年过节的时候, 他＿＿＿＿＿＿＿＿＿＿＿＿＿＿＿＿。(想家)

(2) ＿＿＿＿＿＿＿＿＿＿＿＿＿＿＿, 他就到公園走走。(心情不好)

＿＿＿＿＿＿＿＿＿＿＿＿＿＿＿, 他就到公园走走。(心情不好)

(3) 每當學生在學習上有問題的時候, 王老師都＿＿＿＿＿＿＿＿＿＿＿。

每当学生在学习上有问题的时候, 王老师都＿＿＿＿＿＿＿＿＿＿＿。

打球有益於身體健康。／打球有益于身体健康。

▼▼▼▼▼▼▼▼▼▼▼▼▼▼▼▼▼▼▼▼▼▼▼▼▼▼▼▼▼▼▼▼▼▼▼▼▼

5. 所以..., 是因為... ／ 所以..., 是因为...

EXAMPLE:　張天明認為人們所以參加體育運動, 是因為運動有益於身體
健康。

　　　　　張天明认为人们所以参加体育运动, 是因为运动有益于身体
健康。

(1)　張天明的母親所以希望他學醫,＿＿＿＿＿＿＿＿＿＿＿＿＿＿＿＿。

　　　張天明的母亲所以希望他学医,＿＿＿＿＿＿＿＿＿＿＿＿＿＿＿＿。

(2)　很多家長所以不讓孩子看電視,＿＿＿＿＿＿＿＿＿＿＿＿＿＿＿。

　　　很多家长所以不让孩子看电视,＿＿＿＿＿＿＿＿＿＿＿＿＿＿＿。

(3)　張天明所以搬出宿舍,＿＿＿＿＿＿＿＿＿＿＿＿＿＿＿。

　　　张天明所以搬出宿舍,＿＿＿＿＿＿＿＿＿＿＿＿＿＿＿。

Pinyin Texts

NARRATIVE

　　Zhāng Tiānmíng bān chū xuéshēng sùshè yǐjīng hǎo jǐ ge yuè le. Tā yí ge rén zhù zài xiàowài bǐ zhù zài xiàonèi ānjìng duō le, yǒu hěn duō shíjiān zuò gōngkè. Kěshì yǒude shíhou yí ge rén yě huì juéde jìmò. Zhè tiān wǎnshang Zhāng Tiānmíng zuò wán le gōngkè, xián zhe méi shì, jiù gěi Āndésēn dǎ le yí ge diànhuà.

DIALOGUE

Zhāng Tiānmíng:	Wèi, Āndésēn ma?
Āndésēn:	Duì, wǒ shì Āndésēn. Qǐng wèn nín shì...
Zhāng Tiānmíng:	Zěnme, nǐ lián wǒ de shēngyīn dōu tīng bu chulai le?
Āndésēn:	À, Tiānmíng, shì nǐ! Kàn jīntiān wǎnshang de qiúsài le ma?
Zhāng Tiānmíng:	Qiúsài? Jīntiān wǎnshang wǒ gēnběn méi kàn diànshì.
Āndésēn:	Zěnme, lián zhème zhòngyào de lánqiú bǐsài nǐ dōu bú kàn.
Zhāng Tiānmíng:	Shéi gēn shéi bǐsài?

▼▼▼

Āndésēn:	Zánmen xuéxiào gēn Mìxīgēn.
Zhāng Tiānmíng:	Jiéguǒ zěnmeyàng?
Āndésēn:	Ài, zánmen shū le.
Zhāng Tiānmíng:	Yòu shū le? Tài ràng rén shīwàng le.
Āndésēn:	Kě bú shì, Mìxīgēn Duì gè gè shēn qiáng tǐ zhuàng, tèbié shì tāmen de wǔ hào, sùdù kuài jí le...
Zhāng Tiānmíng:	Wǒ tīngshuō zánmen duì de sùdù yě bú màn ya, érqiě wǒmen de jiàoliàn de jīngyàn bǐ tāmen de fēngfù duō le.
Āndésēn:	Shì a. Běnlái zánmen yìzhí lǐngxiān, kěshì hòulái rénjia bǎ bǐfēn mànmàn de zhuī shanglai le. Zuì jǐnzhāng de shì zuìhòu èrshí miǎozhōng, bǐfēn shì bāshí bǐ bāshí. Zhè shíhou tāmen de wǔ hào yòu jìn yìqiú, qiú gāng yí jìn lán, shíjiān jiù dào le. Bāshí èr bǐ bāshí, rénjia yíng le.
Zhāng Tiānmíng:	Shū yí cì yě méi shénme, fǎnzhèng bú shì juésài.
Āndésēn:	Zhè dào yě shì. Qíshí, zánmen duì dǎ de háishi búcuò de, jiùshì bǐsài jīngyàn méiyǒu tāmen duō. Dǎ de zuìhǎo de shì zánmen de sān hào, tā dé le sānshí fēn.
Zhāng Tiānmíng:	Shéi shì sān hào?
Āndésēn:	Nǐ lián sān hào dōu bù zhīdao? Jiùshì nǚháizi dōu xǐhuan de nàwèi "shuàigē".
Zhāng Tiānmíng:	Ò, wǒ xiǎng qilai le. Xiàcì zài yǒu jīngcǎi de bǐsài, bié wàng le gàosù wǒ.
Āndésēn:	Hǎo!
Zhāng Tiānmíng:	Zàijiàn.

READING

    Shàngge xīngqī, Zhāng Tiānmíng shōu dào biǎogē cóng Nánjīng jì lái de yì fēng xìn, xìn zhōng tídào Zhōngguó tǐyù yùndòng de qíngkuàng. Bāshí niándài yǐlái, Zhōngguó de tǐyù yùndòng yǒu le hěn dà de fāzhǎn, Zhōngguó yùndòngyuán zài Àolínpǐkè yùndònghuì shang ná dào le hěn duō jīnpái hé yínpái, bù shǎo rén hái dǎ pò le shìjiè jìlù. Hěn duō Zhōngguórén wèi cǐ gǎn dào hěn jiāo'ào, juéde zhè shì zhěnggè guójiā de guāngróng. Měi dāng Zhōngguó yùndòngyuán zài guójì bǐsài zhōng qǔdé hǎo chéngjī shí, jiù yǒu chéng qiān shàng wàn de rén shàng jiē qìngzhù. Biǎogē tán dào zhèxiē shìqing shí hěn jīdòng. Kěshì Zhāng Tiānmíng rènwéi, rénmen suǒyǐ cānjiā tǐyù yùndòng, shì yīnwèi yùndòng yǒuyì yú shēntǐ jiànkāng, bú shì wèi le gěi guójiā zhēng róngyù. Érqiě yīnwèi yíng le yì liǎng kuài jīnpái jiù shàng jiē qìngzhù, shízài méi yǒu bìyào.

Discussion Topic: Sports

Anderson did a wonderful job describing the basketball game to Tianming. Do the same with the help of the drawings.

第十四課 ▲ 家庭

◉ **NARRATIVE**

　　過幾天就是感恩節了,學校放一個星期假。張天明回家去看爸爸媽媽,他坐飛機到了波士頓,他的父親開車來機場接他。在車上,父子倆聊了起來。

◉ **DIALOGUE**

張父：　　　天明,這個學期忙不忙?

張天明：　　還好。只是有時候中文課的功課多一點。

張父：　　　那電腦課呢?

張天明：　　我沒選電腦課。

張父：　　　為什麼?你知道,靠你的中文課和歷史課,以後是賺不了多少錢的。要想找個鐵飯碗,就得學工程技術。要不然,聽你媽的,學醫也行。

張天明：　　可是我的興趣不在那個方面。

第十四课 ▲ 家庭

NARRATIVE

　　过几天就是感恩节了,学校放一个星期假。张天明回家去看爸爸妈妈,他坐飞机到了波士顿,他的父亲开车来机场接他。在车上,父子俩聊了起来。

DIALOGUE

张父：　　　天明,这个学期忙不忙?

张天明：　　还好。只是有时候中文课的功课多一点。

张父：　　　那电脑课呢?

张天明：　　我没选电脑课。

张父：　　　为什么?你知道,靠你的中文课和历史课,以后是赚不了多少钱的。要想找个铁饭碗,就得学工程技术。要不然,听你妈的,学医也行。

张天明：　　可是我的兴趣不在那个方面。

張父：　　你要知道，過日子靠的是錢，而不是興趣。

張天明：　可是有些東西有錢也買不到。

張父：　　好了，好了，不說這些了，反正再過幾年，你就得獨立了。...對了，天明，還記得惠敏嗎？

張天明：　當然記得，不就是李叔叔的女兒嗎？

張父：　　是的。你這次回來，去看看她，最好把你們的關係定下來。

張天明：　爸爸...

張父：　　我知道你在學校裏有個女朋友。可是人家是美國人...

張天明：　我也是美國人啊！

張父：　　可你首先是中國人啊。中國人還是跟中國人結婚嘛。東方人和西方人生活習慣不一樣。你看，天華和湯姆就是因為文化背景不同分手的。

張天明：　爸爸，他們分手是因為湯姆喝酒，不是因為文化背景的關係。再說，我不是小孩子了，我的事情我自己知道該怎麼辦。您別操心了。

我們是一家人。／我们是一家人。

张父：   你要知道，过日子靠的是钱，而不是兴趣。

张天明：   可是有些东西有钱也买不到。

张父：   好了，好了，不说这些了，反正再过几年，你就得独立了。… 对了，
          天明，还记得惠敏吗？

张天明：   当然记得，不就是李叔叔的女儿吗？

张父：   是的。你这次回来，去看看她，最好把你们的关系定下来。

张天明：   爸爸…

张父：   我知道你在学校里有个女朋友。可是人家是美国人…

张天明：   我也是美国人啊！

张父：   可你首先是中国人啊。中国人还是跟中国人结婚嘛。东方人和
          西方人生活习惯不一样。你看，天华和汤姆就是因为文化背景不
          同分手的。

张天明：   爸爸，他们分手是因为汤姆喝酒，不是因为文化背景的关系。再说，
          我不是小孩子了，我的事情我自己知道该怎么办。您别操心了。

小家庭

READING

　　張天明的姑父幾年前去世了。姑媽今年六十歲,剛從一家工廠退休。這幾年姑媽一直覺得很寂寞,工廠裏的老朋友想幫她找個老伴兒。可是表嫂覺得姑媽找老伴兒是一件很丟人的事。姑媽覺得表嫂管得太多,說話太衝,所以婆媳關係變得緊張起來。她們本來住在一起,後來表哥和表嫂就帶著女兒玲玲搬出去住了。

　　玲玲今年八歲,很聰明,在學校裏成績不錯。可是她一放學回家,她媽媽不是要她去學鋼琴,就是要她去學畫畫兒。有時候玲玲想玩一會兒,她媽媽就罵她太懶。玲玲常常哭著跑到奶奶那兒去告狀。

　　張天明的表哥工作很忙,抽不出多少時間來管女兒的事。表嫂因此常和表哥吵架。要不是表嫂覺得單親家庭對小孩的影響不好,說不定早就鬧離婚了。張天明沒想到中國的家庭居然也有這麼多問題。

READING

　　张天明的姑父几年前去世了。姑妈今年六十岁,刚从一家工厂退休。这几年姑妈一直觉得很寂寞,工厂里的老朋友想帮她找个老伴儿。可是表嫂觉得姑妈找老伴儿是一件很丢人的事。姑妈觉得表嫂管得太多,说话太冲,所以婆媳关系变得紧张起来。她们本来住在一起,后来表哥和表嫂就带着女儿玲玲搬出去住了。

　　玲玲今年八岁,很聪明,在学校里成绩不错。可是她一放学回家,她妈妈不是要她去学钢琴,就是要她去学画画儿。有时候玲玲想玩一会儿,她妈妈就骂她太懒。玲玲常常哭着跑到奶奶那儿去告状。

　　张天明的表哥工作很忙,抽不出多少时间来管女儿的事。表嫂因此常和表哥吵架。要不是表嫂觉得单亲家庭对小孩的影响不好,说不定早就闹离婚了。张天明没想到中国的家庭居然也有这么多问题。

VOCABULARY

1.	家庭		jiātíng	n	family
2.	父子		fùzǐ	n	father and son
3.	歷史	历史	lìshǐ	n	history
4.	賺(錢)*	赚(钱)	zhuàn (qián)	vo	to make/to earn (money)
5.	鐵飯碗	铁饭碗	tiěfànwǎn	n	iron rice bowl (metaphor: secure job)
6.	工程		gōngchéng	n	engineering
7.	技術	技术	jìshù	n	technology
8.	方面		fāngmiàn	n	aspect
9.	過日子	过日子	guò rìzi	vo	(col) to live; to get by; to survive
10.	而		ér	conj	and; but
11.	獨立	独立	dúlì	adj	independent
12.	叔叔		shūshu	n	father's younger brother; 爸爸的弟弟
13.	定下來		dìng xialai	vc	to fix; to clarify (a relationship)
14.	首先		shǒuxiān	adv	first and foremost
15.	結婚	结婚	jié hūn	vo	to get married

他姐姐明年結婚。／他姐姐明年结婚。

她哥哥跟一個英國人結婚了。／她哥哥跟一个英国人结婚了。

16.	嘛		ma	p	indicating evident and clear reasoning
17.	分手		fēn shǒu	vo	to part company

天華跟湯姆分手了。／天华跟汤姆分手了。

他們分手以後就再也沒说過話。／他们分手以后就再也没说过话。

18.	操心		cāo xīn	vo	to trouble and worry about; "to exercise" or tax one's mind over something

父母常常為子女操心。／父母常常为子女操心。

這件事你別操心。／这件事你别操心。

19.	姑父		gūfu	n	father's sister's husband
20.	去世		qùshì	v	to pass away; to die
21.	工廠	工厂	gōngchǎng	n	factory
22.	退休		tuìxiū	v	to retire
23.	老伴兒	老伴儿	lǎobànr	n	(col) husband or wife of an old married couple
24.	表嫂		biǎosǎo	n	older cousin's wife; 表哥的太太
25.	丟人		diū rén	vo	to lose face; to be disgraced

他大學念了七年還畢不了業，覺得很丟人。

他大学念了七年还毕不了业，觉得很丢人。

| 26. | 衝 | 冲 | chòng | adj | abrupt; blunt |

弟弟說話很衝。／弟弟说话很冲。

你說話別那麼衝。／你说话别那么冲。

27.	婆媳		póxí	n	mother-in-law and daughter-in-law
28.	聰明*	聪明	cōngming	adj	bright; clever
29.	成績*	成绩	chéngjì	n	grades
30.	放學	放学	fàng xué	vo	to get out of school; school lets out
31.	鋼琴*	钢琴	gāngqín	n	piano
32.	畫畫兒	画画儿	huà huàr	vo	to paint; to draw
33.	罵	骂	mà	v	to scold
34.	懶	懒	lǎn	adj	lazy
35.	奶奶*		nǎinai	n	paternal grandmother
36.	告狀	告状	gào zhuàng	vo	(lit) to file a lawsuit against somebody; to lodge a complaint with somebody's superior
37.	抽		chōu	v	to pull out; to set aside (time)

你抽時間給媽媽打個電話吧。／你抽时间给妈妈打个电话吧。

我很忙，抽不出時間。／我很忙，抽不出时间。

38.	因此		yīncǐ	conj	because of this; therefore
39.	吵架*		chǎo jià	vo	to quarrel
40.	要不是		yàobúshì	conj	were it not for the fact that
41.	單親	单亲	dānqīn	adj	single parent
42.	離婚	离婚	lí hūn	vo	to divorce
43.	居然		jūrán	adv	to one's surprise

PROPER NOUNS

1.	感恩節	感恩节	Gǎn'ēnjié	n	Thanksgiving
2.	惠敏		Huìmǐn		a feminine name
3.	玲玲		Língling		a feminine name

ENLARGED CHARACTERS FOR EASIER VIEWING AND COMPARING

鐵　嘛　衝　聰　鋼　畫　離
铁　嘛　冲　聪　钢　画　离

兩個人不寂寞。／两个人不寂寞。

▼▼

Grammar

1. DIRECTIONAL COMPLEMENT (III): INDICATING CHANGE IN STATE

Directional complements can indicate a change in state. There are several kinds of directional complements:

A. Directional complements indicate a change from inaction to action, or the initiation of an action and its continuation (上, 起, 起來 / 起来, 開/开).

(1) 他一到辦公室就打起電話來。/ 他一到办公室就打起电话来。

   He began to make phone calls as soon as he got to the office.

(2) 孩子從學校一回家就彈起鋼琴來了。

   孩子从学校一回家就弹起钢琴来了。

   The child began to play the piano as soon as he got home from school.

(3) 兩個老朋友坐下以後, 就聊起天來了。

   两个老朋友坐下以后, 就聊起天来了。

   The two old friends sat down and began to chat.

起來 / 起来 can also indicate a change in speed, light, temperature, weight, etc. For instance,

(4) 天氣慢慢暖和起來了。/ 天气慢慢暖和起来了。

   The weather began to warm up.

(5) 汽車開得快起來了。/ 汽车开得快起来了。

   The car began to accelerate.

(6) 打開燈, 房間一下子亮起來了。/ 打开灯, 房间一下子亮起来了。

   After the light was turned on, the room brightened up.

(7) 這幾年學中文的學生多起來了。/ 这几年学中文的学生多起来了。

   In the last few years the number of students studying Chinese has begun to increase.

Note: If there is an object, it should be between 起 and 來/来. See examples (1) and (2) above.

上 and 開/开 can also indicate the start of an action or state. However, while 起來 / 起来 can be combined with many adjectives, 上 and 開/开 can only be combined with a limited number of verbs.

(1)　我們在上課, 你怎麼唱上歌了? / 我们在上课, 你怎么唱上歌了?

　　　我們在上課, 你怎麼唱開歌了? / 我们在上课, 你怎么唱开歌了?

　　　We are having class. Why have you started to sing?

(2)　她剛才還很高興, 現在怎麼哭上了? / 她刚才还很高兴, 现在怎么哭上了?

　　　她剛才還很高興, 現在怎麼哭開了? / 她刚才还很高兴, 现在怎么哭开了?

　　　She was very happy just a moment ago. How come she's crying now?

(3)　他一回家就唱上了。

　　　The minute he got home he started to sing.

(4)　他聽了我的話以後就笑開了。 / 他听了我的话以后就笑开了。

　　　After he heard what I said, he burst out laughing.

B. 下來 / 下来 suggests a gradual diminution or decrease in terms of speed, temperature, brightness, tempo, etc. Examples of V +下來 / 下来:

(1)　汽車停下來了。 / 汽车停下来了。

　　　The car slowed down to a halt.

(2)　關上燈, 房間一下子暗 (àn) 下來了。 / 关上灯, 房间一下子暗 (àn) 下来了。

　　　After the light was switched off, the room began to darken.

(3)　音樂怎麼慢下來了? / 音乐怎么慢下来了?

　　　How come the music is slowing down?

下去 indicates the continuation of an action or state:

(1)　張天明不好意思不聽下去。 / 张天明不好意思不听下去。

　　　Zhang Tianming could not bring himself to stop listening (out of a sense of politeness).

(2)　说下去! / 说下去!

　　　Keep on talking!

▼▼

(3)　天再熱下去, 我就受不了了。／天再热下去, 我就受不了了。

　　　If the temperature keeps on rising, I won't be able to take it [anymore].

2. POTENTIAL COMPLEMENT (V) + 不／得 + 了 (liǎo)

Potential complements, which appear in the pattern (V) + 不／得 + 了 (liǎo), can be construed as the equivalent of 不能／能. For instance,

(1)　外面在下雨, 比賽不了了。／外面在下雨, 比赛不了了。

　　　It's raining outside. The game's off.

(2)　孩子病了, 上不了學了。／孩子病了, 上不了学了。

　　　The child is sick and can't go to school anymore.

(3)　一百塊錢買不了幾本書。／一百块钱买不了几本书。

　　　A hundred bucks can't buy more than a couple of books.

This kind of complement is used mainly in negative sentences, and is interchangeable with the pattern 能／不能 + V.

V + 不／得 + 了 can also mean V + 不／得 + 完, e.g., 吃不了 (cannot eat it all up). Compare the following:

(4)　水果壞了, 吃不了了。／水果坏了, 吃不了了。

　　　The fruit is spoiled. You shouldn't eat it.

(5)　飯給得太多了, 我吃不了。／饭给得太多了, 我吃不了。

　　　You've given me too much rice. I can't finish it.

3. 要 (應該／应该)

要 can mean "should" or "need to," e.g.,

(1)　過去中國人認為孩子要聽父母的話, 幫助媽媽帶弟弟妹妹。

　　　过去中国人认为孩子要听父母的话, 帮助妈妈带弟弟妹妹。

　　　In the old days, Chinese people thought that children should listen to their parents and help their mother take care of their younger siblings.

(2)   明天早上有考試, 你們要早一點起床。

       明天早上有考试, 你们要早一点起床。

       There's a test tomorrow morning. You have to get up earlier (than you normally do).

(3)   你跟他借的錢要還給他。/ 你跟他借的钱要还给他。

       You need to pay back the money that you borrowed from him.

Use 不用 or 不必 to negate:

(4)   你跟我借的錢, 不必還了。/ 你跟我借的钱, 不必还了。

       You don't have to pay back the money you borrowed from me.

(5)   明天是週末, 不用早起。/ 明天是周末, 不用早起。

       Tomorrow is the weekend. There's no need to get up early.

4. 下來 / 下来: INDICATING RESULT

下來 / 下来 denotes separation or adherence, e.g., 拿下來 / 拿下来 (take down), 住下來 / 住下来 (settle down), 待下來 / 待下来 (stay), 決定下來 / 决定下来 (decide on), 記下來 / 记下来 (note down), 定下來 / 定下来 (decide), 撕下來 / 撕下来 (sī xialai: tear off), 摘下來 / 摘下来 (zhāi xialai: pull down), and 揭下來 / 揭下来 (jiē xialai: pull off).

(1)   我們在這兒住下來吧。/ 我们在这儿住下来吧。

       Let's settle down here.

(2)   請把領事館的電話和地址記下來。/ 请把领事馆的电话和地址记下来。

       Please write down the phone number and the address of the consulate.

記下來 / 记下来 suggests setting down in writing what already exists, in this case, phone number and address, through an act of transference from another source.

(3)   你學什麼專業應該早一點定下來。/ 你学什么专业应该早一点定下来。

       You should decide on your major as soon as possible.

▼ ▼

Notice that 出來／出来 suggests emergence. 把你的想法寫出來／把你的想法写出来 means making known your ideas to others through writing—in other words, revealing your private thoughts, making them emerge or "come out" from the recesses of your brain, as it were. 起來／起来 as in 想起來／想起来, on the other hand, suggests connecting with the past through recollection—in other words, by retrieving from the storehouse of past memories.

5. TOPICS (II)

In a sentence, if a noun signifies something that is already known, and the adjective describing it conveys new information, one should place the noun at the beginning of the sentence, i.e., treat it as a topic, and put the adjective after the noun. Compare the following examples and pay particular attention to the difference between Chinese and English:

(1a)   只是有時候歷史課的功課比較多。／只是有时候历史课的功课比较多。

It's just that sometimes there's rather too much homework for the history class.

We don't say,

(1b)   *只是有時候歷史課有比較多的功課。

*只是有时候历史课有比较多的功课。

(2a)   東方人和西方人生活習慣不一樣。／东方人和西方人生活习惯不一样。

The lifestyles/customs of people in the East and West differ.

We don't say,

(2b)   *東方人和西方人有不同的生活習慣。

*东方人和西方人有不同的生活习惯。

(3a)   你看, 天華和湯姆就是因為文化背景不同分手的。

你看, 天华和汤姆就是因为文化背景不同分手的。

You see, Tianhua and Tom broke up precisely because of the differences in their cultural backgrounds.

We don't say,

(3b)   *你看, 天華和湯姆就是因為有不同的文化背景分手的。

*你看, 天华和汤姆就是因为有不同的文化背景分手的。

▼▼▼

6. COHESION (IV): 了 (le) AS A COMPLETION MARKER

了 (le) at the end of a sentence signals the completion of a sentence. There is a significant pause after it in speech.

(1)   A: 昨天上午你去哪兒了？/ 昨天上午你去哪儿了？

            Where did you go yesterday morning?

        B: 昨天上午我進城了。/ 昨天上午我进城了。

            Yesterday morning I went to the city.

(2)   做完功課以後我就睡覺了。/ 做完功课以后我就睡觉了。

      I went to bed after finishing my homework.

了 (le) after a verb is quite different. Compare,

(3)   昨天我先在一個飯館吃了飯, 然後又去買了一些東西, 後來就回家了。

        昨天我先在一个饭馆吃了饭, 然后又去买了一些东西, 后来就回家了。

      Yesterday I first ate at a restaurant and then did some shopping. After that I went home.

Note: If a sentence is not yet complete, or if it is immediately followed by another clause, 了 generally goes after the verb. If the sentence is complete, 了 should go at the end of the sentence. [See G5 of Lesson 5, G6 of Lesson 8, and G2 of Lesson 10 in *Integrated Chinese*, Level 1; see G1 of Lesson 1 in *Integrated Chinese*, Level 2.]

We cap the recitation of a series of actions with 了 to signal the completion of the narration. Notice the omission of 了 after the verbs until the last clause in the following example. Where 了 is optional, we have written it as (了).

(4a)   去年我去中國旅行。先到南京遊覽(了)中山陵、夫子廟、和玄武湖公園, 後來到西安遊覽(了)名勝古蹟, 最後去上海買東西, 在中國待了差不多一個月。

        去年我去中国旅行。先到南京游览(了)中山陵、夫子庙、和玄武湖公园, 后来到西安游览(了)名胜古迹, 最后去上海买东西, 在中国待了差不多一个月。

      Last year I took a trip to China. First, [I] went to Nanjing and toured Sun Yat-sen's Mausoleum, the Confucian Temple, and Lake Xuanwu. Then [I] went to Xi'an and saw [some] famous historic sights. Finally, [I] went shopping in Shanghai. [I] stayed in China for almost a month.

南 京 西 安 上海

The recitation of the itinerary consists of two sentences in Chinese whereas in English five sentences are required. That is because in the Chinese passage, you can leave out the subject 我 after its initial appearance. See Lesson 8 Cohesion (1).

(5a) 昨天早上我起床以後先吃早飯, 然後去(了)圖書館借書。我問圖書館的工作人員書可以借幾天, 她說可以借一個月。辦完(了)借書手續以後, 我就回宿舍了。

昨天早上我起床以后先吃早饭, 然后去(了)图书馆借书。我问图书馆的工作人员书可以借几天, 她说可以借一个月。办完(了)借书手续以后, 我就回宿舍了。

Yesterday morning after I got up, I had breakfast first, and then I went to the library to check out [a] book. I asked the librarian how long I could borrow the book for. She said that I could borrow it for a month. After completing the procedures for borrowing the book, I went back to the dorm.

If we were to add 了 after each clause, then we would end up with a collection of discrete sentences rather than two cohesive paragraphs.

(4b) 去年我去中國旅行了。 / 去年我去中国旅行了。

Last year I took a trip to China.

先到南京遊覽中山陵、夫子廟、和玄武湖公園了。
先到南京游览中山陵、夫子庙、和玄武湖公园了。

First [I] went to Nanjing to visit Sun Yat-sen's Mausoleum, the Confucian Temple, and Lake Xuanwu.

後來到西安游覽名勝古蹟了。 / 后来到西安游览名胜古迹了。

Then [I] went to Xi'an and saw [some] famous historic sights.

最後去上海買東西了。 / 最后去上海买东西了。

Finally, [I] went shopping in Shanghai.

在中國待了差不多一個月。／在中国待了差不多一个月。

I stayed in China for almost a month.

(5b) 昨天早上我起床以後吃早飯了。／昨天早上我起床以后吃早饭了。

Yesterday morning after I got up, I had breakfast.

然後去圖書館借書了。／然后去图书馆借书了。

Then I went to the library to check out [a] book.

我問圖書館的工作人員書可以借幾天, 她說可以借一個月。

我问图书馆的工作人员书可以借几天, 她说可以借一个月。

I asked the librarian how long I could borrow the book for. She said that I could borrow the book for a month.

辦完借書手續以後, 我就回宿舍了。／办完借书手续以后, 我就回宿舍了。

After completing the procedures for borrowing the book, I went back to the dorm.

Important Words & Phrases

1. 而

而 is a conjunction that shows contrast between the first and the second clauses. It usually occurs in written or formal Chinese.

EXAMPLE: 過日子靠的是錢, 而不是興趣。

过日子靠的是钱, 而不是兴趣。

你的興趣是彈(tán)鋼琴還是畫畫兒? ／你的兴趣是弹(tán)钢琴还是画画儿?

▼▼

(1)　他們分手是因為＿＿＿＿＿＿＿＿, 而不是因為＿＿＿＿＿＿＿＿。

　　　他们分手是因为＿＿＿＿＿＿＿＿, 而不是因为＿＿＿＿＿＿＿＿。

(2)　小林畢業以後想＿＿＿＿＿＿＿, 而不想＿＿＿＿＿＿＿＿＿。

　　　小林毕业以后想＿＿＿＿＿＿＿, 而不想＿＿＿＿＿＿＿＿＿。

(3)　過端午節應該吃＿＿＿＿＿＿＿, 而不應該吃＿＿＿＿＿＿＿。

　　　过端午节应该吃＿＿＿＿＿＿＿, 而不应该吃＿＿＿＿＿＿＿。

2. 最好 (HAD BETTER; IT'S BEST THAT)

EXAMPLE:　你這次回來, 去看看她, 最好把你們的關係定下來。

　　　　　你这次回来, 去看看她, 最好把你们的关系定下来。

(1)　吃完飯後, ＿＿＿＿＿＿＿＿＿＿＿。(馬上運動)

　　　吃完饭后, ＿＿＿＿＿＿＿＿＿＿＿。(马上运动)

(2)　要是這個包裹很重要, 怕寄丟, ＿＿＿＿＿＿＿＿＿＿。(掛號)

　　　要是这个包裹很重要, 怕寄丢, ＿＿＿＿＿＿＿＿＿＿。(挂号)

(3)　這部電影很吸引人, 看的人多, 如果想看, ＿＿＿＿＿＿＿＿＿。

　　　这部电影很吸引人, 看的人多, 如果想看, ＿＿＿＿＿＿＿＿＿。

3. 要不是 (IF IT WERE NOT FOR)

EXAMPLE:　要不是表嫂覺得單親家庭對小孩的影響不好, 說不定早就鬧離婚了。

　　　　　要不是表嫂觉得单亲家庭对小孩的影响不好, 说不定早就闹离婚了。

(1)　要不是＿＿＿＿＿＿＿＿＿＿＿, 張天明不知道為什麼端午節吃粽子。

　　　要不是＿＿＿＿＿＿＿＿＿＿＿, 张天明不知道为什么端午节吃粽子。

(2) _____, 張天明肯定選文學做他的專業。

_____, 张天明肯定选文学做他的专业。

(3) 要不是_____, 屈原是不會投江自殺的。

要不是_____, 屈原是不会投江自杀的。

4. 說不定 / 说不定 (PROBABLY; PERHAPS)

EXAMPLE: 要不是表嫂覺得單親家庭對小孩的影響不好, 说不定早就鬧離婚了。

要不是表嫂觉得单亲家庭对小孩的影响不好, 说不定早就闹离婚了。

(1) 過節坐飛機的人多, 機票_____。

过节坐飞机的人多, 机票_____。

(2) A: 下個學期我真不知道應該選些什麼課?

下个学期我真不知道应该选些什么课?

B: 你怎麼不跟你的指導教授談談?_____。

你怎么不跟你的指导教授谈谈?_____。

(3) 雖然我們的籃球隊已經輸了五場了, 可是今天打得不錯,_____。

虽然我们的篮球队已经输了五场了, 可是今天打得不错,_____。

5. 沒想到 (DIDN'T EXPECT)

EXAMPLE: 張天明沒想到中國的家庭居然也有這麼多問題。

张天明没想到中国的家庭居然也有这么多问题。

(1) 他們結婚才兩個月,_____。

他们结婚才两个月,_____。

▼▼▼

(2) 我們都以為小王是八十年代從北京移民來美國的，＿＿＿＿＿＿＿＿＿。
(七十年代)

我们都以为小王是八十年代从北京移民来美国的，＿＿＿＿＿＿＿＿＿。
(七十年代)

(3) 大家都说西岸大學的學費貴，＿＿＿＿＿＿＿＿＿。(東岸)

大家都说西岸大学的学费贵，＿＿＿＿＿＿＿＿＿。(东岸)

Pinyin Texts

NARRATIVE

Guò jǐ tiān jiùshì Gǎn'ēn Jié le, xuéxiào fàng yí ge xīngqī jià. Zhāng Tiānmíng huí jiā qù kàn bàba māma, tā zuò fēijī dào le Bōshìdùn, tā de fùqin kāi chē lái jīcháng jiē tā. Zài chē shang, fùzǐ liǎ liáo le qǐlai.

DIALOGUE

Zhāngfù: Tiānmíng, zhège xuéqī máng bu máng?

Zhāng Tiānmíng: Hái hǎo. Zhǐshì yǒu shíhou Zhōngwén kè de gōngkè duō yì diǎn.

Zhāngfù: Nà diànnǎo kè ne?

Zhāng Tiānmíng: Wǒ méi xuǎn diànnǎo kè.

Zhāngfù: Wèi shénme? Nǐ zhīdao, kào nǐ de Zhōngwén kè hé lìshǐ kè, yǐhòu shì zhuàn bu liǎo duōshǎo qián de. Yào xiǎng zhǎo ge tiěfànwǎn, jiù děi xué gōngchéng jìshù. Yàoburán, tīng nǐ mā de, xué yī yě xíng.

Zhāng Tiānmíng: Kěshì wǒ de xìngqù bú zài nàge fāngmiàn.

Zhāngfù: Nǐ yào zhīdao, guò rìzi kào de shì qián, ér bú shì xìngqù.

Zhāng Tiānmíng: Kěshì yǒu xiē dōngxi yǒu qián yě mǎi bu dào.

Zhāngfù: Hǎo le, hǎo le, bù shuō zhèxiē le, fǎnzhèng zài guò jǐn nián, nǐ jiù děi dúlì le...Duì le, Tiānmíng, hái jìde Huìmǐn ma?

Zhāng Tiānmíng: Dāngrán jìde, bú jiùshì Lǐ shūshu de nǚ'ér ma?

Zhāngfù: Shìde. Nǐ zhècì huí lái, qù kàn kan tā, zuìhǎo bǎ nǐmen de guānxi dìng xialai.

Zhāng Tiānmíng: Bàba...

Zhāngfù: Wǒ zhīdao nǐ zài xuéxiào li yǒu ge nǚpéngyou. Kěshì rénjia shì Měiguórén...

Zhāng Tiānmíng: Wǒ yě shì Měiguórén a!

Zhāngfù: Kě nǐ shǒuxiān shì Zhōngguórén a. Zhōngguórén háishì gēn Zhōngguórén jié hūn ma. Dōngfāngrén hé Xīfāngrén shēnghuó xíguàn bù yíyàng. Nǐ kàn, Tiānhuá hé Tāngmǔ jiùshì yīnwèi wénhuà bèijǐng bùtóng fēn shǒu de.

Zhāng Tiānmíng: Bàba, tāmen fēn shǒu shì yīnwèi Tāngmǔ hē jiǔ, bú shì yīnwèi wénhuà bèijǐng de guānxi. Zàishuō, wǒ bú shì xiǎoháizi le, wǒ de shìqing wǒ zìjǐ zhīdao gāi zěnmebàn. Nín bié cāo xīn le.

READING

Zhāng Tiānmíng de gūfu jǐ nián qián qùshì le. Gūmā jīnnián liùshí suì, gāng cóng yì jiā gōngchǎng tuìxiū. Zhè jǐ nián gūmā yìzhí juéde hěn jìmò, gōngchǎng li de lǎopéngyou xiǎng bāng tā zhǎo ge lǎobànr. Kěshì biǎosǎo juéde gūmā zhǎo lǎobànr shì yí jiàn hěn diū rén de shì. Gūmā juéde biǎosǎo guǎn de tài duō, shuō huà tài chòng, suǒyǐ póxí guānxì biàn de jǐnzhāng qǐ lai. Tāmen běnlái zhù zài yìqǐ, hòulái biǎogē hé biǎosǎo jiù dài zhe nǚ'ér Língling bān chuqu zhù le.

Língling jīnnián bā suì, hěn cōngming, zài xuéxiào li chéngjì búcuò. Kěshì tā yí fàng xué huí jiā, tā māma búshì yào tā qù xué gāngqín, jiùshì yào tā qù xué huàhuàr. Yǒu shíhou Língling xiǎng wánr yíhuìr, tā māma jiù mà tā tài lǎn. Língling chángcháng kū zhe pǎo dào nǎinai nàr qù gào zhuàng.

Zhāng Tiānmíng de biǎogē gōngzuò hěn máng, chōu bu chū duōshǎo shíjiān lái guǎn nǚ'ér de shì. Biǎosǎo yīncǐ cháng hé biǎogē chǎo jià. Yàobúshì biǎosǎo juéde dānqīn jiātíng duì xiǎoháir de yǐngxiǎng bù hǎo, shuōbudìng zǎojiù nào lí hūn le. Zhāng Tiānmíng méi xiǎng dào Zhōngguó de jiātíng jūrán yě yǒu zhème duō wèntí.

Discussion Topic: Family

Do you think Tianming will listen to his father? What was his father's advice?

第十五課 ▲ 男女平等

DIALOGUE

麗莎： 天明，昨天晚上我高中的一個女同學來電話，說她懷了孕，快生孩子了。她已經把工作辭了，待在家裏做起家庭主婦來了。

張天明： 這不很好嗎？

麗莎： 好什麼？她是護士，才工作一年。真不公平，生孩子是整個社會的事，為什麼擔子都在女人身上？

張天明： 麗莎，你這麼說，我看有點沒道理。難道讓我們男人生孩子嗎？

麗莎： 誰讓你們生孩子了？我的意思是，一個女人生了孩子以後，不管她願意不願意，都得辭了工作在家裏帶孩子。這不是太不公平了嗎？為什麼不讓丈夫在家裏帶孩子呢？

張天明： 你真的這麼想嗎？讓女的辭職，待在家裏當然不好；可是反過來，讓男的在家裏帶孩子，也不見得公平。應該想一個更好的辦法來解決這個問題。

第十五课 ▲ 男女平等

DIALOGUE

丽莎： 天明，昨天晚上我高中的一个女同学来电话，说她怀了孕，快生孩子了。她已经把工作辞了，待在家里做起家庭主妇来了。

张天明： 这不很好吗？

丽莎： 好什么？她是护士，才工作一年。真不公平，生孩子是整个社会的事，为什么担子都在女人身上？

张天明： 丽莎，你这么说，我看有点没道理。难道让我们男人生孩子吗？

丽莎： 谁让你们生孩子了？我的意思是，一个女人生了孩子以后，不管她愿意不愿意，都得辞了工作在家里带孩子。这不是太不公平了吗？为什么不让丈夫在家里带孩子呢？

张天明： 你真的这么想吗？让女的辞职，待在家里当然不好；可是反过来，让男的在家里带孩子，也不见得公平。应该想一个更好的办法来解决这个问题。

麗莎： 等你想出好辦法以後，恐怕我都老了。實際上，男女不平等的現象還有很多。比如，做同樣的工作，女的薪水往往比男的少。

張天明： 這倒是。

麗莎： 還有，在美國當主管的，有幾個是女的？職位越高，婦女越少，這不是歧視婦女嗎？

張天明： 你說的有道理。不過，我想隨著社會的發展，婦女的地位會不斷得到提高的。

麗莎： 我不像你那麼樂觀。

張天明： 哎，麗莎，我覺得在家庭裏，男女已經很平等了。就拿我家來說吧，我爸爸跟媽媽分擔家務，教育孩子也主要是爸爸。親戚朋友都說我爸爸是一個模範丈夫。

麗莎： 我看你姐夫對你姐姐也很體貼。

張天明： 我姐夫比我爸爸更"模範"，見了姐姐，就像老鼠見了貓。我很看不慣。

麗莎： 男女平等這個問題，大概是很難討論清楚的。

READING

在歷史上，特別是從宋朝開始，中國就是一個重男輕女的社會。在家裏，女子出嫁以前要服從父親，出嫁以後要服從丈夫，丈夫死了還要服從兒子。那個時候，婚姻完全由父母做主，有的還指腹為婚。有的地方，如果女孩還沒長大，未婚夫就死了，就不讓這個女孩跟別人結婚，甚至叫死了未婚夫的女孩跟一個木刻的"男人"結婚。

五十年代開始，中國婦女的情況有了很大的變化。特別是在城市裏，女孩子和男孩子一樣有受教育的機會；在工作方面，同工同酬；婦女的社會地位也有很大的提高。

丽莎： 　等你想出好办法以后，恐怕我都老了。实际上，男女不平等的现象还有很多。比如，做同样的工作，女的薪水往往比男的少。

张天明：这倒是。

丽莎： 　还有，在美国当主管的，有几个是女的？职位越高，妇女越少，这不是歧视妇女吗？

张天明：你说的有道理。不过，我想随着社会的发展，妇女的地位会不断得到提高的。

丽莎： 　我不像你那么乐观。

张天明：哎，丽莎，我觉得在家庭里，男女已经很平等了。就拿我家来说吧，我爸爸跟妈妈分担家务，教育孩子也主要是爸爸。亲戚朋友都说我爸爸是一个模范丈夫。

丽莎： 　我看你姐夫对你姐姐也很体贴。

张天明：我姐夫比我爸爸更"模范"，见了姐姐，就像老鼠见了猫。我很看不惯。

丽莎： 　男女平等这个问题，大概是很难讨论清楚的。

READING

　　在历史上，特别是从宋朝开始，中国就是一个重男轻女的社会。在家里，女子出嫁以前要服从父亲，出嫁以后要服从丈夫，丈夫死了还要服从儿子。那个时候，婚姻完全由父母做主，有的还指腹为婚。有的地方，如果女孩还没长大，未婚夫就死了，就不让这个女孩跟别人结婚，甚至叫死了未婚夫的女孩跟一个木刻的"男人"结婚。

　　五十年代开始，中国妇女的情况有了很大的变化。特别是在城市里，女孩子和南孩子一样有受教育的机会；在工作方面，同工同酬；妇女的社会地位也有很大的提高。

　　但是，改革開放以來，男女不平等的問題又突出起來。比如，升學或找工作的時候，女生都比男生難得多；在一些工廠和公司又出現了同工不同酬的現象；職位高的婦女人數明顯減少了。不過，在一般年輕的夫婦中，大部份丈夫十分體貼、照顧妻子。所以，也許家庭是男女平等體現得最多的地方。

跟木刻的"男人"結婚／跟木刻的"男人"結婚

　　但是，改革开放以来，男女不平等的问题有突出起来。比如，升学或找工作的时候，女生都比男生难得多；在一些工厂和公司又出现了同工不同酬的现象；职位高的妇女人数明显减少了。不过，在一般年轻的夫妇中，大部分丈夫十分体贴、照顾妻子。所以，也许家庭是男女平等体现得最多的地方。

指腹為婚／指腹为婚

VOCABULARY

1. 男女 nánnǚ n men and women; male and female

2. 平等 píngděng adj equal

3. 懷孕　怀孕 huái yùn vo to be pregnant

4. 辭　辞 cí v to resign

5. 家庭主婦　家庭主妇 jiātíng zhǔfù n housewife

6. 護士　护士 hùshi n nurse

7. 公平 gōngpíng adj fair

你們的老師對大家很公平。/ 你们的老师对大家很公平。

不公平的事大家都會反對。/ 不公平的事大家都会反对。

8. 社會　社会 shèhuì n society

9. 擔子　担子 dànzi n loaded carrying pole; burden

10. 女人 nǚrén n (col) woman

11. 不管 bùguǎn conj no matter how

12. 帶　带 dài v (col) to raise, to take care of (a child)

有些人覺得帶孩子很麻煩。/ 有些人觉得带孩子很麻烦。

13. 丈夫 zhàngfu n husband

14. 辭職　辞职 cí zhí vo to resign from a position

15. 反過來　反过来 fǎn guò lái conversely

16. 辦法*　办法 bànfǎ n method; way (to solve a problem)

17. 解決　解决 jiějué v to resolve

他們兩個人的矛盾已經解決了。/ 他们两个人的矛盾已经解决了。

我學習上有很多困難, 你能幫助我解決嗎?

我学习上有很多困难, 你能帮助我解决吗?

18. 現象　现象 xiànxiàng n phenomenon

19.	比如		bǐrú	v	for example
20.	薪水		xīnshuǐ	n	salary
21.	往往		wǎngwǎng	adv	often (indicating tendency rather than frequency)
22.	主管		zhǔguǎn	n/v	person in charge; to preside over
23.	職位	职位	zhíwèi	n	(professional) position
24.	婦女	妇女	fùnǚ	n	woman; women in general
25.	歧視	歧视	qíshì	v	to discriminate against
26.	隨著	随着	suí zhe	conj	in the wake of; following [see G2]
27.	地位		dìwèi	n	status
28.	不斷	不断	búduàn	adv	constantly

電話不斷地響, 真吵。/ 电话不断地响, 真吵。

上課時, 他總是不斷地問老師問題。

上课时, 他总是不断地问老师问题。

29.	得到		dé dào	vc	to obtain
30.	提高*		tígāo	vc	to improve; to lift

婦女的社會地位有很大的提高。/ 妇女的社会地位有很大的提高。

去中國待了一年, 我的中文水平明顯提高了。

去中国待了一年, 我的中文水平明显提高了。

31.	樂觀	乐观	lèguān	adj	be optimistic
32.	分擔	分担	fēndān	v	to share (burden, responsibilities)
33.	家務	家务	jiāwù	n	household duties
34.	主要		zhǔyào	adj/adv	main, chief; mainly, chiefly

他這次去中國主要目的是參加體育比賽。

他这次去中国主要目的是参加体育比赛。

我主要在學校上學, 週末出去工作。

我主要在学校上学, 周末出去工作。

35.	親戚*	亲戚	qīnqi	n	relatives
36.	模範	模范	mófàn	adj/n	model
37.	姐夫		jiěfu	n	姐姐的丈夫; older sister's husband
38.	體貼	体贴	tǐtiē	adj	considerate
39.	老鼠		lǎoshǔ	n	mouse; rat
40.	貓	猫	māo	n	cat

貓追老鼠／猫追老鼠

41.	看不慣	看不惯	kàn bu guàn	vc	cannot bear the sight of; to frown upon
42.	大概		dàgài	adv	probably

會已經開完了,他大概不會來了。／会已经开完了,他大概不会来了。

你大概不認識他吧,他是我哥哥。／你大概不认识他吧,他是我哥哥。

43.	重男輕女	重男轻女	zhòng nán qīng nǚ		to regard males as superior to females
44.	女子		nǚzǐ	n	(formal) woman
45.	出嫁		chū jià	v	(of a woman) to get married
46.	服從	服从	fúcóng	v	to obey
47.	婚姻		hūnyīn	n	marriage
48.	由		yóu	prep	by; up to (indicating agency in written Chinese)

▼▼▼▼▼▼▼▼▼▼▼▼▼▼▼▼▼▼▼▼▼▼▼▼▼▼

49.	做主		zuò zhǔ	vo	decide; take the responsibility for a decision (lit., "act as the master")
50.	指腹為婚	指腹为婚	zhǐ fù wéi hūn		to arrange a marriage (for the sake of the unborn child)
51.	未婚夫		wèihūnfū	n	fiancé
52.	甚至		shènzhì	adv	even; even to the point [see G4]
53.	木刻		mùkè		carved in wood; wood carving
54.	變化	变化	biànhuà	n/v	change; to change
55.	城市*		chéngshì	n	city
56.	機會	机会	jīhuì	n	opportunity

你最近有機會去東岸嗎？/ 你最近有机会去东岸吗？

去中國工作是提高中文水平的好機會。

去中国工作是提高中文水平的好机会。

57.	同工同酬		tóng gōng tóng chóu		equal pay for equal work
58.	改革開放	改革开放	gǎigé kāifàng		to reform and open up
59.	突出		tūchū	adj/v	be prominent; to stand out
60.	升學	升学	shēng xué	vo	to advance to a higher level of schooling
61.	女生		nǚshēng	n	female student
62.	男生		nánshēng	n	male student
63.	出現	出现	chūxiàn	v	to arise; to appear

最近這兒出現了一些奇怪的現象。/ 最近这儿出现了一些奇怪的现象。

最近他們倆在生活中出現了一些矛盾。

最近他们俩在生活中出现了一些矛盾。

64.	人數	人数	rénshù	n	number of people
65.	明顯	明显	míngxiǎn	adj	obvious
66.	減少	减少	jiǎnshǎo	v	to decrease
67.	年輕	年轻	niánqīng	adj	young

68.	夫婦	夫妇	fūfù	n	husband and wife
69.	大部份	大部分	dà bùfen		majority
70.	照顧	照顾	zhàogu	v	to take care of; to look after
71.	妻子		qīzi	n	wife
72.	體現	体现	tǐxiàn	v	to embody; to manifest

PROPER NOUN

| 宋朝 | | Sòngcháo | Song dynasty (960–1279) |

ENLARGED CHARACTERS FOR EASIER VIEWING AND COMPARING

| 懷 | 辭 | 護 | 擔 | 職 | 隨 |
| 怀 | 辞 | 护 | 担 | 职 | 随 |

| 斷 | 範 | 鼠 | 酬 | 顯 | 顧 |
| 断 | 凡 | 鼠 | 酬 | 显 | 顾 |

模範夫妻 / 模范夫妻

Grammar

1. 同樣／同样 AND 一樣／一样

同樣／同样 is a pre-nominal modifier, i.e., it always appears before the nouns that it modifies, whereas 一樣／一样 is used as a predicate or complement.

(1)   A: 這本字典的價錢跟那本一樣。／这本字典的价钱跟那本一样。

           The price of this dictionary is the same as that one.

      B: 我想用同樣的價錢, 也買一本你這樣的字典。

            我想用同样的价钱, 也买一本你这样的字典。

           I'd like to pay the same amount [of money] for a dictionary like yours.

(2)   A: 我跟我同屋對很多問題的看法一樣。

            我跟我同屋对很多问题的看法一样。

           My roommate and I share the same point of view on many issues.

      B: 你們常常看同樣的書, 看法一樣一點也不奇怪。

            你们常常看同样的书, 看法一样一点也不奇怪。

           You often read the same books. No wonder you have the same opinions.

(3)   姐姐跟妹妹長得一樣。／姐姐跟妹妹长得一样。

      The older sister looks exactly like the younger one.

(4)   哥哥和弟弟在一個班, 上同樣的課。

      哥哥和弟弟在一个班, 上同样的课。

      The brothers are in the same class and take the same courses.

2. 隨著…／随着 … (ALONG WITH…; FOLLOWING …; IN CONJUNCTION WITH…)

隨著／随着 is used in a subordinate clause to indicate a changed circumstance. The main clause introduces a corresponding development.

(1)   隨著經濟的發展, 人民的生活水平也提高了。

      随着经济的发展, 人民的生活水平也提高了。

      With economic development, people's living standards improved as well.

(2)　隨著他們交往的時間越長, 兩個人相處得越好。

　　隨着他们交往的时间越长, 两个人相处得越好。

The longer they socialize together, the better they get along with each other.

(3)　隨著他中文水平的提高, 他看中文報的速度越來越快。

　　随着他中文水平的提高, 他看中文报的速度越来越快。

As his proficiency in Chinese improves, he is able to read Chinese newspapers faster and faster.

3. 在...方面 (IN THE AREA OF; AS FOR)

在...方面 mainly denotes an aspect or scope. Verbs and some disyllabic abstract nouns can be inserted between 在 and 方面.

(1)　在男女平等方面, 這個國家還有很大的問題。

　　在男女平等方面, 这个国家还有很大的问题。

In the area of gender equity, there is still a big problem in this country.

(2)　在穿的方面, 他不太在乎, 可是在吃的方面, 他非常挑剔。

He's not too particular about clothes, but he's very finicky about food.

(3)　在體育運動方面, 中國最近幾年發展很快。

　　在体育运动方面, 中国最近几年发展很快。

China has advanced a great deal in sports in recent years.

(4)　MIT可以說是在工程技術方面最有名的大學了。

　　MIT可以说是在工程技术方面最有名的大学了。

MIT can be said to be the most famous college in the area of engineering and technology.

4. 甚至

The conjunction 甚至 is used to single out an item for emphasis in order to stress the speaker's point of view:

(1)　弟弟很聰明, 才五歲, 不但能看書, 甚至能寫詩。

　　弟弟很聪明, 才五岁, 不但能看书, 甚至能写诗。

▼▼▼

My younger brother is really bright. He's only five, but he can read and even write poetry.

(Writing poetry is used to demonstrate his intelligence.)

(2)　　他很會做中國菜, 甚至連月餅都會做。

　　　　他很会做中国菜, 甚至连月饼都会做。

He's good at making Chinese food. He even knows how to make moon cakes.

(His ability to make moon cakes, which are almost always store bought in China, shows he really knows how to make Chinese food.)

(3)　　A:　你看過電影《白毛女》嗎? / 你看过电影《白毛女》吗?

Have you seen the movie, *The White-Haired Girl*?

　　　　B:　沒有, 什麼《白毛女》? 我甚至都沒聽說過。

　　　　　　没有, 什么《白毛女》? 我甚至都没听说过。

No. What *White-Haired Girl*? I've never even heard of it.

(The speaker has never heard of the film, let alone seen it.)

(4)　　他對中國的節日一點都不清楚, 甚至連春節都不知道。

　　　　他对中国的节日一点都不清楚, 甚至连春节都不知道。

He doesn't know anything about Chinese holidays. He hasn't even heard of the Spring Festival.

(His ignorance of the most well-known holiday, the Spring Festival, shows how little he knows about Chinese holidays.)

Note: 甚至 is often used together with 連...也/都... / 连...也/都...

5. WORD ORDER IN CHINESE (III)

We have already discussed Chinese word order in previous lessons. In this lesson we will summarize what we have learned. The normal word order in Chinese is:

(attributive) subj.—time—place—other adverbials—verb—complement—(attributive) obj.

Here, by complement we mean resultative complements and directional complements (for the position of directional complements and objects, see G4 of Lesson 6 and G5 of Lesson 7.) When there is a complement introduced by 得 and an object at the same time, one must repeat the verb. Similarly, if a phrase after a verb indicates the duration of the action or the number of times it has occurred, one must repeat the verb.

(1)   我昨天在電影院看了一個新電影。／我昨天在电影院看了一个新电影。

I saw a new [newly-released] movie at the movie theater yesterday.

(2)   明天我上完課就去圖書館。／明天我上完课就去图书馆。

Tomorrow I'll go to the library as soon as classes are over.

(3)   他學中文學了三年多了。／他学中文学了三年多了。

He has been studying Chinese for more than three years now.

(4)   我寫字寫得很慢。／我写字写得很慢。

I write (Chinese characters) very slowly.

If somebody or something has already been mentioned, under normal circumstances we should treat the noun denoting that person or thing as a topic and put it at the beginning of the sentence, or after 把.

(5)   你告訴我的那件事情我已經知道了。

你告诉我的那件事情我已经知道了。

The thing that you told me about, I already knew.

(6)   請你把桌子上的地圖給我。／请你把桌子上的地图给我。

Please give me the map that is on the table.

誰在家裏帶孩子？／谁在家里带孩子？

▼▼▼▼▼▼▼▼▼▼▼▼▼▼▼▼▼▼▼▼▼▼▼▼▼▼▼▼▼▼▼▼▼▼▼▼▼▼

Important Words & Phrases

1. 反過來 / 反过来 (CONVERSELY)

EXAMPLE: 可是反過來, 讓男的在家裏帶孩子, 也不見得公平。

可是反过来, 让男的在家里带孩子, 也不见得公平。

(1) 小明, 妹妹罵你當然不對, ＿＿＿＿＿＿＿＿＿＿＿＿＿。(你打她)

小明, 妹妹骂你当然不对, ＿＿＿＿＿＿＿＿＿＿＿＿＿。(你打她)

(2) 丈夫不做家務事當然不好, 可是,＿＿＿＿＿＿＿＿＿＿。(妻子不體貼丈夫)

丈夫不做家务事当然不好, 可是,＿＿＿＿＿＿＿＿＿＿。(妻子不体贴丈夫)

(3) 我認為大國不應該打小國,＿＿＿＿＿＿＿＿＿＿＿。(小國不講道理)

我认为大国不应该打小国,＿＿＿＿＿＿＿＿＿＿＿。(小国不讲道理)

2. 實際上 / 实际上 (ACTUALLY, IN FACT, IN REALITY)

EXAMPLE: 實際上, 男女不平等的現象還有很多。比如, 做同樣的工作, 女的薪水往往比男的少。

实际上, 男女不平等的现象还有很多。比如, 做同样的工作, 女的薪水往往比男的少。

(1) 很多人以為張天華和湯姆是因為文化背景不同分手的。

＿＿＿＿＿＿＿＿＿,＿＿＿＿＿＿＿＿＿＿＿＿＿＿＿。

很多人以为张天华和汤姆是因为文化背景不同分手的。

＿＿＿＿＿＿＿＿＿,＿＿＿＿＿＿＿＿＿＿＿＿＿＿＿。

(2) 報上文章說中國菜太油,＿＿＿＿＿＿＿＿, ＿＿＿＿＿＿＿＿＿。

报上文章说中国菜太油,＿＿＿＿＿＿＿＿, ＿＿＿＿＿＿＿＿＿。

(3) 有人說身上戴個荷包就不會生病,＿＿＿＿＿＿＿＿＿＿＿＿,

＿＿＿＿＿＿＿＿＿＿＿＿＿＿＿＿＿＿＿＿＿＿＿＿＿。

有人说身上戴个荷包就不会生病,＿＿＿＿＿＿＿＿＿＿＿＿,

＿＿＿＿＿＿＿＿＿＿＿＿＿＿＿＿＿＿＿＿＿＿＿＿＿。

3. 就拿...來說 / 就拿...来说 (TAKE SOMEBODY OR SOMETHING FOR EXAMPLE)

EXAMPLE: ...在家庭裏,男女已經很平等了。就拿我家來說吧,我爸爸跟媽媽
           分擔家務 ...。

          ...在家庭里,男女已经很平等了。就拿我家来说吧,我爸爸跟妈妈
           分担家务 ...。

(1) 天華和她男朋友的興趣非常不一樣。＿＿＿＿＿＿＿＿＿＿＿＿,

＿＿＿＿＿＿＿＿＿＿＿＿＿＿＿＿＿＿＿。

天华和她男朋友的兴趣非常不一样。＿＿＿＿＿＿＿＿＿＿＿＿,

＿＿＿＿＿＿＿＿＿＿＿＿＿＿＿＿＿＿＿。

(2) 張天明買衣服很挑剔。＿＿＿＿＿＿＿＿＿,＿＿＿＿＿＿＿＿＿＿＿。(牌子)

張天明买衣服很挑剔。＿＿＿＿＿＿＿＿＿,＿＿＿＿＿＿＿＿＿＿＿。(牌子)

(3) 南京有許多的名勝古蹟。＿＿＿＿＿＿＿＿＿＿,＿＿＿＿＿＿＿＿＿＿＿,很吸引
人。(夫子廟)

南京有许多的名胜古迹。＿＿＿＿＿＿＿＿＿＿,＿＿＿＿＿＿＿＿＿＿＿,很吸引
人。(夫子庙)

▼▼▼

4. 明顯 / 明显 (APPRECIABLY; OBVIOUSLY)

EXAMPLE:　職位高的婦女人數明顯減少了。／职位高的妇女人数明显减少了。

(1)　這幾年＿＿＿＿＿＿＿＿＿＿。(中國人的生活水平提高)

　　這几年＿＿＿＿＿＿＿＿＿。(中国人的生活水平提高)

(2)　最近十幾年來,＿＿＿＿＿＿＿＿＿＿＿＿＿＿＿＿＿＿。
(很多國家婦女的地位提高了)

　　最近十几年来,＿＿＿＿＿＿＿＿＿＿＿＿＿＿＿＿＿＿。
(很多国家妇女的地位提高了)

(3)　那個孩子最近電視看得太多,＿＿＿＿＿＿＿＿＿＿。(學習受影響)

　　那个孩子最近电视看得太多,＿＿＿＿＿＿＿＿＿。(学习受影响)

5. COMPARE ...以後 / 以后 AND ...以來 / 以来

... 以後 / 以后 (after a certain point in time), e.g.,

(1)　上大學以後, 我們一直沒有見過她。

　　上大学以后, 我们一直没有见过她。

(2)　她跟我吵架以後, 我就不喜歡她了。／她跟我吵架以后, 我就不喜欢她了。

(3)　一上大學我們就住在一個宿舍, 一年以後我搬走了。

　　一上大学我们就住在一个宿舍, 一年以后我搬走了。

... 以來 / 以来 (from a certain point in the past to the present), e.g.,

(1)　我跟他認識以來, 從來沒有見他吸過煙。

　　我跟他认识以来, 从来没有见他吸过烟。

(2)　開學以來, 我一直沒有見過她。／开学以来, 我一直没有见过她。

(3)　畢業以來, 他已經換了五個工作了。／毕业以来, 他已经换了五个工作了。

Pinyin Texts

DIALOGUE

Lìshā:	Tiānmíng, zuótiān wǎnshang wǒ gāozhōng de yí ge nǚ tóngxué lái diànhuà, shuō tā huái le yùn, kuài shēng háizi le. Tā yǐjīng bǎ gōngzuò cí le, dāi zài jiālǐ zuò qǐ jiātíng zhǔfù lái le.
Zhāng Tiānmíng:	Zhè bù hěn hǎo ma?
Lìshā:	Hǎo shénme? Tā shì hùshi, cái gōngzuò yì nián. Zhēn bù gōngpíng, shēng háizi shì zhěnggè shèhuì de shì, wèishénme dànzi dōu zài nǚrén shēnshang?
Zhāng Tiānmíng:	Lìshā, nǐ zhème shuō, wǒ kàn yǒu diǎn méi dàoli. Nándào ràng wǒmen nánrén shēng háizi ma?
Lìshā:	Shéi ràng nǐmen shēng háizi le? Wǒ de yìsi shì, yí ge nǚrén shēng le háizi yǐhòu, bùguǎn tā yuànyì bu yuànyì, dōu děi cí le gōngzuò zài jiālǐ dài háizi. Zhè bú shì tài bù gōngpíng le ma? Wèi shénme bú ràng zhàngfu zài jiālǐ dài háizi ne?
Zhāng Tiānmíng:	Nǐ zhēnde zhème xiǎng ma? Ràng nǚde cí zhí, dāi zài jiālǐ dāngrán bù hǎo; kěshì fǎn guò lái, ràng nán de zài jiālǐ dài háizi, yě bú jiàn de gōngpíng. Yīnggāi xiǎng yí ge gèng hǎo de bànfǎ lái jiějué zhè ge wèntí.
Lìshā:	Děng nǐ xiǎng chū hǎo bànfǎ yǐhòu, kǒngpà wǒ dōu lǎo le. Shíjì shang, nánnǚ bù píngděng de xiànxiàng hái yǒu hěn duō. Bǐrú, zuò tóngyàng de gōngzuò, nǚ de xīnshui wǎngwǎng bǐ nán de shǎo.
Zhāng Tiānmíng:	Zhè dào shì.
Lìshā:	Háiyǒu, zài Měiguó dāng zhǔguǎn de, yǒu jǐ ge shì nǚ de? Zhíwèi yuè gāo, fùnǚ yuè shǎo, zhè bú shì qíshì fùnǚ ma?
Zhāng Tiānmíng:	Nǐ shuō de yǒu dàoli. Búguò, wǒ xiǎng suízhe shèhuì de fāzhǎn, fùnǚ de dìwèi huì búduàn dédào tígāo de.
Lìshā:	Wǒ bú xiàng nǐ nàme lèguān.
Zhāng Tiānmíng:	Ài, Lìshā, wǒ juéde zài jiātíng li, nánnǚ yǐjīng hěn píngděng le. Jiù ná wǒ jiā lái shuō ba, wǒ bàba gēn māma fēndān jiāwù, jiàoyù háizi yě zhǔyào shì bàba. Qīnqi péngyou dōu shuō wǒ bàba shì yí ge mófàn zhàngfu.
Lìshā:	Wǒ kàn nǐ jiěfu duì nǐ jiějie yě hěn tǐtiē.
Zhāng Tiānmíng:	Wǒ jiěfu bǐ wǒ bàba gèng "mófàn", jiàn le jiějie, jiù xiàng lǎoshǔ jiàn le māo. Wǒ hěn kàn bu guàn.
Lìshā:	Nánnǚ píngděng zhège wèntí, dàgài shì hěn nán tǎolùn qīngchu de.

READING

Zài lìshǐ shang, tèbié shì cóng Sòngcháo kāishǐ, Zhōngguó jiùshì yí ge zhòng nán qīng nǚ de shèhuì. Zài jiālǐ, nǚzǐ chū jià yǐqián yào fúcóng fùqīn, chū jià yǐhòu yào fúcóng zhàngfu, zhàngfu sǐ le hái yào fúcóng érzi. Nàge shíhou, hūnyīn wánquán yóu fùmǔ zuò zhǔ, yǒude hái zhǐ fù wéi hūn. Yǒude dìfang, rúguǒ nǚháir hái méi zhǎng dà, wèihūnfū jiù sǐ le, jiù bú ràng zhège nǚháir gēn bié rén jié hūn, shènzhì jiào sǐ le wèihūnfū de nǚháir gēn yí ge mùkè de "nánrén" jié hūn.

Wǔshí niándài kāishǐ, Zhōngguó fùnǚ de qíngkuàng yǒu le hěn dà de biànhuà. Tèbié shì zài chéngshì li, nǚháizi hé nánháizi yíyàng yǒu shòu jiàoyù de jīhuì; zài gōngzuò fāngmiàn, tóng gōng tóng chóu; fùnǚ de shèhuì dìwèi yě yǒu hěn dà de tígāo.

Dànshì, gǎigé kāifàng yǐlái, nánnǚ bù píngděng de wèntí yòu tūchū qilai. Bǐrú, shēng xué huò zhǎo gōngzuò de shíhou, nǚshēng dōu bǐ nánshēng nán de duō; zài yìxiē gōngchǎng hé gōngsī yòu chūxiàn le tóng gōng bù tóng chóu de xiànxiàng; zhíwèi gāo de fùnǚ rénshù míngxiǎn jiǎnshǎo le. Búguò, zài yìbān niánqīng de fūfù zhōng, dà bùfen zhàngfu shífēn tǐtiē, zhàogu qīzi. Suǒyǐ, yěxǔ jiātíng shì nánnǚ píngděng tǐxiàn de zuì duō de dìfang.

Discussion Topic: Gender Equality

What examples did Lisa and Tianming use when commenting on equality of the sexes? What does it mean for men and women to be equal?

第十六課 ▲ 健康與保險

看哪一科?

張天明： 麗莎,這個星期五我不能陪你去看電影了,我得去機場接我姑媽,
　　　　她要來我們大學醫院看病。

麗莎： 哪個姑媽?

張天明： 多倫多的那個。

麗莎： 她為什麼不在加拿大看病?我聽說加拿大的醫療保險很好,醫
　　　　院也不錯。她來這兒看病不是得自己花錢嗎?

張天明： 加拿大的保險制度是不錯,人人都有保險。可是如果不是急病
　　　　的話,看病得等很長時間。我姑媽的心臟病雖然不太嚴重,可是
　　　　她不願意再等下去了。加上她聽說我們學校醫院的心臟科很有名,
　　　　所以決定來這兒做手術。聽說很多加拿大人來美國看病。

麗莎： 可是,如果你是個窮人的話,你就會覺得美國的醫療制度不如加
　　　　拿大的好,因為在加拿大至少你不必擔心付不起醫療費。

張天明： 在美國,政府每年拿出很多錢照顧窮人。你沒有錢醫院也會給
　　　　你看病。

麗莎： 能得到政府幫助的人畢竟很少。很多人沒有買保險,有了病,受了
　　　　傷,也不敢看醫生,等病重了才去看。有保險的人,保險費越來越高,
　　　　實際上是替那些沒有保險的人付醫藥費。

第十六课 ▲ 健康与保险

🔘 **DIALOGUE**

张天明： 丽莎,这个星期五我不能陪你去看电影了,我得去机场接我姑妈,她要来我们大学医院看病。

丽莎： 哪个姑妈?

张天明： 多伦多的那个。

丽莎： 她为什么不在加拿大看病?我听说加拿大的医疗保险很好,医院也不错。她来这儿看病不是得自己花钱吗?

张天明： 加拿大的保险制度是不错,人人都有保险。可是如果不是急病的话,看病得等很长时间。我姑妈的心脏病虽然不太严重,可是她不愿意再等下去了。加上她听说我们学校医院的心脏科很有名,所以决定来这儿做手术。听说很多加拿大人来美国看病。

丽莎： 可是,如果你是个穷人的话,你就会觉得美国的医疗制度不如加拿大的好,因为在加拿大至少你不必担心付不起医疗费。

张天明： 在美国,政府每年拿出很多钱照顾穷人。你没有钱医院也会给你看病。

丽莎： 能得到政府帮助的人毕竟很少。很多人没有买保险,有了病,受了伤,也不敢看医生,等病重了才去看。有保险的人,保险费越来越高,实际上是替那些没有保险的人付医药费。

張天明： 如果你有工作，工作單位會給你買保險，你自己只出一部份。

麗莎： 可是不是所有的單位都給它的工作人員買保險。而且"羊毛出在羊身上"，公司會提高產品價格，再把錢賺回來，最後還是咱們自己出錢。這也正是美國藥比別的國家貴的原因。

張天明： 你說的不錯。可是你也得讓製藥公司有錢可賺哪！要不然美國怎麼會有世界上最好的藥呢？

麗莎： 如果你沒有錢的話，藥無論多好，對你也是毫無意義的。反正我覺得美國的保險制度應該改革。對了，你姑媽什麼時候動手術？

張天明： 還不知道呢。你想不想見她？她以前在台灣還是個電影明星呢。聽我爸爸說，她拍了很多武打片。

麗莎： 是嗎？那我真想見見她，我們星期六請她吃飯怎麼樣？

張天明： 好啊。就這麼說定了。

羊毛出在羊身上？

张天明： 如果你有工作，工作单位会给你买保险，你自己只出一部份。

丽莎： 可是不是所有的单位都给它的工作人员买保险。而且"羊毛出在羊身上"，公司会提高产品价格，再把钱赚回来，最后还是咱们自己出钱。这也正是美国药比别的国家贵的原因。

张天明： 你说的不错。可是你也得让制药公司有钱可赚哪！要不然美国怎么会有世界上最好的药呢？

丽莎： 如果你没有钱的话，药无论多好，对你也是毫无意义的。反正我觉得美国的保险制度应该改革。对了，你姑妈什么时候动手术？

张天明： 还不知道呢。你想不想见她？她以前在台湾还是个电影明星呢。听我爸爸说，她拍了很多武打片。

丽莎： 是吗？那我真想见见她，我们星期六请她吃饭怎么样？

张天明： 好啊。就这么说定了。

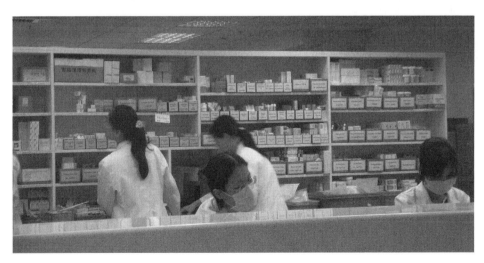

各種各樣的藥／各种各样的药

READING

　　在現在的世界上，當然還有人在為吃飯發愁。可是對不少人來說，他們擔心的已經不是營養不足，而是營養過剩的問題。隨著生活水平的提高，人們越來越關心自己的健康與身材。吃素的人越來越多，另外也有不少人減肥。可是有些人過份節食，結果患上營養不良症。營養專家指出，應該注意攝取多種營養，因為只有營養均衡，才能保證身體健康。

READING

在现在的世界上，当然还有人在为吃饭发愁。可是对不少人来说，他们担心的已经不是营养不足，而是营养过剩的问题。随着生活水平的提高，人们越来越关心自己的健康与身材。吃素的人越来越多，另外也有不少人减肥。可是有些人过份节食，结果患上营养不良症。营养专家指出，应该注意摄取多种营养，因为只有营养均衡，才能保证身体健康。

VOCABULARY

1.	與	与	yǔ	conj	(formal) and
2.	保險*	保险	bǎoxiǎn	n/v	insurance; to insure
3.	醫院	医院	yīyuàn	n	hospital
4.	看病*		kàn bìng	vo	to see a doctor
5.	醫療	医疗	yīliáo	n	medical treatment
6.	花錢*	花钱	huā qián	vo	to spend money
7.	制度		zhìdù	n	system
8.	急病		jíbìng	n	serious illness; illness that needs immediate medical attention
9.	心臟病	心脏病	xīnzàng bìng		heart disease

太太得了心臟病,他很著急。／太太得了心脏病,他很着急。

10.	嚴重	严重	yánzhòng	adj	serious; grave

孩子不能上學是一個嚴重的問題。／孩子不能上学是一个严重的问题。

奶奶的病很嚴重。／奶奶的病很严重。

11.	加上		jiāshàng	vc	to add to; in addition
12.	心臟科	心脏科	xīnzàng kē		cardiology department
13.	有名		yǒumíng	adj	famous
14.	決定	决定	juédìng	v/n	to decide; decision

他決定大學畢業以後上醫學院。／他决定大学毕业以后上医学院。

我們討論以後,做出了一個重要的決定。

我们讨论以后,做出了一个重要的决定。

15.	手術	手术	shǒushù	n	surgery
16.	窮人	穷人	qióngrén	n	poor people
17.	不如		bùrú		not as... [see G4]

18.	至少		zhìshǎo	adv	at least
19.	不必		búbì		not necessary; no need to

老師病了,今天我們不必考試了。

老师病了,今天我们不必考试了。

他的事你不必操心。

20.	擔心*	担心	dān xīn	vo	to worry
21.	付*		fù	v	to pay
22.	付不起		fù bu qǐ	vc	cannot afford [see G6]
23.	...費*	...费	fèi		fee
24.	政府		zhèngfǔ	n	government
25.	畢竟	毕竟	bìjìng	adv	after all
26.	受傷*	受伤	shòu shāng	vo	to get wounded; to be injured
27.	替		tì	prep	for; on behalf of
28.	所有		suǒyǒu		all
29.	單位	单位	dānwèi	n	(work) unit
30.	一部份	一部分	yí bùfen		one part
31.	人員	人员	rényuán	n	personnel; staff
32.	羊毛		yángmáo	n	wool; fleece
33.	出		chū	v	to come out; to appear
34.	產品	产品	chǎnpǐn	n	product
35.	價格	价格	jiàgé	n	price (formal)
36.	藥*	药	yào	n	medicine
37.	原因		yuányīn	n	cause; reason
38.	製藥	制药	zhì yào	vo	to manufacture drugs
39.	毫無	毫无	háowú		not an iota; not in the least

40.	意義	意义	yìyì	n	sense; meaning
41.	動手術	动手术	dòng shǒushù	vo	to have an operation; to perform an operation
42.	明星		míngxīng	n	"bright star"; (movie, etc.) star
43.	拍		pāi	v	to make (a film); to shoot (a film, photograph)

拍電影; 拍電視; 拍攝 (shè) ／ 拍电影; 拍电视; 拍摄 (shè)

| 44. | 武打片 | | wǔdǎpiàn | n | martial arts movie |
| 45. | 發愁 | 发愁 | fā chóu | vo | worry |

他畢業以後一直找不到工作, 每天都在發愁。

他毕业以后一直找不到工作, 每天都在发愁。

他發愁的不是工作, 而是孩子的教育。

他发愁的不是工作, 而是孩子的教育。

46.	營養	营养	yíngyǎng	n	nutrition; nourishment
47.	不足		bùzú	adj	not sufficient; not enough
48.	過剩	过剩	guòshèng	v	excess; surplus
49.	水平		shuǐpíng	n	(water) level; standard
50.	關心	关心	guān xīn	vo	to be concerned with/about

營養不良 vs. 營養過剩 ／ 营养不良 vs. 营养过剩

51.	身材		shēncái	n	bodily figure
52.	吃素*		chī sù	vo	to eat vegetarian food; to be a vegetarian
53.	減肥	减肥	jiǎn féi	vo	to lose weight
54.	過份	过分	guòfèn	adj	excessive
55.	節食	节食	jiéshí	v	to restrict one's food intake; to be on a diet
56.	患		huàn	v	to contract (an illness)
57.	營養不良	营养不良	yíngyǎng bùliáng		malnutrition
58.	...症		zhèng		disease; symptoms
59.	專家	专家	zhuānjiā	n	expert
60.	指出		zhǐchū	vc	to point out
61.	注意		zhùyì	v	to pay attention to

上課應該注意聽課, 這樣可以節省很多時間。

上课应该注意听课, 这样可以节省很多时间。

這件事已經引起學校的注意。／这件事已经引起学校的注意。

62.	攝取	摄取	shèqǔ	v	to absorb, assimilate (nutrients, water, etc.)
63.	只有		zhǐyǒu	conj	only if
64.	均衡		jūnhéng	adj	balanced; proportionate
65.	保證	保证	bǎozhèng	v/n	to guarantee; guarantee

這本書我保證你喜歡。／这本书我保证你喜欢。

健康是成功的保證之一。(成功: success)

健康是成功的保证之一。

PROPER NOUNS

1.	多倫多	多伦多	Duōlúnduō	Toronto
2.	加拿大		Jiā'nádà	Canada
3.	台灣*	台湾	Táiwān	Taiwan

▼▼

ENLARGED CHARACTERS FOR EASIER VIEWING AND COMPARING

醫　療　臟　窮　費　製　藥　養　攝　衡

医　疗　脏　穷　费　制　药　养　摄　衡

Grammar

1. MULTIPLE ATTRIBUTIVES

A noun can be preceded by several attributives. The order of attributives follows certain rules. First, descriptive attributives must appear after those that denote possession or other non-descriptive attributives. Numerals plus measure words, and demonstrative pronouns plus measure words, are sandwiched between these descriptive and non-descriptive attributives.

(1)　在中國, 我們遊覽了北京的幾個最大的公園, 以及南京的那個有名的
　　　夫子廟。

　　　在中国, 我们游览了北京的几个最大的公园, 以及南京的那个有名的
　　　夫子庙。

　　　In China we toured several of the biggest parks in Beijing and that famous Confucian Temple in Nanjing.

北京 and 南京 indicate places; they are non-descriptive. They appear first. 最大 and 有名 are descriptive. They appear last. 幾個／几个 and 那個／那个 are inserted between these two kinds of attributives. More examples:

(2)　媽媽昨天給妹妹講了一個非常有意思的故事。

　　　妈妈昨天给妹妹讲了一个非常有意思的故事。

　　　Yesterday Mother told my younger sister a very interesting story.

(3)　我給姐姐買的那件襯衫很漂亮。

　　　我给姐姐买的那件衬衫很漂亮。

　　　The shirt that I bought for my older sister was very pretty.

(4)　我從來不看電視裏播的那些亂七八糟的新聞。

　　　我从来不看电视里播的那些乱七八糟的新闻。

　　　I never watch those junky news (programs) on TV.

▼▼

Among descriptive attributives, attributives that do not require 的 are closest to the nouns that they modify, e.g., 好的中文老師／好的中文老师 (a good Chinese teacher), 很新的木頭椅子／很新的木头椅子 (a very new wooden chair). When both attributives are adjectives, simple adjectives follow more complex ones, e.g., 窄窄的小河 (a little narrow river), 胖胖的圓臉／胖胖的圆脸 (a chubby round face), 很大的綠樹／很大的绿树 (a huge green tree). Finally, when both attributives are adjectives, those that describe colors follow other kinds of adjectives, e.g., 大紅毛衣／大红毛衣 (a big red shirt), 小白貓／小白猫 (a small white cat).

2. 是 (shì) INDICATING EMPHASIS OR CONFIRMATION

In Chinese when the predicate of a sentence is an adjective, there is no need for a linking verb before it. Only when we wish to reaffirm a point, do we use 是 before the adjective. In this context 是 receives its full fourth tone to indicate stress.

(1) A: 今天天氣不錯。／今天天气不错。

The weather today is rather nice.

B: 今天天氣是不錯, 咱們出去玩玩吧?

今天天气是不错, 咱们出去玩玩吧?

The weather today *is* rather nice. Shall we go out and play?

(2) 你剛才說現在男女不平等。對, 現在男女是還不夠平等, 可是已經比從前好多了。

你刚才说现在男女不平等。对, 现在男女是还不够平等, 可是已经比从前好多了。

You just said that men and women are unequal today. You're right. There is gender inequity today, but it's much better than before.

(3) A: 這個女孩鋼琴彈(tán)得真好。／这个女孩钢琴弹(tán)得真好。

This girl plays the piano really well.

B: 她鋼琴彈得是好, 連我都被她吸引住了。

她钢琴弹得是好, 连我都被她吸引住了。

She does play the piano well. Even I was captivated by her.

3. REDUPLICATION OF MEASURE WORDS

Measure words can be reduplicated to stress all inclusiveness or universality among constituent elements of a collective entity. In other words, all the individual members of a group share the same qualities or exist in the same state. The emphasis, therefore, is on commonality. A few nouns like 人, 年, and 天 can also be reduplicated.

(1)   今天過年, 人人都很高興。／今天过年, 人人都很高兴。

   (emphasizes commonality)

   Today is New Year's Day. Everybody is very happy.

(2)   我們班的學生, 雖然個個都很聰明, 可是不都很用功。

   我们班的学生, 虽然个个都很聪明, 可是不都很用功。

   (emphasizes commonality)

   Although each and every one of the students in our class is very smart, they are not all very hard-working.

(3)   他頓頓飯都吃魚。／他顿顿饭都吃鱼。

   He eats fish at every meal.

A. The word 每 differs from reduplicated measure words. Depending on the context, 每 can imply either commonality or individuality.

(4)   端午節的時候, 每家都吃粽子。／端午节的时候, 每家都吃粽子。

   During the Dragon Boat Festival, every family eats dumplings. (emphasizes commonality)

(5)   我們姐妹三人, 每個人的興趣不同。

   我们姐妹三人, 每个人的兴趣不同。

   Each one of us three sisters has her own interests. (emphasizes individuality)

   *我們姐妹三人, 人人的興趣不同。／*我们姐妹三人, 人人的兴趣不同。

This sentence is incorrect because 人人 emphasizes commonality rather than difference. Note that examples (1) through (4) all denote sameness: each and every person shares the same happy feeling on New Year's Day, each and every student shares the same characteristic of intelligence, each and every meal is fish, and every family eats the same meal during the Dragon Boat Festival. But in example (5), the sisters do not share any common interest. This is why 人人 and 不同 do not belong together, and why 每 has to be used.

B. Unlike 每, reduplicated measure words generally cannot modify an object or serve as an object.

Compare:

(6)　你要把信寄給班上每一個人。／你要把信寄给班上每一个人。

You must send a letter to everyone in our class.

*你要把信寄給班上人人。／*你要把信寄给班上人人。

(7)　請你把信送到每一家的門口。／请你把信送到每一家的门口。

Please deliver the letter to each family's doorstep.

*請你把信送到家家的門口。／*请你把信送到家家的门口。

4. USING 不如 TO MAKE COMPARISONS

不如 can be used to compare, e.g.,

(1)　今天的天氣不如昨天。／今天的天气不如昨天。

The weather today is not as good as yesterday's.

(2)　他覺得美國的健康保險制度不如加拿大好。
他觉得美国的健康保险制度不如加拿大好。

He feels that the American health insurance system is not as good as Canada's.

(3)　這部電影不如昨天看的那部有意思。
这部电影不如昨天看的那部有意思。

This film is not as interesting as the one we saw yesterday.

A. When using 不如, we can omit the adjective 好, as in example (1).

B. The adjectives used in this kind of sentence are usually positive, such as 好 (good), 大 (big), 長／长 (long), 厚 (thick), 重 (heavy), and 亮 (bright), rather than their opposites, 壞／坏 (bad), 小 (small), 短 (short), 薄 (thin), 輕／轻 (light), and 暗 (àn: dark).

(4)　我的成績不如他。／我的成绩不如他。

My grades are not as good as his.

(5)   你的指導教授不如我的指導教授負責任。

   你的指导教授不如我的指导教授负责任。

   Your adviser is not as responsible as mine.

(6)   打字機不如電腦方便。／打字机不如电脑方便。

   Typewriters are not as convenient as computers.

This form is similar to the 沒有 form (see Lesson 13), but 不如 can stand alone. See examples (1) and (4). In that case, it means "not as good as..."

One can also use 不比 to make comparisons. However, 不比 is usually used to contradict someone else's opinion. Usually, there is a previous occurrence of 比.

(7)   A: 我姐姐比你高。／我姐姐比你高。

      My sister is taller than you are.

      B: 不, 你姐姐不比我高。／不, 你姐姐不比我高。

      No, your sister is no taller than I am.

(8)   A: 日文比中文難。／日文比中文难。

      Japanese is more difficult to learn than Chinese.

      B: 我覺得日文不比中文難。／我觉得日文不比中文难。

      I don't think that Japanese is any more difficult to learn than Chinese.

Note that 沒有 and 不比 have quite different meanings. While 沒有 means "not as (much) as," 不比 means "not more than."

(9)   小張沒有你高。／小张没有你高。

   Little Zhang is not as tall as you.

   (You're taller than my sister.)

   小張不比你高。／小张不比你高。

   Little Zhang is no taller than you.

   (Little Zhang is shorter than you or the same height as you.

When making comparisons, we can often omit some words and phrases if the omissions will not lead to any misunderstanding. See examples (1), (2), and (4) above.

▼▼

5. MODAL VERB 會/会

The modal verb 會/会 has several meanings. One common meaning is "to know how to do something by learning," or "to be able to do something after receiving instruction," e.g., 我會説漢語 / 我会说汉语 (I can speak Chinese); 你會開車嗎 / 你会开车吗 (Can you drive?); and 我妹妹不會畫畫兒 / 我妹妹不会画画儿 (My sister doesn't know how to draw). Tasks that one can perform without formal or prior instruction are not expressed with會/会. In this lesson, we introduce a new meaning of 會/会 as indicating future probability.

(1) A: 我沒有錢了, 你説我跟小王借, 他會借給我嗎?

　　　我没有钱了, 你说我跟小王借, 他会借给我吗?

　　　I don't have any money left. Do you think Little Wang would lend some to me if I asked him?

　　B: 我想他會借給你。/ 我想他会借给你。

　　　I think he would.

(2) A: 飛機是九點的, 現在走會晚嗎? / 飞机是九点的, 现在走会晚吗?

　　　The plane is (scheduled for take-off) at nine o'clock. Would it be too late to leave now?

　　B: 別著急, 不會晚。/ 别着急, 不会晚。

　　　Don't worry. [We/you] won't be late.

6. V+不/得+起

The pattern V + 不/得 + 起 is used to tell whether one can afford the money or time.

(1) A: 戲票那麼貴, 他買得起買不起? / 戏票那么贵, 他买得起买不起?

　　　The tickets to the play are so expensive. Can he afford them?

　　B: 我猜他買不起。/ 我猜他买不起。

　　　I guess not.

(2) 多穿點兒, 別病了。我們沒保險, 看不起病。

　　多穿点儿, 别病了。我们没保险, 看不起病。

　　Put on more clothes. Don't get sick. We don't have health insurance and we can't afford to see a doctor.

(3) 那家飯館的菜貴得不得了, 咱們吃不起。

那家饭馆的菜贵得不得了, 咱们吃不起。

That restaurant is impossibly expensive. We can't afford to eat there.

(4) 我每天那麼忙, 你讓我陪你去看電影, 我陪不起。

我每天那么忙, 你让我陪你去看电影, 我陪不起。

I'm so busy every day. I couldn't find the time to go to the movies with you, even if you did ask me.

7. 畢竟 / 毕竟

The adverb 畢竟 is used to mean "after all, in the final analysis" or to emphasize the cause or special characteristics of something.

(1) 你畢竟在家裏常常聽父母説中文, 學中文比我容易多了。

你毕竟在家里常常听父母说中文, 学中文比我容易多了。

After all, you hear your parents speak Chinese at home. For you, learning Chinese is much easier than it is for me.

(2) 媽媽畢竟是媽媽, 怎麼會不愛自己的孩子?

妈妈毕竟是妈妈, 怎么会不爱自己的孩子?

A mom is a mom after all. How could she not love her own kids?

(3) 現在畢竟是春天了, 天氣無論多冷, 也跟冬天不一樣。

现在毕竟是春天了, 天气无论多冷, 也跟冬天不一样。

After all, it's spring now. No matter how cold it is, it's not the same as winter.

Important Words & Phrases

1. 加上 (IN ADDITION)

EXAMPLE: 她不願意等, 加上她聽説我們學校醫院的心臟科很有名, 所以決定來這兒做手術。

她不愿意等, 加上她听说我们学校医院的心脏科很有名, 所以决定来这儿做手术。

(1) 林先生跟林太太賺的錢都很多,＿＿＿＿＿＿＿＿,兩個人日子過得很舒服。(沒有孩子)

　　林先生跟林太太賺的钱都很多,＿＿＿＿＿＿＿＿,两个人日子过得很舒服。(没有孩子)

(2) 他平常營養過剩, 又不運動,＿＿＿＿＿＿＿＿,
大家都很擔心他的身體健康。

　　他平常营养过剩, 又不运动,＿＿＿＿＿＿＿＿,
大家都很担心他的身体健康。

(3) 張先生去世了,＿＿＿＿＿＿＿＿, 張太太一個人在家實在太寂寞了。

　　张先生去世了,＿＿＿＿＿＿＿＿, 张太太一个人在家实在太寂寞了。

2. 至少 (AT LEAST)

EXAMPLE:　在加拿大至少你不必擔心付不起醫療費。

　　　　　在加拿大至少你不必担心付不起医疗费。

(1) 他做事雖然做得很慢,＿＿＿＿＿, 比你只說不做好。(他在做)

　　他做事虽然做得很慢,＿＿＿＿＿, 比你只说不做好。(他在做)

(2) 雖然社會上還有許多男女不平等的現象, 但是＿＿＿＿＿。(比以前好多了)

　　虽然社会上还有许多男女不平等的现象, 但是＿＿＿＿＿。(比以前好多了)

(3) 這次考試他雖然考得不太好, 但是＿＿＿＿＿,不要罵他了。(他復習了)

　　这次考试他虽然考得不太好, 但是＿＿＿＿＿,不要骂他了。(他复习了)

3. 毫無 ／ 毫无 (NOT AT ALL, HAVE NONE WHATSOEVER)

EXAMPLE:　如果你沒有錢的話, 藥無論多好, 對你也是毫無意義的。

　　　　　如果你没有钱的话, 药无论多好, 对你也是毫无意义的。

▼▼▼▼▼▼▼▼▼▼▼▼▼▼▼▼▼▼▼▼▼▼▼▼▼▼▼▼▼▼▼▼

(1) 他的女兒不上學, 也不工作, 但是他＿＿＿＿＿＿。(辦法)

   他的女儿不上学, 也不工作, 但是他＿＿＿＿＿＿。(办法)

(2) 我們已經離婚了, 他跟我之間＿＿＿＿＿＿。(關係)

   我们已经离婚了, 他跟我之间＿＿＿＿＿＿。(关系)

(3) 他大學剛畢業, 也沒實習過,＿＿＿＿＿＿。(工作經驗)

   他大学刚毕业, 也没实习过,＿＿＿＿＿＿。(工作经验)

4. (沒) 有 + N + 可 + V

EXAMPLE: 可是你也得讓製藥公司有錢可賺哪!

   可是你也得让制药公司有钱可赚哪!

(1) 你不是閑著沒事嗎? 咱們明天搬家, 這樣就＿＿＿＿＿＿＿＿。(有事)

   你不是闲着没事吗? 咱们明天搬家, 这样就＿＿＿＿＿＿＿＿。(有事)

(2) 他們的看法太不同了, 坐在一起＿＿＿＿＿＿＿＿。(沒有話)

   他们的看法太不同了, 坐在一起＿＿＿＿＿＿＿＿。(没有话)

(3) 春節快到了, 小朋友＿＿＿＿＿＿＿＿。(有新衣服)

   春节快到了, 小朋友＿＿＿＿＿＿＿＿。(有新衣服)

5. 只有..., 才... (ONLY WHEN...)

EXAMPLE: 只有營養均衡, 才能保證身體健康。

   只有营养均衡, 才能保证身体健康。

(1) 下學期的課只有你的指導教授簽字了, 才能＿＿＿＿＿＿。

   下学期的课只有你的指导教授签字了, 才能＿＿＿＿＿＿。

(2) 在美國只有買了保險才＿＿＿＿＿＿＿＿＿＿。

   在美国只有买了保险才＿＿＿＿＿＿＿＿＿＿。

(3) 這幾年工作不容易找,只有念電腦或者工程技術才＿＿＿＿＿＿＿＿＿＿。

   这几年工作不容易找,只有念电脑或者工程技术才＿＿＿＿＿＿＿＿＿＿。

在美國看病,為什麼發愁?／在美国看病,为什么发愁?

Pinyin Texts

DIALOGUE

Zhāng Tiānmíng: Lìshā, zhège xīngqīwǔ wǒ bù néng péi nǐ qù kàn diànyǐng le, wǒ děi qù jīchǎng jiē wǒ gūmā, tā yào lái wǒmen dàxué yīyuàn kàn bìng.

Lìshā: Nǎge gūmā?

Zhāng Tiānmíng: Duōlúnduō de nàge.

Lìshā: Tā wèishénme bú zài Jiānádà kàn bìng? Wǒ tīngshuō Jiānádà de yīliáo bǎoxiǎn hěn hǎo, yīyuàn yě búcuò. Tā lái zhèr kàn bìng bú shì děi zìjǐ huā qián ma?

Zhāng Tiānmíng:	Jiānádà de bǎoxiǎn zhìdù shì búcuò, rénrén dōu yǒu bǎoxiǎn. Kěshì rúguǒ bú shì jíbìng de huà, kànbìng děi děng hěn cháng shíjiān. Wǒ gūmā de xīnzàng bìng suīrán bú tài yánzhòng, kěshì tā bú yuànyì zài děng xiàqu le. Jiāshàng tā tīngshuō wǒmen xuéxiào yīyuàn de xīnzàng kē hěn yǒumíng, suǒyǐ juédìng lái zhèr zuò shǒushù. Tīngshuō hěn duō Jiānádàrén lái Měiguó kàn bìng.
Lìshā:	Kěshì, rúguǒ nǐ shì ge qióngrén de huà, nǐ jiù huì juéde Měiguó de yīliáo zhìdù bùrú Jiānádà de hǎo, yīnwèi zài Jiānádà zhìshǎo nǐ búbì dān xīn fù bu qǐ yīliáofèi.
Zhāng Tiānmíng:	Zài Měiguó, zhèngfǔ měinián ná chū hěn duō qián zhàogù qióngrén. Nǐ méiyǒu qián yīyuàn yě huì gěi nǐ kàn bìng.
Lìshā:	Néng dé dào zhèngfǔ bāngzhù de rén bìjìng hěn shǎo. Hěn duō rén méiyǒu mǎi bǎoxiǎn, yǒu le bìng, shòu le shāng, yě bù gǎn kàn yīshēng, děng bìng zhòng le cái qù kàn. Yǒu bǎoxiǎn de rén, bǎoxiǎnfèi yuè lái yuè gāo, shíjì shang shì tì nàxiē méiyǒu bǎoxiǎn de rén fù yīyàofèi.
Zhāng Tiānmíng:	Rúguǒ nǐ yǒu gōngzuò, gōngzuò dānwèi huì gěi nǐ mǎi bǎoxiǎn, nǐ zìjǐ zhǐ chū yí bùfen.
Lìshā:	Kěshì búshì suǒyǒu de dānwèi dōu gěi tā de gōngzuò rényuán mǎi bǎoxiǎn. Érqiě "yángmáo chū zài yáng shēnshang", gōngsī huì tígāo chǎnpǐn jiàgé, zài bǎ qián zhuàn huílai, zuìhòu háishi zánmen zìjǐ chū qián. Zhè yě zhèng shì Měiguó yào bǐ bié de guójiā guì de yuányīn.
Zhāng Tiānmíng:	Nǐ shuō de búcuò. Kěshì nǐ yě děi ràng zhǐ yào gōngsī yǒu qián kě zhuàn na! Yàobùrán Měiguó zěnme huì yǒu shìjiè shang zuì hǎo de yào ne?
Lìshā:	Rúguǒ nǐ méiyǒu qián de huà, yào wúlùn duō hǎo, duì nǐ yě shì háo wú yìyì de. Fǎnzhèng wǒ juéde Měiguó de bǎoxiǎn zhìdù yīnggāi gǎigé. Duì le, nǐ gūmā shénme shíhou dòng shǒushù?
Zhāng Tiānmíng:	Hái bù zhīdao ne. Nǐ xiǎng bu xiǎng jiàn tā? Tā yǐqián zài Táiwān háishi ge diànyǐng míngxīng ne. Tīng wǒ bàba shuō, tā pāi le hěn duō wǔdǎpiàn.
Lìshā:	Shì ma? Nà wǒ zhēn xiǎng jiàn jian tā, wǒmen xīngqīliù qǐng tā chī fàn zěnmeyàng?
Zhāng Tiānmíng:	Hǎo a. Jiù zhème shuō dìng le.

 ## READING

     Zài xiànzài de shìjiè shang, dāngrán hái yǒu rén zài wèi chī fàn fāchóu. Kěshì duì bù shǎo rén lái shuō, tāmen dān xīn de yǐjīng bú shì yíngyǎng bùzú, érshì yíngyǎng guòshèng de wèntí. Suízhe shēnghuó shuǐpíng de tígāo, rénmen yuè lái yuè guānxīn zìjǐ de jiànkāng yǔ shēncái. Chī sù de rén yuè lái yuè duō, lìngwài yě yǒu bù shǎo rén jiǎn féi. Kěshì yǒu xiē rén guòfèn jiéshí, jiéguǒ huànshang yíngyǎng bùliáng zhèng. Yíngyǎng zhuānjiā zhǐchū, yīnggāi zhùyì shèqǔ duōzhǒng yíngyǎng, yīnwèi zhǐyǒu yíngyǎng jūnhéng, cái néng bǎozhèng shēntǐ jiànkāng.

Discussion Topic: Medical Care in America

Explain in Chinese why Tianming's aunt is coming to the United States. State whether you think the American model of medical care is better than the Canadian model, and why.

第十七課 ▲ 教育

DIALOGUE

張天明： 姐姐，記得以前爸爸常說，在美國念小學太舒服，太輕鬆了，每天放學以後都沒有什麼功課，他很不以為然。

張天星： 可是老師說，對小孩子，不應該用填鴨式的教育方式。等孩子們長大了，就會比較成熟，自然就會有上進心了。

張天明： 爸爸不同意老師的觀點，認為無論如何，基礎一定得打好。基礎不好，沒有本領，將來用什麼跟人競爭？

張天星： 對了，他還經常跟老師辯論，批評美國的小學教育，不是說老師不夠嚴，就是說學生態度不夠認真。害得老師無話可說，也讓我們很不好意思。

張天明： 我覺得美國的中小學教育的確有一些缺點。

張天星： 但是中國的教育也有問題。我在中國念小學一年級的時候，壓力大得受不了。來美國上小學以後，簡直樂壞了，功課又少，老師也

第十七课 ▲ 教育

🔘 **DIALOGUE**

张天明： 姐姐，记得以前爸爸常说，在美国念小学太舒服，太轻松了，每天放学以后都没有什么功课，他很不以为然。

张天星： 可是老师说，对小孩子，不应该用填鸭式的教育方式。等孩子们长大了，就会比较成熟，自然就会有上进心了。

张天明： 爸爸不同意老师的观点，认为无论如何，基础一定得打好。基础不好，没有本领，将来用什么跟人竞争？

张天星： 对了，他还经常跟老师辩论，批评美国的小学教育，不是说老师不够严，就是说学生态度不够认真。害得老师无话可说，也让我们很不好意思。

张天明： 我觉得美国的中小学教育的确有一些缺点。

张天星： 但是中国的教育也有问题。我在中国念小学一年级的时候，压力大得受不了。来美国上小学以后，简直乐坏了，功课又少，老师也不那麼嚴。但是我得承認,要是沒有爸爸媽媽的督促,只靠在學校學的東西,我上學不會這麼順利。

張天明: 美國的教育重視讓孩子自由發展,發揮孩子的想像力。但是這樣的教育方式並不適合每個孩子。有的孩子不夠自覺,需要老師的指導,要不然很快就會被淘汰。

張天星: 可是中國的教育走另一個極端,從來不考慮學生的特點,對每個學生的要求都一樣,加上升學的壓力,使許多學生變成考試機器,只會死讀書。

張天明: 看來這兩種教育方式各有優缺點。

張天星: 以前我不懂為什麼爸爸媽媽每天都讓我們做那麼多的數學習題,現在才理解他們的苦心。

張天明: 中國人說,"望子成龍,望女成鳳",我們的父母為了子女的教育,實在是用心良苦啊。

認真讀書／认真读书

不那么严。但是我得承认，要是没有爸爸妈妈的督促，只靠在学校学的东西，我上学不会这么顺利。

张天明： 美国的教育重视让孩子自由发展，发挥孩子的想像力。但是这样的教育方式并不适合每个孩子。有的孩子不够自觉，需要老师的指导，要不然很快就会被淘汰。

张天星： 可是中国的教育走另一个极端，从来不考虑学生的特点，对每个学生的要求都一样，加上升学的压力，使许多学生变成考试机器，只会死读书。

张天明： 看来这两种教育方式各有优缺点。

张天星： 以前我不懂，为什么爸爸妈妈每天都让我们做那么多的数学习题，现在才理解他们的苦心。

张天明： 中国人说，"望子成龙，望女成凤"，咱们的父母为了子女的教育，实在是用心良苦啊。

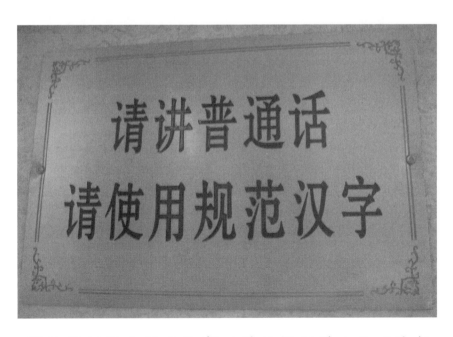

學校督促學生做兩件事／学校督促学生做两件事

READING

　　在中國，學生負擔很重。白天上學，晚上還得上補習班或者請家庭教師，連週末都不能休息。中國的教育目標及方式與美國十分不同。在中國，"升學是教學的指揮棒"，教學總是隨著升學考試走。老師強調死記硬背。家庭作業更是壓得人喘不過氣來。但是學生"尊師重道"，即使有意見也不敢提。在美國，一般來說，老師重視自由發展。強調啟發式教育，鼓勵學生多思考，也很少留家庭作業。許多從中國移民到美國來的家長，以為美式教育能給孩子一個自由、快樂的童年。可是看著孩子放學回家沒什麼功課，他們就擔心孩子的基礎打不好，將來無法跟別人競爭。這時候，他們又想起中國的教育方式來了。

READING

在中国，学生负担很重。白天上学，晚上还得上补习班或者请家庭教师，连周末都不能休息。中国的教育目标及方式与美国十分不同。在中国，"升学是教学的指挥棒"，教学总是随着升学考试走。老师强调死记硬背。家庭作业更是压得人喘不过气来。但是学生"尊师重道"，即使有意见也不敢提。在美国，一般来说，老师重视自由发展。强调启发式教育，鼓励学生多思考，也很少留家庭作业。许多从中国移民到美国来的家长，以为美式教育能给孩子一个自由、快乐的童年。可是看着孩子放学回家没什么功课，他们就担心孩子的基础打不好，将来无法跟别人竞争。这时候，他们又想起中国的教育方式来了。

▼▼▼▼▼▼▼▼▼▼▼▼▼▼▼▼▼▼▼▼▼▼▼▼▼▼▼▼▼▼▼▼

VOCABULARY

1.	小學	小学	xiǎoxué	n	elementary school
2.	輕鬆	轻松	qīngsōng	adj	relaxed; easygoing

他每天工作六小時, 很輕鬆。／他每天工作六小时, 很轻松。

我妹妹很輕鬆地考上了理想的大學。

我妹妹很轻松地考上了理想的大学。

3.	不以為然	不以为然	bù yǐ wéi rán		to disapprove of; to object to [see G1]
4.	填鴨式	填鴨式	tiányāshì		cramming method (in teaching); (lit) "force feeding duck style"
5.	方式		fāngshì	n	method
6.	成熟		chéngshú	adj	mature
7.	自然		zìrán	adj/adv	natural; naturally
8.	上進心	上进心	shàngjìnxīn	n	the desire to be better; aspiration
9.	觀點	观点	guāndiǎn	n	point of view
10.	無論如何	无论如何	wúlùn rúhé		under any circumstances, no matter what
11.	打基礎	打基础	dǎ jīchǔ	vo	to establish a foundation
12.	本領	本领	běnlǐng	n	skill; capability
13.	將來*	将来	jiānglái	t	in the future
14.	競爭	竞争	jìngzhēng	v	to compete

在這個學校裏, 孩子競爭得很厲害。

在这个学校里, 孩子竞争得很厉害。

一個人應該有競爭精神。／一个人应该有竞争精神。

15.	辯論	辩论	biànlùn	v	to debate; to argue

我們明天辯論男女平等的問題。／我们明天辩论男女平等的问题。

你说话没有道理, 我不跟你辩论了。／你说话没有道理, 我不跟你辩论了。

▼▼▼▼▼▼▼▼▼▼▼▼▼▼▼▼▼▼▼▼▼▼▼▼▼▼▼▼▼▼▼▼▼▼▼

16. 批評　批评　pīpíng　v　to criticize

今天老師批評我學習不認真。／今天老师批评我学习不认真。

17. 嚴　严　yán　adj　strict

18. 態度　态度　tàidu　n　attitude

他做什麼事態度都很認真。／他做什么事态度都很认真。

你對奶奶的態度不好, 趕快說對不起。

你对奶奶的态度不好, 赶快说对不起。

19. 認真　认真　rènzhēn　adj　earnest; serious

20. 害　　hài　v　to do harm to; to cause trouble to

21. 的確　的确　díquè　adv　indeed; really

22. 缺點　缺点　quēdiǎn　n　shortcoming

23. 壓力　压力　yālì　n　pressure

24. 簡直　简直　jiǎnzhí　adv　simply [see G2]

25. 樂壞了　乐坏了　lè huài le　vc　to be thrilled to pieces [see G3]

26. 承認　承认　chéngrèn　v　to admit; to acknowledge

他跟父母承認自己錯了。／他跟父母承认自己错了。

你打了他, 怎麼不承認? ／你打了他, 怎么不承认?

27. 督促　　dūcù　v　to supervise and urge

28. 上學　上学　shàng xué　vo　to go to school

29. 重視　重视　zhòngshì　v　to take seriously; to view as important

30. 發揮　发挥　fāhuī　v　to give free rein to

31. 想像力　　xiǎngxiànglì　n　imagination

32. 適合　适合　shìhé　v　to suit; to fit [see G4]

33. 自覺　自觉　zìjué　adj　self-aware; self-motivated

34. 淘汰　　táotài　v　to eliminate through selection or competition

35. 極端　极端　jíduān　n　the extreme; an extreme

36.	特點	特点	tèdiǎn	n	special feature; distinguishing feature
37.	要求		yāoqiú	n	demand
38.	使		shǐ	v	to cause/make (someone do something)
39.	變成	变成	biàn chéng	vc	to change into
40.	機器	机器	jīqì	n	machine; machinery
41.	讀書	读书	dú shū	vo	to study; to read
42.	看來	看来	kànlái		to appear; to seem
43.	優缺點	优缺点	yōuquēdiǎn	n	merits and demerits; advantages and disadvantages
44.	數學	数学	shùxué	n	mathematics
45.	習題	习题	xítí	n	exercises
46.	理解		lǐjiě	v	to understand; to comprehend

你女朋友跟你吵架了，你心情不好，我能理解。

這個孩子的理解力很強。/ 这个孩子的理解力很强。

47.	苦心	苦心	kǔxīn	n	painstaking efforts
48.	望子成龍	望子成龙	wàng zǐ chéng long		hope for one's son to be very successful; (lit) hope for one's son to become a dragon
49.	望女成鳳	望女成凤	wàng nǚ chéng fèng		hope for one's daughter to be very successful; (lit) hope for one's daughter to become a phoenix
50.	子女		zǐnǚ	n	sons and daughters
51.	用心良苦		yòngxīn liángkǔ		have really given much thought to the matter; well-meaning
52.	負擔	负担	fùdān	n	burden; load
53.	白天		báitiān	n	daytime
54.	補習班	补习班	bǔxíbān	n	"cram" school
55.	家庭教師	家庭教师	jiātíng jiàoshī		private tutor

▼▼▼▼▼▼▼▼▼▼▼▼▼▼▼▼▼▼▼▼▼▼▼▼▼▼▼▼▼▼▼▼▼▼

56.	休息		xiūxi	v	to rest
57.	目標	目标	mùbiāo	n	goal; target
58.	及		jí	conj	(formal) and
59.	教學	教学	jiàoxué	n	teaching; education
60.	指揮棒	指挥棒	zhǐhuībàng	n	conductor's baton
61.	強調	强调	qiángdiào	v	to stress; to emphasize
62.	死記硬背	死记硬背	sǐ jì yìng bèi		mechanical memorizing
63.	作業	作业	zuòyè	n	(formal) homework
64.	喘氣	喘气	chuǎn qì	vo	to pant; to gasp for breath
65.	尊師重道	尊师重道	zūn shī zhòng dào		to respect the teacher and value the Way
66.	即使		jíshǐ	conj	even; even if
67.	一般來說	一般来说	yìbān lái shuō		generally speaking
68.	啟發	启发	qǐfā	v	to enlighten; to inspire
69.	鼓勵	鼓励	gǔlì	v	to encourage
70.	思考		sīkǎo	v	to think about; to ponder
71.	留*		liú	v	to leave (a note); to assign (homework)
72.	童年		tóngnián	n	childhood
73.	無法	无法	wúfǎ		unable; incapable; 沒有辦法 / 没有办法

ENLARGED CHARACTERS FOR EASIER VIEWING AND COMPARING

| 鬆 | 礎 | 辯 | 嚴 | 壓 | 壞 |
| 松 | 础 | 辩 | 严 | 压 | 坏 |

| 優 | 數 | 龍 | 鳳 | 尊 | 勵 |
| 优 | 数 | 龙 | 凤 | 尊 | 励 |

望子成龍, 望女成鳳 / 望子成龙, 望女成凤

Grammar

1. 很不以為然 / 很不以为然

不以為然 / 不以为然 means "do not approve." Its literal definition in classical Chinese is, "do not think it is so." 很 modifies 不以為然 / 不以为然. 很不以為然 / 很不以为然 means "do not approve at all." However, in mainland China 不以為然/不以为然 has acquired a new meaning in recent years: to shrug off, e.g., "His mother told him children shouldn't smoke. He just shrugged off (her remark)." In this lesson, the expression is used in its original sense.

2. 簡直 / 简直

簡直 / 简直 means "simply," or "completely." It often carries a sense of exaggeration.

(1) 他們結婚才半年就要離婚, 簡直開玩笑。

他们结婚才半年就要离婚, 简直开玩笑。

They have been married for only half a year and now want to divorce. It's simply a joke.

(They're almost treating marriage as if it were a joke.)

(2)　他居然做這樣的事, 簡直不是人。 / 他居然做这样的事, 简直不是人。

I can't believe that he actually did this. He's simply not human.

(3)　他減肥以後, 我簡直認不出他來了。 / 他减肥以后, 我简直认不出他来了。

After he lost weight, I simply couldn't recognize him anymore.

(I almost didn't recognize him.)

3. V + 壞/坏 + 了 INDICATING DEGREE

壞/坏 can be used after certain verbs in colloquial Chinese to indicate an extreme degree, e.g., 急壞了 / 急坏了 (worried sick), 餓壞了 / 饿坏了 (starved), 累壞了 / 累坏了 (utterly exhausted), 氣壞了 / 气坏了 (really mad), and 樂壞了 / 乐坏了 (tickled to death).

4. 適合 / 适合 AND 合適 / 合适 COMPARED

In Lesson 4 we learned 合適 / 合适 as an adjective meaning "suitable." In this lesson we have 適合 / 适合, which means "to suit." It is a verb, which must be followed by an object or a clause in which the noun object of 適合 / 适合 is a "pivot" and also serves as the subject of the following clause.

Note the contrasting functions of these two words in the following sentences:

(1)　這條牛仔褲不適合你穿, 你媽媽穿可能合適。

這条牛仔裤不适合你穿, 你妈妈穿可能合适。

This pair of jeans does not suit you. It might be suitable for your mom.

(2)　這種傢俱適合家裏用, 放在辦公室不合適。

这种家具适合家里用, 放在办公室不合适。

This kind of furniture is suitable for homes. It's not suitable for an office.

(3)　這部武打片對小孩不合適, 我們還是看卡通片吧。

这部武打片对小孩不合适, 我们还是看卡通片吧。

This martial arts movie is not suitable for kids. Let's watch a cartoon.

(4)　這個專業不適合你, 你還是選別的專業吧。

这个专业不适合你, 你还是选别的专业吧。

This major does not suit you. You'd better pick another major.

5. THE PREPOSITION 被, A MARKER OF PASSIVE VOICE

In Chinese one does not need to use any specific word to indicate passivity.

(1) 水果都吃完了，該去買了。／水果都吃完了，该去买了。

There's no fruit left. [We] should get some more.

(2) 功課做錯了，他只好再做一次。／功课做错了，他只好再做一次。

He made a mess of his homework and had to do it again.

(3) 房子租好了，明天就可以搬家了。／房子租好了，明天就可以搬家了。

The apartment is already rented. [We/you] can move in tomorrow.

In the above sentences, 水果, 功課／功课, and 房子 are all objects of the actions and topicalized. These sentences all express the idea of passivity even though no words such as 被, 叫, and 讓／让 are used. In fact, 水果, 功課／功课, and 房子 are topics in these sentences, and 被, 叫, or 讓／让 cannot be used.

The passive marker prepositions 被, 叫, and 讓／让 often occur in sentences expressing something unpleasant that has happened to a person or something that has been lost.

(1) 屈原被楚國國王趕到南方去了。／屈原被楚国国王赶到南方去了。

The King of Chu expelled Qu Yuan to the South.

(Qu Yuan was expelled to the South by the King of Chu.)

(2) 書叫郵局寄丟了。／书叫邮局寄丢了。

The post office lost the book.

(The book was lost by the post office.)

(3) 他讓壞人打了一頓。／他让坏人打了一顿。

He got beaten up by bad people.

However, these terms also occur in sentences that have no such negative connotations. See the following two examples:

(4) 王朋被同學選為班長。／王朋被同学选为班长。

Wang Peng was elected class president by his classmates.

(5)　哥哥被派 (pài) 到國外去了。 / 哥哥被派 (pài) 到国外去了。

　　[My] brother was sent abroad.

叫 and 讓/让 occur mostly in colloquial usage, while 被 is somewhat more formal. Especially in written styles, 被 has come to be used more and more frequently in recent years, perhaps to some extent because of the influence of English.

Like in the 把 structure, there has to be a complement indicating result, change, or a 了 after the verb in a 被 sentence.

6. 從來 / 从来

從來 / 从来 means "unchanged from the past to the present." It is often used in negative sentences for emphasis.

(1)　A:　我的作業是不是你拿去了? / 我的作业是不是你拿去了?

　　　　Did you take my homework?

　　B:　沒有啊, 我從來不拿你的東西。 / 没有啊, 我从来不拿你的东西。

　　　　No, I didn't. I never touch your stuff.

(2)　我從來沒買過健康保險, 因為我買不起。
　　我从来没买过健康保险, 因为我买不起。

　　I've never had health insurance because I can't afford it.

(3)　我跟我的哥哥從來沒有在一起打過球。
　　我跟我的哥哥从来没有在一起打过球。

　　I've never played ball together with my older brother.

(4)　這件事情我從來沒聽說過。
　　这件事情我从来没听说过。

　　I've never heard of this matter.

從來 / 从来 is also sometimes used in affirmative sentences, in which case it is often followed by 都是 or 是.

(1) 這個人從來都是這樣, 見到人不愛打招呼。

這个人从来都是这样, 见到人不爱打招呼。

This guy has always been like this, rather stand-offish.

(2) 他從來是看別人怎麼做, 他就怎麼做。

他从来是看别人怎么做, 他就怎么做。

He always watches what others do and then follows suit.

學生都放學回家了。/学生都放学回家了。

Important Words & Phrases

1. 自然 (NATURALLY, OVER THE COURSE OF TIME)

EXAMPLE: 等孩子們長大了, 就會比較成熟, 自然就會有上進心了。

等孩子们长大了, 就会比较成熟, 自然就会有上进心了。

(1) A: 我學中文的時候很注意發音, 可是還是說得不標準。我的發音怎麼才
能進步呢?

我学中文的时候很注意发音, 可是还是说得不标准。我的发音怎么才能进步呢?

B: 你多聽錄音, 说話的時候多注意, 發音＿＿＿＿＿＿＿＿＿＿。

你多听录音, 说话的时候多注意, 发音＿＿＿＿＿＿＿＿＿＿。

(2) 電腦看起來難學, 實際上, 多上幾次機,＿＿＿＿＿＿＿＿＿。

电脑看起来难学, 实际上, 多上几次机,＿＿＿＿＿＿＿＿＿。

(3) 很多人剛移民到美國來的時候, 吃不慣美國菜, 但時間久了,

＿＿＿＿＿＿＿＿＿＿＿＿＿＿＿＿＿＿＿＿＿＿＿。

很多人刚移民到美国来的时候, 吃不惯美国菜, 但时间久了,

＿＿＿＿＿＿＿＿＿＿＿＿＿＿＿＿＿＿＿＿＿＿＿。

2. 不是..., 就是... (IF NOT..., THEN...)

EXAMPLE: 不是說老師不夠嚴, 就是說學生態度不夠認真。

不是说老师不够严, 就是说学生态度不够认真。

(1) 我週末不是＿＿＿＿＿＿, 就是＿＿＿＿＿＿, 一點也不能休息。

我周末不是＿＿＿＿＿＿, 就是＿＿＿＿＿＿, 一点也不能休息。

(2) 來參加晚會的不是＿＿＿＿＿＿, 就是＿＿＿＿＿＿, 他都認識。

来参加晚会的不是＿＿＿＿＿＿, 就是＿＿＿＿＿＿, 他都认识。

(3) A: 你們常常吃牛肉嗎? / 你们常常吃牛肉吗?

B: 不, 我們不是＿＿＿＿＿＿, 就是＿＿＿＿＿＿, 不吃牛肉。

3. 害得... (CAUSING SOME NEGATIVE IMPACT OR HARMFUL RESULT)

EXAMPLE: 他還常常跟老師辯論, 批評美國的小學教育, 不是說老師不夠嚴, 就是說學生不夠認真。害得老師無話可說, 也讓我們很不好意思。

他还常常跟老师辩论, 批评美国的小学教育, 不是说老师不够严, 就是说学生不够认真。害得老师无话可说, 也让我们很不好意思。

(1) 湯姆喝酒的問題, _____。

湯姆喝酒的问题, _____。

(2) 波士頓的房租越來越貴, _____。

波士顿的房租越来越贵, _____。

(3) 張天明隔壁的同學看球賽的時候老大喊大叫,

_____

張天明隔壁的同学看球赛的时候老大喊大叫,

_____

4. 的確 / 的确 (TRULY)

EXAMPLE: 我覺得美國的中小學教育的確有一些缺點。

我觉得美国的中小学教育的确有一些缺点。

(1) 學生: 老師, 這一篇課文太難了, 我看了好幾次還是不懂。

学生: 老师, 这一篇课文太难了, 我看了好几次还是不懂。

老師: 這一篇課文_____。不過你要是把那幾個長句子看懂了, 整篇課文也就容易了。

老师: 这一篇课文_____。不过你要是把那几个长句子看懂了, 整篇课文也就容易了。

▼▼

(2) 人們都説南京的中山陵很壯觀, 我去年去那兒旅行, 覺得中山陵

_____。

人们都说南京的中山陵很壮观, 我去年去那儿旅行, 觉得中山陵

_____。

(3) 你説這本書很有意思, _____, 我看得都不想吃飯, 不想
睡覺了。

你说这本书很有意思, _____, 我看得都不想吃饭, 不想
睡觉了。

5. 看來 / 看来 (TO SEEM)

EXAMPLE: 看來這兩種教育方式各有優缺點。

看来这两种教育方式各有优缺点。

(1) A: 咱們不是説今天一起去看紅葉的嗎? 走吧!

咱们不是说今天一起去看红叶的吗? 走吧!

B: 外邊下起雨來了, _____。

外边下起雨来了, _____。

(2) 老師: 小明, 你今天上課怎麼一點精神也沒有, _____。

老师: 小明, 你今天上课怎么一点精神也没有, _____。

小明: 是的, 老師, 我昨天晚上的確沒睡好覺。

小明: 是的, 老师, 我昨天晚上的确没睡好觉。

(3) 小林: 今天晚上的球賽是決賽, 那麼多人排隊買票,
_____, 別排了, 反正電視會播。

小林: 今天晚上的球賽是決賽, 那麼多人排隊買票,
　　　_____, 別排了, 反正電視會播。

小張: 那倒也是, 那我們還是回宿舍看電視轉播吧。

小张: 那倒也是, 那我们还是回宿舍看电视转播吧。

6. 即使...也 (EVEN IF)

EXAMPLE:　但是學生 "尊師重道", 即使有意見也不敢提。

但是学生 "尊师重道", 即使有意见也不敢提。

(1)　那個中國電影故事很簡單,_____。(不懂中文)

那个中国电影故事很简单,_____。(不懂中文)

(2)　中國的名勝古蹟太多了,_____。(一年)

中国的名胜古迹太多了,_____。(一年)

(3)　他明年要考大學, 壓力很大,_____。(週末)

他明年要考大学, 压力很大,_____。(周末)

Pinyin Texts

DIALOGUE

Zhāng Tiānmíng:　Jiějie, jìde yǐqián bàba cháng shuō, zài Měiguó niàn xiǎoxué tài shūfu, tài qīngsōng le, měitiān fàng xué yǐhòu dōu méiyǒu shénme gōngkè, tā hěn bù yǐ wéi rán.

Zhāng Tiānxīng:　Kěshì lǎoshī shuō, duì xiǎoháizi, bù yīnggāi yòng tiányāshì de jiàoyù fāngshì. Děng háizimen zhǎng dà le, jiù huì bǐjiào chéngshú, zìrán jiù huì yǒu shàngjìnxīn le.

Zhāng Tiānmíng:　Bàba bù tóngyì lǎoshī de guāndiǎn, rènwéi wúlùn rúhé, jīchǔ yídìng děi dǎ hǎo. Jīchǔ bù hǎo, méiyǒu běnlǐng, jiānglái yòng shénme gēn rén jìngzhēng?

▼▼

Zhāng Tiānxīng:	Duì le, tā hái jīngcháng gēn lǎoshī biànlùn, pīpíng Měiguó de xiǎoxué jiàoyù, búshì shuō lǎoshī bú gòu yán, jiùshì shuō xuésheng tàidu bú gòu rènzhēn. Hàide lǎoshī wú huà kě shuō, yě ràng wǒmen hěn bù hǎo yìsi.
Zhāng Tiānmíng:	Wǒ juéde Měiguó de zhōng xiǎoxué jiàoyù díquè yǒu yìxiē quēdiǎn.
Zhāng Tiānxīng:	Dànshì Zhōngguó de jiàoyù yě yǒu wèntí. Wǒ zài Zhōngguó niàn xiǎoxué yì niánjí de shíhou, yālì dà de shòu bu liǎo. Lái Měiguó shàng xiǎoxué yǐhòu, jiǎnzhí lè huài le, gōngkè yòu shǎo, lǎoshī yě bú nàme yán. Dànshì wǒ děi chéngrèn, yàoshì méiyǒu bàba māma de dūcù, zhǐ kào zài xuéxiào xué de dōngxi, wǒ shàng xué bú huì zhème shùnlì.
Zhāng Tiānmíng:	Měiguó de jiàoyù zhòngshì ràng háizi zìyóu fāzhǎn, fāhuī háizi de xiǎngxiànglì. Dànshì zhèyàng de jiàoyù fāngshì bìng bú shìhé měi ge háizi. Yǒude háizi bú gòu zìjué, xūyào lǎoshī de zhǐdǎo, yàobùrán hěn kuài jiù huì bèi táotài.
Zhāng Tiānxīng:	Kěshì Zhōngguó de jiàoyù zǒu lìng yí ge jíduān, cónglái bù kǎolǜ xuésheng de tèdiǎn, duì měige xuésheng de yāoqiú dōu yíyàng, jiāshàng shēng xué de yālì, shǐ xǔduō xuésheng biàn chéng kǎoshì jīqì, zhǐ huì sǐ dú shū.
Zhāng Tiānmíng:	Kànlái zhè liǎng zhǒng jiàoyù fāngshì gè yǒu yōuquēdiǎn.
Zhāng Tiānxīng:	Yǐqián wǒ bù dǒng wèishénme bàba māma měitiān dōu ràng wǒmen zuò nàme duō de shùxué xítí, xiànzài cái lǐjiě tāmen de kǔxīn.
Zhāng Tiānmíng:	Zhōngguórén shuō, "wàng zǐ chéng lóng, wàng nǚ chéng fèng," zánmen de fùmǔ wèile zǐnǚ de jiàoyù, shízài shì yòngxīn liángkǔ a.

READING

Zài Zhōngguó, xuésheng fùdān hěn zhòng. Báitiān shàng xué, wǎnshang hái děi shàng bǔxíbān huòzhě qǐng jiātíng jiàoshī, lián zhōumò dōu bù néng xiūxi.

Zhōngguó de jiàoyù mùbiāo jí fāngshì yǔ Měiguó shífēn bùtóng. Zài Zhōngguó, "shēng xué shì jiàoxué de zhǐhuībàng", jiàoxué zǒngshì suí zhe shēng xué kǎoshì zǒu. Lǎoshī qiángdiào sǐ jì yìng bèi. Jiātíng zuòyè gèng shì yā de rén chuǎn bu guò qì lái. Dànshì xuésheng "zūn shī zhòng dào", jíshǐ yǒu yìjiàn yě bù gǎn tí. Zài Měiguó, yìbān lái shuō, lǎoshī zhòngshì zìyóu fāzhǎn. Qiángdiào qǐfā shì jiàoyù, gǔlì xuésheng duō sīkǎo, yě hěn shǎo liú jiātíng zuòyè. Xǔduō cóng Zhōngguó yímín dào Měiguó lái de jiāzhǎng, yǐwéi Měishì jiàoyù néng gěi háizi yí ge zìyóu, kuàilè de tóngnián. Kěshì kàn zhe háizi fàng xué huí jiā méi shénme gōngkè, tāmen jiù dān xīn háizi de jīchǔ dǎ bu hǎo, jiānglái wúfǎ gēn biérén jìngzhēng. Zhè shíhou, tāmen yòu xiǎng qǐ Zhōngguó de jiàoyù fāngshì lái le.

Discussion Topic: Teaching Approaches in China and the United States

The following drawings show the Zhang family's impressions of the education systems of both the United States and China. Practice in Chinese concurring with or disputing what they said.

第十八課 ▲ 槍枝與犯罪

DIALOGUE

約翰：　　這枝槍是誰的？張天明，槍是你的嗎？

張天明：　對，是我的。這是我給我哥哥買的生日禮物。他喜歡打獵。

約翰：　　你把槍放好，別亂放，不然太危險了。我們這兒進進出出的人那麼多，萬一不小心，槍走了火怎麼辦？

張天明：　你緊張什麼?!我馬上把槍收好，行了吧？

約翰：　　我只是讓你小心點兒。

張天明：　我知道。

約翰：　　你也會用槍嗎？

張天明：　會，我是跟我哥哥學的。你呢？

約翰：　　我不會。槍這東西我連碰都不想碰。我爸爸有三枝槍，我媽和我常為這件事跟我爸爸吵架。那麼多人有槍，買槍那麼容易，我

第十八课 ▲ 枪支与犯罪

DIALOGUE

约翰： 这支枪是谁的？张天明，枪是你的吗？

张天明： 对，是我的。这是我给我哥哥买的生日礼物。他喜欢打猎。

约翰： 你把枪放好，别乱放，不然太危险了。我们这儿进进出出的人那么多，万一不小心，枪走了火怎么办？

张天明： 你紧张什么?! 我马上把枪收好，行了吧？

约翰： 我只是让你小心点儿。

张天明： 我知道。

约翰： 你也会用枪吗？

张天明： 会，我是跟我哥哥学的。你呢？

约翰： 我不会。枪这东西我连碰都不想碰。我爸爸有三支枪，我妈和我常为这件事跟我爸爸吵架。那么多人有枪，买枪那么容易，我們這個社會簡直快沒有理智了！我看世界上沒有哪個國家的人像美國人這麼愛舞刀弄槍的。

張天明： 正因為那麼多人有槍，你也得有槍保護自己啊。萬一出了什麼事，你還等著警察來救你的命？

約翰： 如果警察不夠，我們可以要求政府多僱一些警察呀。你不是不知道，有很多罪犯，前腳出了監獄，後腳就進槍店，買了槍就到處殺人。槍店也不查買槍的是什麼人，不管他是不是殺過人放過火，腦子正常不正常，只要給錢，他們就賣。

張天明： 你別這麼說，已經有法律規定，賣槍的時候一定要調查買槍人的背景。

約翰： 算了吧，有幾個槍店會認真執行這些法律？槍這種東西應該全面禁止，私人不應該有槍，電視裏也應禁止播賣槍的廣告。

張天明： 美國人可以買槍來保護自己，這和言論自由、集會自由一樣，是憲法保障的權利，不應該受到限制。難道你願意像羔羊一樣任人宰割嗎？

们这个社会简直快没有理智了！我看世界上没有哪个国家的人像美国人这么爱舞刀弄枪的。

张天明： 正因为那么多人有枪，你也得有枪保护自己啊。万一出了什么事，你还等着警察来救你的命？

约翰： 如果警察不够，我们可以要求政府多雇一些警察呀。你不是不知道，有很多罪犯，前脚出了监狱，后脚就进枪店，买了枪就到处杀人。枪店也不查买枪的是什么人，不管他是不是杀过人放过火，脑子正常不正常，只要给钱，他们就卖。

张天明： 你别这么说，已经有法律规定，卖枪的时候一定要调查买枪人的背景。

约翰： 算了吧，有几个枪店会认真执行这些法律？枪这种东西应该全面禁止，私人不应该有枪，电视里也应禁止播卖枪的广告。

张天明： 美国人可以买枪来保护自己，这和言论自由、集会自由一样，是宪法保障的权利，不应该受到限制。难道你愿意像羔羊一样任人宰割吗？

READING

　　一九四九年以後，中國禁止賭博和販賣毒品，並取締妓女，打擊偷竊搶劫。中國政府通過強制教育等各種手段，使毒品、妓女在中國消失了，賭博的現象也基本上消滅了，偷竊、搶劫等犯罪也大大減少了。但是改革開放後，尤其是九十年代以來，中國的經濟發展得很快，各種社會問題也隨之產生。如貧富不均、價值觀念紊亂、經濟法規不健全等等。各種犯罪現象也開始出現了。不過總的來說，中國仍然是世界上犯罪率比較低的國家之一，基本上還是比較安全的。

READING

一九四九年以后，中国禁止赌博和贩卖毒品，并取缔妓女，打击偷窃抢劫。中国政府通过强制教育等各种手段，使毒品、妓女在中国消失了，赌博的现象也基本上消灭了，偷窃、抢劫等犯罪也大大减少了。但是改革开放后，尤其是九十年代以来，中国的经济发展得很快，各种社会问题也随之产生。如贫富不均、价值观念紊乱、经济法规不健全等等。各种犯罪现象也开始出现了。不过总的来说，中国仍然是世界上犯罪率比较低的国家之一，基本上还是比较安全的。

VOCABULARY

1.	槍枝	枪支	qiāngzhī	n	firearms
2.	犯罪		fàn zuì	vo	to commit a crime
3.	枝	支	zhī	m	measure word (for pens, rifles, etc.)
4.	槍	枪	qiāng	n	gun (rifle, pistol, etc.); spear
5.	打獵	打猎	dǎ liè	vo	to go hunting
6.	亂放	乱放	luàn fang		to put (things) all over the place
7.	不然		bùrán	conj	otherwise
8.	危險*	危险	wēixiǎn	adj/n	dangerous; danger
9.	小心*		xiǎoxīn	adj	careful
10.	走火		zǒu huǒ	vo	to discharge (firearms) accidentally
11.	收好		shōu hǎo	vc	to put things away in their proper places
12.	碰		pèng	v	to touch; to bump
13.	理智		lǐzhì	n/adj	reason; intellect; rational

他到處殺人,簡直沒有理智了。/他到处杀人,简直没有理智了。

你應該理智一點兒,不要太激動。/你应该理智一点儿,不要太激动。

14.	舞刀弄槍	舞刀弄枪	wǔ dāo nòng qiāng		to brandish swords and spears
15.	正		zhèng	adv	just; precise; precisely [see G3]
16.	保護	保护	bǎohù	v	to protect
17.	出事		chū shì	vo	to have an accident; something bad happens
18.	警察		jǐngchá	n	police
19.	救命		jiù mìng	vo	to save (someone's) life

20.	僱	雇	gù	v	to hire; to employ
21.	罪犯		zuìfàn	n	criminal
22.	監獄	监狱	jiānyù	n	jail; prison
23.	前腳...後腳...	前脚...后脚...	qiánjiǎo...hòujiǎo...		no sooner...than...
24.	到處	到处	dàochù	adv	everywhere; at all places
25.	殺人	杀人	shā rén	vo	to kill someone
26.	查		chá	v	to investigate, check
27.	放火		fàng huǒ	vo	to set fire to
28.	腦子	脑子	nǎozi	n	brain; mind
29.	正常		zhèngcháng	adj	normal

他的腦子有點兒不正常。／他的脑子有点儿不正常。

我認為正常的人都會喜歡旅行。／我认为正常的人都会喜欢旅行。

30.	只要		zhǐyào	conj	so long as
31.	法律		fǎlǜ	n	the law
32.	規定	规定	guīdìng	v/n	to stipulate; stipulation; rule
33.	調查	调查	diàochá	v/n	to investigate, check; investigation

那件事情正在調查, 還沒有結果。／那件事情正在调查, 还没有结果。

請你把調查結果告訴我。／请你把调查结果告诉我。

34.	執行	执行	zhíxíng	v	to implement; to execute (a plan, decision, or policy)
35.	全面		quánmiàn	adj	comprehensive
36.	禁止		jìnzhǐ	v	to prohibit

禁止吸煙。／禁止吸烟。

美國政府禁止學生帶槍上學。／美国政府禁止学生带枪上学。

37.	私人		sīrén	n	private individual
38.	言論	言论	yánlùn	n	opinion on public affairs; speech
39.	集會	集会	jíhuì	n/v	assembly; to assemble
40.	憲法	宪法	xiànfǎ	n	constitution
41.	保障		bǎozhàng	v	to ensure; to safeguard
42.	權利	权利	quánlì	n	right
43.	受到		shòu dào	vc	to receive (influence, restriction, etc.)
44.	限制		xiànzhì	n/v	restriction; to restrict, limit

那個國家婦女工作受到很多限制。／那个国家妇女工作受到很多限制。

填鴨式的教育限制兒童想像力的發揮。

填鸭式的教育限制儿童想像力的发挥。

45.	羔羊		gāoyáng	n	lamb
46	任人宰割		rèn rén zǎigē		to allow oneself to be slaughtered or trampled upon
47.	賭博	赌博	dǔbó	v	to gamble
48.	販賣	贩卖	fànmài	v	to peddle; to sell at a profit; (often derogatory) to traffic in
49.	毒品		dúpǐn	n	narcotic drugs
50.	並	并	bìng	conj	and; furthermore [see G4]
51.	取締	取缔	qǔdì	v	to ban; to suppress
52.	妓女		jìnǚ	n	prostitute

53.	打擊	打击	dǎjī	v	to strike, hit; to attack
54.	偷竊	偷窃	tōuqiè	v	to steal; to pilfer
55.	搶劫	抢劫	qiǎngjié	v	to rob; to loot
56.	通過	通过	tōngguò	prep	through (a method); by means of
57.	強制	强制	qiángzhì	v	to force; to coerce; to compel
58.	手段		shǒuduàn	n	means, method; trick, artifice
59.	消失		xiāoshī	v	to disappear, vanish, dissolve
60.	基本上		jīběnshang		basically
61.	消滅	消灭	xiāomiè	v	to perish; to die out; to eradicate
62.	尤其是		yóuqí shì		particularly; especially
63.	經濟*	经济	jīngjì	n/adj	economy; economical
64.	隨之	随之	suí zhī		along with it (之 here derives from its function in classical Chinese as a pronoun)
65.	產生	产生	chǎnshēng	v	to produce; to emerge; to give rise to
66.	如		rú	v	such as; like; for example
67.	貧富不均	贫富不均	pín fù bù jūn		unequal distribution of wealth; (lit) "poor and rich are unequal"
68.	價值觀念	价值观念	jiàzhí guānniàn		values; concepts or system of values
69.	紊亂	紊乱	wěnluàn	adj	disorderly; chaotic
70.	法規	法规	fǎguī	n	laws and regulations
71.	健全		jiànquán	adj	well-developed (of laws, institutions); sound
72.	仍然		réngrán	adv	still
73.	...率		lǜ		rate
74.	低		dī	adj	low

ENLARGED CHARACTERS FOR EASIER VIEWING AND COMPARING

憲　　　獄　　　監　　　察　　　警　　　獵
宪　　　狱　　　监　　　察　　　警　　　猎

案　　　滅　　　竊　　　擊　　　博　　　權
案　　　灭　　　窃　　　击　　　博　　　权

法律規定槍店需要調查買槍人的背景。／法律规定枪店需要调查买枪人的背景。

Grammar

1. CONJUNCTION OMISSION

In Chinese, conjunctions are often omitted; the exact relationship between two clauses can only be determined from the context. Therefore, the listener or reader has to fill in the gaps to infer the exact meaning. For instance, in the following example sentence the conjunction 如果 or 要是 is left out.

我們這兒進進出出的人那麼多, 萬一不小心, 槍走了火怎麼辦?

我们这儿进进出出的人那么多, 万一不小心, 枪走了火怎么办?

Here is the same sentence with 如果 or 要是 retained:

我們這兒進進出出的人那麼多, (如果／要是)萬一不小心, 槍走了火
怎麼辦?

我们这儿进进出出的人那么多, (如果／要是)万一不小心, 枪走了火
怎么办?

We have so many people coming and going here. [If] someone is careless and lets the gun go off, what would we do?

2. 槍走了火／枪走了火

Semantically, 走火 is one word. However, grammatically, it is a verb phrase. Particles such as 了, 過／过, or number-measure expressions can be inserted in between the verb and its object or complement. Similar words are 睡覺／睡觉, 洗澡, 跳舞, 唱歌, and 見面／见面. Remember what you have learned about the internal construction of such expressions and do not erroneously add objects or complements after the expression.

(1)　*我以前沒見面過他。　→　我以前沒跟他見過面。

　　　*我以前没见面过他。　→　我以前没跟他见过面。

　　　I've never met him before.

(2)　*昨天晚上我跳舞了一個鐘頭。　→　昨天晚上我跳了一個鐘頭舞。

　　　*昨天晚上我跳舞了一个钟头。　→　昨天晚上我跳了一个钟头舞。

　　　I danced for an hour last night.

(3)　*一個星期洗澡三次。　→　一個星期洗三次澡。

　　*一个星期洗澡三次。　→　一个星期洗三次澡。

　　Bathe three times a week.

(4)　*你應該幫忙小張。　→　你應該幫小張忙。

　　*你应该帮忙小张。　→　你应该帮小张忙。

　　You should help Little Zhang.

(5)　*他已經結婚小李了。　→　他已經跟小李結婚了。

　　*他已经结婚小李了。　→　他已经跟小李结婚了。

　　He already married Little Li.

3. THE ADVERB 正

The adverb 正 can mean "it so happens, coincidentally, precisely," etc.

(1)　學生: 老師, 這個題我不會做, 可以不做嗎?

　　学生: 老师, 这个题我不会做, 可以不做吗?

　　Teacher, I don't know how to answer this question. Can I skip it?

　　老師: 正因為你不會做, 才更應該做。不懂的地方可以問我。

　　老师: 正因为你不会做, 才更应该做。不懂的地方可以问我。

　　Precisely because you don't know how to answer it, that's all the more reason that you should
　　[try to] do it. If there's something you don't understand, you can ask me.

(2)　今天正好我沒有事, 我們出去看電影好嗎?

　　今天正好我没有事, 我们出去看电影好吗?

　　I happen to be free today. Shall we go out and see a movie?

(3)　A:　這本書借我看看可以嗎? / 这本书借我看看可以吗?

　　　　Could I borrow this book?

▼▼

B:　對不起, 這本書我也正要看, 我看完了你再看吧。

　　對不起, 这本书我也正要看, 我看完了你再看吧。

Sorry, it so happens that I want to read it, too. You can borrow it after I'm done.

4. THE CONJUNCTION 並／并

The conjunction 並／并 means "in addition, furthermore." It is synonymous with 並且／并且 and can connect two verbs or verb phrases or two clauses. It is used primarily in more formal speech or in written language.

(1)　昨天上課, 老師教我們生詞並介紹了語法。

　　昨天上课, 老师教我们生词并介绍了语法。

Yesterday in class our teacher taught us new vocabulary. Moreover, he/she introduced the grammar.

(2)　最近報上介紹中國的文章很多, 其中有一篇提到了中國經濟發展很快的原因, 並指出了現有的問題。

　　最近报上介绍中国的文章很多, 其中有一篇提到了中国经济发展很快的原因, 并指出了现有的问题。

Recently, there have been many newspaper articles about China. One of them talked about the reasons for the rapid development of China's economy. In addition, [the article] pointed out the existing problems.

(3)　學校昨天開會, 討論老師以及學生提出的問題, 並研究了解決的辦法。

　　学校昨天开会, 讨论老师以及学生提出的问题, 并研究了解决的办法。

Yesterday the school had a meeting and went over issues raised by the teachers and the students; in addition, they discussed ways of solving (the problems).

Note: In the above sentences, one cannot use 和 to replace 並／并.

5. 等(等)

等 is used at the end of enumerative phrases.

(1)　參加討論會的有中國、美國、法國等三個國家。

　　参加讨论会的有中国、美国、法国等三个国家。

The conference participants came from China, America, and France.

(2)　奧林匹克運動會今天的比賽有籃球、游泳、跳水等等。

　　　奥林匹克运动会今天的比赛有篮球、游泳、跳水等等。

　　　Competitive events at the Olympics today include basketball, swimming, diving, and so on.

(3)　上半年我去了北京、上海、南京等五個城市。

　　　上半年我去了北京、上海、南京等五个城市。

　　　In the first six months of this year I went to five cities: Beijing, Shanghai, Nanjing, and so on.

The enumeration can be complete as in example (1) or partial as in examples (2) and (3). 等 and 等等 can be used interchangeably.

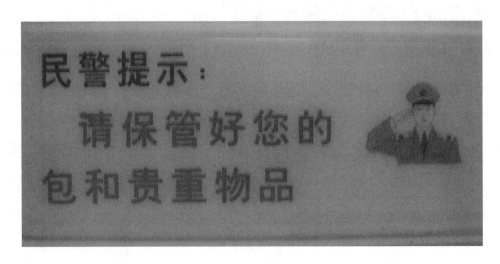

Important Words & Phrases

1. 萬一 / 万一 (IN CASE)

EXAMPLE:　萬一出了什麼事,你還等著警察來救你的命?

　　　　　万一出了什么事,你还等着警察来救你的命?

(1)　我反對男女兩個人還沒結婚就生活在一起, _____, 怎麼辦?

　　　我反对男女两个人还没结婚就生活在一起, _____, 怎么办?

(2)　A:　今天要買那麼多東西, 多帶點現金。

　　　　　今天要买那么多东西, 多带点现金。

B: 沒關係, _____, 我就用信用卡。

没关系, _____, 我就用信用卡。

(3) 別玩火柴, _____, 可不是開玩笑的。

别玩火柴, _____, 可不是开玩笑的。

2. 只要 (SO LONG AS)

EXAMPLE: 槍店也不查買槍的是什麼人, 不管他是不是殺過人放過火, 腦子正常不正常, 只要給錢他們就賣。

枪店也不查买枪的是什么人, 不管他是不是杀过人放过火, 脑子正常不正常, 只要给钱他们就卖。

(1) A: 明天端午節, 你去不去看賽龍舟?

明天端午节, 你去不去看赛龙舟?

B: _____, 我就去。

(2) A: 醫生, 怎麼樣才能睡好覺?

医生, 怎么样才能睡好觉?

B: _____, 就能睡好覺。

_____, 就能睡好觉。

(3) A: 怎麼樣發音才會好?

怎么样发音才会好?

B: _____, 你的發音就會越來越好。

_____, 你的发音就会越来越好。

3. 難道／难道 (INTRODUCING A RHETORICAL QUESTION: DO YOU MEAN TO SAY...?)

EXAMPLE: 難道你願意像羔羊一樣任人宰割嗎?

             难道你愿意像羔羊一样任人宰割吗?

(1)   馬上就要畢業了, 你怎麼還不開始申請工作,_____?

     马上就要毕业了, 你怎么还不开始申请工作,_____?

(2)   孩子教育得不好, 家長不是怪老師督促得不夠, 就是怪社會的影響不好,
_____?

     孩子教育得不好, 家长不是怪老师督促得不够, 就是怪社会的影响不好,
_____?

(3)   妻子: 你不分擔家務, 不幫忙帶孩子, 整天只知道喝茶、看報紙,
_____?

     妻子: 你不分担家务, 不帮忙带孩子, 整天只知道喝茶、看报纸,
_____?

4. 通過／通过 (BY MEANS OF, THROUGH, BY)

EXAMPLE: 政府通過強制教育等各種手段, 使毒品、妓女在中國消失了。

             政府通过强制教育等各种手段, 使毒品、妓女在中国消失了。

(1)   _____, 張天明的電腦總算修好了。(柯林的幫助)

          _____, 张天明的电脑总算修好了。(柯林的帮助)

(2)   _____, 我們對中國的文化有了更深的認識。(這次旅行)

          _____, 我们对中国的文化有了更深的认识。(这次旅行)

(3)   _____, 我哥哥順利地寫完了他的論文。(教授的指導)

          _____, 我哥哥顺利地写完了他的论文。(教授的指导)

Pinyin Texts

DIALOGUE

Yuēhàn:	Zhèzhī qiāng shì shéi de? Zhāng Tiānmíng, qiāng shì nǐ de ma?
Zhāng Tiānmíng:	Duì, shì wǒ de. Zhè shì wǒ gěi wǒ gēge mǎi de shēngrì lǐwù. Tā xǐhuan dǎ liè.
Yuēhàn:	Nǐ bǎ qiāng fàng hǎo, bié luàn fàng, bùrán tài wēixiǎn le. Wǒmen zhèr jìn jìn chū chū de rén nàme duō, wànyī bù xiǎoxīn, qiāng zǒu le huǒ zěnme bàn?
Zhāng Tiānmíng:	Nǐ jǐnzhāng shénme?! Wǒ mǎshàng bǎ qiāng shōu hǎo, xíng le ba?
Yuēhàn:	Wǒ zhǐshì ràng nǐ xiǎoxīn diǎnr.
Zhāng Tiānmíng:	Wǒ zhīdao.
Yuēhàn:	Nǐ yě huì yòng qiāng ma?
Zhāng Tiānmíng:	Huì, wǒ shì gēn wǒ gēge xué de. Nǐ ne?
Yuēhàn:	Wǒ bú huì. Qiāng zhè dōngxi wǒ lián pèng dōu bù xiǎng pèng. Wǒ bàba yǒu sān zhī qiāng, wǒ mā hé wǒ cháng wèi zhèjiàn shì gēn wǒ bàba chǎo jià. Nàme duō rén yǒu qiāng, mǎi qiāng nàme róngyì, wǒmen zhège shèhuì jiǎnzhí kuài méiyǒu lǐzhì le! Wǒ kàn shìjiè shang méiyǒu nǎge guójiā de rén xiàng Měiguórén zhème ài wǔ dāo nòng qiāng de.
Zhāng Tiānmíng:	Zhèng yīnwèi nàme duō rén yǒu qiāng, nǐ yě děi yǒu qiāng bǎohù zìjǐ a. Wànyī chū le shénme shì, nǐ hái děng zhe jǐngchá lái jiù nǐ de mìng?
Yuēhàn:	Rúguǒ jǐngchá bú gòu, wǒmen kěyǐ yāoqiú zhèngfǔ duō gù yìxiē jǐngchá ya. Nǐ bú shì bù zhīdao, yǒu hěn duō zuìfàn, qián jiǎo chū le jiānyù, hòu jiǎo jiù jìn qiāng diàn, mǎi le qiāng jiù dàochù shā rén. Qiāng diàn yě bù chá mǎi qiāng de shì shénme rén, bùguǎn tā shì bu shì shā guò rén fàng guò huǒ, nǎozi zhèngcháng bu zhèngcháng, zhǐyào gěi qián, tāmen jiù mài.
Zhāng Tiānmíng:	Nǐ bié zhème shuō, yǐjīng yǒu fǎlǜ guīdìng, mài qiāng de shíhou yídìng yào diàochá mǎi qiāng rén de bèijǐng.
Yuēhàn:	Suàn le ba, yǒu jǐ ge qiāng diàn huì rènzhēn zhíxíng zhèxiē fǎlǜ? Qiāng zhè zhǒng dōngxi yīnggāi quánmiàn jìnzhǐ, sīrén bù yīnggāi yǒu qiāng, diànshì li yě yīng jìnzhǐ bō mài qiāng de guǎnggào.
Zhāng Tiānmíng:	Měiguórén kěyǐ mǎi qiāng lái bǎohù zìjǐ, zhè hé yánlùn zìyóu, jíhuì zìyóu yíyàng, shì xiànfǎ bǎozhàng de quánlì, bù yīnggāi shòudào xiànzhì. Nándào nǐ yuànyì xiàng gāoyáng yíyàng rèn rén zǎigē ma?

READING

Yī jiǔ sì jiǔ nián yǐhòu, Zhōngguó jìnzhǐ dǔbó hé fànmài dúpǐn, bìng qǔdì jìnǔ, dǎjī tōuqiè qiǎngjié. Zhōngguó zhèngfǔ tōngguò qiángzhì jiàoyù děng gèzhǒng shǒuduàn, shǐ dúpǐn, jìnǔ zài Zhōngguó xiāoshī le, dǔbó de xiànxiàng yě jīběn shang xiāomiè le, tōuqiè, qiǎngjié děng fànzuì yě dàdà jiǎnshǎo le. Dànshì gǎigé kāifàng hòu, yóuqí shì jiǔshí niándài yǐlái, Zhōngguó de jīngjì fāzhǎn de hěn kuài, gè zhǒng shèhuì wèntí yě suí zhī chǎnshēng. Rú pín fù bù jūn, jiàzhí guānniàn wěnluàn, jīngjì fǎguī bú jiànquán děng děng. Gè zhǒng fànzuì xiànxiàng yě kāishǐ chūxiàn le. Búguò zǒng de lái shuō, Zhōngguó réngrán shì shìjiè shang fànzuìlǜ bǐjiào dī de guójiā zhīyī, jīběn shang háishì bǐjiào ānquán de.

Discussion Topic: Is Gun Control a Good Idea?

Zhang Tianming, John, and their families have different views on gun ownership in the United States. State those views in Chinese.

第十九課 ▲ 動物與人

DIALOGUE

張天明： 你今天下午去哪兒了？我找了你半天都沒找到。

柯林： 我到生物系抗議去了。

張天明： 抗議什麼？

柯林： 校報說，生物系的一個教授為了研究老年癡呆症，解剖猴腦，很多猴子就這樣死了，實在太可憐了，因此我們組織大家去生物系抗議。幾天前我們還去了紐約，在幾家大的裘皮服裝店門前抗議，向他們的顧客扔雞蛋，剪她們的裘皮大衣。對了，還有幾個電影明星也跟我們一起抗議。後天我們準備去包圍生物系的動物房，你想去嗎？

張天明： 我沒空兒。我好不容易弄到兩張票，想找你後天一起去看全國大學籃球決賽。

柯林： 那糟了，我已經說好要去包圍動物房了，只能犧牲這場球了。算了，你去找別人吧。

第十九课 ▲ 动物与人

DIALOGUE

张天明： 你今天下午去哪儿了？我找了你半天都没找到。

柯林： 我到生物系抗议去了。

张天明： 抗议什么？

柯林： 校报说，生物系的一个教授为了研究老年痴呆症，解剖猴脑，很
多猴子就这样死了，实在太可怜了，因此我们组织大家去生物系
抗议。几天前我们还去了纽约，在几家大的裘皮服装店门前抗议，
向他们的顾客仍鸡蛋，剪他们的裘皮大衣。对了，还有几个电影
明星也跟我们一起抗议。后天我们准备去包围生物系的动物房，
你想去吗？

张天明： 我没空儿。我好不容易弄到两张票，想找你后天一起去看全国大
学篮球决赛。

柯林： 那糟了，我已经说好要去包围动物房了，只能牺牲这场球了。算了，
你去找别人吧。

張天明： 你可別後悔啊！哎，柯林，你不覺得你們扔雞蛋，剪人家的裘皮
大衣，包圍動物房，有點太過份了嗎？我同意，我們人對動物也
應該講人道，但我覺得動物實驗是很有用的。很多藥只有通過
動物實驗，才能知道對人是不是安全。

柯林： 你這種想法是錯誤的。現在已經可以不通過動物實驗來做研究
了。都二十一世紀了，這麼虐待動物，實在是太野蠻，太不人道了！

張天明： 你的想法也太極端了。你不覺得人比動物更重要嗎？科學家也
不是有意要虐待動物。讓那麼多人死於癌症、艾滋病，也不見得
就人道。

柯林： 你憑什麼說人比動物更重要？正是因為我們有這種想法，才去破
壞大自然。現在熱帶雨林一天比一天少，很多珍稀動物瀕臨滅絕，
生態失去平衡，我們不是已經開始自食其果了嗎？

動物與人 / 动物与人

▼▼▼▼▼▼▼▼▼▼▼▼▼▼▼▼▼▼▼▼▼▼▼▼▼▼▼▼▼▼▼▼▼▼▼▼▼▼

张天明：你可别后悔啊！哎，柯林，你不觉得你们扔鸡蛋，剪人家的裘皮大衣，包围动物房，有点太过份了吗？我同意，我们人对动物也应该讲人道，但我觉得动物实验是很有用的。很多药只有通过动物实验，才能知道对人是不是安全。

柯林：你这种想法是错误的。现在已经可以不通过动物实验来做研究了。都二十一世纪了，这么虐待动物，实在是太野蛮，太不人道了！

张天明：你的想法也太极端了。你不觉得人比动物更重要吗？科学家也不是有意要虐待动物。让那么多人死于癌症、艾滋病，也不见得就人道。

柯林：你凭什么说人比动物更重要？正是因为我们有这种想法，才去破坏大自然。现在热带雨林一天比一天少，很多珍稀动物濒临灭绝，生态失去平衡，我们不是已经开始自食其果了吗？

中國的珍稀動物之一：熊貓／中国的珍稀动物之一：熊猫

張天明：　我承認你說的有點道理。如果可以避免用動物做實驗，當然應該避免。實在避免不了的話，也應該儘量減少動物的痛苦。但為了虛榮而穿裘皮大衣，那就大可不必了。

柯林：　你這不是自相矛盾嗎？為了虛榮而殺動物和為了救我們自己而犧牲動物，有什麼區別呢？

張天明：　我覺得很多事情不像你想的那樣黑白分明。好了，好了，我不跟你辯論了。既然你不去看球賽，我就去找別人了。

READING

中國有許多稀有動物，其中有不少是十分珍貴的。但由於人口不斷增加，動物生存的空間越來越小，有些動物，如華南虎等已瀕臨滅絕。最近幾年中國採取了一些保護珍稀動物的措施，並設立了許多動物保護區。中國的國寶大熊貓，也得到了很好的保護。但大多數中國人的動物保護意識還很薄弱。很多人常常為了發展經濟而忽略動物保護，甚至認為動物保護和發展經濟是互相矛盾的。因此，在發展經濟的同時注意動物保護，是中國政府面臨的一大難題。

张天明：　我承认你说的有点道理。如果可以避免用动物做实验，当然应该避免。实在避免不了的话，也应该尽量减少动物的痛苦。但为了虚荣而穿裘皮大衣，那就大可不必了。

柯林：　　你这不是自相矛盾吗？为了虚荣而杀动物和为了救我们自己而牺牲动物，有什么区别呢？

张天明：　我觉得很多事情不像你想的那样黑白分明。好了，好了，我不跟你辩论了。既然你不去看球赛，我就去找别人了。

READING

　　中国有许多稀有动物，其中有不少是十分珍贵的。但由于人口不断增加，动物生存的空间越来越小，有些动物，如华南虎等已濒临灭绝。最近几年中国采取了一些保护珍稀动物的措施，并设立了许多动物保护区。中国的国宝大熊猫，也得到了很好的保护。但大多数中国人的动物保护意识还很薄弱。很多人常常为了发展经济而忽略动物保护，甚至认为动物保护和发展经济是互相矛盾的。因此，在发展经济的同时注意动物保护，是中国政府面临的一大难题。

VOCABULARY

1. 動物*   动物   dòngwù   n   animal

2. 生物   shēngwù   n   biology; living thing, organism

3. 抗議   抗议   kàngyì   v   to protest

   美國政府向日本政府提出抗議。／美国政府向日本政府提出抗议。

   我們抗議你們虐待動物的行為。／我们抗议你们虐待动物的行为。

4. 研究   yánjiū   v   to research

5. 老年癡呆症   老年痴呆症   lǎonián chīdāi zhèng   n   Alzheimer's disease

6. 解剖   jiěpōu   v   to dissect

7. 猴腦   猴脑   hóunǎo   n   monkey brain

8. 猴子   hóuzi   n   monkey

9. 可憐   可怜   kělián   adj/v   pitiable; to pity

   那個孩子沒有父母,很可憐。／那个孩子没有父母,很可怜。

   可憐的妹妹,功課壓得她喘不過氣來。

   可怜的妹妹,功课压得她穿不过气来。

10. 組織   组织   zǔzhī   v/n   to organize; organization

    她組織同學上街抗議。／她组织同学上街抗议。

    紅十字會是一個很有名的組織。／红十字会是一个很有名的组织。

11. 裘皮   qiúpí   n   fur

12. 服裝   服装   fúzhuāng   n   (formal) clothing

13. 顧客   顾客   gùkè   n   customer

14. 扔   rēng   v   to throw

15. 雞蛋   鸡蛋   jīdàn   n   chicken egg

16. 剪   jiǎn   v   to cut (with scissors)

▼▼▼▼▼▼▼▼▼▼▼▼▼▼▼▼▼▼▼▼▼▼▼▼▼▼▼▼▼▼▼▼▼▼

17.	大衣		dàyī	n	overcoat; long coat
18.	包圍	包围	bāowéi	v	to surround; to encircle
19.	動物房	动物房	dòngwùfáng	n	room where animals are housed
20.	弄		nòng	v	(col) to get; to do
21.	糟了		zāo le		(col) oh no; shoot; darn
22.	犧牲	牺牲	xīshēng	v	to sacrifice
23.	講	讲	jiǎng	v	(col) to stress; to pay attention to
24.	人道		réndào	n/adj	humanitarianism; humane
25.	實驗	实验	shíyàn	n/v	experiment; to experiment
26.	錯誤	错误	cuòwù	n	mistake
27.	世紀	世纪	shìjì	n	century
28.	虐待		nüèdài	v	to abuse
29.	野蠻	野蛮	yěmán	adj	barbarous; uncivilized
30.	科學家	科学家	kēxuéjiā	n	scientist
31.	有意		yǒuyì	adv	intentionally; on purpose

他有意讓女朋友不高興。／他有意让女朋友不高兴。

我做錯了，但不是有意的。／我做错了，但不是有意的。

32.	癌症		áizhèng	n	cancer
33.	艾滋病		Àizībìng	n	AIDS
34.	憑	凭	píng	prep	based on
35.	破壞	破坏	pòhuài	v	to destroy
36.	大自然		dà zìrán	n	nature
37.	熱帶雨林	热带雨林	rèdài yǔlín	n	tropical rain forest
38.	珍稀動物	珍稀动物	zhēnxī dòngwù		precious and rare animals

39.	瀕臨	濒临	bīnlín	v	to be on the verge of
40.	滅絕	灭绝	mièjué	v	to exterminate; to become extinct
41.	生態	生态	shēngtài	n	ecology
42.	失去		shīqù	v	to lose
43.	平衡		pínghéng	adj	balanced

你賺錢少, 花錢多, 收支不平衡。／你赚钱少, 花钱多, 收支不平衡。

看到別人考得比自己好, 他心裏有點兒不平衡。

看到别人考得比自己好, 他心里有点儿不平衡。

44.	自食其果		zì shí qí guǒ		to suffer the consequences of one's own actions
45.	避免		bìmiǎn	v	to avoid

為了避免犯錯誤, 他做事十分小心。

为了避免犯错误, 他做事十分小心。

他總是想辦法避免跟以前的女朋友見面。

他总是想办法避免跟以前的女朋友见面。

46.	儘量	尽量	jǐnliàng	adv	to the best of one's ability
47.	痛苦		tòngkǔ	adj	painful
48.	虛榮	虚荣	xūróng	n	vanity
49.	大可不必		dà kě búbì		no need whatsoever
50.	區別	区别	qūbié	n/v	distinction; to distinguish

這兩個詞有什麼區別?／这两个词有什么区别?

你應該能區別"合適"和"適合"這兩個詞的用法。

你应该能区别"合适"和"适合"这两个词的用法。

51.	黑白分明		hēibái fēnmíng		with black and white sharply contrasted; clear cut

52.	稀有		xīyǒu	adj	rare
53.	珍貴	珍贵	zhēnguì	adj	valuable; precious
54.	由於	由于	yóuyú	prep	due to; owing to
55.	增加		zēngjiā	v	to increase
56.	生存		shēngcún	v	to exist; to survive
57.	空間	空间	kōngjiān	n	space
58.	華南虎	华南虎	Huánán hǔ	n	South Chinese tiger
59.	已		yǐ	adv	already; 已經／已经
60.	採取	采取	cǎiqǔ	v	to take/adopt (measures, methods, steps)
61.	措施		cuòshī	n	measure; step
62.	設立	设立	shèlì	v	to establish; to set up
63.	保護區	保护区	bǎohùqū	n	protected area; conservation area
64.	國寶	国宝	guóbǎo	n	national treasure
65.	(大)熊貓	(大)熊猫	(dà) xióngmāo	n	(great) panda
66.	大多數	大多数	dà duōshù		most; the great majority
67.	意識	意识	yìshí	n	consciousness
68.	薄弱	薄弱	bóruò	adj	weak; frail
69.	忽略		hūlüè	v	to overlook; to neglect
70.	互相矛盾		hùxiāng máodùn		contradictory; to contradict each other
71.	在...同時	在...同时	zài...tóngshí		at the same time as
72.	面臨	面临	miànlín	v	to face; to be confronted with
73.	難題	难题	nántí	n	difficult problem; dilemma

PROPER NOUN

紐約*	纽约	Niǔyuē	New York

ENLARGED CHARACTERS FOR EASIER VIEWING AND COMPARING

解　憐　圍　犧　蠻　瀕　寶　薄
解　怜　围　牺　蛮　濒　宝　薄

Notes

▲1▲ The pronunciation of 癌症 was changed in mainland China from yánzhèng to áizhèng to avoid confusion with the homonymous 炎症 (inflammation). The old pronunciation can still be heard in Taiwan.

▲2▲ Although in both mainland China and Taiwan AIDS is known as "Àizībìng," mainland China has opted for the more neutral looking character 艾, instead of 愛/爱, which is used in Taiwan. 滋 literally means "to breed, propagate; to cause, create."

保護動物 vs. 發展經濟 / 保护动物 vs. 发展经济

▼▼▼▼▼▼▼▼▼▼▼▼▼▼▼▼▼▼▼▼▼▼▼▼▼▼▼▼▼▼▼▼▼▼▼▼

Grammar

1. 為了／为了 AND 因為／因为

為了／为了 denotes purpose; 因為／因为 denotes cause.

(1) 為了中文學得更好, 我明年要去中國。

   为了中文学得更好, 我明年要去中国。

   In order to improve (my) Chinese, I'm going to China next year.

(2) 因為在中國學中文環境更好, 所以我明年去中國學習。

   因为在中国学中文环境更好, 所以我明年去中国学习。

   Because the environment in China is better for learning Chinese, I'm going to China to study next year.

(3) 為了解決人口問題, 中國政府只讓每個家庭生一個孩子。

   为了解决人口问题, 中国政府只让每个家庭生一个孩子。

   In order to solve the problem of over-population, the Chinese government only allows every family to have one child.

(4) 因為中國的人口太多, 所以中國政府只讓一家生一個孩子。

   因为中国的人口太多, 所以中国政府只让一家生一个孩子。

   Because there are too many people in China, the Chinese government only allows every family to have one child.

(5) 我買槍是為了保護自己。／我买枪是为了保护自己。

   The reason I bought the gun is to protect myself.

(6) 因為這兒不安全, 所以我買了一枝槍。

   因为这儿不安全, 所以我买了一枝枪。

   I bought a gun because it's not safe here.

(7) 因為這個學校很有名, 所以我申請。

   因为这个学校很有名, 所以我申请。

   Because this school is very famous, I'm going to apply to it.

(8) 我申請這個學校, 是為了能跟我的女朋友在一起。

我申请这个学校, 是为了能跟我的女朋友在一起。

I'm applying to this school so that I can be with my girlfriend.

2. THE ADVERB 可 IN 你可別後悔 / 你可別后悔

In imperative sentences, 可 denotes caution or admonition, and is often followed by such modal verbs as 要, 能, 不能, 不要, and 應該 / 应该, and a particle of mood. In 你可別後悔 / 你可別后悔, the 別 is another way of saying 不要.

(1) 那兒很危險, 你可要注意啊! / 那儿很危险, 你可要注意啊!

It's very dangerous there. Please be careful!

(2) 明天的會特別重要, 你可不能忘了。/ 明天的会特别重要, 你可不能忘了。

Tomorrow's meeting is extremely important. Make sure that you don't forget [to come]!

(3) 這件事你同意了, 可別後悔呀。/ 这件事你同意了, 可别后悔呀。

You've agreed to this. Don't regret [your decision]!

(4) 我買槍的事, 你可別告訴我媽媽。/ 我买枪的事, 你可别告诉我妈妈。

Don't tell my mom that I bought a gun.

This usage of 可 occurs frequently in spoken Chinese.

3. 於 / 于

Here the preposition 於 / 于 denotes cause. It is used in written or formal language.

(1) 每年不少人死於艾滋病或者癌症。

每年不少人死于艾滋病或者癌症。

Every year many people die of AIDS or cancer.

(2) 最近我忙於寫論文, 沒有時間給你打電話。

最近我忙于写论文, 没有时间给你打电话。

I've been busy writing my thesis. [That's why] I haven't had the time to call you.

4. 而

而 can connect a phrase denoting a target or cause with a verb. It is usually preceded by such words as 由於 ／ 由于 or 因為 ／ 因为 and is used in written language.

(1)　我們為國家而工作。／ 我们为国家而工作。

We work for our country.

(The verb is 工作. 為國家 ／ 为国家 denotes the target or client.)

(2)　他們因為贏得了金牌而驕傲起來。／ 他们因为赢得了金牌而骄傲起来。

They became arrogant because they had won a gold medal.

(The verb and outcome is 驕傲起來 ／ 骄傲起来. 贏得金牌 ／ 赢得金牌 denotes the reason.)

(3)　他們由於表現太差而被淘汰。

他们由于表现太差而被淘汰。

They were iliminated due to poor performance.

(The cause of 被淘汰 is 表現太差 ／ 表现太差.)

5. 其中

其中 means "among." 其 is a possessive pronoun from classical Chinese, so the phrase literally means "in its/their midst." In this expression it refers to a group of persons or things.

(1)　三年級有十五個學生, 其中有三個是日本人, 三個是韓國人, 其他的是美國人。

三年级有十五个学生, 其中有三个是日本人, 三个是韩国人, 其他的是美国人。

The third year (class) has fifteen students. Among those, three are Japanese, three are Korean, and the rest are American.

(2)　學校附近有很多中國餐館, 其中有一家是從芝加哥搬來的。

学校附近有很多中国餐馆, 其中有一家是从芝加哥搬来的。

There are many Chinese restaurants near the school. One of them moved here from Chicago.

(3)   老師問了我不少問題, 其中只有一個很容易, 我會, 別的我都不會。

               老师问了我不少问题, 其中只有一个很容易, 我会, 别的我都不会。

The teacher asked me many questions. Only one of them was easy for me. I couldn't answer the rest.

Note: When using 其中, there must be a preceding sentence, and in that sentence there must be a phrase denoting multiple people or things, e.g., fifteen students in example (1), many Chinese restaurants in example (2), and many questions in example (3). 其中 is placed in the second clause to indicate "in the midst of" those fifteen students, many Chinese restaurants, and many questions.

動物的生存空間 / 动物的生存空间

Important Words & Phrases

1. 抗議 / 抗议 (TO PROTEST)

EXAMPLE: 柯林: 我到生物系抗議去了。 / 柯林: 我到生物系抗议去了。

                  張天明: 抗議什麼? / 张天明: 抗议什么?

(1)   六十年代, 美國有很多大學生上街_____。

       六十年代, 美国有很多大学生上街_____。

▼▼

(2) 醫療保險一年比一年貴,老百姓向政府抗議,希望＿＿＿＿＿＿＿＿＿。

医疗保险一年比一年贵,老百姓向政府抗议,希望＿＿＿＿＿＿＿＿＿。

(3) 這州的商品稅居然提高到百分之九,許多人打算去州政府前＿＿＿＿＿＿
＿＿＿＿＿。

这州的商品税居然提高到百分之九,许多人打算去州政府前＿＿＿＿＿
＿＿＿＿＿。

2. 說好 / 说好 (TO COME TO AN AGREEMENT)

EXAMPLE: 我已經說好要去包圍動物房了。/ 我已经说好要去包围动物房了。

(1) 那對年輕夫婦結婚以前就＿＿＿＿＿＿＿＿＿,
什麼都考慮到了。

那对年轻夫妇结婚以前就＿＿＿＿＿＿＿＿＿,
什么都考虑到了。

(2) 張天明和麗莎遊覽完中山陵,兩個人＿＿＿＿＿＿＿＿＿。

张天明和丽莎游览完中山陵,两个人＿＿＿＿＿＿＿＿＿。

(3) 籃球比賽的時候,教練得先跟球員說好怎麼打,要不然＿＿＿＿＿＿＿。

篮球比赛的时候,教练得先跟球员说好怎么打,要不然＿＿＿＿＿＿＿。

3. 憑什麼 / 凭什么 (WHY ON EARTH? ON WHAT BASIS DO YOU...?)

EXAMPLE: 你憑什麼說人比動物更重要?/ 你凭什么说人比动物更重要?

(1) 哥哥: 妹妹,別看卡通了,該去睡覺了。

哥哥: 妹妹,别看卡通了,该去睡觉了。

妹妹:＿＿＿＿＿＿＿＿＿? 你也在看啊!

(2) 教練: 小柯打了很長時間, 太累了, 小王, 輪到你上場了。

教练: 小柯打了很长时间, 太累了, 小王, 轮到你上场了。

小王: 不公平, 我剛才打的時間比他更長,＿＿＿＿＿＿＿＿?

小王: 不公平, 我刚才打的时间比他更长,＿＿＿＿＿＿＿＿?

(3) 我和他合租一套公寓, 我們的房間一樣大, 我的房租是六百五十, 他的是
六百,＿＿＿＿＿＿＿＿＿?

我和他合租一套公寓, 我们的房间一样大, 我的房租是六百五十, 他的是
六百,＿＿＿＿＿＿＿＿＿?

4. 儘量 / 尽量 (AS MUCH AS POSSIBLE)

EXAMPLE: 如果可以避免用動物做實驗, 當然應該避免。避免不了的話, 應該
儘量減少動物的痛苦。

如果可以避免用动物做实验, 当然应该避免。避免不了的话, 应该
尽量减少动物的痛苦。

(1) 學中文應該＿＿＿＿＿＿＿＿＿。

学中文应该＿＿＿＿＿＿＿＿＿。

(2) 我的老師的教學方式是＿＿＿＿＿＿＿＿, 並不強調死記硬背。

我的老师的教学方式是＿＿＿＿＿＿＿＿, 并不强调死记硬背。

(3) 懷孕的時候要＿＿＿＿＿＿＿＿。

怀孕的时候要＿＿＿＿＿＿＿＿。

進入熱帶雨林的門票／进入热带雨林的门票

(See the Appendix of Alternate Character Versions for traditional characters.)

Pinyin Texts

DIALOGUE

Zhāng Tiānmíng: Nǐ jīntiān xiàwǔ qù nǎr le? Wǒ zhǎo le nǐ bàntiān dōu méi zhǎo dào.

Kē Lín: Wǒ dào shēngwùxì kàngyì qù le.

Zhāng Tiānmíng: Kàngyì shénme?

Kē Lín: Xiǎobǎo shuō, shēngwùxì de yí ge jiàoshòu wèile yánjiū lǎonián chīdāi zhèng, jiěpōu hóunǎo, hěn duō hóuzi jiù zhèyàng sǐ le, shízài tài kělián le, yīncǐ wǒmen zǔzhī dàjiā qù shēngwùxì kàngyì. Jǐ tiān qián wǒmen hái qù le Niǔyuē, zài jǐ jiā dà de qiúpí fúzhuāng diàn ménqián kàngyì, xiàng tāmen de gùkè rēng jīdàn, jiǎn tāmen de qiúpí dàyī. Duì le, háiyǒu jǐ ge diànyǐng míngxīng yě gēn wǒmen yìqǐ kàngyì. Hòutiān wǒmen zhǔnbèi qù bāowéi shēngwùxì de dòngwùfáng, nǐ xiǎng qù ma?

Zhāng Tiānmíng: Wǒ méi kòngr. Wǒ hǎo bù róngyì nòng dào liǎng zhāng piào, xiǎng zhǎo nǐ hòutiān yìqǐ qù kàn quánguó dàxué lánqiú juésài.

Kē Lín: Nà zāo le, wǒ yǐjīng shuō hǎo yào qù bāowéi dòngwùfáng le, zhǐnéng xīshēng zhè chǎng qiú le. Suàn le, nǐ qù zhǎo biérén ba.

Zhāng Tiānmíng: Nǐ kě bié hòuhuǐ a! Āi, Kē Lín, nǐ bù juéde nǐmen rēng jīdàn, jiǎn rénjia de qiúpí dàyī, bāowéi dòngwùfáng, yǒu diǎn tài guòfèn le ma? Wǒ tóngyì, wǒmen rén duì dòngwù yě yīnggāi jiǎng réndào, dàn wǒ juéde dòngwù shíyàn shì hěn yǒuyòng de. Hěn duō yào zhǐyǒu tōngguò dòngwù shíyàn, cáinéng zhīdao duì rén shì bu shì ānquán.

▼▼▼▼▼▼▼▼▼▼▼▼▼▼▼▼▼▼▼▼▼▼▼▼▼▼▼▼▼▼▼▼▼▼▼▼▼▼

Kē Lín:	Nǐ zhèzhǒng xiǎngfǎ shì cuòwù de. Xiànzài yǐjīng kěyǐ bù tōngguò dòngwù shíyàn lái zuò yánjiū le. Dōu èrshí yī shìjì le, zhème nüèdài dòngwù, shízài shì tài yěmán, tài bù réndào le!
Zhāng Tiānmíng:	Nǐ de xiǎngfǎ yě tài jíduān le. Nǐ bù juéde rén bǐ dòngwù gèng zhòngyào ma? Kēxuéjiā yě bú shì yǒuyì yào nüèdài dòngwù. Ràng nàme duō rén sǐ yú áizhèng, Àizībìng, yě bú jiàn de jiù réndào.
Kē Lín:	Nǐ píng shénme shuō rén bǐ dòngwù gèng zhòngyào? Zhèng shì yīnwèi wǒmen yǒu zhèzhǒng xiǎngfǎ, cái qù pòhuài dàzìrán. Xiànzài rèdài yǔlín yì tiān bǐ yì tiān shǎo, hěn duō zhēnxī dòngwù bīnlín mièjué, shēngtài shīqù pínghéng, wǒmen bú shì yǐjīng kāishǐ zì shí qí guǒ le ma?
Zhāng Tiānmíng:	Wǒ chéngrèn nǐ shuō de yǒu diǎn dàoli. Rúguǒ kěyǐ bìmiǎn yòng dòngwù zuò shíyàn, dāngrán yīnggāi bìmiǎn. Shízài bìmiǎn bu liǎo de huà, yě yīnggāi jǐnliàng jiǎnshǎo dòngwù de tòngkǔ. Dàn wèile xūróng ér chuān qiúpí dàyī, nà jiù dà kě bú bì le.
Kē Lín:	Nǐ zhè bú shì zìxiāng máodùn ma? Wèile xūróng ér shā dòngwù hé wèile jiù wǒmen zìjǐ ér xīshēng dòngwù, yǒu shénme qūbié ne?
Zhāng Tiānmíng:	Wǒ juéde hěn duō shìqing bú xiàng nǐ xiǎng de nàyàng hēibái fēnmíng. Hǎo le, hǎo le, wǒ bù gēn nǐ biànlùn le. Jìrán nǐ bú qù kàn qiúsài, wǒ jiù qù zhǎo biérén le.

🔘 READING

Zhōngguó yǒu xǔduō xīyǒu dòngwù, qízhōng yǒu bù shǎo shì shífēn zhēnguì de. Dàn yóuyú rénkǒu búduàn zēngjiā, dòngwù shēngcún de kōngjiān yuè lái yuè xiǎo, yǒuxiē dòngwù, rú Huánán hǔ děng yǐ bīnlín mièjué. Zuìjìn jǐ nián Zhōngguó cǎiqǔ le yìxiē bǎohù zhēnxī dòngwù de cuòshī, bìng shèlì le xǔduō dòngwù bǎohùqū. Zhōngguó de guóbǎo dà xióngmāo, yě dé dào le hěn hǎo de bǎohù. Dàn dà duōshù Zhōngguó rén de dòngwù bǎohù yìshí hái hěn bóruò. Hěnduō rén chángcháng wèi le fāzhǎn jīngjì ér hūlüè dòngwù bǎohù, shènzhì rènwéi dòngwù bǎohù hé fāzhǎn jīngjì shì hùxiāng máodùn de. Yīncǐ, zài fāzhǎn jīngjì de tóngshí zhùyì dòngwù bǎohù, shì Zhōngguó zhèngfǔ miànlín de yí dà nántí.

Discussion Topic: Do Animals Have Rights?

In Chinese, describe the two protests and what Ke Lin did during them. Do you agree with Ke Lin's actions?

第二十課 ▲ 環境保護

張天明： 這兩天你在忙些什麼呀,怎麼總見不到你?

李哲： 我這學期在化學系參加了一項研究,是州政府給的錢,要幫助解決這裏的工業廢氣、廢水、廢渣問題。化學系僱了幾個學生做化學分析,這兩天我天天在實驗室裏做實驗、寫報告。

張天明： 難怪我連你的影子都見不到,打了幾次電話也沒人接。這兒的工業三廢問題嚴重嗎?這個小地方有什麼工業?不就是個大學城嗎?

李哲： 這兒有一個很大的化工廠,工廠排出的三廢對我們這個地方造成了嚴重的污染。因為聯邦環境保護法越來越嚴,所以州政府讓工廠解決他們的三廢問題。可是工廠說他們沒有能力解決這個問題,因為解決這個問題會增加成本,產品就會競爭不過外國。工廠要求州政府幫助他們解決這個問題,還威脅說,要是州政府不幫他們解決,他們就搬到墨西哥去。後來,州政府申請到一筆錢,委託我們學校化學系幫助化工廠解決污染問題。

第二十课 ▲ 环境保护

DIALOGUE

张天明：　这两天你在忙些什么呀，怎么总见不到你？

李哲：　　我这学期在化学系参加了一项研究，是州政府给的钱，要帮助解决这里的工业废气、废水、废渣问题。化学系雇了几个学生做化学分析，这两天我天天在实验室里做实验、写报告。

张天明：　难怪我连你的影子都见不到，打了几次电话也没人接。这儿的工业三废问题严重吗？这个小地方有什么工业？不就是个大学城吗？

李哲：　　这儿有一个很大的化工厂，工厂排出的三废对我们这个地方造成了严重的污染。因为联邦环境保护法越来越严，所以州政府让工厂解决他们的三废问题。可是工厂说他们没有能力解决这个问题，因为解决这个问题会增加成本，产品就会竞争不过外国。工厂要求州政府帮助他们解决这个问题，还威胁说，要是州政府不帮他们解决，他们就搬到墨西哥去。后来，州政府申请到一笔钱，委托我们学校化工系帮助化工厂解决污染问题。

張天明： 噢，原來如此。怪不得這裏的松樹林死了一大片，我以為是有害蟲呢。

李哲： 這兒比山下好多了，山下面的污染更屬害。山下那個湖裏不是有魚嗎？以前大家都不知道湖裏的魚有毒不能吃，結果有人吃了被毒死了。

張天明： 哎，環保這件事情真難辦。你不治理環境吧，不行，治理吧，往往得花很多錢，有時還會造成一些人失業。

李哲： 可是如果我們現在不注意環保的話，將來可能就太晚了。像臭氧層、酸雨這些問題，如果現在不管，將來後果會不堪設想。

一片松樹林 / 一片松树林

张天明： 噢，原来如此。怪不得这里的松树林死了一大片，我以为是有害虫呢。

李哲： 这儿比山下好多了，山下面的污染更厉害。山下那个湖里不是有鱼吗？以前大家都不知道湖里的鱼有毒不能吃，结果有人吃了被毒死了。

张天明： 哎，环保这件事情真难办。你不治理环境吧，不行，治理吧，往往得花很多钱，有时还会造成一些人失业。

李哲： 可是如果我们现在不注意环保的话，将来可能就太晚了。像臭氧层、酸雨这些问题，如果现在不管，将来后果会不堪设想。

一個湖／一个湖

READING

　　中國是世界上的能源大國之一，煤產量居世界第一位。由於石油比煤貴，核電站造價高、週期長，所以中國的發電廠大多用煤發電。這些發電廠每年排放大量的二氧化硫，對環境造成很大的污染。在中國，除發電廠外，另一個污染源是很多城市居民使用的煤爐。這些大大小小的污染源，對人體健康造成很大的危害。隨著中國工業化速度的加快，對能源的需求量也與日俱增。如果不採取有效措施，中國的空氣污染將會日益加劇，自然，人民的健康也會受到更大的威脅。

汽車廢氣會造成空氣污染／汽车废气会造成空气污染

READING

　　中国是世界上的能源大国之一，煤产量居世界第一位。由于石油比煤贵，核电站造价高、周期长，所以中国的发电厂大多用煤发电。这些发电厂每年排放大量的二氧化硫，对环境造成很大的污染。在中国，除发电厂外，另一个污染源是很多城市居民使用的煤炉。这些大大小小的污染源，对人体健康造成很大的危害。随着中国工业化速度的加快，对能源的需求量也与日俱增。如果不采取有效措施，中国的空气污染将会日益加剧，自然，人民的健康也会受到更大的威胁。

为了节约能源和人身安全，当你离开房间时，请锁门、熄灯、关闭空调，　谢　谢！

VOCABULARY

1.	環境*	环境	huánjìng	n	environment
2.	總	总	zǒng	adv	always; 總是 / 总是
3.	化學	化学	huàxué	n	chemistry
4.	項	项	xiàng	m	measure word for projects, tasks, etc.
5.	工業	工业	gōngyè	n	industry
6.	廢氣	废气	fèiqì	n	waste gas or steam
7.	廢水	废水	fèishuǐ	n	waste water
8.	廢渣	废渣	fèizhā	n	waste residue; solid waste
9.	分析		fēnxī	v	to analyze
10.	實驗室*	实验室	shíyànshì	n	laboratory
11.	影子		yǐngzi	n	shadow
12.	接(電話)	接(电话)	jiē (diànhuà)	v(o)	to answer (the phone)
13.	三廢	三废	sānfèi	n	three types of waste; 廢氣, 廢水, 廢渣 / 废气, 废水, 废渣
14.	化工		huàgōng	n	chemical engineering; chemical industry
15.	排出		pái chū	vc	to discharge; to emit
16.	造成		zàochéng	v	to cause; to lead to

大雨下了五天, 造成了嚴重的水災。/ 大雨下了五天, 造成了严重的水灾。

州政府不給我們學校錢了, 造成了很大的困難。

州政府不给我们学校钱了, 造成了很大的困难。

17.	污染		wūrǎn	v	to pollute
18.	聯邦	联邦	liánbāng	n	federation
19.	能力		nénglì	n	ability; capacity
20.	成本		chéngběn	n	cost

21.	筆	笔	bǐ	m	an amount of money or money related matters

一筆生意 ／ 一笔生意

22.	委託	委托	wěituō	v	to commission; to entrust
23.	原來如此	原来如此	yuánlái rúcǐ		so that's the reason, so that's how it is
24.	怪不得		guàibude		no wonder
25.	松樹林	松树林	sōngshù lín		pine grove/forest
26.	害蟲	害虫	hàichóng	n	harmful insect
27.	湖*		hú	n	lake
28.	毒		dú	n/v	toxin, poison; to poison
29.	環保	环保	huánbǎo	n	environmental protection;

環境保護 ／ 环境保护

30.	難辦	难办	nán bàn		hard to handle

這件事真難辦。 ／ 这件事真难办。

這個人誰的話都不聽, 很難辦。 ／ 这个人谁的话都不听, 很难办。

31.	治理		zhìlǐ	v	to bring under control; to manage
32.	有時	有时	yǒushí		sometimes; 有的時候 ／ 有的时候
33.	失業	失业	shī yè	vo	be out of work; to lose one's job
34.	臭氧層	臭氧层	chòuyǎngcéng	n	ozone layer; ozonosphere
35.	酸雨		suānyǔ	n	acid rain
36.	後果	后果	hòuguǒ	n	consequence; aftermath
37.	不堪設想	不堪设想	bùkān shèxiǎng		(too) dreadful to contemplate

小明天天喝醉酒, 這樣下去, 學習成績將不堪設想。

小明天天喝醉酒, 这样下去, 学习成绩将不堪设想。

38.	能源		néngyuán	n	energy resources
39.	煤		méi	n	coal

40. 產量	产量	chǎnliàng	n	output
41. 居		jū	v	to occupy (a certain position)
42. 石油		shíyóu	n	petroleum
43. 核電站	核电站	hédiànzhàn	n	nuclear power plant
44. 造價	造价	zàojià	n	manufacturing cost
45. 週期	周期	zhōuqī	n	cycle
46. 發電廠	发电厂	fādiànchǎng	n	power plant
47. 大多		dàduō	adv	mostly
48. 排放		páifàng	v	to discharge; to emit
49. 大量		dàliàng	adj	in large quantity
50. 二氧化硫		èryǎnghuàliú	n	sulfur dioxide
51. 污染源		wūrǎnyuán	n	source of pollution
52. 居民		jūmín	n	resident
53. 使用		shǐyòng	v	to use; 用
54. 煤爐	煤炉	méilú	n	coal stove
55. 人體	人体	réntǐ	n	human body; 人的身體／人的身体
56. 危害		wēihài	v	to harm
57. 加快		jiākuài	v	to quicken, speed up
58. 需求量		xūqiú liàng		volume of demand
59. 與日俱增	与日俱增	yǔ rì jù zēng		to grow with each passing day
60. 有效		yǒuxiào	adj	effective
61. 空氣	空气	kōngqì	n	air
62. 將	将	jiāng		will; shall
63. 日益加劇	日益加剧	rìyì jiājù		to become more aggravated day by day
64. 人民*		rénmín	n	the people

▼▼

ENLARGED CHARACTERS FOR EASIER VIEWING AND COMPARING

廢	實	驗	聯	蟲	層	酸	爐
废	实	验	联	虫	层	酸	炉

Grammar

1. 怎麼 ／ 怎么 AND 為什麼 ／ 为什么

怎麼 ／ 怎么 is an interrogative pronoun used to inquire about the manner of an action, as in, "How do you write that character?" 怎麼 ／ 怎么 can also be used to inquire about the reason for something, e.g., "How come I haven't seen you for the past couple of days?" How does the second 怎麼 ／ 怎么 differ from 為什麼 ／ 为什么? The answer is that 怎麼 ／ 怎么 generally implies surprise or bewilderment.

(1)　三點了, 他應該來了, 怎麼還沒來? ／ 三点了, 他应该来了, 怎么还没来?

It's three o'clock. He should have gotten here. How come he is still not here?

(2)　明天考試? 我怎麼不知道? ／ 明天考试? 我怎么不知道?

There's an exam tomorrow? How come I didn't know?

(3)　怎麼? 他沒來上課? ／ 怎么? 他没来上课?

What? He didn't come to the class?

為什麼 ／ 为什么, on the other hand, does not necessarily imply bewilderment. It is used primarily to inquire about reasons. In the first example, 為什麼 ／ 为什么 can be substituted for 怎麼 ／ 怎么. The tone will shift from puzzlement to reproach. In the second example, 怎麼 ／ 怎么 cannot be replaced without the meaning substantially changing as well. If 為什麼 ／ 为什么 were used, it would sound as if the speaker were complaining.

(4)　這麼重要的事情, 你為什麼不告訴我?

這么重要的事情, 你为什么不告诉我?

Why didn't you tell me about such an important thing?

(5)　　飛機為什麼會飛?／飞机为什么会飞?

Why can airplanes fly?

(6)　　他為什麼不來? 為什麼? 為什麼?／他为什么不来? 为什么? 为什么?

Why isn't he coming? Why? Why?

In (4), 怎麼／怎么 can be substituted for 為什麼／为什么, but there would be a slight difference in meaning. 怎麼／怎么 would connote curiosity rather than reproach. In (5), 怎麼／怎么 cannot be substituted for 為什麼／为什么. The tone of voice is neutral; the sentence is dealing with an objective inquiry and could have been taken from a physics textbook. As a general rule, 怎麼／怎么 cannot be used at the end of an utterance, unlike 為什麼／为什么 in (6). And 為什麼／为什么 cannot be used at the beginning of an utterance by itself, unlike 怎麼／怎么 in example (3).

2. (好)多了 AND (好)得多

When making a comparison, one can use 多了 or 得多 after the adjective to indicate an extreme degree.

(1)　　這兒的天氣比東岸熱多了。／这儿的天气比东岸热多了。

The weather here is much hotter than on the East Coast.

(2)　　中國的人口比美國多得多。／中国的人口比美国多得多。

China's population is much larger than that of the United States.

(3)　A:　你姐姐的病好一點了嗎?／你姐姐的病好一点了吗?

Is your sister [her illness] a little better?

　　B:　好多了。

Much better.

(* 好得多 would be incorrect here.)

A. In these comparative sentences the adjectives cannot be preceded by modifiers, e.g., we do not say, *他比我很好, etc. We can put 一點兒／一点儿, 得很, 得多, 多了, and 很多, etc. after the adjectives. However, we cannot combine any two of 一點兒／一点儿, 得很, 得多,

▼▼▼

多了, and 很多 after the adjectives in these comparative sentences, e.g., we do not say, *他比我好得多了.

B. If there are no words that indicate comparison, such as 比, the adjectives can only be followed by 一點兒／一点儿 or 多了. See example (3) above.

3. …吧, …吧,…

This construction, usually found in spoken Chinese, suggests two alternative hypotheses, and is used to indicate that the speaker is in a dilemma and unable to make a decision.

(1)　我的車舊了, 最近老有問題。買新的吧, 沒有錢, 不買新的吧, 舊車又不可靠, 真難辦。

　　　我的车旧了, 最近老有问题。买新的吧, 没有钱, 不买新的吧, 旧车又不可靠, 真难办。

My car is old, and lately it's been having many problems. I could buy a new one, but I don't have the money. I could keep [this] old one, but it is not reliable. [This problem is] really difficult to resolve.

(2)　晚上有一場籃球賽, 可是今天作業很多。看吧, 怕作業做不完, 不看吧, 又覺得很可惜。(kěxī: it's a pity)

　　　晚上有一场篮球赛, 可是今天作业很多。看吧, 怕作业做不完, 不看吧, 又觉得很可惜。(kěxī: it's a pity)

There's a basketball game tonight, but I have a lot of homework. If I watch the game, I'm afraid I won't finish my homework, but if I don't watch it, it will be such a pity.

(3)　他的女朋友的妹妹明天舉行生日晚會。他想, 去吧, 沒有錢買禮物, 不去吧, 又怕女朋友生氣。怎麼辦呢?

　　　他的女朋友的妹妹明天举行生日晚会。他想, 去吧, 没有钱买礼物, 不去吧, 又怕女朋友生气。怎么办呢?

His girlfriend's sister is having a birthday party tomorrow. He thinks if he goes, he won't have the money to buy a present, but he's afraid that if he doesn't go his girlfriend will be angry. What should he do?

4. 往往 AND 常常

Both 往往 and 常常 indicate high frequency, but they differ in degree.

A. 往往 usually indicates a higher frequency than 常常.

B. 往往 is used in reference to predictable patterns, and cannot be used with verbs that denote subjective desire. 常常 is placed in front of a verb and indicates constant recurrence that is not necessarily predictable. It can be used with verbs that denote subjective desire, e.g.,

(1)　過去我常常希望他來, 現在怕他來。

　　　过去我常常希望他来, 现在怕他来。

　　　In the past I often hoped he would come visit. Now I dread the prospect of his coming.

　　　*過去我往往希望他來, 現在怕他來。

　　　*过去我往往希望他来, 现在怕他来。

(2)　我希望你以後常常來。／ 我希望你以后常常来。

　　　I hope you'll come often.

　　　*我希望你以後往往來。／*我希望你以后往往来。

(3)　週末他往往不在家。／ 周末他往往不在家。

　　　On weekends, more often than not, he's not at home. (indicates a tendency)

　　　週末他常常不在家。／ 周末他常常不在家。

　　　On weekends he's often not at home. (indicates frequency)

Note: The two sentences in (3) are different.

C. 往往 can only be used in reference to the past or to situations in which time is not a factor. This restriction does not apply to 常常.

　　　我以後星期六會常常來。／ 我以后星期六会常常来。

　　　From now on I will come often on Saturdays.

　　　Incorrect: *我以後星期六會往往來。／*我以后星期六会往往来。

Important Words & Phrases

1.(競爭)不過 ／(竞争)不过 (CANNOT COMPETE WITH; BE NO MATCH FOR)

EXAMPLE:　產品將競爭不過外國。／ 产品将竞争不过外国。

(1)　我妹妹很會說話, 每次和人辯論, 別人_____。(說)

　　　我妹妹很会说话, 每次和人辩论, 别人_____。(说)

(2)　他每天都練長跑, 你讓我跟他比賽, 我肯定_____。(跑)

　　　他每天都练长跑, 你让我跟他比赛, 我肯定_____。(跑)

(3)　她在中國待了三年, 能說不少中文, 而我從來沒去過中國, 所以在聽說方
　　　面, _____。(比)

　　　她在中国待了三年, 能说不少中文, 而我从来没去过中国, 所以在听说方
　　　面, _____。(比)

2. 委託 ／ 委托 (COMMISSION; ENTRUST)

EXAMPLE:　州政府...委託我們學校化學系幫助化工廠解決污染問題。

　　　　　州政府...委托我们学校化学系帮助化工厂解决污染问题。

(1)　校長不能參加今年的畢業典禮, 所以他_____
　　　_____。(張教授, 講話)

　　　校长不能参加今年的毕业典礼, 所以他_____
　　　_____。(张教授, 讲话)

(2)　美國的電視公司常常_____。
　　　(蓋洛普Gallup公司, 做民意調查)

　　　美国的电视公司常常_____。
　　　(盖洛普Gallup公司, 做民意调查)

▼▼

(3)　美國政府＿＿＿＿＿＿＿＿＿＿＿＿＿＿＿＿＿＿＿。(她, 參加世界環保大會)

　　　美国政府＿＿＿＿＿＿＿＿＿＿＿＿＿＿＿＿＿＿＿。(她, 参加世界环保大会)

3. 原來如此 / 原来如此 (SO THAT'S HOW IT IS; SO THAT'S WHY)

EXAMPLE:　...噢, 原來如此。怪不得這裏的松樹林死了一大片。

　　　　　...噢, 原来如此。怪不得这里的松树林死了一大片。

(1)　A:　他過生日的時候, 我送了他一個鐘, 他好像有些不高興。

　　　　他过生日的时候, 我送了他一个钟, 他好像有些不高兴。

　　B:　在中國送禮物是不能送鐘的。

　　　　在中国送礼物是不能送钟的。

　　A:　為什麼? / 为什么?

　　B:　因為 "送鐘" 和 "送終" (bury a parent or a senior member of the family) 發音一樣, 所以中國人覺得送鐘非常不合適。(終 zhōng: end)

　　　　因为 "送钟" 和 "送终" (bury a parent or a senior member of the family) 发音一样, 所以中国人觉得送钟非常不合适。(终 zhōng: end)

　　A:　噢, ＿＿＿＿＿＿＿, 難怪他不高興。

　　　　噢, ＿＿＿＿＿＿＿, 难怪他不高兴。

(2)　A:　他為什麼這兩天沒來上課?

　　　　他为什么这两天没来上课?

　　B:　他的奶奶病了, 他去波士頓看奶奶去了。

　　　　他的奶奶病了, 他去波士顿看奶奶去了。

▼▼▼▼▼▼▼▼▼▼▼▼▼▼▼▼▼▼▼▼▼▼▼▼▼▼▼▼▼▼▼▼▼▼▼▼

A:　噢,＿＿＿＿＿＿＿＿。希望他奶奶很快就好起來。

　　噢,＿＿＿＿＿＿＿＿。希望他奶奶很快就好起来。

4. 不就是 (ISN'T IT JUST...?)

不就是 means "只是" or "只有" and introduces a rhetorical question).

EXAMPLE:　這個小地方有什麼工業? 不就是一個大學城嗎?

　　　　　这个小地方有什么工业? 不就是一个大学城吗?

(1)　他不就是個研究生嗎? 他的論文為什麼＿＿＿＿＿＿? (有影響)

　　　他不就是个研究生吗? 他的论文为什么＿＿＿＿＿＿? (有影响)

(2)　今天的考試＿＿＿＿＿＿? 你不要那麼緊張。(生詞小考)

　　　今天的考试＿＿＿＿＿＿? 你不要那么紧张。(生词小考)

(3)　他們＿＿＿＿＿＿? 你別那麼激動。(贏了場球)

　　　他们＿＿＿＿＿＿? 你别那么激动。(赢了场球)

Pinyin Texts

DIALOGUE

Zhāng Tiānmíng:	Zhè liǎng tiān nǐ zài máng xiē shénme ya, zěnme zǒng jiàn bu dào nǐ?
Lǐ Zhé:	Wǒ zhè xuéqī zài huàxuéxì cānjiā le yí xiàng yánjiū, shì zhōu zhèngfǔ gěi de qián, yào bāngzhù jiějué zhèlǐ de gōngyè fèiqì, fèishuǐ, fèizhā wèntí. Huàxuéxì gù le jǐge xuésheng zuò huàxué fēnxī, zhè liǎng tiān wǒ tiāntiān zài shíyànshì li zuò shíyàn, xiě bàogào.
Zhāng Tiānmíng:	Nánguài wǒ lián nǐ de yǐngzi dōu jiàn bu dào, dǎ le jǐ cì diànhuà yě méi rén jiē. Zhèr de gōngyè sānfèi wèntí yánzhòng ma? Zhège xiǎo dìfang yǒu shénme gōngyè? Bú jiùshì ge dàxuéchéng ma?
Lǐ Zhé:	Zhèr yǒu yí ge hěn dà de huàgōngchǎng, gōngchǎng pái chū de sānfèi duì wǒmen zhège dìfang zàochéng le yánzhòng de wūrǎn. Yīnwèi liánbāng huánjìng bǎohù fǎ

yuè lái yuè yán, suǒyǐ zhōu zhèngfǔ ràng gōngchǎng jiějué tāmen de sānfèi wèntí. Kěshì gōngchǎng shuō tāmen méiyǒu nénglì jiějué zhège wèntí, yīnwèi jiějué zhège wèntí huì zēngjiā chéngběn, chǎnpǐn jiù huì jìngzhēng bu guò wàiguó. Gōngchǎng yāoqiú zhōu zhèngfǔ bāngzhù tāmen jiějué zhège wèntí, hái wēixié shuō, yàoshi zhōu zhèngfǔ bù bāng tāmen jiějué, tāmen jiù bān dào Mòxīgē qù. Hòulái, zhōu zhèngfǔ shēnqǐng dào yì bǐ qián, wěituō wǒmen xuéxiào huàxuéxì bāngzhù huàgōngchǎng jiějué wūrǎn wèntí.

| Zhāng Tiānmíng: | Ō, yuánlái rúcǐ. Guàibude zhèlǐ de sōngshùlín sǐ le yí dà piàn, wǒ yǐwéi shì yǒu hàichóng ne. |

| Lǐ Zhé: | Zhèr bǐ shānxià hǎo duō le, shān xiàmian de wūrǎn gèng lìhai. Shānxià nàge hú li bú shì yǒu yú ma? Yǐqián dàjiā dōu bù zhīdao hú li de yú yǒu dú bù néng chī, jiéguǒ yǒu rén chī le bèi dú sǐ le. |

| Zhāng Tiānmíng: | Ài, huánbǎo zhèjiàn shìqing zhēn nán bàn. Nǐ bú zhìlǐ huánjìng ba, bù xíng, zhìlǐ ba, wǎngwǎng děi huā hěn duō qián, yǒushí hái huì zàochéng yìxiē rén shīyè. |

| Lǐ Zhé: | Kěshì rúguǒ wǒmen xiànzài bú zhùyì huánbǎo de huà, jiānglái kěnéng jiù tài wǎn le. Xiàng chòuyǎngcéng, suānyǔ zhèxiē wèntí, rúguǒ xiànzài bù guǎn, jiānglái hòuguǒ huì bùkān shèxiǎng. |

READING

Zhōngguó shì shìjièshang de néngyuán dà guó zhī yī, méi chǎnliàng jū shìjiè dì yī wèi. Yóuyú shíyóu bǐ méi guì, hédiànzhàn zàojià gāo, zhōuqī cháng, suǒyǐ Zhōngguó de fādiànchǎng dàduō yòng méi fā diàn. Zhèxiē fādiànchǎng měinián páifàng dàliàng de èryǎnghuàliú, duì huánjìng zàochéng hěn dà de wūrǎn. Zài Zhōngguó, chú fādiànchǎng wài, lìng yí ge wūrǎnyuán shì hěn duō chéngshì jūmín shǐyòng de méilú. Zhèxiē dà dà xiǎo xiǎo de wūrǎnyuán, duì réntǐ jiànkāng zàochéng hěn dà de wēihài. Suí zhe Zhōngguó gōngyèhuà sùdù de jiākuài, duì néngyuán de xūqiú liàng yě yǔ rì jù zēng. Rúguǒ bù cǎiqǔ yǒuxiào cuòshī, Zhōngguó de kōngqì wūrǎn jiāng huì rìyì jiājù, zìrán, rénmín de jiànkāng yě huì shòu dào gèng dà de wēixié.

Discussion Topic: Is Sustainable Development Achievable?

Use the drawings to talk about the environmental hazards mentioned in the dialogue. Can developing countries grow their economies without sacrificing the environment?

APPENDIX: MEASURE WORDS

1. The collocation of nouns and measure words can be quite complex. In this appendix, we list mainly those measure words and nouns introduced in Levels 1 and 2 of *Integrated Chinese*. Table I lists—in alphabetical order—all of the nominal measure words (measure words that count people or objects denoted by nouns) in the *Integrated Chinese* series. It does not, however, include indefinite measure words, such as 點 / 点 and 些. Nor does it include verbal measure words that count the iteration of an action, such as 次 and 趟.

2. 個 / 个 can be used with many nouns. Table I includes only the main nouns introduced in the *Integrated Chinese* series. It is true that in informal contexts 個 / 个 can sometimes function as a less precise substitute for other measure words. For instance, 一個桌子 / 一个桌子 can take the place of 一張桌子 / 一张桌子. However, one should always remember which specific measure words go with which nouns, and be careful not to overuse 個 / 个, as it is difficult to predict when it is unacceptable, as in *一個紙 / 一个纸.

3. The measure words in Table II are not found in the *Integrated Chinese* series, but can be combined with the nouns introduced in the series.

4. Some nouns can be combined with more than one measure word, with little or no difference in meaning, e.g., 一條黃瓜 / 一条黄瓜 and 一根 gēn 黄瓜. However, sometimes different measure words convey different meanings, e.g., 一朵 duǒ 花 (a flower), 一枝花 (a flower with its stem intact), and 一束花 (a bouquet of flowers).

TABLE I: MEASURE WORDS INTRODUCED IN THE *INTEGRATED CHINESE* SERIES

1. 把   objects that can be grasped: 刀, 椅子, 手槍 / 手枪

2. 本   books: 書 / 书, 詞典 / 词典, 字典, 小说 / 小说 (novel);

                 bound documents or paper products: 護照 / 护照, 相册 (photo album)

3. 杯   cups/glasses of liquid: 咖啡, 茶, 水, 果汁, 可樂 / 可乐

4. 部   books or artistic products: 電影 / 电影, 紀錄片 / 纪录片, 卡通片, 商業片 / 商业片, 藝術片 / 艺术片, 小说 / 小说;

                 automobiles: 汽車 / 汽车

5. 筆 / 笔   "brush," by association, counts of money, business deals, transactions: 錢 / 钱, 生意, 買賣 / 买卖

6. 層 / 层   "layer", stories of a building: 樓 / 楼

7. 棟 / 栋   buildings: 房子, 樓 / 楼, 大樓 / 大楼

▼▼▼▼▼▼▼▼▼▼▼▼▼▼▼▼▼▼▼▼▼▼▼▼▼▼▼▼▼▼▼▼▼▼▼

8. 封   Originally used to refer to wrapped and sealed objects (from the verb "to seal"); "wrapped and sealed objects," now mostly letters, correspondences: 信, 電報 / 电报, 電子郵件 / 电子邮件

9. 個 / 个   people: 老師 / 老师, 學生 / 学生, 朋友, 女孩;

     a wide variety of concrete objects: 杯子, 位子, 地方, 窗戶, 門 / 门, 餃子 / 饺子, 衣櫃 / 衣柜, 漢字 / 汉字, 生詞 / 生词, 歌劇 / 歌剧, 號碼 / 号码;

     a wide variety of abstract matters: 方法, 意見 / 意见, 建議 / 建议, 計劃 / 计划, 變化 / 变化, 活動 / 活动, 錯誤 / 错误, 標準 / 标准

10. 家   commercial establishments or enterprises: 公司, 商店, 旅行社, 餐館 / 餐馆, 電影院 / 电影院, 旅館 / 旅馆, 銀行 / 银行, 醫院 / 医院

11. 間 / 间   rooms: 屋子, 房子, 教室, 臥室 / 卧室

12. 件   upper garments, overcoats: 衣服, 毛衣, T恤衫, 大衣;

     items of objects: 行李, 東西 / 东西, 傢俱 / 家具, 禮物 / 礼物, 首飾 / 首饰;

     things: 事情, 心事

13. 節 / 节   "joint," "section," class periods: 課 / 课

14. 塊 / 块   block-like objects: 豆腐, 牛肉, 香皂, 地毯, 金牌, 銀牌 / 银牌, 餅乾 / 饼干, 月餅 / 月饼

15. 門 / 门   academic courses: 課 / 课

16. 盤 / 盘   things on plates: 菜, 青菜, 餃子 / 饺子, 糖醋魚 / 糖醋鱼;

     round, plate-like objects: 錄音帶 / 录音带, 錄像帶 / 录像带, 磁帶 / 磁带 cídài (audio tape)

17. 篇   written texts or entries: 課文 / 课文, 日記 / 日记, 文章

18. 片   flat and thin objects: 紅葉 / 红叶, 樹葉 / 树叶, 藥 / 药, 麵包 / 面包 (bread)

▼▼▼▼▼▼▼▼▼▼▼▼▼▼▼▼▼▼▼▼▼▼▼▼▼▼▼▼▼▼

	expanses of land, water, scenery, etc.: 樹林 / 树林, 樹海 / 树海, 熱帶雨林 / 热带雨林, 商店
19. 瓶	bottled liquid: 水, 果汁, 醋, 酒, 可樂 / 可乐
20. 束	bundled, elongated objects: 花
21. 雙 / 双	paired objects: 手, 腳 / 脚, 眼睛, 耳朵 ěrduo (ears), 鞋, 筷子
22. 台	machines, equipment: 機器 / 机器, 電腦 / 电脑, 洗衣機 / 洗衣机, 烘乾機 / 烘干机, 電視機 / 电视机
23. 套	sets of objects: 房子, 公寓, 傢俱 / 家具, 運動服 / 运动服, 設備 / 设备
24. 條 / 条	elongated—but not overly thin—objects: 黃瓜, 船, 毛巾, 浴巾, 腿, 褲子 / 裤子, 牛仔褲 / 牛仔裤, 江, 河, 街, 路, 馬路 / 马路, 走廊, 路線 / 路线 (also see 根 gēn in Table II)
	some animals: 狗, 龍 / 龙, 魚 / 鱼, 蛇 shé (snake);
	discrete abstract items: 法律, 法規 / 法规, 新聞 / 新闻, 意見 / 意见, 建議 / 建议
25. 位	"position," "seat"; polite references to people: 朋友, 教授, 老師 / 老师, 同學 / 同学, 記者 / 记者
26. 碗	objects, mainly food, in bowls: 水, 米飯 / 米饭, 湯 / 汤, 酸辣湯 / 酸辣汤
27. 項 / 项	systematic schemes or plans: 研究, 計劃 / 计划
28. 枝 / 支	long, hard, stick-like objects: 筆 / 笔, 毛筆 / 毛笔, 槍 / 枪, 花
29. 張 / 张	(from the verb "to stretch, extend, or open") objects with flat surfaces: 床, 桌子, 書桌 / 书桌, 臉 / 脸, 報紙 / 报纸, 飛機票 / 飞机票, 地圖 / 地图, 畫 / 画, 明信片, 信用卡, 電話卡 / 电话卡, 支票, 旅行支票, 郵票 / 邮票
	objects that can be closed and opened: 嘴, 弓
30. 隻 / 只	animals: 雞 / 鸡, 鴨子 / 鸭子, 羊, 熊貓 / 熊猫, 華南虎 / 华南虎, 老鼠, 貓 / 猫, 猴子

▼▼

one of a pair of organs or appendages of the body: 眼睛, 手, 腳 / 脚

boats, ships: 船, 龍舟 / 龙舟

31. 種/种   varieties (of fruits, trees, products, customs, skills, methods, tastes, pain, etc.):
水果, 水果, 樹 / 树, 産品 / 产品, 風俗 / 风俗, 本領 / 本
领, 方式, 味道, 痛苦

32. 座   "seat", solid-looking natural and man-made structures; mountains and
buildings: 山, 城市, 大樓 / 大楼, 建築 / 建筑

TABLE II: ADDITIONAL MEASURE WORDS

1. 班   regularly scheduled services of public transport: 船, 飛機 / 飞机, 火車 /
火车, 汽車 / 汽车

2. 床   被(子) quilts

3. 袋 dài   bagged objects: 米, 洗衣粉

4. 道   questions/problems, exercises, dilemmas; courses of a meal: 題 / 题, 習題 /
习题, 難題 / 难题, 菜

5. 滴 dī   drops of liquid: 水, 眼淚 / 眼泪

6. 頂 / 顶 dǐng   帽子 màozi (hats, caps)

7. 對 / 对   pairs, couples: 夫婦 / 夫妇, 父子

8. 朵 duǒ   (originally, "drooping flowers and fruit") flowers, clouds: 花, 雲

9. 番 fān   time, round, time and effort expended: 苦心 (pains; trouble taken)

10. 根 gēn   "root", elongated, mostly very thin objects: 黃瓜, 火柴, 針 / 针, 頭髮 /
头发 tóufa (hair on the human head)

11. 盒 hé   boxed objects: 火柴, 糖

12. 架   "frame," "rack," or "stand"; supported objects: 飛機 / 飞机, 鋼琴 / 钢琴

13. 口   "mouth": 人, 猪

14. 列 liè   (a line or file of) passenger or freight cars: 火車 / 火车

▼ ▼

15. 輛 / 辆 liàng　(originally, a "two-wheeled chariot"), vehicles: 汽車 / 汽车, 自行車 / 自行车, 出租車 / 出租车

16. 面　face: 鏡子 / 镜子, 墙 / 墙

17. 匹 pī　horses or mules: 馬 / 马;

　　bolts or lengths of fabrics: 布 bù

18. 頭 / 头　牛, 猪 zhū (pigs)

19. 艘 sōu　ships, boats: 船

20. 扇 shàn　"fan," (leaf of) windows, doors, or screens: 窗户, 門 / 门

21. 首 shǒu　songs, poems: 歌, 詩 / 诗

22. 所 suǒ　institutions: 學校 / 学校, 高中

23. 盞 / 盏 zhǎn　"small cup": 燈 / 灯

VOCABULARY INDEX (CHINESE-ENGLISH)

Traditional	Simplified	Pinyin	Part of Speech	English	Lesson
▲A▲					
哎呀		āiyā	exc	(an exclamation indicating suprise) gosh; oh	4
癌症		áizhèng	n	cancer	19
唉		ài	exc	(an exclamation indicating resignation) oh well	5
愛國	爱国	àiguó	adj	patriotic	12
艾滋病		Àizībìng	n	AIDS	19
安好		ānhǎo	adj	safe and sound	11
安靜	安静	ānjìng	adj	quiet	2
安全		ānquán	adj/n	safe; safety	1
▲B▲					
白天		báitiān	n	daytime	17
擺	摆	bǎi	v	to put; to place	2
百分之x		bǎifēn zhī		x percent	4
拜年		bài nián	vo	to pay a New Year call; to wish someone a happy New Year	12
搬		bān	v	to move (objects, or to a new home)	1
搬家		bān jiā	vo	to move (to a different house)	1
辦	办	bàn	v	to handle; to do	1
辦法	办法	bànfǎ	n	method; way (to solve a problem)	15
辦公	办公	bàn gōng	vo	to work (in an office); open for business	10
包		bāo	v	to include	6
包裹		bāoguǒ	n	parcel	10
包圍	包围	bāowéi	v	to surround; to encircle	19
保護	保护	bǎohù	v	to protect	18
保護區	保护区	bǎohù qū	n	protected area; conservation area	19
保險	保险	bǎoxiǎn	n/v	insurance; to insure	16
保障		bǎozhàng	v	to ensure; to safeguard	18
保證	保证	bǎozhèng	v/n	to guarantee; guarantee	16
杯子		bēizi	n	cup; drinking glass	4
背景		bèijǐng	n	background	7
被子		bèizi	n	comforter; quilt	2
本來	本来	běnlái	adv	at first; originally	13
本領	本领	běnlǐng	n	skill; capability	17
筆	笔	bǐ	m	"an amount" of money or money related matters	20
比分		bǐfēn	n	score (of a basketball match, etc.)	13

Traditional	Simplified	Pinyin	Part of Speech	English	Lesson
比如		bǐrú	v	for example	15
比賽	比赛	bǐsài	n/v	competition; to compete	6
必要		bìyào	n/adj	necessity; necessary	13
畢竟	毕竟	bìjìng	adv	after all	16
畢業	毕业	bì yè	vo	to graduate	5
避免		bìmiǎn	v	to avoid	19
鞭炮		biānpào	n	firecracker; a long string of small firecrackers	12
變成	变成	biàn chéng	vc	to change into	17
辯論	辩论	biànlùn	v	to debate; to argue	17
變化	变化	biànhuà	n/v	change; to change	15
標準	标准	biāozhǔn	n/adj	criterion; standard	4
表弟		biǎodì	n	(younger male) cousin (of different surname, i.e., on mother's side of the family)	11
表哥		biǎogē	n	(elder male) cousin	13
表面上		biǎomiàn shang	adv	on the surface	12
表嫂		biǎosǎo	n	older cousin's wife; 表哥的太太	14
表現	表现	biǎoxiàn	v	to display; to manifest	12
憋死		biē sǐ	vc	to suffocate; to feel stifled	7
別具風格	别具风格	biéjù fēnggé		have a distinctive style	11
瀕臨	濒临	bīnlín	v	on the verge of	19
餅乾	饼干	bǐnggān	n	cookies; crackers	10
病人		bìngrén	n	"sick person"; patient	5
並	并	bìng	conj	and; furthermore	18
播		bō	v	to broadcast	8
菠菜		bōcài	n	spinach	3
薄弱		bóruò	adj	weak; frail	19
補習班	补习班	bǔxíbān	n	"cram" school	17
不必		bùbì		not necessary; no need to	16
不斷	不断	bùduàn	adv	constantly	15
不管		bùguǎn	conj	no matter how	15
不過	不过	bùguò	conj	but; however	5
不過	不过	bùguò	adv	no more than; just; only	9
不見得	不见得	bù jiàn de		not necessarily	1
不堪設想	不堪设想	bùkān shèxiǎng		too dreadful to contemplate	20
不然		bùrán	conj	otherwise	18
不如		bùrú		not as...	16
不同		bùtóng	adj/n	different; difference	7
不以為然	不以为然	bù yǐ wéi rán		disapprove of; object to	17
不足		bùzú		not sufficient; not enough	16
部		bù	m	measure word (for movies, multivolume books, etc.)	7

▼▼

Traditional	Simplified	Pinyin	Part of Speech	English	Lesson
▲**C**▲					
猜對了	猜对了	cāi duì le	vc	guessed correctly	2
採取	采取	cǎiqǔ	v	to take/adopt (measures, methods, steps)	19
菜單	菜单	càidān	n	menu	3
餐館	餐馆	cānguǎn	n	restaurant	2
餐廳	餐厅	cāntīng	n	cafeteria	2
參加	参加	cānjiā	v	to attend; to take part in	13
操心		cāo xīn	vo	to trouble or worry about; "to exercise" or tax one's mind over something	14
廁所	厕所	cèsuǒ	n	restroom; toilet	2
層	层	céng	m	measure word for floors	2
曾經	曾经	céngjīng	adv	(indicating that something happened before) once	9
查		chá	v	to investigate; to check	18
產量	产量	chǎnliàng	n	output	20
產品	产品	chǎnpǐn	n	product	16
產生	产生	chǎnshēng	v	to produce; to emerge; to give rise to	18
常客		chángkè	n	frequent patron; regular	3
長	长	cháng	adj	long	1
長短	长短	chángduǎn	n	length	4
長途	长途	chángtú	n	long distance	10
吵		chǎo	adj	noisy	2
吵		chǎo	v	to disturb; to make noise	6
吵架		chǎo jià	vo	to quarrel	7, 14
趁		chèn	prep	take advantage of (an opportunity or situation)	10
稱	称	chēng	v	to weigh	10
成本		chéngběn	n	cost	20
成績	成绩	chéngjì	n	achievement	13
成績	成绩	chéngjì	n	grades	14
成千上萬	成千上万	chéng qiān shàng wàn		tens of thousands	13
成熟		chéngshú	adj	mature	17
城市		chéngshì	n	city	15
程度		chéngdù	n	degree; extent	11
承認	承认	chéngrèn	v	to admit; to acknowledge	17
吃醋		chī cù	vo	(col) to be jealous (because of rivalry in love); (lit) eat vinegar	9
吃素		chī sù	vo	to eat vegetarian food; to be a vegetarian	16
衝	冲	chòng	adj	abrupt; blunt	14

▼▼▼▼▼▼▼▼▼▼▼▼▼▼▼▼▼▼▼▼▼▼▼▼▼▼▼▼▼▼▼▼▼▼▼

Traditional	Simplified	Pinyin	Part of Speech	English	Lesson
抽		chōu	v	to pull out; to set aside (time)	14
臭氧層	臭氧层	chòuyǎng céng	n	ozone layer; ozonosphere	20
出		chū	v	to come out; to appear	16
出差		chū chāi	vo	to go on a business trip	10
出國	出国	chū guó	vo	go abroad	9
出嫁		chūjià	v	(of a woman) to get married	15
出門	出门	chū mén	vo	to be away from home; to go out	1
出生		chūshēng	v	to be born	1
出事		chūshì	vo	to have an accident; something bad happens	18
出現	出现	chūxiàn	v	to arise; to appear	15
出租		chūzū	v	to rent out; to let	6
廚房	厨房	chúfáng	n	kitchen	6
除非		chúfēi	conj	unless; only if	9
穿		chuān	v	to wear	4
傳統	传统	chuántǒng	adj/n	traditional; tradition	12
喘氣	喘气	chuǎn qì	vo	to pant; to gasp (for breath)	17
窗戶		chuānghu	n	window	2
床		chuáng	n	bed	2
吹		chuī	v	(col) to break up; (lit) blow	7
純棉(的)	纯棉(的)	chúnmián (de)	adj	pure cotton; 100% cotton	4
辭	辞	cí	v	to resign	15
辭職	辞职	cí zhí	vo	to resign from a position	15
聰明	聪明	cōngming	adj	bright; clever	14
從來	从来	cónglái	adv	ever (usually followed by a negative)	7
催		cuī	v	to hurry; to urge	11
措施		cuòshī	n	measure; step	19
錯誤	错误	cuòwù	n	mistake	19

▲D▲

Traditional	Simplified	Pinyin	Part of Speech	English	Lesson
打擊	打击	dǎjī	v	to strike, to hit; to attack	18
打基礎	打基础	dǎ jīchǔ	vo	to establish a foundation	17
打交道		dǎ jiāodào	vo	to deal with (usually persons)	5
打獵	打猎	dǎ liè	vo	to go hunting	18
打破		dǎ pò	vc	to break into pieces	7
打算		dǎsuàn	v/n	to plan; plan	5
打聽	打听	dǎtīng	v	to ask about; to inquire about	9
打通		dǎ tōng	vc	to go through; to make a successful connection (on the telephone)	10
打招呼		dǎ zhāohu	vo	to greet	6
打折		dǎ zhé	vo	to discount (from a set of list price)	4
大半		dàbàn	n	more than half; most	5
大部份	大部分	dà bùfen		majority	15

▼▼

Traditional	Simplified	Pinyin	Part of Speech	English	Lesson
大多		dàduō	adv	mostly	20
大多數	大多数	dà duōshù		most; the great majority	19
大概		dàgài	adv	probably	15
大官		dà guān	n	high-ranking official	12
大喊大叫		dà hǎn dà jiào		yell and shout	6
大可不必		dà kě búbì		no need whatsoever	19
大量		dàliàng	adj	in large quantity	20
大樓	大楼	dàlóu	n	tall building	10
大陸	大陆	dàlù	n	mainland; continent	9
大人		dàren	n	adult	8
大人物		dàrénwù		important person	11
大聲	大声	dàshēng	adv	loudly; in a big voice	6
大小		dàxiǎo	n	size	4
(大)熊貓	(大)熊猫	(dà) xióngmāo	n	(great) panda	19
大衣		dàyī	n	overcoat; long coat	19
大自然		dàzìrán	n	nature	19
待		dāi	v	to stay	9
戴		dài	v	to wear (jewelry, hat, watch, glasses, etc.)	12
帶	带	dài	v	to take or bring somebody along	2
帶	带	dài	v	to be equipped with; to come with	6
帶	带	dài	v	(col) to raise; to take care of (a child)	15
單親	单亲	dānqīn	adj	single parent	14
單位	单位	dānwèi	n	(work) unit	16
擔心	担心	dān xīn	vo	to worry	16
擔子	担子	dànzi	n	loaded carrying pole; burden	15
當	当	dāng	v	to work as; to be	5
當年	当年	dāngnián		in those years; at that time	11
當時	当时	dāngshí		at that time; of that time	12
導遊	导游	dǎoyóu	n	tour guide	9
道理		dàoli	n	reason; sense	1
到處	到处	dàochù	adv	everywhere; at all places	18
倒也是		dào yě shì		That's true (indicating concession)	13
...的話	...的话	dehuà		if	6
得		dé	v	to get	13
得到		dé dào	vc	to obtain	15
燈	灯	dēng	n	lantern; lamp	12
等		děng	v	to wait	7
等等		děng děng		etc.	4
瞪		dèng	v	to glower at	11
低		dī	adj	low	18
的確	的确	díquè	adv	indeed; really	17
地道		dìdao	adj	authentic	2

▼▼▼▼▼▼▼▼▼▼▼▼▼▼▼▼▼▼▼▼▼▼▼▼▼▼▼▼▼▼▼▼▼▼▼▼

Traditional	Simplified	Pinyin	Part of Speech	English	Lesson
地毯		dìtǎn	n	carpet	6
地位		dìwèi	n	status	15
地址		dìzhǐ	n	address	9
點(菜)	点(菜)	diǎn (cài)	v	to order (food)	3
電報	电报	diànbào	n	telegram	10
電話卡	电话卡	diànhuàkǎ	n	phone card	10
電腦	电脑	diànnǎo	n	computer	5
電影院	电影院	diànyǐngyuàn	n	cinema; movie theater	7
電子郵件	电子邮件	diànzi yóujiàn	n	email	10
調查	调查	diàochá	v/n	to investigate, to check; investigation	18
訂	订	dìng	v	to reserve; to book	9
定下來		dìng xialai	vc	to fix; to clarify (the relationship)	14
丟人		diū rén	vo	to lose face; to be disgraced	14
東岸	东岸	dōng'àn	n	east coast; east shore	9
東方	东方	dōngfāng	n	east; the Orient	9
東亞史	东亚史	Dōngyàshǐ	n	East Asian history	5
棟	栋	dòng	m	measure word for buildings	2
動手術	动手术	dòng shǒushù	vo	to have an operation; to perform an operation	16
動人	动人	dòngrén	adj	moving; touching	12
動物	动物	dòngwù	n	animal	19
動物房	动物房	dòngwùfáng	n	room where animals are housed	19
豆腐		dòufu	n	bean curd; tofu	3
督促		dūcù	v	to supervise and urge	17
毒		dú	n/v	toxin; poison; to poison	20
毒品		dúpǐn	n	narcotic drugs	18
獨立	独立	dúlì	adj	independent	14
讀書	读书	dú shū	vo	to study; to read	17
賭博	赌博	dǔbó	v	to gamble	18
端		duān	v	to carry something held level with both hands	12
隊	队	duì	n	team	13
對...來說	对...来说	duì...lái shuō		as to...; so far as... is concerned	5
對面	对面	duìmiàn	n	opposite; the other side	10
頓	顿	dùn	m	measure word for meals	3
多半		duōbàn	adv	mostly	8

▲E▲

而		ér	conj	and; but	14
兒童	儿童	értóng	n	(formal) children	8
二氧化硫		èryǎnghuàliú	n	sulfur dioxide	20

▲F▲

發愁	发愁	fā chóu	vo	to worry	16
發電廠	发电厂	fādiànchǎng	n	power plant	20

Traditional	Simplified	Pinyin	Part of Speech	English	Lesson
發揮	发挥	fāhuī	v	to give free rein to	17
發展	发展	fāzhǎn	n/v	development; to develop	13
法規	法规	fǎguī	n	laws and regulations	18
法律		fǎlǜ	n	the law	18
翻到		fān dào	vc	to turn to	6
反對	反对	fǎnduì	v	to oppose	8
反而		fǎn'ér	adv	on the contrary	8
反復	反复	fǎnfù	adv	repeatedly	5
反過來	反过来	fǎn guò lái		conversely	15
反正		fǎnzhèng	conj	anyway	13
販賣	贩卖	fànmài	v	to peddle; to sell at a profit (often derogatory: "traffic in")	18
犯罪		fàn zuì	vo	to commit a crime	18
飯錢	饭钱	fànqian		money for food	5
方便		fāngbiàn	adj	convenient	1
方面		fāngmiàn	n	aspect	14
方式		fāngshì	n	method	17
房子		fángzi	n	house	6
房租		fángzū	n	rent (for house or apartment)	5
放火		fàng huǒ	vo	to set fire to	18
放假		fàng jià	vo	to have a holiday/vacation; to have a day off	7
放心		fàngxīn	vo	to relax; to rest assured	10
放學	放学	fàng xué	vo	to get out of school; school lets out	14
非...不可		fēi...bùkě		to have to be; nothing other than would do	4
飛機	飞机	fēijī	n	airplane	1
費	费	fèi	n	fee	16
廢氣	废气	fèiqì	n	waste gas or steam	20
廢水	废水	fèishuǐ	n	waste water	20
廢渣	废渣	fèizhā	n	waste residue; solid waste	20
分擔	分担	fēndān	v	to share (burden; responsibilities)	15
分手		fēn shǒu	vo	to part company	14
分析		fēnxī	v	to analyze	20
封		fēng	m	measure word for letters	13
豐富	丰富	fēngfù	adj	abundant	13
豐盛	丰盛	fēngshèng	adj	sumptuous (meal)	12
風俗	风俗	fēngsú	n	folk customs	12
否則	否则	fǒuzé	conj	otherwise	9
夫婦	夫妇	fūfù	n	husband and wife	15
服從	服从	fúcóng	v	to obey	15
服裝	服装	fúzhuāng	n	(formal) clothing	19
付		fù	v	to pay	16
付不起		fù bu qǐ	vc	cannot afford	16

▼▼

Traditional	Simplified	Pinyin	Part of Speech	English	Lesson
付錢	付钱	fù qián	vo	to pay (for a purchase)	4
父子		fùzǐ	n	father and son	14
負擔	负担	fùdān	n	burden; load	17
負責任	负责任	fù zérèn	vo	to take responsibility	8
婦女	妇女	fùnǚ	n	woman; women in general	15

▲G▲

Traditional	Simplified	Pinyin	Part of Speech	English	Lesson
該	该	gāi	av	應該; should	9
改革開放	改革开放	gǎigé kāifàng	v	to reform and open up	15
敢		gǎn	v	to dare	8
趕	赶	gǎn	v	to drive away	12
趕緊	赶紧	gǎnjǐn	adv	in a hurried fashion; right away	6
趕快	赶快	gǎnkuài	adv	quickly	9
感到		gǎn dào	vc	to feel	13
鋼琴	钢琴	gāngqín	n	piano	14
羔羊		gāoyáng	n	lamb	18
高中		gāozhōng	n	senior high school	7
告狀	告状	gào zhuàng	vo	(lit) to file a lawsuit against somebody; to lodge a complaint with somebody's superior	14
隔壁		gébì	n	next door	6
各		gè	pr	every; various	1
各種各樣	各种各样	gèzhǒng gèyàng		of various kinds	12
跟		gēn	v	to follow	3
根本		gēnběn	adv	fundamentally; (often used in the negative form) not at all	12
弓		gōng	n	bow	1
工廠	工厂	gōngchǎng	n	factory	14
工程		gōngchéng	n	engineering	14
工學院	工学院	gōngxuéyuàn	n	school of engineering	5
工業	工业	gōngyè	n	industry	20
功課	功课	gōngkè	n	homework	3
公平		gōngpíng	adj	fair	15
公司		gōngsī	n	company	9
購物中心	购物中心	gòuwù zhōngxīn		shopping center	4
姑父		gūfu	n	father's sister's husband	14
姑媽	姑妈	gūmā	n	aunt (father's sister)	9
古城墻	古城墙	gǔ chéngqiáng		ancient city wall	11
古典音樂	古典音乐	gǔdiǎn yīnyuè		classical music	7
鼓勵	鼓励	gǔlì	v	to encourage	17
僱	雇	gù	v	to hire; to employ	18
顧客	顾客	gùkè	n	customer	19

▼▼

Traditional	Simplified	Pinyin	Part of Speech	English	Lesson
故事		gùshì	n	story	11
掛	挂	guà	v	to hang	2
掛號	挂号	guà hào	vo	to register (mail)	10
怪		guài	v	to blame	8
怪不得		guài bu de		no wonder	20
觀點	观点	guāndiǎn	n	point of view	17
關心	关心	guān xīn	vo	to be concerned with/about	16
管		guǎn	v	(col) to control, manage; mind, care about	5
管理學院	管理学院	guǎnlǐ xuéyuàn		school of management	5
光榮	光荣	guāngróng	n/adj	glory; glorious	13
廣告欄	广告栏	guǎnggào lán		ad columns; classified ads	6
逛街		guàng jiē	vo	to go window shopping; to stroll (in the city)	10
規定	规定	guīdìng	v/n	to stipulate; stipulation; rule	18
櫃子	柜子	guìzi	n	cabinet; cupboard	2
國寶	国宝	guóbǎo	n	national treasure	19
國際	国际	guójì	n	international	13
國家	国家	guójiā	n	country	13
國王	国王	guówáng	n	king	12
過份	过分	guòfèn	adj	excessive	16
過幾天	过几天	guò jǐ tiān		in a few days	2
過節	过节	guòjié	vo	to celebrate a festival or holiday	12
...過去	...过去	…guò qu	(v)c	...toward	10
過日子	过日子	guò rìzi	vo	(col) to live; to get by; to survive	14
過剩	过剩	guòshèng	v	excess; surplus	16

▲ **H** ▲

Traditional	Simplified	Pinyin	Part of Speech	English	Lesson
哈哈大笑		hāhā dà xiào		laugh heartily	11
孩子		háizi	n	child	5
海		hǎi	n	ocean	11
海運	海运	hǎiyùn	v	transport by sea	10
害蟲	害虫	hàichóng	n	harmful insect	20
害		hài	v	to do harm to; to cause trouble to	17
航空公司		hángkōng gōngsī		airline	9
毫無	毫无	háowú		not an iota; not in the least	16
好處	好处	hǎochù	n	advantage; benefit	1
好看		hǎokàn	adj	nice looking; attractive	4
好像		hǎoxiàng		as if; seem to be	4
好奇		hàoqí	adj	curious	10
喝醉酒		hē zuì jiǔ	vc	to get drunk	7
河		hé	n	river	6
荷包		hébāo	n	embroidered pouch; pouch; purse	12

Traditional	Simplified	Pinyin	Part of Speech	English	Lesson
核電站	核电站	hédiànzhàn	n	nuclear power plant	20
合適	合适	héshì	adj	suitable	4
黑白分明		hēibái fēnmíng		with black and white sharply contrasted; clear cut	19
狠狠地		hěnhěn de	adv	vigorously; with a great deal of intensity	11
烘乾機	烘干机	hōnggānjī	n	(clothes) dryer	2
猴腦	猴脑	hóunǎo	n	monkey brain	19
猴子		hóuzi	n	monkey	19
厚薄		hòubó	n	thickness	4
後果	后果	hòuguǒ	n	consequence; aftermath	20
後悔	后悔	hòuhuǐ	v	to regret	7
後面	后面	hòumian		in the back; back	6
後天	后天	hòutiān	t	the day after tomorrow	5
忽略		hūlüè	v	to overlook; to neglect	19
湖		hú	n	lake	11, 20
護士	护士	hùshi	n	nurse	15
護照	护照	hùzhào	n	passport	9
互相矛盾		hùxiāng máodùn		contradictory; contradict each other	19
花錢	花钱	huā qián	vo	to spend money	16
划船		huá chuán	vo	to row/paddle a boat	11
華南虎	华南虎	Huánán hǔ		the South Chinese tiger	19
化工		huàgōng	n	chemical engineering; chemical industry	20
化學	化学	huàxué	n	chemistry	20
化妝品	化妆品	huàzhuāng pǐn	n	cosmetic products	4
畫畫兒	画画儿	huà huàr	vo	to paint; to draw	14
懷孕	怀孕	huái yùn	vo	to be pregnant	15
環保	环保	huánbǎo		environmental protection; 環境保護 / 环境保护	20
環境	环境	huánjìng	n	environment; surroundings	6, 20
患		huàn	v	contract (an illness)	16
會	会	huì	av	to be good at; to know how to	3
婚姻		hūnyīn	n	marriage	15
火		huǒ	n	fire	8
火柴		huǒchái	n	match	8
火車	火车	huǒchē	n	train	9
火爐	火炉	huǒlú	n	furnace	9
火災	火灾	huǒzāi	n	fire (disaster)	8
或		huò	conj	or	6

▲ J ▲

激動	激动	jīdòng	adj	excited	6
基本上		jīběnshang		basically	18

Traditional	Simplified	Pinyin	Part of Speech	English	Lesson
幾乎	几乎	jīhū	adv	almost	8
機場	机场	jīchǎng	n	airport	9
機會	机会	jīhuì	n	opportunity	15
機票	机票	jīpiào	n	plane ticket	9
機器	机器	jīqì	n	machine; machinery	17
雞	鸡	jī	n	chicken	12
雞蛋	鸡蛋	jīdàn	n	chicken egg	19
集會	集会	jíhuì	n/v	assembly; to assemble	18
及		jí	conj	(formal) and	17
極端	极端	jíduān	n	the extreme; an extreme	17
急病		jíbìng	n	serious illness; illness that needs immediate medical attention	16
急躁		jízào	adj	impetuous; impatient	7
即使		jíshǐ	conj	even; even if	17
擠	挤	jǐ	adj/v	crowded; to squeeze, press, push against	11
擠下來	挤下来	jǐ xialai	vc	to squeeze one's way down; to push one's way off	11
技術	技术	jìshù	n	technology	14
寂寞		jìmò	adj	lonely	13
妓女		jìnǔ	n	prostitute	18
寄		jì	v	to send by mail	10
寄丟了		jì diū le	vc	to get lost in the mail	10
祭祀		jìsì	v	to offer sacrifices to	12
既然		jìrán	conj	since; now that	9
記者	记者	jìzhě	n	reporter	3
記住	记住	jì zhù	vc	to remember; to fix in the memory	5
紀錄片	纪录片	jìlùpiàn	n	documentary film	8
家庭		jiātíng	n	family	14
家庭教師	家庭教师	jiātíng jiàoshī		private tutor	17
家庭主婦	家庭主妇	jiātíng zhǔfù	n	housewife	15
家務	家务	jiāwù	n	household duties	15
家長	家长	jiāzhǎng	n	parent; head of a family	8
傢俱	家具	jiājù	n	furniture	2
加快		jiākuài	v	to quicken; to speed up	20
加上		jiāshang	vc	to add to; in addition	16
價格	价格	jiàgé	n	price (formal)	16
價錢	价钱	jiàqian	n	price	4
價值觀念	价值观念	jiàzhí guānniàn		values; concepts or system of values	18
假期	假期	jiàqī	n	vacation; "vacation period"	9
間	间	jiān	m	measure word for rooms	6
監獄	监狱	jiānyù	n	jail; prison	18
簡直	简直	jiǎnzhí	adv	simply	17

Traditional	Simplified	Pinyin	Part of Speech	English	Lesson
剪		jiǎn	v	to cut (with scissors)	19
減肥	减肥	jiǎn féi	vo	to lose weight	16
減價	减价	jiǎn jià	vo	to discount; on sale	4
減少	减少	jiǎnshǎo	v	to decrease	15
見面	见面	jiàn miàn	vo	to meet; to get together	7
建議	建议	jiànyì	v/n	to suggest; suggestion	5
建築	建筑	jiànzhù	n/v	architecture; to build	11
健康		jiànkāng	adj/n	healthy; health	3
健全		jiànquán	adj	well developed (of laws, institutions); sound	18
將	将	jiāng		will; shall	20
將來	将来	jiānglái	t	in the future	17
江		jiāng	n	river	12
講	讲	jiǎng	v	(col) stress; pay attention to	19
交通		jiāotōng	n	transportation; communications	6
交往		jiāowǎng	v	to socialize; to have dealings with	7
驕傲	骄傲	jiāo'ào	adj	proud	13
教練	教练	jiàoliàn	n	coach	13
教學	教学	jiàoxué	n	teaching; education	17
教育		jiàoyù	v/n	to educate; education	8
叫(菜)		jiào (cài)	v	to order (food); to call	3
接		jiē	v	to pick up (somebody)	3
接(電話)	接(电话)	jiē (diànhuà)	v(o)	to answer (the phone)	20
街		jiē	n	street	6
節目	节目	jiémù	n	(TV, radio) program; performance	7
節日	节日	jiérì	n	festival; holiday	12
節食	节食	jiéshí	v	to restrict one's food intake; to be on a diet	16
結果	结果	jiéguǒ	conj/n	as a result; result	8, 13
結婚	结婚	jié hūn	vo	to get married	14
結束	结束	jiéshù	v	to end	1
解決	解决	jiějué	v	to resolve	15
解剖		jiěpōu	v	to dissect	19
姐夫		jiěfu	n	older sister's husband	15
芥蘭	芥兰	jièlán	n	Chinese broccoli	3
(找)藉口	(找)借口	(zhǎo) jièkǒu	vo	(look for) an excuse	8
金牌		jīnpái	n	gold medal	13
緊張	紧张	jǐnzhāng	adj	tense; nervous	13
禁止		jìnzhǐ	v	to prohibit	18
儘可能	尽可能	jǐnkěnéng	adv	try one's best	12
儘量	尽量	jǐnliàng	adv	to the best of one's ability	19
精彩		jīngcǎi	adj	spectacular; exciting	13
精神		jīngshén	n	spirit	12
經常	经常	jīngcháng	adv	frequently	7

▼ ▼

Traditional	Simplified	Pinyin	Part of Speech	English	Lesson
經濟	经济	jīngjì	n/adj	economy; economical	18
經驗	经验	jīngyàn	n	experience	5
警察		jǐngchá	n	police	18
敬祝		jìngzhù	v	to wish respectfully	11
鏡子	镜子	jìngzi	n	mirror	7
競爭	竞争	jìngzhēng	v	to compete	17
酒吧		jiǔbā	n	bar	7
救		jiù	v	to save (life)	12
救命		jiù mìng	vo	to save (someone's) life	18
舊	旧	jiù	adj	(of things) old	2
居		jū	v	to occupy (a certain position)	20
居民		jūmín	n	resident	20
居然		jūrán	adv	to one's surprise	14
據說	据说	jùshuō		it is said that; allegedly	8
決定	决定	juédìng	v/n	to decide; decision	16
決賽	决赛	juésài	n	final match	13
均衡		jūnhéng	adj	balanced; proportionate	16
▲**K**▲					
卡路里		kǎlùlǐ	n/m	calorie	3
卡通		kǎtōng	n	cartoon	8
開朗	开朗	kāilǎng	adj	outgoing and cheerful	7
開槍	开枪	kāi qiāng	vo	to fire a gun	8
開玩笑	开玩笑	kāi wánxiào	vo	to joke; to joke around	6
開學	开学	kāi xué	vo	new semester begins	1
看病		kàn bìng	vo	to see a doctor	16
看不慣	看不惯	kàn bu guàn	vc	cannot bear the sight of; to frown upon	15
看法		kànfǎ	n	point of view	3
看來	看来	kànlái		appear; seem	17
抗議	抗议	kàngyì	v	to protest	19
考慮	考虑	kǎolǜ	v	to consider; to think over	5
靠		kào	v	to depend	1
靠		kào	v	to lean against	2
科學家	科学家	kēxuéjiā	n	scientist	19
可不是		kě bú shì		Isn't that the truth?	13
可靠		kěkào	adj	reliable	10
可憐	可怜	kělián	adj/v	pitiable; to pity	19
可怕		kěpà	adj	terrible	9
肯		kěn	av	to be willing to	11
肯定		kěndìng	adv	definitely	5
空		kōng	adj	empty	2
空間	空间	kōngjiān	n	space	19
空氣	空气	kōngqì	n	air	20
空調	空调	kōngtiáo	n	air-conditioning	2

Traditional	Simplified	Pinyin	Part of Speech	English	Lesson
空運	空运	kōngyùn	v	transport by air	10
恐怕		kǒngpà	adv	I'm afraid that; I think perhaps; probably	2
苦心	苦心	kǔxīn	n	painstaking efforts	17
▲L▲					
來對了	来对了	lái duì le	vc	(it was a) right (decision) to come	10
來不及	来不及	lái bu jí	vc	there's not enough time (for)	9
籃	籃	lán	n	basket	13
籃球	籃球	lánqiú	n	basketball	6
懶	懒	lǎn	adj	lazy	14
老百姓		lǎobǎixìng	n	"old hundred names;" ordinary folks	12
老闆	老板	lǎobǎn	n	boss; owner	3
老伴兒	老伴儿	lǎobànr	n	(col) husband or wife of an old married couple	14
老年癡呆症	老年痴呆症	lǎonián chīdāi zhèng		Alzheimer's disease	19
老生		lǎoshēng	n	returning student	1
老鼠		lǎoshǔ	n	mouse; rat	15
樂觀	乐观	lèguān	adj	be optimistic	15
樂壞了	乐坏了	lè huài le	vc	thrilled to pieces	17
離婚	离婚	lí hūn	vo	to get divorced	14
離開	离开	líkāi	vc	to leave	1
理解		lǐjiiě	v	to understand; to comprehend	17
理想		lǐxiǎng	n/adj	ideal	6
理智		lǐzhì	n/adj	reason; intellect; rational	18
禮拜	礼拜	lǐbài	n	week	9
禮堂	礼堂	lǐtáng	n	auditorium	8
厲害	厉害	lìhai	adj	terrible; severe	7
歷史	历史	lìshǐ	n	history	14
聯邦	联邦	liánbāng	n	federation	20
戀戀不捨	恋恋不舍	liànliàn bù shě		(to leave) reluctantly	11
亮		liàng	adj	bright	12
聊		liáo	v	to chat	5
陵墓		língmù	n	mausoleum; tomb	11
領事館	领事馆	lǐngshìguǎn	n	consulate	9
領先	领先	lǐngxiān	v	(in ball games) to lead	13
另		lìng	pr	the other; another	8
留		liú	v	to leave (a note); to assign (homework)	17
龍舟	龙舟	lóngzhōu	n	dragon boat	12
樓梯	楼梯	lóutī	n	stairway	6
樓下	楼下	lóuxià		downstairs	2
路上		lùshang	n	on the way	10
路線	路线	lùxiàn	n	route	9

Traditional	Simplified	Pinyin	Part of Speech	English	Lesson
陸空聯運	陆空联运	lùkōng liányùn		land-air linked transport	10
旅行社		lǚxíngshè	n	travel agency	9
率		lǜ	n	rate; proportion	18
履歷	履历	lǚlì	n	curriculum vitae; résumé	5
亂放	乱放	luàn fàng		put (things) all over the place	18
亂七八糟	乱七八糟	luàn qī bā zāo		messy; messed up	8
輪到	轮到	lún dào	vc	become the turn of	10

▲M▲

Traditional	Simplified	Pinyin	Part of Speech	English	Lesson
麻煩	麻烦	máfan	v/adj	to trouble; troublesome	3
馬路	马路	mǎlù	n	road	2
馬上	马上	mǎshàng	adv	immediately; right away	3
罵	骂	mà	v	to scold	14
嘛		ma	p	indicating evident and clear reasoning	14
瞞	瞞	mán	v	to hide the truth from; to obscure	6
貓	猫	māo	n	cat	15
毛衣		máoyī	n	woolen sweater	4
煤	煤	méi	n	coal	20
煤爐	煤炉	méilú	n	coal stove	20
每當...時	每当...时	měi dāng...shí		whenever	13
門	门	mén	m	measure word for (academic) courses	5
門口	门口	ménkǒu	n	doorway; entrance	3
米		mǐ	n	(uncooked) rice	12
秘密		mìmì	n/adj	secret	11
面臨	面临	miànlín	v	to face; to be confronted with	19
秒鐘	秒钟	miǎozhōng	n	second (of time)	13
妙齡	妙龄	miàolíng	adj	(of young girls) the wonderful age	11
滅絕	灭绝	mièjué	v	to exterminate; to become extinct	19
明顯	明显	míngxiǎn	adj	obvious	15
明信片		míngxìnpiàn	n	postcard	10
明星		míngxīng	n	bright star; (movie, etc.) star	16
名牌		míngpái	n	famous brand; name brand	4
名勝古蹟	名胜古迹	míngshèng gǔjì		famous scenic spots and ancient historic sites	11
模范	模范	mófàn	adj/n	model	15
模仿		mófǎng	v	to imitate	8
母親	母亲	mǔqin	n	mother	10
墓碑		mùbēi	n	tombstone	11
目標	目标	mùbiāo	n	goal; target	17
木刻		mùkè		carved in wood; wood carving	15

▲N▲

Traditional	Simplified	Pinyin	Part of Speech	English	Lesson
拿手		náshǒu	adj	good at; adept	3
那樣	那样	nàyàng	pr	that manner; that kind	8

Traditional	Simplified	Pinyin	Part of Speech	English	Lesson
奶奶		nǎinai	n	paternal grandmother	14
南方		nánfāng	n	the south	12
男女		nánnǚ	n	men and women; male and female	15
男生		nánshēng	n	male student	15
難辦	难办	nán bàn		hard to handle	20
難道	难道	nándào	adv	(introducing a rhetorical question) Do you mean to say?	4
難怪	难怪	nánguài	adv	no wonder	7
難免	难免	nánmiǎn	adv	inevitably; hard to avoid	8
難題	难题	nántí	n	difficult problem; dilemma	19
難聽	难听	nántīng	adj	ugly to listen to	7
腦子	脑子	nǎozi	n	brains; mind	18
鬧翻	闹翻	nào fān	vc	to have a falling out (with somebody)	7
嫩		nèn	adj	tender	3
能力		nénglì	n	ability; capacity	20
能源		néngyuán	n	energy resources	20
嗯		ng	exc	interjection indicating minor regret over an otherwise satisfactory situation	6
膩(了)	腻(了)	nì(le)	v	(col) to be bored with doing something; to be sick of doing something	9
年代		niándài	n	decade	9
年級	年级	niánjí	n	grade; year	1
年輕	年轻	niánqīng	adj	young	15
牛肉		niúròu	n	beef	3
牛仔褲	牛仔裤	niúzǎikù	n	jeans; "cowboy pants"	4
農曆	农历	nónglì	n	"agricultural" calendar; lunar calendar	12
弄		nòng	v	(col) to get	19
女孩兒	女孩儿	nǚháir	n	a girl; a young woman	3
女人		nǚrén	n	(col) woman	15
女生		nǚshēng	n	female student	15
女子		nǚzǐ	n	(formal) woman	15
虐待		nüèdài	v	to abuse	19

▲O▲

| 噢 | | ō | exc | oh | 7 |
| 偶爾 | 偶尔 | ǒu'ěr | adv | occasionally | 8 |

▲P▲

怕		pà	v	to be afraid	9
拍		pāi	v	to make (a film); to shoot (a film, photograph)	16
拍		pāi	v	to send (a telegram); to pat	10

▼▼▼▼▼▼▼▼▼▼▼▼▼▼▼▼▼▼▼▼▼▼▼▼▼▼▼▼▼▼▼▼▼▼▼▼

Traditional	Simplified	Pinyin	Part of Speech	English	Lesson
排出		pái chū	vc	to discharge; to emit	20
排隊	排队	pái duì	vo	to stand in line; to line up	10
排放		páifàng	v	to discharge; to emit	20
牌子		páizi	n	brand	4
盤	盘	pán	m	plate; platter	12
陪		péi	v	to accompany; to go with someone	4
碰		pèng	v	to touch; to bump	18
批評	批评	pīpíng	v	to criticize	17
脾氣	脾气	píqi	n	temper; temperament	7
片		...piàn		film	8
片面		piànmiàn	adj	one-sided	3
漂亮		piàoliang	adj	pretty	3
頻道	频道	píndào	n	TV channel	8
貧富不均	贫富不均	pín fù bù jūn		unequal distribution of wealth; (lit) "poor and rich are unequal"	18
平等		píngděng	adj	equal	15
平衡		pínghéng	adj	balanced	19
憑	凭	píng	prep	based on	19
婆媳		póxí	n	mother-in-law and daughter in-law	14
破壞	破坏	pòhuài	v	to destroy	19

▲**Q**▲

Traditional	Simplified	Pinyin	Part of Speech	English	Lesson
妻子		qīzi	n	wife	15
其實	其实	qíshí	adv	actually	3
其他		qítā	pr	other	5
奇怪		qíguài	adj	strange; unfamiliar	10
歧視	歧视	qíshì	v	to discriminate against	15
啟發	启发	qǐfā	v	to enlighten; inspire	17
千萬	千万	qiānwàn	adv	be sure to	11
簽證	签证	qiānzhèng	n	visa	9
簽字	签字	qiān zì	vo	to sign one's name	4
前邊	前边	qiánbian	in front		1
前腳...後腳...	前脚...后脚...	qiánjiǎo...hòujiǎo...		no sooner...than...	18
前天		qiántiān	t	the day before yesterday	2
槍	枪	qiāng	n	gun (rifle, pistol, etc.); spear	18
槍枝	枪枝	qiāngzhī	n	firearms	18
強調	强调	qiángdiào	v	to stress; to emphasize	17
強制	强制	qiángzhì	v	to force; to coerce; to compel	18
強壯	强壮	qiángzhuàng	adj	strong	13
搶劫	抢劫	qiǎngjié	v	to rob; to loot	18
親朋好友	亲朋好友	qīn péng hǎo yǒu		good friends and dear relatives	12
親戚	亲戚	qīnqi	n	relatives	15
青菜		qīngcài	n	green leafy vegetables	3

Traditional	Simplified	Pinyin	Part of Speech	English	Lesson
清淡		qīngdàn	adj	light in flavor	3
清蒸		qīngzhēng	v	to steam (food without heavy sauce)	3
輕鬆	轻松	qīngsōng	adj	relaxed; easygoing	17
情況	情况	qíngkuàng	n	situation	7
慶祝	庆祝	qìngzhù	v	to celebrate	13
窮人	穷人	qióngrén	n	poor people	16
裘皮		qiúpí	n	fur, i.e., animal skin with fur attached	19
球場	球场	qiúchǎng	n	ball court	6
球迷		qiúmí	n	fan (of ball games: basketball, football, etc.)	6
球賽	球赛	qiúsài	n	ball game (match)	13
區別	区别	qūbié	n/v	distinction; to distinguish	19
取得		qǔdé	v	to obtain	13
取締	取缔	qǔdì	v	to ban; to suppress	18
去世		qùshì	v	to pass away, die	14
權利	权利	quánlì	n	right	18
全面		quánmiàn		comprehensive	18
缺點	缺点	quēdiǎn	n	shortcoming	17
卻	却	què	conj	however	10
確實	确实	quèshí	adv	indeed; in truth	9

▲R▲

Traditional	Simplified	Pinyin	Part of Speech	English	Lesson
然後	然后	ránhòu		then; after that; next	9
熱帶雨林	热带雨林	rèdài yǔlín	n	tropical rain forest	19
人道		réndào	n/adj	humanitarianism; humane	19
人家		rénjia	pr	others; they	13
人口		rénkǒu	n	population	11
人老珠黃	人老珠黄	rén lǎo zhū huáng		(metaphor) women grow old and pearls turn yellow; not as beautiful as before	11
人們	人们	rénmen	n	people	12
人民		rénmín	n	the people	20
人山人海		rén shān rén hǎi		huge crowds of people	11
人數	人数	rénshù	n	the number of people	15
人體	人体	réntǐ	n	human body	20
人物		rénwù	n	character in a play, story, etc.	8
人員	人员	rényuán	n	personnel; staff	16
忍不住		rěn bu zhù	vc	unable to bear, can't help but	11
任人宰割		rèn rén zǎigē		allow oneself to be slaughtered or trampled upon	18
認為	认为	rènwéi	v	to hold (the opinion that)	3
認真	认真	rènzhēn	adj	earnest; serious	17

▼▼▼▼▼▼▼▼▼▼▼▼▼▼▼▼▼▼▼▼▼▼▼▼▼▼▼▼▼▼▼▼▼▼▼▼▼▼▼

Traditional	Simplified	Pinyin	Part of Speech	English	Lesson
扔		rēng	v	to throw	19
仍然		réngrán	adv	still	18
日程		rìchéng	n	schedule; itinerary	10
日益加劇	日益加剧	rìyì jiājù		become more aggravated day by day	20
日用品		rìyòngpǐn	n	daily household necessities	2
日子		rìzi	n	day; time; life	12
榮譽	荣誉	róngyù	n	honor	13
如		rú	v	such as; like; for example	18

▲**S**▲

Traditional	Simplified	Pinyin	Part of Speech	English	Lesson
賽	赛	sài	v	to race; to compete	12
三廢	三废	sānfèi	n	three types of waste	20
散步		sàn bù	vo	to take a walk	9
沙發	沙发	shāfā	n	sofa	8
殺人	杀人	shā rén	vo	to kill someone	18
商店		shāngdiàn	n	shop	2
商量		shāngliang	v	to discuss; to negotiate	9
商業片	商业片	shāngyèpiàn	n	commercial film	8
賞月	赏月	shǎng yuè	vo	to admire the full moon	12
上街		shàng jiē	vo	to go into the streets	12
上進心	上进心	shàngjìnxīn	n	the desire to be better; aspiration	17
上學	上学	shàng xué	vo	to go to school	17
上演		shàngyǎn	v	(of plays or movies) to show	8
稍微		shāowēi	adv	a little bit; somewhat	6
燒死	烧死	shāo sǐ	vc	to burn to death	8
少		shǎo	adv	(of quantity) less	3
少女		shàonǚ	n	young girl	11
社會	社会	shèhuì	n	society	15
設備	设备	shèbèi	n	facilities; equipment	2
設立	设立	shèlì	v	to establish; to set up	19
攝取	摄取	shèqǔ	v	to absorb, assimilate (nutrients, water, etc.)	16
深		shēn	adj	deep	11
申請	申请	shēnqǐng	v	to apply (for admission to school; for job)	5
身材		shēncái	n	bodily figure	16
身強體壯	身强体壮	shēn qiáng tǐ zhuàng		(of a person) strong; sturdy	13
身上		shēnshang		on the body	12
身體	身体	shēntǐ	n	body	13
什麼樣	什么样	shénmeyàng		what kind	6
甚至		shènzhì	adv	even; even to the point	15
聲音	声音	shēngyīn	n	voice	13
生存		shēngcún	v	to exist; to survive	19

▼▼▼▼▼▼▼▼▼▼▼▼▼▼▼▼▼▼▼▼▼▼▼▼▼▼▼▼▼▼▼▼

Traditional	Simplified	Pinyin	Part of Speech	English	Lesson
生氣	生气	shēng qì	vo	to be angry	11
生態	生态	shēngtài	n	ecology	19
生物		shēngwù	n	biology; living thing, organism	19
升學	升学	shēng xué	vo	to advance to a higher level of schooling	15
省錢	省钱	shěng qián	vo	to save money	1
省下來	省下来	shěng xialai	vc	to save (money, time)	5
詩	诗	shī	n	poem; poetry	12
詩人	诗人	shīrén	n	poet	12
失去		shīqù	v	to lose	19
失望		shīwàng	v/adj	disappointed	13
失業	失业	shī yè	vo	out of work; to lose one's job	20
十分		shífēn	adv	very	7
石油		shíyóu	n	petroleum	20
實際上	实际上	shíjì shang	adv	actually, in fact, in reality	12
實習	实习	shíxí	v	to work as an intern	5
實驗	实验	shíyàn	n/v	experiment; to experiment	19
實驗室	实验室	shíyànshì	n	laboratory	20
實在	实在	shízài	adv	indeed; really	13
使		shǐ	v	to cause/make (someone do something)	17
使用		shǐyòng	v	to use	20
室		shì	n	room	6
試	试	shì	v	to try	6
世紀	世纪	shìjì	n	century	19
世界紀錄	世界纪录	shìjiè jìlù		world record	13
適合	适合	shìhé	v	to suit; to fit	17
適應	适应	shìyìng	v	to adapt; to become accustomed to	1
收好		shōu hǎo	vc	to put things away in their proper places	18
收據	收据	shōujù	n	receipt	4
手段		shǒuduàn	n	means, method; trick, artifice	18
手機	手机	shǒujī	n	cell phone	10
手術	手术	shǒushù	n	surgery	16
手續	手续	shǒuxù	n	procedure	1
首先		shǒuxiān		first and foremost	14
受不了		shòu bu liǎo	vc	cannot take it	5
受到		shòu dào	vc	to receive (influence, restriction, etc.)	18
受傷	受伤	shòu shāng	vo	to get wounded; to be injured	16
受影響	受影响	shòu yǐngxiǎng	vo	to be affected	6
輸	输	shū	v	to lose (a competition)	13
叔叔		shūshu	n	爸爸的弟弟; father's younger brother	14

▼▼▼▼▼▼▼▼▼▼▼▼▼▼▼▼▼▼▼▼▼▼▼▼▼▼▼▼▼▼▼▼▼▼▼▼▼

Traditional	Simplified	Pinyin	Part of Speech	English	Lesson
書架	书架	shūjià	n	bookshelf	2
熟悉		shúxi	v	to be familiar with	2
暑假		shǔjià	n	summer vacation	1
樹林	树林	shùlín	n	woods	6
數學	数学	shùxué	n	mathematics	17
帥哥	帅哥	shuàigē	n	(col) handsome young guy	13
雙學位	双学位	shuāng xuéwèi		"double degree"; double major	5
水電	水电	shuǐdiàn	n	water and electricity	6
水平		shuǐpíng	n	(water) level; standard	16
睡不好覺	睡不好觉	shuì bu hǎo jiào	vc	not able to sleep well	6
稅		shuì	n	tax	4
順便	顺便	shùnbiàn	adv	in passing; on the way; conveniently	9
順利	顺利	shùnlì	adj	without a hitch, smooth	10
說定	说定	shuō dìng	vc	to agree on; to settle	11
說法	说法	shuōfǎ		way of saying a thing; statement	3
思考		sīkǎo	v	to think about; to ponder	17
私人		sīrén	n	private individual	18
死		sǐ	v	to die	11
死記硬背	死记硬背	sǐ jì yìng bèi		mechanical memorizing	17
松樹林	松树林	sōngshùlín	n	pine grove/forest	20
素菜		sùcài	n	vegetable dishes	3
速度		sùdù	n	speed	13
酸雨		suānyǔ	n	acid rain	20
算		suàn	v	to count; to be counted as	6
隨著	随着	suízhe	conj	in the wake of; following	15
隨之	随之	suí zhī		along with it	18
所有		suǒyǒu		all	16

▲**T**▲

Traditional	Simplified	Pinyin	Part of Speech	English	Lesson
台		tái	m	measure word for machines	2
台灣	台湾	Táiwān	n	Taiwan	16
態度	态度	tàidù	n	attitude	17
談	谈	tán	v	to talk; to discuss	7
毯子		tǎnzi	n	blanket	2
湯	汤	tāng	n	soup	3
糖果		tángguǒ	n	candies	10
趟		tàng	m	measure word for round trips	9
淘汰		táotài	v	to eliminate through selection or competition	17
討論	讨论	tǎolùn	v	to discuss	5
套		tào	m	suite; set	4, 6
特產	特产	tèchǎn	n	unique local product	10
特地		tèdì	adv	specially	10

▼ ▼

Traditional	Simplified	Pinyin	Part of Speech	English	Lesson
特點	特点	tèdiǎn	n	special feature; distinguishing feature	17
T恤衫		tīxùshān	n	T shirt	4
提		tí	v	to mention	5
提高		tígāo	vc	to improve; to lift	15
體會到	体会到	tǐhuì dào	vc	to learn from experience; to realize	11
體貼	体贴	tǐtiē	adj	considerate	15
體現	体现	tǐxiàn	v	to embody; to manifest	15
體育	体育	tǐyù	n	physical education; sports	7
體育場	体育场	tǐyùchǎng	n	sports field	6
替		tì	prep	for; on behalf of	16
填鴨式	填鸭式	tiányāshì		cramming method (in teaching); (lit) "force feeding duck style"	17
挑剔		tiāoti	adj	picky; fastidious	4
鐵飯碗	铁饭碗	tiěfànwǎn	n	iron rice bowl (metaphor: secure job)	14
廳	厅	tīng	n	room; living room; an "outer" or more "public" room of a house	6
聽說	听说	tīngshuō	v	to be told; to hear of	2
挺		tǐng	adv	(col) quite; rather	7
通過	通过	tōngguò	prep	through (a method); by means of	18
童年		tóngnián	n	childhood	17
同工同酬		tóng gōng tóng chóu		equal pay for equal work	15
同屋		tóngwū	n	roommate	2
同意		tóngyì	v	to agree	3
統計學	统计学	tǒngjìxué	n	statistics	5
痛苦		tòngkǔ	adj	painful	19
偷竊	偷窃	tōuqiè	v	to steal; to pilfer	18
投		tóu	v	to throw	12
投江		tóu jiāng	vo	to jump into the river	12
突出		tūchū	adj/v	to be prominent; to stand out	15
突然		tūrán	adv	suddenly	11
圖	图	tú	v	to seek; to pursue	4
團圓	团圆	tuányuán	v	to reunite as a family	12
退休		tuìxiū	v	to retire	14

▲ W ▲

Traditional	Simplified	Pinyin	Part of Speech	English	Lesson
外面		wàimian		outside	12
完全		wánquán	adv	completely	8
萬一	万一	wànyī	adv	in case; in the highly unlikely event that…	10
往往		wǎngwǎng	adv	often (indicating tendency rather than frequency)	15
忘不了		wàng bu liǎo	vc	cannot forget; unable to forget	9

Traditional	Simplified	Pinyin	Part of Speech	English	Lesson
望女成鳳	望女成凤	wàng nǚ chéng fèng		hope for one's daughter to be very successful	17
望子成龍	望子成龙	wàng zǐ chéng lóng		hope for one's son to be very successful	17
威脅	威胁	wēixié	v/n	to threaten; threat	8
危害		wēihài	v	to harm	20
危險	危险	wēixiǎn	adj/n	dangerous; danger	18
為此	为此	wèi cǐ		of this; for this	13
偉大	伟大	wěidà	adj	great; mighty	11
委託	委托	wěituō	v	to commission; to entrust	20
未婚夫		wèihūnfū	n	fiancé	15
為	为	wèi	prep	for	5
喂		wèi/wéi	exc	(on the phone) hello	6
味道		wèidao	n	taste	3
味精		wèijīng	n	MSG (monosodium glutamate)	3
胃口		wèikǒu	n	appetite	2
衛生紙	卫生纸	wèishēngzhǐ	n	"sanitary paper"; toilet paper	4
文化		wénhuà	n	culture	7
文具		wénjù	n	stationery; writing supplies	2
文科		wénkē	n	humanities	5
文學	文学	wénxué	n	literature	5
文章		wénzhāng	n	article	3
紊亂	紊乱	wěnluàn	adj	disorderly; chaotic	18
臥室	卧室	wòshì	n	bedroom	6
屋裏	屋里	wūli		inside the room	7
污染		wūrǎn	v	to pollute	20
污染源		wūrǎnyuán	n	source of pollution	20
無法	无法	wúfǎ		unable; incapable; 沒有辦法/没有办法	17
無論	无论	wúlùn	conj	regardless of...; whether it be...	4
無論如何	无论如何	wúlùn rúhé		under any circumstances; no matter what	17
武打片		wǔdǎpiān	n	martial arts movie	16
舞刀弄槍	舞刀弄枪	wǔ dāo nòng qiāng		brandish swords and spears	18
物理		wùlǐ	n	physics	5
物美價廉	物美价廉	wùměi jià lián		attractive goods at inexpensive prices	4

▲X▲

Traditional	Simplified	Pinyin	Part of Speech	English	Lesson
西岸		xī'àn	n	west coast; west shore	9
西方		Xīfāng	n	the West	5
吸煙	吸烟	xī yān	vo	smoke	3
吸引		xīyǐn	v	to attract	11
犧牲	牺牲	xīshēng	v	to sacrifice	19

▼ ▼

Traditional	Simplified	Pinyin	Part of Speech	English	Lesson
稀有		xīyǒu	adj	rare	19
媳婦	媳妇	xífu	n	daughter-in-law; wife	11
習慣	习惯	xíguàn	n/v	usual practice; to be accustomed to	12
習題	习题	xítí	n	exercises	17
洗衣粉		xǐyī fěn	n	laundry powder	4
洗衣機	洗衣机	xǐyījī	n	washing machine	2
洗澡		xǐ zǎo	vo	to bathe; to take a bath/shower	11
系		xì	n	department (of a university)	5
戲	戏	xì	n	play; drama	7
戲迷	戏迷	xìmí	n	theater buff	7
閑著沒事	闲着没事	xián zhe méi shì		idle with nothing to do	8
現金	现金	xiànjīn	n	cash	4
現象	现象	xiànxiàng	n	phenomenon	15
憲法	宪法	xiànfǎ	n	constitution	18
限制		xiànzhì	n/v	restriction; to restrict; to limit	18
香		xiāng	adj	fragrant; nice smelling	3
香皂		xiāngzào	n	"scented soap"; bath soap; facial soap	4
相處	相处	xiāngchǔ	v	to get along; to interact	7
詳細	详细	xiángxì	adj	detailed; in detail	7
想法		xiǎngfǎ	n	idea; opinion	5
想起來		xiǎng qilai	vc	to realize; to recall	4
想像		xiǎngxiàng	v	to imagine; to visualize	11
想像力		xiǎngxiànglì	n	imagination	17
向		xiàng	prep	toward	8
項	项	xiàng	m	measure word for projects, tasks, etc.	20
像		xiàng	v	such as	4
象徵	象征	xiàngzhēng	v/n	to symbolize; symbol	12
消滅	消灭	xiāomiè	v	to perish; to die out; to eradicate	18
消失		xiāoshī	v	to disappear, to vanish, to dissolve	18
小白菜		xiǎo báicài	n	small Chinese cabbage	3
小孩兒	小孩儿	xiǎoháir	n	child	8
小男孩		xiǎo nánhái	n	a little boy	8
小心		xiǎoxīn	adj	careful	18
小學	小学	xiǎoxué	n	elementary school	17
校內		xiàonèi		on campus	1
校外		xiàowài		off campus	1
校園	校园	xiàoyuán	n	campus	7
薪水	薪水	xīnshui	n	salary	15
新生		xīnshēng	n	new student	1
新聞	新闻	xīnwén	n	news	8
新鮮	新鲜	xīnxian	adj	fresh	3

▼▼▼▼▼▼▼▼▼▼▼▼▼▼▼▼▼▼▼▼▼▼▼▼▼▼▼▼▼▼▼▼▼▼▼▼

Traditional	Simplified	Pinyin	Part of Speech	English	Lesson
心情		xīnqíng	n	mood	7
心事		xīnshì	n	something weighing on one's mind	7
心臟病	心脏病	xīnzàng bìng		heart disease	16
心臟科	心脏科	xīnzàng kē		cardiology department	16
信筒		xìntǒng	n	street mailbox for posting mail	10
信用卡		xìnyòng kǎ	n	credit card	4
行		xíng	v	(col) will work; will do	4
行李		xíngli	n	luggage	1
行為	行为	xíngwéi	n	behavior	8
性格		xìnggé	n	personality; disposition	7
興趣	兴趣	xìngqu	n	hobbies	7
休息		xiūxi	v	rest	17
需求量		xūqiú liàng		volume of demand	20
需要		xūyào	v/n	to need; need	4
虛榮	虚荣	xūróng	adj	vanity	19
許多	许多	xǔduō		many; a lot	11
選	选	xuǎn	v	choose	5
選好	选好	xuǎn hǎo	vc	to finish choosing	5
選課	选课	xuǎn kè	vo	to select/register for courses	5
學到	学到	xué dào	vc	to learn; to acquire	5
學分	学分	xuéfēn	n	academic credit	5

▲**Y**▲

Traditional	Simplified	Pinyin	Part of Speech	English	Lesson
鴨	鸭	yā	n	duck	12
壓力	压力	yālì	n	pressure	17
壓歲錢	压岁钱	yāsuìqián	n	money given to children as a lunar New Year gift	12
牙膏		yágāo	n	toothpaste	4
鹽	盐	yán	n	salt	3
嚴	严	yán	adj	strict	17
嚴重	严重	yánzhòng	adj	serious; grave	16
研究		yánjiū	v	to research	19
研究所		yánjiūsuǒ	n	graduate school	5
言論	言论	yánlùn	n	opinion on public affairs; speech	18
演		yǎn	v	(of plays or movies) to show	7
羊毛		yángmáo	n	wool; fleece	16
樣子	样子	yàngzi	n	style	4
搖滾樂	摇滚乐	yáogǔnyuè	n	rock 'n' roll music	7
藥	药	yào	n	medicine	16
要不然		yàobùrán	conj	otherwise	3
要不是		yàobúshì	conj	were it not for the fact that	14
要麼...要麼...	要么...要么...	yàome... yàome...	conj	if it's not A, it's B; either...or	5
要求		yāoqiú	n	demand	17
野蠻	野蛮	yěmán	adj	barbarous; uncivilized	19

Traditional	Simplified	Pinyin	Part of Speech	English	Lesson
也許	也许	yěxǔ	adv	perhaps	3
衣服		yīfu	n	clothes	4
衣櫃	衣柜	yīguì	n	wardrobe	2
一般		yìbān	adv	generally	2
一般來說	一般来说	yìbān lái shuō		generally speaking	17
一本正經	一本正经	yī běn zhèngjīng		in all seriousness	11
一部份	一部分	yī bùfen		one part	16
一刻鐘	一刻钟	yí kè zhōng	t	a quarter (of an hour)	3
一下子		yí xiàzi		at one go; in a short while	10
一向		yíxiàng	adv	consistently; always	10
一直		yīzhí	adv	continuously	6
醫療	医疗	yīliáo	n	medical treatment	16
醫學院	医学院	yīxuéyuàn	n	school of medicine	5
醫院	医院	yīyuàn	n	hospital	16
移民		yímín	v/n	to emigrate or immigrate; immigrant	9
已		yǐ	adv	already; 已經/已经	19
以及		yǐjí	conj	(formal) and	4
以來	以来	yǐlái	n	since	7
以為	以为	yǐwéi	v	to think erroneously	8
意見	意见	yìjiàn	n	opinion	5
意識	意识	yìshí	n	consciousness	19
意義	意义	yìyì	n	sense; meaning	16
藝術片	艺术片	yìshùpiàn	n	art film	8
因此		yīncǐ	conj	because of this; therefore	14
銀牌	银牌	yínpái	n	silver medal	13
引起		yǐnqǐ	v	to give rise to; to arouse; to provoke	8
印象		yìnxiàng	n	impression	11
贏	赢	yíng	v	to win (a prize, a game, etc.)	13
營養	营养	yíngyǎng	n	nutrition; nourishment	16
營養不良	营养不良	yíngyǎng bùliáng		malnutrition	16
影響	影响	yǐngxiǎng	n/v	influence; to influence	8
影子		yǐngzi	n	shadow	20
用處	用处	yòngchu	n	use	12
用心良苦	用心良苦	yòngxīn liángkǔ		have really given much thought to the matter; well-meaning	17
憂國憂民	忧国忧民	yōu guó yōu mín		concerned about one's country and one's people	12
優缺點	优缺点	yōuquēdiǎn	n	merits and demerits; advantages and disadvantages	17
油		yóu	n/adj	oil; oily	3

▼▼▼▼▼▼▼▼▼▼▼▼▼▼▼▼▼▼▼▼▼▼▼▼▼▼▼▼▼▼▼▼▼▼

Traditional	Simplified	Pinyin	Part of Speech	English	Lesson
由		yóu	prep	by; up to (indicating agency in written Chinese)	15
由於	由于	yóuyú	prep	due to; owing to	19
遊客	游客	yóukè	n	tourist	11
遊覽	游览	yóulǎn	v	to go sight-seeing	11
尤其是		yóuqí shì		particularly, especially	18
郵電局	邮电局	yóudiànjú	n	post and telecommunications office	10
郵簡	邮简	yóujiǎn	n	aerogram	10
郵局	邮局	yóujú	n	post office	9, 10
郵票	邮票	yóupiào	n	stamp	10
有益於	有益于	yǒuyì yú	vc	good for	13
有空		yǒu kòngr	vo	to have free time	7
有名		yǒumíng	adj	famous	16
有時	有时	yǒushí		sometimes	20
有效		yǒuxiào	adj	effective	20
有意		yǒuyì	adv	intentionally; on purpose	19
魚	鱼	yú	n	fish	3
於是	于是	yúshì	conj	so; therefore	4
與	与	yǔ	conj	(formal) and	16
與日俱增	与日俱增	yǔ rì jù zēng		grow with each passing day	20
浴巾		yùjīn	n	bath towel	4
浴室		yùshì	n	bathroom (a room for bathing)	2
元宵		yuánxiāo	n	night of the fifteenth of the first lunar month; sweet dumplings made of glutinous rice, eaten on this date	12
原來	原来	yuánlái	adv/adj	as it turns out; formerly; former	3
原來如此	原来如此	yuánlái rúcǐ		so that's the reason, so that's how it is	20
原因		yuányīn	n	cause; reason	16
圓	圆	yuán	adj	round	12
願意	愿意	yuànyi	av	to want to; to be willing to	5
院子		yuànzi	n	courtyard	12
月餅	月饼	yuèbǐng	n	moon cake	12
月亮		yuèliang	n	the moon	12
運動服	运动服	yùndòng fú	n	sportswear; sports clothes	4
運動會	运动会	yùndòng huì	n	sports meet	13
運動員	运动员	yùndòngyuán	n	athlete	13

▲Z▲

再三		zàisān	adv	over and over again	11
再說	再说	zàishuō	conj	besides; moreover	1
在乎		zàihu	v	mind; care	4
在...同時	在...同时	zài...tóngshí		at the same time as	19

▼▼▼▼▼▼▼▼▼▼▼▼▼▼▼▼▼▼▼▼▼▼▼▼▼▼▼▼▼▼▼▼▼▼▼▼

Traditional	Simplified	Pinyin	Part of Speech	English	Lesson
咱們	咱们	zánmen	pr	we (including the listener; 我們 does not necessarily include the listener)	5
葬		zàng	v	to bury (a person)	11
糟了		zāo le		(col) oh no; shoot; darn	19
早晨		zǎochen	t	early morning	12
早晚		zǎowǎn	adv	sooner or later	12
造成		zàochéng	v	to cause; to lead to	20
造價	造价	zàojià	n	manufacturing cost	20
增加		zēngjiā	v	to increase	19
炸		zhà	v	to bomb	8
窄		zhǎi	adj	narrow	11
長大	长大	zhǎng dà	vc	to grow up	1
長得	长得	zhǎng de		to look; to grow to be	3
丈夫		zhàngfu	n	husband	15
著急	着急	zháo jí	vo	to feel restless or impatient as a result of worrying about sth.	2
找不到		zhǎo bu dào	vc	to not be able to find	6
(找)藉口	(找)借口	(zhǎo) jièkǒu	vo	(to look for) an excuse	8
照顧	照顾	zhàogu	v	to take care of; to look after	15
照相		zhào xiàng	vo	to have a picture taken; to take a picture	9
哲學	哲学	zhéxué	n	philosophy	5
這樣	这样	zhèyàng	pr	in this way	5
真的		zhēnde	adv	really; truly	2
珍貴	珍贵	zhēnguì	adj	valuable; precious	19
珍稀動物	珍稀动物	zhēnxī dòngwù		precious and rare animals	19
爭	争	zhēng	v	to fight for; to strive for	13
爭論	争论	zhēnglùn	v	to argue	4
爭先恐后	争先恐后	zhēng xiān kǒng hòu		strive to be the first and fear to lag behind; vie with one another	12
正月		zhēngyuè	n	the first month of the lunar calendar	12
整個	整个	zhěnggè		entire	13
整天		zhěngtiān		all day long	5
正		zhèng	adv	just; precise; precisely	18
正常		zhèngcháng	adj	normal	18
正好		zhènghǎo	adv	coincidentally	3
政府		zhèngfǔ	n	government	16
症		zhèng	n	disease; symptoms	16
枝		zhī	m	measure word (for pens, rifles, etc.)	18
之一		zhīyī		one of	12
直飛	直飞	zhí fēi		fly directly	9
職位	职位	zhíwèi	n	(professional) position	15

▼▼▼▼▼▼▼▼▼▼▼▼▼▼▼▼▼▼▼▼▼▼▼▼▼▼▼▼▼▼▼▼▼▼▼

Traditional	Simplified	Pinyin	Part of Speech	English	Lesson
執行	执行	zhíxíng	v	to implement; to execute (a plan, decision or policy)	18
指出		zhǐchū	v	point out	16
指導教授	指导教授	zhǐdǎo jiàoshòu	n	guiding professor; academic advisor	5
指腹為婚	指腹为婚	zhǐ fù wéi hūn		to arrange a marriage (for the sake of the unborn child)	15
指揮棒	指挥棒	zhǐhuī bàng	n	conductor's baton	17
只好		zhǐhǎo	adv	have to; be forced to	3
只要		zhǐyào	conj	so long as	18
只有		zhǐyǒu	conj	only if	16
至少		zhìshǎo	adv	at least	16
至於	至于	zhìyú	conj	as for; as to	5
制度		zhìdù	n	system	16
質量	质量	zhìliàng	n	quality	4
治理		zhìlǐ	v	to bring under control; to manage	20
製藥	制药	zhì yào	vo	to manufacture drugs	16
中國城	中国城	zhōngguó chéng	n	Chinatown	3
重男輕女	重男轻女	zhòng nán qīng nǚ		regard males as superior to females	15
重視	重视	zhòngshì	v	to take seriously; to view as important	17
重要		zhòngyào	adj	important	13
州		zhōu	n	state	4
週末	周末	zhōumò	n	weekend	3
週期	周期	zhōuqī	n	cycle	20
竹筒		zhútǒng	n	bamboo tube	12
主管		zhǔguǎn	n/v	person-in-charge; to preside over	15
主要		zhǔyào	adj/adv	main, chief; mainly, chiefly	15
注意		zhùyì	v	to pay attention to	16
註冊	注册	zhù cè	vo	to register; to matriculate	1
專家	专家	zhuānjiā	n	expert	16
專業	专业	zhuānyè	n	major; specialization	5
賺錢	赚钱	zhuàn qián	vo	to make/earn money	5, 14
壯觀	壮观	zhuàngguān	adj	(of buildings, monuments, scenery etc.) grand	11
追		zhuī	v	to catch up; to chase, pursue	13
準備	准备	zhǔnbèi	v	to prepare	5
子女		zǐnǚ	n	sons and daughters	17
自從	自从	zìcóng		ever since; since	6
自覺	自觉	zìjué	adj	self-aware; self-motivated	17
自然		zìrán	adj/adv	natural; naturally	17
自殺	自杀	zìshā	v	to commit suicide	12

Traditional	Simplified	Pinyin	Part of Speech	English	Lesson
自食其果		zì shí qí guǒ		suffer the consequences of one's own doing	19
自相矛盾		zìxiāng máodùn		contradict oneself; self-contradictory	8
自由		zìyóu	adj	free; unrestricted	1
總	总	zǒng	adv	always	20
總的來说	总的来说	zǒng de lái shuō		generally speaking; on the whole	3
總算	总算	zǒngsuàn	adv	finally; in the end	11
走火		zǒu huǒ	vo	to discharge (firearms) accidentally	18
走廊		zǒuláng	n	hallway	6
租*		zū	v	to rent	6
租金		zūjīn	n	rent money	6
祖籍		zǔjí	n	ancestral home	1
組織	组织	zǔzhī	v/n	to organize; organization	19
醉		zuì	adj	drunk	7
罪犯		zuìfàn	n	criminal	18
尊師重道	尊师重道	zūn shī zhòng dào		respect the teacher and value the Way	17
坐		zuò	v	to sit; to travel by	1
做生意		zuò shēngyì	vo	to do business	9
做主		zuò zhǔ	vo	to decide; to take the responsibility for a decision (lit., "act as the master")	15
作業	作业	zuòyè	n	(formal) homework	17
粽子		zòngzi	n	a kind of dumpling wrapped in bamboo leaves eaten during the Dragon Boat Festival	12

▼ ▼

PROPER NOUNS

Traditional	Simplified	Pinyin	English	Lesson
阿迪達斯	阿迪达斯	Ādídásī	Adidas	4
安德森		Āndésēn	Anderson	6
奧林匹克		Àolínpǐkè	Olympics	13
波士頓	波士顿	Bōshìdùn	Boston	1
楚國	楚国	Chǔguó	the State of Chu (740-330 BCE)	12
春節	春节	Chūn Jié	the Spring Festival	12
燈節	灯节	Dēng Jié	the Lantern Festival	12
東亞史	东亚史	Dōngyàshǐ	East Asian history	5
端午節	端午节	Duānwǔ Jié	the Dragon Boat Festival	12
多倫多	多伦多	Duōlúnduō	Toronto	16
夫子廟	夫子庙	Fūzǐ Miào	The Temple of Confucius	11
感恩節	感恩节	Gǎn'ēnjié	Thanksgiving	14
韓國	韩国	Hánguó	(South) Korea	9
華清池	华清池	Huáqīng Chí	Huaqing Springs, a famous hot spring outside Xi'an	11
華盛頓	华盛顿	Huáshèngdùn	Washington	2
惠敏		Huìmǐn	a feminine name	14
加拿大		Jiā'nádà	Canada	16
加州		Jiāzhōu	(abbr.) the state of California	8
柯林		Kē Lín	Colin	1
李哲		Lǐ Zhé	a masculine name	5
麗莎	丽莎	Lìshā	Lisa	7
林雪梅		Lín Xuěméi	a feminine name	3
玲玲		Língling	a feminine name	14
南京		Nánjīng	Nanjing	9
紐約	纽约	Niǔyuē	New York	19
密西根		Mìxīgēn	Michigan	13
墨西哥	墨西哥	Mòxīgē	Mexico	9
秦國	秦国	Qínguó	the State of Qin (879-221 BCE)	12
秦淮河		Qínhuái Hé	The Qinhuai River	11
屈原		Qū Yuán	Qu Yuan (343-290 BCE)	12
斯蒂夫		Sīdìfū	Steve	9
宋朝		Sòngcháo	the Song Dynasty (960-1279)	15
孫中山	孙中山	Sūn Zhōngshān	Sun Yat-sen	11
台灣	台湾	Táiwān	Taiwan	16
湯姆	汤姆	Tāngmǔ	Tom	7
天華	天华	Tiānhuá	a unisex name	7
西安		Xī'ān	Xi'an, famous historic city in western China	10
香港		Xiānggǎng	Hong Kong	9
中國城	中国城	Zhōngguóchéng	Chinatown	3

Traditional	Simplified	Pinyin	English	Lesson
小陳	小陈	Xiǎo Chén	"Little" Chen	3
玄武湖		Xuánwǔ Hú	Lake Xuanwu, a scenic lake in Nanjing	11
楊貴妃	杨贵妃	Yáng Guìfēi	Imperial Concubine Yang	11
元宵節	元宵节	Yuánxiāo Jié	the Lantern Festival	12
約翰	约翰	Yuēhàn	John	2
張天明	张天明	Zhāng Tiānmíng	a masculine name	1
芝加哥		Zhījiāgē	Chicago	9
芝蔴街	芝麻街	Zhīmajiē	Sesame Street (TV Program)	8
中秋節	中秋节	Zhōngqiū Jié	the Mid-Autumn Festival	12
中山陵		Zhōngshān Líng	Sun Yat-sen's Mausoleum	11
中山路		Zhōngshān Lù	Zhongshan Road	10

VOCABULARY INDEX (ENGLISH-CHINESE)

English	Traditional	Simplified	Pinyin	Part of Speech	Lesson
▲A▲					
ability; capacity	能力		nénglì	n	20
abrupt; blunt	衝	冲	chòng	adj	14
absorb, assimilate (nutrients, water, etc.)	攝取	摄取	shèqǔ	v	16
abundant	豐富	丰富	fēngfù	adj	13
abuse	虐待		nüèdài	v	19
academic credit	學分	学分	xuéfēn	n	5
accompany; go with someone	陪		péi	v	4
achievement	成績	成绩	chéngjì	n	13
acid rain	酸雨		suānyǔ	n	20
actually	其實	其实	qíshí	adv	3
actually; in fact; in reality	實際上	实际上	shíjì shang	adv	12
ad columns; classified ads	廣告欄	广告栏	guǎnggào lán		6
adapt; become accustomed to	適應	适应	shìyìng	v	1
add to; in addition	加上		jiāshàng		16
address	地址		dìzhǐ	n	9
admire the full moon	賞月	赏月	shǎng yuè	vo	12
admit; acknowledge	承認	承认	chéngrèn	v	17
adult	大人		dàren	n	8
advance to a higher level of schooling	升學	升学	shēng xué	vo	15
advantage; benefit	好處	好处	hǎochù	n	1
aerogram	郵簡	邮简	yóujiǎn	n	10
after all	畢竟	毕竟	bìjìng	adv	16
agree	同意		tóngyì	v	3
agree on	說定	说定	shuō dìng	vc	11
AIDS	艾滋病		Àizībìng	n	19
air	空氣	空气	kōngqì	n	20
air-conditioning	空調	空调	kōngtiáo	n	2
airline	航空公司		hángkōng gōngsī		9
airplane	飛機	飞机	fēijī	n	1
airport	機場	机场	jīchǎng	n	9
all	所有		suǒyǒu		16
all day long	整天		zhěngtiān		5
allow oneself to be slaughtered or trampled upon	任人宰割		rèn rén zǎigē		18
almost	幾乎	几乎	jīhū	adv	8
along with it	隨之	随之	suí zhī		18
already	已		yǐ	adv	19

English	Traditional	Simplified	Pinyin	Part of Speech	Lesson
always	總	总	zǒng	adv	20
Alzheimer's disease	老年癡呆症	老年痴呆症	lǎonián shīdāizhèng	n	19
"an amount" of money or money related matters	筆	笔	bǐ	m	20
analyze	分析		fēnxī	v	20
ancestral home	祖籍		zǔjí	n	1
ancient city wall	古城牆	古城墙	gǔ chéngqiáng		11
and	及		jí	conj	17
and	以及		yǐjí	conj	4
and	與	与	yǔ	conj	16
and; but	而		ér	conj	14
and; furthermore	並	并	bìng	conj	18
angry	生氣	生气	shēngqì	v	11
animal	動物	动物	dòngwù	n	19
answer (the phone)	接(電話)	接(电话)	jiē (diànhuà)	v(o)	20
anyway	反正		fǎnzhèng	conj	13
appear; seem	看來	看来	kàn lái		17
appetite	胃口		wèikǒu	n	2
apply (for admission to school; for job)	申請	申请	shēnqǐng	v	5
architecture; to build	建築	建筑	jiànzhù	n/v	11
argue	爭論	争论	zhēnglùn	v	4
arise; appear	出現	出现	chūxiàn	v	15
arrange a marriage (for the sake of the unborn child)	指腹為婚	指腹为婚	zhǐ fù wěi hūn		15
art film	藝術片	艺术片	yìshùpiàn	n	8
article	文章		wénzhāng	n	3
as a result; result	結果	结果	jiéguǒ	conj/n	8, 13
as for; as to	至於	至于	zhìyú	conj	5
as if; seem to be	好像		hǎoxiàng		4
as it turns out; formerly; former	原來	原来	yuánlái	adv/adj	3
as to; so far as…is concern	對…來説	对…来说	duì…lái shuō		5
ask about; inquire about	打聽	打听	dǎtīng	v	9
aspect	方面		fāngmiàn	n	14
assembly; assemble	集會	集会	jíhuì	n/v	18
at first; originally	本來	本来	běnlái		13
at least	至少		zhìshǎo	adv	16
at one go; in a short while	一下子		yíxiàzi		10
at that time	當時	当时	dāngshí		12
at the same time as	在…同時	在…同时	zài…tóngshí		19
athlete	運動員	运动员	yùndòngyuán	n	13
attend; take part in	參加	参加	cānjiā	v	13
attitude	態度	态度	tàidù	n	17

▼▼▼▼▼▼▼▼▼▼▼▼▼▼▼▼▼▼▼▼▼▼▼▼▼▼▼▼▼▼▼▼▼▼▼▼▼

English	Traditional	Simplified	Pinyin	Part of Speech	Lesson
attract	吸引		xīyǐn	v	11
attractive goods at inexpensive prices	物美價廉	物美价廉	wù měi jià lián		4
auditorium	禮堂	礼堂	lǐtáng	n	8
aunt (father's sister)	姑媽	姑妈	gūmā	n	9
authentic	地道		dìdao	adj	2
avoid		避免	bìmiǎn	v	19
▲B▲					
background	背景		bèijǐng	n	7
balanced	平衡		pínghéng	adj	19
balanced; proportionate	均衡		jūnhéng	adj	16
ball court	球場	球场	qiúchǎng	n	6
ball game	球賽	球赛	qiúsài	n	13
bamboo tube	竹筒		zhú tǒng	n	12
ban; suppress	取締	取缔	qǔdì	v	18
bar	酒吧		jiǔbā	n	7
barbarous; uncivilized	野蠻	野蛮	yěmán	adj	19
based on	憑	凭	píng	prep	19
basically	基本上		jīběnshang		18
basket	籃	篮	lán	n	13
basketball	籃球	篮球	lánqiú	n	6
bath towel	浴巾		yùjīn	n	4
bathe; take a bath/shower	洗澡		xǐ zǎo	vo	11
bathroom	浴室		yùshì	n	2
be accustomed to	習慣	习惯	xíguàn	v	12
be affected	受影響	受影响	shòu yǐngxiǎng	vo	6
be afraid	怕		pà	v	9
be away from home	出門	出门	chū mén	v	1
be born	出生		chūshēng	v	1
be sure to	千萬	千万	qiānwàn	adv	11
be told; hear of	聽說	听说	tīngshuō	v	2
bean curd; tofu	豆腐		dòufu	n	3
because of this	因此		yīncǐ	conj	14
become more aggravated day by day	日益加劇	日益加剧	rìyì jiājù		20
become the turn of	輪到	轮到	lún dào	vc	10
bed	床		chuáng	n	2
bedroom	臥室	卧室	wòshì	n	6
beef	牛肉		niúròu	n	3
behavior	行為	行为	xíngwéi	n	8
besides	再說	再说	zàishuō	conj	1
biology; living thing, organism	生物		shēngwù	n	19
blame	怪		guài	v	8
blanket	毯子		tǎnzi	n	2

English	Traditional	Simplified	Pinyin	Part of Speech	Lesson
bodily figure	身材		shēncái	n	16
body	身體	身体	shēntǐ	n	13
bomb	炸		zhà	v	8
bookshelf	書架	书架	shūjià	n	2
bored with doing something; sick of doing something	V+膩(了)	V+腻(了)	nì(le)		9
boss	老闆	老板	lǎobǎn	n	3
bow	弓		gōng	n	1
brains	腦子	脑子	nǎozi	n	18
brand	牌子		páizi	n	4
brandish swords and spears	舞刀弄槍	舞刀弄枪	wǔ dāo nòng qiāng		18
break into pieces	打破		dǎ pò	vc	7
break up; blow	吹		chuī	v	7
bright	亮		liàng	adj	12
bright; clever	聰明	聪明	cōngming	adj	14
bright star; (movie, etc.) star	明星		míngxīng	n	16
bring under control; manage	治理		zhìlǐ	v	20
broadcast	播		bō	v	8
burden	負擔	负担	fùdān	n	17
burn to death	燒死	烧死	shāo sǐ	vc	8
bury (a person)	葬		zàng	v	11
but	不過	不过	búguò	conj	5
by; up to (indicating agency in written Chinese)	由		yóu	prep	15

▲C▲

English	Traditional	Simplified	Pinyin	Part of Speech	Lesson
cabinet	櫃子	柜子	guìzi	n	2
cafeteria	餐廳	餐厅	cāntīng	n	2
calorie	卡路里		kǎlùlǐ	n/m	3
campus	校園	校园	xiàoyuán	n	7
cancer	癌症		áizhèng	n	19
candies	糖果		tángguǒ	n	10
cannot afford	付不起		fù bu qǐ	vc	16
cannot bear the sight of; frown upon	看不慣	看不惯	kàn bu guàn	vc	15
cannot forget	忘不了		wàng bu liǎo	vc	9
cannot take it	受不了		shòu bu liǎo	vc	5
cardiology department	心臟科	心脏科	xīnzàng kē		16
careful	小心		xiǎoxīn	adj	18
carpet	地毯		dìtǎn	n	6
carry or hold something level with both hands	端		duān	v	12
cartoon	卡通		kǎtōng	n	8
carved in wood; wood carving	木刻		mùkè		15

English	Traditional	Simplified	Pinyin	Part of Speech	Lesson
cash	現金		xiànjīn	n	4
cat	貓	猫	māo	n	15
catch up	追		zhuī	v	13
cause; lead to	造成		zàochéng	v	20
cause/make (someone do something)	使		shǐ	v	17
cause; reason	原因		yuányīn	n	16
celebrate a festival or holiday	過節	过节	guò jié	vo	12
celebrate	慶祝	庆祝	qìngzhù	v	13
century	世紀	世纪	shìjì	n	19
change	變化	变化	biànhuà	n/v	15
change into	變成	变成	biàn chéng	vc	17
character in a play, story, etc.	人物		rénwù	n	8
chat	聊		liáo	v	5
chemical engineering; chemical industry	化工		huàgōng	n	20
chemistry	化學	化学	huàxué	n	20
chicken	雞	鸡	jī	n	12
chicken egg	雞蛋	鸡蛋	jīdàn	n	19
child	孩子		háizi	n	5
child	小孩兒	小孩儿	xiǎoháir	n	8
childhood	童年		tóngnián	n	17
children	兒童	儿童	értóng	n	8
Chinese broccoli	芥蘭	芥兰	jièlán	n	3
choose	選	选	xuǎn	v	5
cinema	電影院	电影院	diànyǐngyuàn	n	7
city	城市		chéngshì	n	15
classical music	古典音樂	古典音乐	gǔdiǎn yīnyuè		7
clothes	衣服		yīfu	n	4
clothing (formal)	服裝	服装	fúzhuāng	n	19
coach	教練	教练	jiàoliàn	n	13
coal	煤		méi	n	20
coal stove	煤爐	煤炉	méilú	n	20
coincidentally	正好		zhèng hǎo	adv	3
come out; appear	出		chū	v	16
comforter	被子		bèizi	n	2
commercial film	商業片	商业片	shāngyèpiàn	n	8
commission; entrust	委託	委托	wěituō	v	20
commit a crime	犯罪		fàn zuì	vo	18
commit suicide	自殺	自杀	zìshā	v	12
company	公司		gōngsī	n	9
compete	競爭	竞争	jìngzhēng	v	17
competition	比賽	比赛	bǐsài	n/v	6
completely	完全		wánquán	adv	8

English	Traditional	Simplified	Pinyin	Part of Speech	Lesson
comprehensive	全面		quánmiàn		18
computer	電腦	电脑	diànnǎo	n	5
concerned about one's country and people	憂國憂民	忧国忧民	yōu guó yōu mín		12
concerned with/about	關心	关心	guān xīn	vo	16
conductor's baton	指揮棒	指挥棒	zhǐhuī bàng	n	17
consciousness	意識	意识	yìshí	n	19
consequence; aftermath	後果	后果	hòuguǒ	n	20
consider	考慮	考虑	kǎolǜ	v	5
considerate	體貼	体贴	tǐtiē	adj	15
consistently	一向		yīxiàng	adv	10
constantly	不斷	不断	bùduàn	adv	15
constitution	憲法	宪法	xiànfǎ	n	18
consulate	領事館	领事馆	lǐngshìguǎn	n	9
continuously	一直		yìzhí	adv	6
contract (an illness)	患		huàn	v	16
contradict oneself; self-contradictory	自相矛盾		zìxiāng máodùn		8
contradictory; contradict each other	互相矛盾		hùxiāng máodùn		19
convenient	方便		fāngbiàn	adj	1
conversely	反過來	反过来	fǎn guò lái		15
cookies	餅乾	饼干	bǐnggān	n	10
cosmetic products	化妝品	化妆品	huàzhuāng pǐn	n	4
cost	成本		chéngběn	n	20
count	算		suàn	v	6
country	國家	国家	guójiā	n	13
courtyard	院子		yuànzi	n	12
cousin (older male) (of different surname, i.e. on mother's side of the family)	表哥		biǎogē	n	13
cousin (younger male)	表弟		biǎodì	n	11
"cram" school	補習班	补习班	bǔxíbān	n	17
cramming method (in teaching)	填鴨式	填鸭式	tiányāshì		17
credit card	信用卡		xìnyòngkǎ	n	4
criminal	罪犯		zuìfàn	n	18
criterion	標準	标准	biāozhǔn	n	4
criticize	批評	批评	pīpíng	n	17
crowded; to squeeze, press, push against	擠	挤	jǐ	adj	11
culture	文化		wénhuà	n	7
cup; drinking glass	杯子		bēizi	n	4
curious	好奇		hàoqí	v	10
curriculum vitae; résumé	履歷	履历	lǚlì	n	5

▼▼▼

English	Traditional	Simplified	Pinyin	Part of Speech	Lesson
customer	顧客	顾客	gùkè	n	19
cut (with scissors)	剪		jiǎn	v	19
cycle	週期	周期	zhōuqī	n	20
▲**D**▲					
daily household necessities	日用品		rìyòngpǐn	n	2
dangerous; danger	危險	危险	wēixiǎn	adj/n	18
dare	敢		gǎn	v	8
daughter-in-law; wife	媳婦	媳妇	xífu	n	11
day; time; life	日子		rìzi	n	12
day after tomorrow	後天	后天	hòutiān	t	5
day before yesterday	前天		qiántiān	t	2
daytime	白天		báitiān	n	17
deal with (usually persons)	打交道		dǎ jiāodào		5
debate; argue	辯論	辩论	biànlùn	v	17
decade	年代		niándài	n	9
decide; decision	決定	决定	juédìng	v	16
decide; take the responsibility for a decision (lit., "act as the master")	做主		zuò zhǔ	vo	15
decrease	減少	减少	jiǎnshǎo	v	15
deep	深		shēn	adj	11
definitely	肯定		kěndìng	adv	5
degree	程度		chéngdù	n	11
demand	要求		yāoqiú	n	17
department (of a university)	系		xì	n	5
depend	靠		kào	v	1
desire to be better; aspiration	上進心	上进心	shàngjìnxīn		17
destroy	破壞	破坏	pòhuài	v	19
detailed; in detail	詳細	详细	xiángxì	adj	7
develop; development	發展	发展	fāzhǎn	n/v	13
different	不同		bùtóng	adj	7
difficult problem; dilemma	難題	难题	nántí	n	19
disappear, vanish, dissolve	消失		xiāoshī	v	18
disappointed	失望		shīwàng	v/adj	13
disapprove of; object to	不以為然	不以为然	bù yǐ wéi rán		17
discharge; emit	排出		pái chū	vc	20
discharge; emit	排放		páifàng	v	20
discharge (firearms) accidentally	走火		zǒu huǒ	vo	18
discount (from a set or list price)	打折		dǎ zhé	vo	4
discount; on sale	減價	减价	jiǎn jià	vo	4
discriminate against	歧視	歧视	qíshì	v	15
discuss	討論	讨论	tǎolùn	v	5
discuss; negotiate	商量		shāngliang	v	9
disease; symptom	症		zhèng	n	16

English	Traditional	Simplified	Pinyin	Part of Speech	Lesson
disorderly; chaotic	紊亂	紊乱	wěnluàn	adj	18
display; manifest	表現	表现	biǎoxiàn	v	12
dissect	解剖		jiěpōu	v	19
distinction; distinguish	區別	区别	qūbié	n/v	19
disturb; make noise	吵		chǎo	v	6
divorce	離婚	离婚	lí hūn	vo	14
do business	做生意		zuò shēngyi	vo	9
do harm to; to cause trouble to	害		hài	v	17
Do you mean to say?	難道	难道	nándào	adv	4
documentary film	紀錄片	纪录片	jìlùpiàn	n	8
doorway	門口	门口	ménkǒu	n	3
double major	雙學位	双学位	shuāng xuéwèi		5
downstairs	樓下	楼下	lóuxià		2
dragon boat	龍舟	龙舟	lóngzhōu	n	12
dryer (clothes)	烘乾機	烘干机	hōnggānjī	n	2
drive away	趕	赶	gǎn	v	12
drunk	醉		zuì	v	7
duck	鴨	鸭	yā	n	12
due to; owing to	由於	由于	yóuyú	conj	19
dumpling wrapped in bamboo leaves	粽子		zòngzi	n	12

▲E▲

English	Traditional	Simplified	Pinyin	Part of Speech	Lesson
early morning	早晨		zǎochen	t	12
earnest; serious	認真	认真	rènzhēn	adj	17
east	東方	东方	dōngfāng	n	9
east coast	東岸	东岸	dōng'àn	n	9
eat vegetarian food; be a vegetarian	吃素		chī sù	vo	16
ecology	生態	生态	shēngtài	n	19
economy; economical	經濟	经济	jīngjì	n/adj	18
educate; education	教育		jiàoyù	v/n	8
effective	有效		yǒuxiào	adj	20
elementary school	小學	小学	xiǎoxué	n	17
eliminate through selection or competition	淘汰		táotài	v	17
embody; manifest	體現	体现	tǐxiàn	v	15
embroidered pouch; pouch; purse	荷包		hébāo	n	12
emigrate	移民		yímín	v/n	9
empty	空		kōng	adj	2
encourage	鼓勵	鼓励	gǔlì	v	17
end	結束	结束	jiéshù	v	1
energy resources	能源		néngyuán	n	20
engineering	工程		gōngchéng	n	14
enlighten; inspire	啟發	启发	qǐfā	v	17

▼▼▼▼▼▼▼▼▼▼▼▼▼▼▼▼▼▼▼▼▼▼▼▼▼▼▼▼▼▼▼▼▼▼

English	Traditional	Simplified	Pinyin	Part of Speech	Lesson
ensure; safeguard	保障		bǎozhàng	v	18
entire	整個	整个	zhěnggè		13
environment	環境	环境	huánjìng	n	6, 20
environmental protection; 環境保護／环境保护	環保	环保	huánbǎo		20
equal	平等		píngděng	adj	15
equal pay for equal work	同工同酬		tóng gōng tóng chóu		15
equipped with	帶	带	dài	v	6
establish	設立	设立	shèlì	v	19
establish a foundation	打基礎	打基础	dǎ jīchǔ	vo	17
etc.	等等		děng děng		4
even; even to the point	甚至		shènzhì	adv	15
even; even if	即使		jíshǐ	conj	17
ever	從來	从来	cónglái	adv	7
ever since	自從	自从	zìcóng	prep	6
every; various	各		gè	pr	1
everywhere; at all places	到處	到处	dàochù	adv	18
excess; surplus	過剩	过剩	guòshèng		16
excessive	過份	过分	guòfèn	adj	16
excited	激動	激动	jīdòng	v	6
(look for an) excuse	(找)藉口	(找)借口	(zhǎo) jièkǒu	vo	8
exercises	習題	习题	xítí	n	17
exist; survive	生存		shēngcún	v	19
experience	經驗	经验	jīngyàn	n	5
experiment	實驗	试验	shíyàn	n/v	19
expert	專家	专家	zhuānjiā	n	16
exterminate; become extinct	滅絕	灭绝	mièjué	v	19

▲**F**▲

English	Traditional	Simplified	Pinyin	Part of Speech	Lesson
face; confronted with	面臨	面临	miànlín	v	19
facilities	設備	设备	shèbèi	n	2
factory	工廠	工厂	gōngchǎng	n	14
fair	公平		gōngpíng	adj	15
familiar with	熟悉		shúxi	v	2
family	家庭		jiātíng	n	14
famous	有名		yǒumíng	adj	16
famous brand; name brand	名牌		míngpái	n	4
fan (of ball games)	球迷		qiúmí	n	6
father and son	父子		fùzǐ	n	14
father's sister's husband	姑父		gūfu	n	14
father's younger brother	叔叔		shūshu	n	14
federation	聯邦	联邦	liánbāng	n	20
fee	費	费	fèi	n	16
feel	感到		gǎn dào	vc	13

English	Traditional	Simplified	Pinyin	Part of Speech	Lesson
feel restless or impatient as a result of worrying about something	著急	着急	zháo jí	vo	2
female student	女生		nǚshēng	n	15
festival	節日	节日	jiérì	n	12
fiancé	未婚夫		wèihūnfū	n	15
fight for	爭	争	zhēng	v	13
file a lawsuit against somebody; lodge a complaint with somebody's superior	告狀	告状	gào zhuàng	vo	14
film	…片		piàn		8
final match	決賽	决赛	juésài	n	13
finally	總算	总算	zǒngsuàn	adv	11
finish choosing	選好	选好	xuǎnhǎo	vc	5
fire	火		huǒ	n	8
fire (disaster)	火災	火灾	huǒzāi	n	8
fire a gun	開槍	开枪	kāi qiāng	vo	8
firearms	槍枝	枪支	qiāngzhī	n	18
firecracker; a long string of small firecrackers	鞭炮		biānpào	n	12
first and foremost	首先		shǒuxiān	adv	14
first month of the lunar calendar	正月		zhēngyuè	n	12
fish	魚	鱼	yú	n	3
fix; clarify (a relationship)	定下來		dìng xialai	vc	14
fly directly	直飛	直飞	zhí fēi		9
folk customs	風俗	风俗	fēngsú	n	12
follow	跟		gēn	v	3
for	為	为	wèi	prep	5
for; on behalf of	替		tì	prep	16
for example	比如		bǐrú	v	15
force; coerce; compel	強制	强制	qiángzhì	v	18
fragrant	香		xiāng	adj	3
free; unrestricted	自由		zìyóu	adj	1
frequent patron	常客		chángkè	n	3
frequently	經常	经常	jīngcháng	adv	7
fresh	新鮮	新鲜	xīnxian	adj	3
fundamentally	根本		gēnběn	adv	12
fur, i.e., animal skin with fur attached	裘皮		qiúpí	n	19
furnace	火爐	火炉	huǒlú	n	9
furniture	家俱	家具	jiājù	n	2

▲ G ▲

| gamble | 賭博 | 赌博 | dǔbó | v | 18 |
| generally | 一般 | | yībān | adj | 2 |

▼▼▼

English	Traditional	Simplified	Pinyin	Part of Speech	Lesson
generally speaking	一般來说	一般来说	yībān lái shuō		17
generally speaking; on the whole	總的来说	总的来说	zǒng de lái shuō		3
get	得		dé	v	13
get	弄		nòng	v	19
get along	相處	相处	xiāngchǔ	v	7
get drunk	喝醉酒		hē zuì jiǔ		7
get lost in the mail	寄丢了		jì diū le		10
get married	結婚	结婚	jiéhūn	vo	14
get married (of a woman)	出嫁		chūjià	v	15
get out of school	放學	放学	fàng xué	vo	14
get wounded; be injured	受傷	受伤	shòu shāng	vo	16
(a) girl; (a) young woman	女孩兒	女孩儿	nǚháir	n	3
give free rein to	發揮	发挥	fāhuī	v	17
give rise to	引起		yǐnqǐ	v	8
glory; glorious	光榮	光荣	guāngróng	n/adj	13
glower at	瞪		dèng	v	11
go abroad	出國	出国	chū guó	vo	9
go hunting	打獵	打猎	dǎ liè	v	18
go on a business trip	出差		chū chāi	vo	10
go sight-seeing	遊覽	游览	yóulǎn	v	11
go through; make a successful connection (on the telephone)	打通		dǎ tōng	vc	10
go to school	上學	上学	shàng xué	vo	17
go into the streets	上街		shàng jiē	vo	12
go window shopping; stroll (in the city)	逛街		guàng jiē	vo	10
goal; target	目標	目标	mùbiāo	n	17
gold medal	金牌		jīnpái	n	13
good at		拿手	náshǒu	adj	3
good at; know how to	會	会	huì	av	3
good for	有益於	有益于	yǒuyì yú		13
good friends and dear relatives	親朋好友	亲朋好友	qīn péng hǎo yǒu		12
gosh	哎呀		āiyā	exc	4
government	政府		zhèngfǔ	n	16
grade	年級	年级	niánjí	n	1
grades	成績	成绩	chéngjì	n	14
graduate	畢業	毕业	bì yè	vo	5
graduate school	研究所		yánjiūsuǒ	n	5
grand	壯觀	壮观	zhuàngguān	adj	11
great	偉大	伟大	wěidà	adj	11
(great) panda	(大)熊貓	(大)熊猫	(dà) xióngmāo	n	19
green leafy vegetables	青菜	青菜	qīngcài	n	3

▼▼▼▼▼▼▼▼▼▼▼▼▼▼▼▼▼▼▼▼▼▼▼▼▼▼▼▼▼▼▼▼▼▼▼▼▼▼

English	Traditional	Simplified	Pinyin	Part of Speech	Lesson
greet		打招呼	dǎ zhāohu	vo	6
grow up	長大	长大	zhǎng dà	vc	1
grow with each passing day	與日俱增	与日俱增	yǔ rǐ jù zēng		20
guarantee	保證	保证	bǎozhèng	v	16
guessed correctly	猜對了	猜对了	cāi duì le	vc	2
guiding professor; academic advisor	指導教授	指导教授	zhǐdǎo jiàoshòu	n	5
gun (rifle, pistol, etc.); spear	槍	枪	qiāng	n	18

▲H▲

English	Traditional	Simplified	Pinyin	Part of Speech	Lesson
hallway	走廊		zǒuláng	n	6
handle; do	辦	办	bàn	v	1
handsome young guy	帥哥	帅哥	shuàigē	adj	13
hang	掛	挂	guà	v	2
hard to handle	難辦	难办	nán bàn		20
harm	危害		wēihài	v	20
harmful insect	害蟲	害虫	hàichóng	n	20
have a falling out (with somebody)	鬧翻	闹翻	nào fān	vc	7
have a holiday/vacation; have a day off	放假		fàng jià	vo	7
have a distinctive style	別具風格	别具风格	bié jù fēnggé		11
have a picture taken	照相		zhào xiàng	v	9
have an accident; something bad happens	出事		chū shì	vo	8
have an operation; perform an operation	動手術	动手术	dòng shǒushù	vo	16
have free time	有空		yǒu kòngr	vo	7
have given much thought to the matter; well-meaning	用心良苦	用心良苦	yòngxīn liángkǔ		17
have to	只好		zhǐhǎo	adv	3
have to be	非…不可		fēi…bù kě		4
healthy; health	健康		jiànkāng	adj/n	3
heart disease	心臟病	心脏病	xīnzàngbìng		16
hello (on the phone)	喂		wèi/wéi	exc	6
hide the truth from	瞞		mán	v	6
high-ranking official	大官		dà guān		12
hire	僱	雇	gù	v	18
history	歷史	历史	lìshǐ	n	14
hobbies	興趣	兴趣	xìngqu	n	7
hold (the opinion that)	認為	认为	rénwéi	v	3
homework	功課	功课	gōngkè	n	3
homework	作業	作业	zuòyè	n	17
honor	榮譽	荣誉	róngyù	n	13
hope for one's daughter to be very successful	望女成鳳	望女成凤	wàng nǚ chéng fèng		17

▼▼▼▼▼▼▼▼▼▼▼▼▼▼▼▼▼▼▼▼▼▼▼▼▼▼▼▼▼▼▼▼▼▼▼▼▼

English	Traditional	Simplified	Pinyin	Part of Speech	Lesson
hope for one's son to be very successful	望子成龍	望子成龙	wàng zǐ chéng lóng		17
hospital	醫院	医院	yīyuàn	n	16
house	房子		fángzi	n	6
household duties	家務	家务	jiāwù	n	15
housewife	家庭主婦	家庭主妇	jiātíng zhǔfù	n	15
however	卻	却	què	adv	10
huge crowds of people	人山人海		rén shān rén hǎi		11
human body	人體	人体	réntǐ	n	20
humanities	文科		wénkē	n	5
humanitarianism; humane	人道		réndào	n/adj	19
hurry	催		cuī	v	11
husband	丈夫		zhàngfu	n	15
husband and wife	夫婦	夫妇	fūfù	n	15
husband or wife of an old married couple	老伴兒	老伴儿	lǎobànr	n	14

▲Ｉ▲

English	Traditional	Simplified	Pinyin	Part of Speech	Lesson
(I'm) afraid that; I think perhaps; probably	恐怕		kǒngpà	adv	2
idea	想法		xiǎngfǎ	n	5
ideal	理想		lǐxiǎng	n/adj	6
idle	閑著沒事	闲着没事	xián zhe méi shì		8
if	...的話	...的话	dehuà		6
if it's not A, it's B	要麼...要麼...	要么...要么...	yàome...yàome...	conj	5
imagination	想像力		xiǎngxiànglì	n	17
imagine	想像		xiǎngxiàng	v	11
imitate	模仿		mófǎng	v	8
immediately; right away	馬上	马上	mǎshàng	adv	3
impetuous	急躁		jízào	adj	7
implement; execute (a plan, decision or policy)	執行	执行	zhíxíng	v	18
important	重要		zhòngyào	adj	13
important person	大人物		dà rénwù		11
impression	印象		yìnxiàng	n	11
improvement; improve; lift	提高		tígāo	n/v	15
in a few days	過幾天	过几天	guò jǐ tiān		2
in a hurried fashion	趕緊	赶紧	gǎnjǐn	adv	6
in all seriousness	一本正經	一本正经	yī běn zhèngjīng		11
in case; in the highly unlikely event that...	萬一	万一	wànyī	adv	10
in front	前邊	前边	qiánbiān		1
in large quantity	大量		dàliàng	adj	20

English	Traditional	Simplified	Pinyin	Part of Speech	Lesson
in passing	順便	顺便	shùnbiàn	adv	9
in the back	後面	后面	hòumiàn		6
in the future	將來	将来	jiānglái	t	17
in the wake of; following	隨著	随着	suí zhe	conj	15
in this way	這樣	这样	zhèyàng	pr	5
in those years; at that time	當年	当年	dāngnián		11
include	包		bāo	v	6
increase	增加		zēngjiā	v	19
indeed	的確	的确	díquè	adv	17
indeed	實在	实在	shízài	adv	13
indeed; in truth	確實	确实	quèshí	adv	9
independent	獨立	独立	dúlì	adj	14
industry	工業	工业	gōngyè	n	20
inevitably; hard to avoid	難免	难免	nánmiǎn	adj	8
influence	影響	影响	yǐngxiǎng	v/n	8
inside the room	屋裏	屋里	wūli		7
insurance; insure	保險	保险	bǎoxiǎn	n/v	16
intentionally; on purpose	有意		yǒuyì	adv	19
interjection indicating minor regret	嗯		ng	exc	6
international	國際	国际	guójì	n	13
investigate; check	查		chá	v	18
investigate, check; investigation	調查	调查	diàochá	v/n	18
iron rice bowl; secure job	鐵飯碗	铁饭碗	tiěfànwǎn	n	14
Isn't that the truth?	可不是		kě bú shì		13
it is said that	據説	据说	jùshuō		8

▲ J ▲

jail	監獄	监狱	jiānyù	n	18
jealous; to eat vinegar	吃醋		chī cù	vo	9
jeans	牛仔褲	牛仔裤	niúzǎikù	n	4
joke around	開玩笑	开玩笑	kāi wánxiào	vo	6
jump into the river	投江		tóu jiāng		12
just; precise; precisely	正		zhèng	adv	18

▲ K ▲

kill someone	殺人	杀人	shā rén	vo	18
king	國王	国王	guówáng	n	12
kitchen	廚房	厨房	chúfáng	n	6

▲ L ▲

laboratory	實驗室	实验室	shíyànshì	n	20
lake	湖		hú	n	11, 20
lamb	羔羊		gāoyáng	n	18
land-air linked transport	陸空聯運	陆空联运	lù kōng liányùn		10

English	Traditional	Simplified	Pinyin	Part of Speech	Lesson
lantern	燈	灯	dēng	n	12
laugh heartily	哈哈大笑		hāhā dà xiào		11
laundry powder	洗衣粉		xǐyīfěn		4
laws and regulations	法規	法规	fǎguī	n	18
lazy	懶	懒	lǎn	adj	14
lean against	靠		kào	v	2
lead (in ball games)	領先	领先	lǐngxiān	v	13
learn	學到	学到	xué dào	vc	5
learn from experience	體會到	体会到	tǐhuì dào	vc	11
leave	離開	离开	lí kāi	vc	1
leave (a note); assign (homework)	留		liú	v	17
length	長短	长短	chángduǎn	n	4
less	少		shǎo	adv	3
level (water); standard	水平		shuǐpíng	n	16
light in flavor	清淡		qīngdàn	adj	3
literature	文學	文学	wénxué	n	5
little bit	稍微		shāowēi	adv	6
little boy	小男孩		xiǎo nánhái	n	8
live	過日子	过日子	guò rìzi	vo	14
loaded carrying pole; burden	擔子	担子	dànzi	n	15
lonely	寂寞		jìmò	adj	13
long	長	长	cháng	adj	1
long distance	長途	长短	chángtú	n	10
look; grow to be	長得	长得	zhǎng de		3
(look for) an excuse	(找)藉口	(找)借口	(zhǎo) jièkǒu	vo	8
lose	失去		shīqù	v	19
lose	輸		shū	v	13
lose face	丟人		diū rén	vo	14
lose weight	減肥	减肥	jiǎn féi	vo	16
loudly; in a big voice	大聲	大声	dàshēng	adv	6
low	低		dī	adj	18
luggage	行李		xíngli	n	1
lunar/"agricultural" calendar	農曆	农历	nónglì	n	12

▲**M**▲

machine	機器	机器	jīqì	n	17
main, chief; mainly, chiefly	主要		zhǔyào	adj/adv	15
mainland	大陸	大陆	dàlù	n	9
major	專業	专业	zhuānyè	n	5
majority	大部份	大部分	dà bùfen		15
make (a film); shoot (a film, photograph)	拍		pāi	v	16
make (money)	賺錢	赚钱	zhuàn qián	vo	5, 14
male student	男生		nánshēng	n	15

▼ ▼

English	Traditional	Simplified	Pinyin	Part of Speech	Lesson
malnutrition	營養不良	营养不良	yíngyǎng bù liáng		16
manufacture drugs	制藥	制药	zhì yào	vo	16
manufacturing cost	造價	造价	zàojià	n	20
many; a lot	許多	许多	xǔduō		11
marriage	婚姻		hūnyīn	n	15
martial arts movie	武打片		wǔdǎpiān	n	16
match	火柴		huǒchái	n	8
mathematics	數學	数学	shùxué		17
mature	成熟		chéngshú	adj	17
mausoleum	陵墓		língmù	n	11
means, method; trick, artifice	手段		shǒuduàn	n	18
measure; step	措施		cuòshī	n	19
measure word for buildings	棟	栋	dòng	m	2
measure word for courses	門	门	mén	m	5
measure word for floors	層	层	céng	m	2
measure word for letters	封		fēng	m	13
measure word for machines	台		tái	m	2
measure word for meals	頓	顿	dùn	m	3
measure word for movies, books, etc.	部		bù	m	7
measure word for pens, rifles, etc.	枝		zhī	m	18
measure word for projects, tasks, etc.	項	项	xiàng	m	20
measure word for rooms	間	间	jiān	m	6
measure word for round trips	趟		tàng	m	9
mechanical memorizing	死記硬背	死记硬背	sǐ jì yìng bèi		17
medical treatment	醫療	医疗	yīliáo	n	16
medicine	藥	药	yào	n	16
meet; get together	見面	见面	jiàn miàn	vo	7
men and women; male and female	男女		nánnǚ	n	15
mention	提		tí	v	5
menu	菜單	菜单	càidan	n	3
merits and demerits; advantages and disadvantages	優缺點	优缺点	yōuquēdiǎn	n	17
messy; messed up	亂七八糟	乱七八糟	luàn qī bā zāo		8
method; way (to solve a problem)	辦法	办法	bànfǎ	n	15
method	方式		fāngshì	n	17
mind	在乎		zàihu	v	4
control, manage; mind about, care about	管		guǎn	v	5
mirror	鏡子	镜子	jìngzi	n	7

English	Traditional	Simplified	Pinyin	Part of Speech	Lesson
mistake	錯誤	错误	cuòwù	n	19
model	模範	模范	mófàn	adj/n	15
money for food	飯錢	饭钱	fànqian		5
money given to children as a lunar New Year gift	壓歲錢	压岁钱	yāsuìqián	n	12
monkey	猴子		hóuzi	n	19
monkey brain	猴腦	猴脑	hóunǎo	n	19
mood	心情		xīnqíng	n	7
moon	月亮		yuèliang	n	12
moon cake	月餅	月饼	yuèbǐng	n	12
more than half	大半		dàbàn	n	5
most; the great majority	大多數	大多数	dà duōshù		19
mostly	大多		dàduō	adv	20
mostly	多半		duōbàn	adv	8
mother	母親	母亲	mǔqin	n	10
mother-in-law and daughter-in-law	婆媳		póxí	n	14
mouse; rat	老鼠		lǎoshǔ	n	15
move	搬		bān	v	1
move (to a different house)	搬家		bān jiā	vo	1
moving; touching	動人	动人	dòngrén	adj	12
MSG (monosodium glutamate)	味精		wèijīng	n	3

▴N▴

English	Traditional	Simplified	Pinyin	Part of Speech	Lesson
narcotic drugs	毒品		dúpǐn	n	18
narrow	窄		zhǎi	adj	11
national treasure	國寶	国宝	guóbǎo	n	19
natural; naturally	自然		zìrán	adj/adv	17
nature	大自然		dàzìrán	n	19
necessity; necessary	必要		bìyào	n/adj	13
need	需要		xūyào	v/n	4
new semester begins; start classes for a school	開學	开学	kāi xué	vo/n	1
new student	新生		xīnshēng	n	1
news	新聞	新闻	xínwén	n	8
next door	隔壁		gébì		6
nice looking	好看		hǎokàn	adj	4
night of the fifteenth of the first lunar month; sweet dumplings made of glutinous rice, eaten on this date	元宵		yuánxiāo	n	12
no matter how	不管		bùguǎn	conj	15
no more than	不過	不过	bùguò	adv	9
no need whatsoever	大可不必		dà kě búbì		19

English	Traditional	Simplified	Pinyin	Part of Speech	Lesson
no sooner...than...	前腳...後腳...	前脚...后脚...	qiánjiǎo... hòujiǎo...		18
no wonder	怪不得		guài bu de		20
no wonder	難怪	难怪	nánguài	v	7
noisy	吵		chǎo	adj	2
normal	正常		zhèngcháng	adj	18
not able to find	找不到		zhǎo bu dào	vc	6
not able to sleep well	睡不好覺	睡不好觉	shuì bu hǎo jiào		6
not an iota; not in the least	毫無	毫无	háowú		16
not as...	不如		bùrú		16
not necessarily	不見得	不见得	bù jiàn de		1
not necessary; no need to	不必		bùbì		16
not sufficient	不足		bùzú		16
nuclear power plant	核電站	核电站	hédiànzhàn	n	20
number of people	人數	人数	rénshù	n	15
nurse	護士	护士	hùshi	n	15
nutrition; nourishment	營養	营养	yíngyǎng	n	16

▲**O**▲

English	Traditional	Simplified	Pinyin	Part of Speech	Lesson
obey	服從	服从	fúcóng	v	15
obtain	得到		dé dào	vc	15
obtain	取得		qǔdé	v	13
obvious	明顯	明显	míngxiǎn	adj	15
occasionally	偶爾	偶尔	ǒu'ěr	adv	8
occupy (a certain position)	居		jū	v	20
ocean	海		hǎi	n	11
of this; for this	為此	为此	wèi cǐ		13
of various kinds	各種各樣	各种各样	gè zhǒng gè yàng		12
off-campus	校外		xiàowài		1
offer sacrifices to	祭祀		jìsì	v	12
often (tendency)	往往		wǎngwǎng	adv	15
oh	噢		ō	exc	7
oh no; shoot; darn	糟了		zāo le		19
oh well	唉		ài	exc	5
oil; oily	油		yóu	n/adj	3
old	舊	旧	jiù	adj	2
older cousin's wife	表嫂		biǎosǎo	n	14
older sister's husband	姐夫		jiěfu	n	15
on-campus	校內		xiàonèi		1
on the body	身上		shēnshang		12
on the contrary	反而		fǎn'ér	adv	8
on the surface	表面上		biǎomiàn shang	adv	12

▼▼▼▼▼▼▼▼▼▼▼▼▼▼▼▼▼▼▼▼▼▼▼▼▼▼▼▼▼▼▼▼▼▼▼▼

English	Traditional	Simplified	Pinyin	Part of Speech	Lesson
on the verge of	瀕臨	濒临	bīnlín	v	19
on the way	路上		lùshang	n	10
once (indicating that something happened before)	曾經	曾经	cēngjīng	adv	9
one of	...之一		zhīyī		12
one part	一部份	一部分	yī bùfen		16
one-sided	片面		piànmiàn	adj	3
only if	只有		zhǐyǒu	conj	16
opinion	意見	意见	yìjiàn	n	5
opinion on public affairs; speech	言論	言论	yánlùn	n	18
opportunity	機會	机会	jīhuì	n	15
oppose	反對	反对	fǎnduì	v	8
opposite	對面	对面	duìmiàn	n	10
optimistic	樂觀	乐观	lèguān	adj	15
or	或		huò	conj	6
order (food)	點(菜)	点(菜)	diǎn (cài)	v	3
order (food); call	叫(菜)		jiào (cài)	v	3
ordinary folks	老百姓		lǎobǎixìng	n	12
organize; organization	組織	组织	zǔzhī	v/n	19
other	另		lìng	adj	8
other	其他		qítā	pr	5
others; they	人家		rénjia	pr	13
otherwise	不然		bùrán	conj	18
otherwise	否則	否则	fǒuzé	conj	9
otherwise	要不然		yàobùrán	conj	3
out of work; lose one's job	失業	失业	shī yè	vo	20
outgoing	開朗	开朗	kāilǎng	adj	7
output	產量	产量	chǎnliàng	n	20
outside	外面		wàimiàn		12
over and over again	再三		zàisān	adv	11
overcoat; long coat	大衣		dàyī	n	19
overlook; neglect	忽略		hūlüè	v	19
owner	老闆	老板	lǎobǎn	n	3
ozone layer; ozonosphere	臭氧層	臭氧层	chòuyǎngcēng	n	20

▲**P**▲

English	Traditional	Simplified	Pinyin	Part of Speech	Lesson
painful	痛苦		tòngkǔ	adj	19
painstaking efforts	苦心	苦心	kǔxīn	n	17
paint	畫畫兒	画画儿	huà huàr	vo	14
pant; gasp for breath	喘氣	喘气	chuǎn qì	vo	17
parcel	包裹		bāoguǒ	n	10
parent	家長	家长	jiāzhǎng	n	8
part company	分手		fēnshǒu	vo	14
particle indicating evident and clear reasoning	嘛		ma	p	14

English	Traditional	Simplified	Pinyin	Part of Speech	Lesson
particularly; especially	尤其是		yóuqí shì		18
pass away	去世		qùshì	v	14
passport	護照	护照	hùzhào	n	9
paternal grandmother	奶奶		nǎinai	n	14
patient	病人		bìngrén	n	5
patriotic	愛國	爱国	àiguó	adj	12
pay	付		fù	v	16
pay (for a purchase)	付錢	付钱	fù qián	vo	4
pay a New Year call	拜年		bài nián	vo	12
pay attention to	注意		zhùyì	v	16
peddle; sell at a profit (often derogatory: "traffic in")	販賣	販卖	fànmài	v	18
people	人們	人们	rénmen	n	12
people, the	人民		rénmín	n	20
percent	百分之		bǎifēn zhī		4
perhaps	也許	也许	yěxǔ	adv	3
perish; die out; eradicate	消滅	消灭	xiāomiè	v	18
person-in-charge; preside over	主管		zhǔguǎn	n/v	15
personality	性格		xìnggé	n	7
personnel; staff	人員	人员	rényuán	n	16
petroleum	石油		shíyóu	n	20
phenomenon	現象	现象	xiànxiàng	n	15
philosophy	哲學	哲学	zhéxué	n	5
physical education; sports	體育	体育	tǐyù	n	7
physics	物理		wùlǐ	n	5
piano	鋼琴	钢琴	gāngqín	n	14
pick up	接		jiē	v	3
picky	挑剔		tiāotì	adj	4
pine grove/forest	松樹林	松树林	sōngshùlín	n	20
pitiable; pity	可憐	可怜	kělián	adj/v	19
plan	打算		dǎsuàn	v/n	5
plane ticket	機票	机票	jīpiào	n	9
plate; platter	盤	盘	pán	m	12
play; drama	戲	戏	xì	n	7
poet	詩人	诗人	shīrén	n	12
poetry	詩	诗	shī	n	12
point of view	看法		kànfǎ	n	3
point of view	觀點	观点	guāndiǎn	n	17
point out	指出		zhǐchū	vc	16
police	警察		jǐngchá	n	18
pollute	污染		wūrǎn	v	20
poor people	窮人	穷人	qióngrén	n	16
population	人口		rénkǒu	n	11
position (professional)	職位	职位	zhíwèi	n	15

English	Traditional	Simplified	Pinyin	Part of Speech	Lesson
post and telecommunications office	郵電局	邮电局	yóudiànjú	n	10
post office	郵局	邮局	yóujú	n	9, 10
postcard	明信片		míngxìnpiàn	n	10
power plant	發電廠	发电厂	fādiànchǎng	n	20
precious and rare animals	珍稀動物	珍稀动物	zhēnxī dòngwù		19
pregnant	懷孕	怀孕	huái yùn	v	15
prepare	準備	准备	zhǔnbèi	v	5
pressure	壓力	压力	yālì	n	17
pretty	漂亮		piàoliang	adj	3
price	價格	价格	jiàgé	n	16
price	價錢	价钱	jiàqian	n	4
private individual	私人		sīrén	n	18
private tutor	家庭教師	家庭教师	jiātíng jiàoshī		17
probably	大概		dàgài	adv	15
procedure	手續	手续	shǒuxù	n	1
produce; emerge; give rise to	產生	产生	chǎnshēng	v	18
product	產品	产品	chǎnpǐn	n	16
program (TV, radio)	節目	节目	jiémù	n	7
prohibit	禁止		jìnzhǐ	v	18
prominent; stand out	突出		tūchū	adj	15
prostitute	妓女		jìnǚ	n	18
protect	保護	保护	bǎohù	v	18
protected area; conservation area	保護區	保护区	bǎohù qū	n	19
protest	抗議	抗议	kàngyì	v	19
proud	驕傲	骄傲	jiāo'ào	adj	13
pull out; set aside (time)	抽		chōu	v	14
pure cotton	純棉(的)	纯棉(的)	chúnmián	adj	4
put	擺	摆	bǎi	v	2
put things away in their proper places	收好		shōu hǎo	vc	18
put (things) all over the place	亂放	乱放	luàn fàng		18

▲Q▲

quality	質量	质量	zhìliàng	n	4
quarrel	吵架		chǎo jià	vo	7, 14
quarter of an hour	一刻鐘	一刻钟	yí kèzhōng		3
quicken; speed up	加快		jiākuài	v	20
quickly	趕快	赶快	gǎnkuài	adv	9
quiet	安靜	安静	ānjìng	adj	2
quite	挺		tǐng	adv	7

▲R▲

| race | 賽 | 赛 | sài | v | 12 |
| raise (a child) | 帶 | 带 | dài | v | 15 |

▼▼▼▼▼▼▼▼▼▼▼▼▼▼▼▼▼▼▼▼▼▼▼▼▼▼▼▼▼▼▼▼

English	Traditional	Simplified	Pinyin	Part of Speech	Lesson
rare	稀有		xīyǒu	adj	19
rate; proportion	率		lǜ	n	18
realize; recall	想起來		xiǎng qilai	vc	4
really	真的	真的	zhēnde		2
reason	道理		dàoli	n	1
reason; intellect; rational	理智		lǐzhì	n/adj	18
receipt	收據	收据	shōujù	n	4
receive	受到		shòu dào	vc	18
reform and opening up	改革開放	改革开放	gǎigé kāifàng	v	15
regard males as superior to females	重男輕女	重男轻女	zhòng nán qīng nǚ		15
regardless of...; whether it be...	無論	无论	wúlùn	conj	4
register	註冊	注册	zhù cè	vo	1
register (mail)	掛號	挂号	guà hào	vo	10
regret	後悔	后悔	hòuhuǐ	v	7
relative	親戚	亲戚	qīnqi	n	15
relaxed; rest assured	放心		fàng xīn	vo	10
relaxed; easegoing	輕鬆	轻松	qīngsōng	adj	17
reliable		可靠	kěkào	adj	10
reluctantly (to leave)	戀戀不捨	恋恋不舍	liànliàn bù shě		11
remember; fix in the memory	記住	记住	jì zhù	vc	5
rent (for house or apartment)	房租		fángzū	n	5
rent	租		zū	v	6
rent money	租金		zūjīn	n	6
rent out	出租		chūzū	v	6
repeatedly	反復	反复	fǎnfù	adv	5
reporter	記者	记者	jìzhě	n	3
research	研究		yánjiū	v	19
reserve	訂	订	dìng	v	9
resident	居民		jūmín	n	20
resign	辭	辞	cí	v	15
resign from a position	辭職	辞职	cí zhí	vo	15
resolve	解決	解决	jiějué	v	15
respect the teacher and value the Way	尊師重道	尊师重道	zūn shī zhòng dào		17
rest	休息		xiūxi	v	17
restaurant	餐館	餐馆	cānguǎn	n	2
restrict one's food intake; on a diet	節食	节食	jiéshí	v	16
restriction; restrict; limit	限制		xiànzhì	n/v	18
restroom; toilet	廁所	厕所	cèsuǒ	n	2
result; as a result	結果	结果	jiéguǒ	conj/n	8, 13
retire	退休		tuìxiū	v	14
returning student	老生		lǎoshēng	n	1

English	Traditional	Simplified	Pinyin	Part of Speech	Lesson
reunite as a family	團圓	团圆	tuányuán	v	12
rice (uncooked)	米		mǐ	n	12
right	權利	权利	quánlì	n	18
(it was a) right (decision) to come	來對了	来对了	lái duì le	vc	10
river	河		hé	n	6
river	江		jiāng	n	12
road	馬路	马路	mǎlù	n	2
rob; loot	搶劫	抢劫	qiǎngjié	v	18
rock 'n' roll music	搖滾樂	摇滚乐	yáogǔnyuè	n	7
room	室		shì	n	6
room; living room; an "outer" or more "public" room of a house	廳	厅	tīng	n	6
room where animals are housed	動物房	动物房	dòngwùfáng	n	19
roommate	同屋		tóngwū	n	2
round	圓	圆	yuán	adj	12
route	路線	路线	lùxiàn	n	9
row/paddle a boat	划船		huá chuán	vo	11

▴**S**▴

English	Traditional	Simplified	Pinyin	Part of Speech	Lesson
sacrifice	犧牲	牺牲	xīshēng	v	19
safe and sound	安好		ānhǎo	adj	11
safe; safety	安全		ānquán	adj/n	1
salary	薪水	薪水	xīnshuǐ	n	15
salt	鹽	盐	yán	n	3
save (life)	救		jiù	v	12
save (someone's) life	救命		jiù mìng	vo	18
save (money, time)	省下來	省下来	shěng xialai	vc	5
save money	省錢	省钱	shěng qián	vo	1
famous scenic spots and ancient historic sites	名勝古蹟	名胜古迹	míngshèng gǔjì		11
scented soap; bath soap; facial soap	香皂		xiāngzào	n	4
schedule	日程		rìchéng	n	10
school of engineering	工學院	工学院	gōng xuéyuàn		5
school of management	管理學院	管理学院	guǎnlǐ xuéyuàn		5
school of medicine	醫學院	医学院	yīxuéyuàn	n	5
scientist	科學家	科学家	kēxuéjiā	n	19
scold	罵	骂	mà	v	14
score	比分		bǐfēn	n	13
second (of time)	秒鐘	秒钟	miǎozhōng	n	13
secret	秘密		mìmì	n/adj	11
see a doctor	看病		kàn bìng	vo	16
seek	圖	图	tú	v	4
select/register for courses	選課	选课	xuǎn kè	vo	5
self-aware; self-motivated	自覺	自觉	zìjué	v	17

English	Traditional	Simplified	Pinyin	Part of Speech	Lesson
send (a telegram); pat	拍		pāi	v	10
send by mail	寄		jì	v	10
senior high school	高中		gāozhōng	n	7
sense; meaning	意義	意义	yìyì	n	16
serious; grave	嚴重	严重	yánzhòng	adj	16
serious illness; illness that needs immediate medical attention	急病		jíbìng	n	16
set fire to	放火		fàng huǒ	vo	18
shadow	影子		yǐngzi	n	20
share	分擔	分担	fēndān	v	15
shop	商店		shāngdiàn	n	2
shopping center	購物中心	购物中心	gòuwù zhōngxīn	n	4
shortcoming	缺點	缺点	quēdiǎn	n	17
should	該	该	gāi	av	9
show (plays or movies)	上演		shàngyǎn	v	8
show (plays or movies)	演		yǎn	v	7
sign one's name	簽字	签字	qiān zì	vo	4
silver medal	銀牌	银牌	yínpái	n	13
simply	簡直	简直	jiǎnzhì	adv	17
since	既然		jìrán	conj	9
since	以來	以来	yǐlái	n	7
single parent	單親	单亲	dānqīn		14
sit; travel by	坐		zuò	v	1
situation	情況	情况	qíngkuàng		7
size	大小		dàxiǎo	n	4
skill; capability	本領		běnlǐng	n	17
small Chinese cabbage	小白菜	小白菜	xiǎo báicài	n	3
smoke	吸煙	吸烟	xī yān	vo	3
so; therefore; thereupon	於是	于是	yúshì	conj	4
so long as	只要		zhǐyào	conj	18
so that's the reason; so that's how it is	原來如此	原来如此	yuánlái rúcǐ		20
socialize	交往		jiāowǎng	v	7
society	社會	社会	shèhuì	n	15
sofa	沙發	沙发	shāfā	n	8
something weighing on one's mind	心事		xīnshì	n	7
sometimes	有時	有时	yǒushí		20
sons and daughters	子女		zǐnǚ	n	17
sooner or later	早晚		zǎowǎn	adv	12
soup	湯	汤	tāng	n	3
source of pollution	污染源		wūrǎnyuán	n	20
south	南方		nánfāng	n	12
South Chinese tiger	華南虎	华南虎	Huánán hǔ		19

English	Traditional	Simplified	Pinyin	Part of Speech	Lesson
space	空間	空间	kōngjiān	n	19
special feature; distinguishing feature	特點	特点	tèdiǎn	n	17
specially	特地		tèdì	adv	10
spectacular	精彩		jīngcǎi	adj	13
speed	速度		sùdù	n	13
spend money	花錢	花钱	huā qián	vo	16
spinach	菠菜	菠菜	bōcài	n	3
spirit	精神		jīngshén	n	12
sports meet	運動會	运动会	yùndònghuì	n	13
sports field	體育場	体育场	tǐyù chǎng	n	6
sportswear	運動服	运动服	yùndòng fú	n	4
squeeze one's way down; push one's way off	擠下來	挤下来	jǐ xialai	vc	11
stairway	樓梯	楼梯	lóutī	n	6
stamp	郵票	邮票	yóupiào	n	10
stand in line	排隊	排队	pái duì	vo	10
state	州		zhōu	n	4
stationery	文具		wénjù	n	2
statistics	統計學	统计学	tǒngjìxué	n	5
status	地位		dìwèi	n	15
stay	待		dāi	v	9
steal; pilfer	偷竊	偷窃	tōuqiè	v	18
steam (food)	清蒸		qīngzhēng	v	3
still	仍然		réngrán	adv	18
stipulate; stipulation; rule	規定	规定	guīdìng	v/n	18
story	故事		gùshì	n	11
strange	奇怪		qíguài	adj	10
street	街		jiē	n	6
street mailbox for posting mail	信筒		xìntǒng	n	10
stress	強調	强调	qiángdiào	v	17
stress; pay attention to	講	讲	jiǎng	v	19
strict	嚴	严	yán	adj	17
strike, hit; attack	打擊	打击	dǎjī	v	18
strive to be the first and fear to lag behind; vie with one another	爭先恐後	争先恐后	zhēng xiān kǒng hòu		12
strong	強壯	强壮	qiángzhuàng	adj	13
strong; sturdy (of a person)	身強體壯	身强体壮	shēn qiáng tǐ zhuàng		13
study; read	讀書	读书	dú shū	vo	17
style	樣子	样子	yàngzi	n	4
such as	像		xiàng	v	4
such as; like; for example	如		rú	v	18

▼▼

English	Traditional	Simplified	Pinyin	Part of Speech	Lesson
suddenly	突然		tūrán	adj	11
suffer the consequences of one's own doing	自食其果		zì shí qí guǒ		19
suffocate	憋死		biē sǐ	v	7
suggest/suggestion	建議	建议	jiànyì	v/n	5
suit; fit	適合	适合	shìhé	v	17
suite; set	套		tào	m	4, 6
suitable	合適	合适	héshì	adj	4
sulfur dioxide	二氧化硫		èryǎnghùliú	n	20
summer vacation	暑假		shǔjià	n	1
sumptuous (meal)	豐盛	丰盛	fēngshèng	adj	12
supervise and urge	督促		dūcù	v	17
surgery	手術	手术	shǒushù	n	16
surround; encircle	包圍	包围	bāowéi	v	19
symbolize; symbol	象徵	象征	xiàngzhēng	v/n	12
system	制度		zhìdù	n	16

▲**T**▲

English	Traditional	Simplified	Pinyin	Part of Speech	Lesson
T shirt	T恤衫		tīxùshān	n	4
Taiwan	台灣	台湾	Táiwān	n	16
take a picture	照相		zhào xiàng	vo	9
take a walk	散步		sàn bù	vo	9
take/adopt (measures, methods, etc.)	採取	采取	cǎiqǔ	v	19
take advantage of (an opportunity or situation)	趁		chèn	prep	10
take care of; look after	照顧	照顾	zhàogu	v	15
take responsibility	負責任	负责任	fù zérèn	vo	8
take or bring somebody along	帶	带	dài	v	2
take seriously; view as important	重視	重视	zhòngshì	v	17
talk	談	谈	tán	v	7
tall building	大樓	大楼	dàlóu	n	10
taste	味道		wèidào	n	3
tax	稅		shuì	n	4
teaching; education	教學	教学	jiàoxué	n	17
team	隊	队	duì	n	13
technology	技術	技术	jìshù	n	14
telegram	電報	电报	diànbào	n	10
temper; temperament	脾氣	脾气	píqi	n	7
tender	嫩		nèn	adj	3
tens of thousands	成千上萬	成千上万	chéng qiān shàng wàn		13
tense; nervous	緊張	紧张	jǐnzhāng	adj	13
terrible	可怕		kěpà	adj	9
terrible	厲害	厉害	lìhai	adj	7

English	Traditional	Simplified	Pinyin	Part of Speech	Lesson
that manner; that kind	那樣	那样	nàyáng	pr	8
that's true	到也是		dào yě shì		13
the extreme; an extreme	極端	极端	jíduān	adj	17
the law	法律		fǎlǜ	n	18
theater buff	戲迷	戏迷	xì mí	n	7
then; after that; next	然後	然后	ránhòu	adv	9
there's not enough time (for)	來不及	来不及	lái bu jí		9
thickness	厚薄	厚薄	hòubó	n	4
think about; ponder	思考		sīkǎo	v	17
think erroneously	以為	以为	yǐwéi	v	8
threaten; threat	威脅	威胁	wēixié	v/n	8
three types of waste	三廢	三废	sānfèi	n	20
thrilled to pieces	樂壞了	乐坏了	lè huài le	vc	17
through; by means of	通過	通过	tōngguò	prep	18
throw	投		tóu	v	12
throw	扔		rēng	v	19
to one's surprise	居然		jūrán	adv	14
to the best of one's ability	儘量	尽量	jǐnliàng	adv	19
toilet paper	衛生紙	卫生纸	wèishēngzhǐ	n	4
tombstone	墓碑		mùbēi	n	11
too dreadful to contemplate	不堪設想	不堪设想	bùkān shèxiǎng		20
toothpaste	牙膏		yágāo	n	4
touch; bump	碰		pèng	v	18
tour guide	導游	导游	dǎoyóu	n	9
tourist	遊客	游客	yóukè	n	11
...toward	...過去	...过去	...guò qu	(v)c	10
toward	向		xiàng	prep	8
toxin; poison	毒		dú	n/v	20
traditional; tradition	傳統	传统	chuántǒng	adj/n	12
train	火車	火车	huǒchē	n	9
transport by air	空運	空运	kōngyùn	v	10
transport by sea	海運	海运	hǎiyùn	v	10
transportation	交通		jiāotōng	n	6
travel agency	旅行社		lǚxíngshè	n	9
tropical rain forest	熱帶雨林	热带雨林	rèdài yǔlín	n	19
trouble	麻煩	麻烦	máfan	v/adj	3
trouble and worry about; "to exercise" or tax one's mind over something	操心		cāo xīn	vo	14
try	試	试	shì	v	6
try one's best	儘可能	尽可能	jǐnkěnéng	adv	12
turn to	翻到		fān dào	vc	6
TV channel	頻道	频道	píndào	n	8

English	Traditional	Simplified	Pinyin	Part of Speech	Lesson
▲U▲					
ugly to listen to	難聽	难听	nántīng	adj	7
unable; incapable; 沒有辦法 / 没有办法	無法	无法	wúfǎ		17
unable to bear	忍不住		rěn bu zhù		11
under any circumstance; no matter what	無論如何	无论如何	wúlùn rúhé		17
understand; comprehend	理解		lǐjiě	v	17
unequal distribution of wealth; (lit) "poor and rich are unequal"	貧富不均	贫富不均	pín fù bù jūn		18
unique local product	特產	特产	tèchǎn	n	10
unit (work)	單位	单位	dānwèi	n	16
unless	除非		chúfēi	conj	9
use	使用		shǐyòng	v	20
use	用處	用处	yòngchu	n	12
usual practice	習慣	习惯	xíguàn	n	12
▲V▲					
vacation; vacation period	假期		jiàqī	n	9
valuable	珍貴	珍贵	zhēnguì	adj	19
values; concepts or system of values	價值觀念	价值观念	jiàzhí guānniàn		18
vanity	虛榮	虚荣	xūróng	adj	19
vegetable dishes	素菜	素菜	sù cài		3
very	十分		shífēn	adv	7
vigorously	狠狠地		hěnhěnde	adv	11
visa	簽證	签证	qiānzhèng	n	9
voice	聲音	声音	shēngyīn	n	13
volume of demand	需求量		xūqiú liàng		20
▲W▲					
wait	等		děng	v	7
want to; willing to	願意	愿意	yuànyi	av	5
wardrobe	衣櫃	衣柜	yīguì	n	2
washing machine	洗衣機	洗衣机	xǐyījī	n	2
waste gas or steam	廢氣	废气	fèiqì	n	20
waste residue; solid waste	廢渣	废渣	fèizhā	n	20
waste water	廢水	废水	fèishuǐ	n	20
water and electricity	水電	水电	shuǐdiàn	n	6
way of saying thing	說法	说法	shuōfa	n	3
we	咱們	咱们	zánmen	pr	5
weak	薄弱	薄弱	bóruò	adj	19
wear	穿		chuān	v	4
wear	戴		dài	v	12
week	禮拜	礼拜	lǐbài	n	9
weekend	週末	周末	zhōumò	n	3

▼▼▼

English	Traditional	Simplified	Pinyin	Part of Speech	Lesson
weigh	稱	称	chēng	v	10
well developed (of laws, institutions); sound	健全		jiànquán	adj	18
were it not for the fact that	要不是		yàobushì	conj	14
West	西方		Xīfāng		5
west coast	西岸		xǐàn	n	9
what kind	什麼樣	什么样	shénmeyàng	pr	6
whenever	每當...	每当...	měi dāng		13
wife	妻子		qīzi	n	15
will; shall	將	将	jiāng		20
will work; will do	行		xíng	v	4
willing to	肯		kěn	av	11
win	贏	赢	yíng	v	13
window	窗戶		chuānghu	n	2
wish respectfully	敬祝		jìng zhù	v	11
with black and white sharply contrasted; clear cut	黑白分明		hēi bái fēnmíng		19
without a hitch	順利	顺利	shùnlì	adj	10
woman	女人		nǚrén	n	15
woman	女子		nǚzǐ	n	15
woman; women in general	婦女	妇女	fùnǚ	n	15
women grow old and pearls turn yellow; not as beautiful as before	人老珠黃	人老珠黄	rén lǎo zhū huáng		11
wonderful age (of young girls)	妙齡	妙龄	miàolíng		11
woods	樹林	树林	shùlín	n	6
wool; fleece	羊毛		yángmáo	n	16
woolen sweater	毛衣		máoyī	n	4
work as	當	当	dāng	v	5
work as an intern	實習	实习	shíxí	v	5
work (in an office); open for business	辦公	办公	bàn gōng	v	10
world record	世界記錄	世界纪录	shìjiè jìlù		13
worry	擔心	担心	dān xīn	vo	16
worry	發愁	发愁	fāchóu	v	16

▲**Y**▲

English	Traditional	Simplified	Pinyin	Part of Speech	Lesson
yell and shout	大喊大叫		dà hǎn dà jiào		6
young	年輕	年轻	niánqīng	adj	15
young girl	少女		shàonǚ		11

PROPER NOUNS

English	Traditional	Simplified	Pinyin	Lesson
Adidas	阿迪達斯	阿迪达斯	Ādídásī	4
Anderson	安德森		Āndésēn	6
Boston	波士頓	波士顿	Bōshìdùn	1
California State	加州		Jiāzhōu	8
Canada	加拿大		Jiā'nádà	16
Chicago	芝加哥		Zhījiāgē	9
Chinatown	中國城	中国城	Zhōngguóchéng	3
Dragon Boat Festival	端午節	端午节	Duānwǔ Jié	12
East Asian history	東亞史	东亚史	Dōngyàshǐ	5
Hong Kong	香港		Xiānggǎng	9
Huaqing Springs, a famous hot spring outside Xi'an	華清池	华清池	Huáqīng Chí	11
Huimin (a feminine name)	惠敏		Huìmǐn	14
Imperial Concubine Yang	楊貴妃	杨贵妃	Yáng Guìfēi	11
John	約翰	约翰	Yuēhàn	2
Ke Lin (Colin)	柯林		Kē Lín	1
(South) Korea	韓國	韩国	Hánguó	9
Lake Xuanwu, a scenic lake in Nanjing	玄武湖		Xuánwǔ Hú	11
Lantern Festival	燈節	灯节	Dēng Jié	12
Lantern Festival	元宵節	元宵节	Yuánxiāo Jié	12
Li Zhe (a masculine name)	李哲		Lǐ Zhé	5
Lin Xuemei (a feminine name)	林雪梅		Lín Xuěméi	3
Lingling (a feminine name)	玲玲		Língling	14
Lisa	麗莎	丽莎	Lìshā	7
Little Chen	小陳	小陈	Xiǎo Chén	3
Mexico	墨西哥		Mòxīgē	9
Michigan	密西根		Mìxīgēn	13
Mid-Autumn Festival	中秋節	中秋节	Zhōngqiū Jié	12
Nanjing	南京		Nánjīng	9
New York	紐約	纽约	Niǔyuē	19
Olympics	奧林匹克		Àolínpǐkè	13
Qinhuai River	秦淮河		Qínhuái Hé	11
Qu Yuan	屈原		Qū Yuán	12
Sesame Street (TV Program)	芝蔴街	芝麻街	Zhīmajiē	8
Song dynasty	宋朝		Sòngcháo	15
Spring Festival	春節	春节	Chūn Jié	12
State of Chu	楚國	楚国	Chǔguó	12
State of Qin	秦國	秦国	Qínguó	12
Steve	斯蒂夫		Sīdìfū	9
Sun Yat-sen, founding father of modern China	孫中山	孙中山	Sūn Zhōngshān	11

English	Traditional	Simplified	Pinyin	Lesson
Sun Yat-sen's Mausoleum	中山陵		Zhōngshān Líng	11
Taiwan	台灣	台湾	Táiwān	16
Temple of Confucius	夫子廟	夫子庙	Fúzǐ Miào	11
Thanksgiving	感恩節	感恩节	Gǎn'ēn Jié	14
Tianhua (a unisex name)	天華	天华	Tiānhuá	7
Tom	湯姆	汤姆	Tāngmǔ	7
Toronto	多倫多	多伦多	Duōlúnduō	16
Washington	華盛頓	华盛顿	Huáshèngdùn	2
Xi'an	西安		Xī'ān	10
Zhang Tianming (a masculine name)	張天明	张天明	Zhāng Tiānmíng	1
Zhongshan Road	中山路		Zhōngshān Lù	10

三　　　層

Page 21

房屋租售　　雅房出租　　中国城公寓

环境舒适、交通便利　交通便　包水电
快速上网、包水电费　单人单房　$230
请电:425 xxxxxxx　双人单房　$265
　　　　　　　　　　206 xxxxxxx
　　　　　　　　　　425 xxxxxxx

Page 117

電視電影節目表
7月13日（星期二）—7月14日（星期三）

Page 154

▼▼▼▼▼▼▼▼▼▼▼▼▼▼▼▼▼▼▼▼▼▼▼▼▼▼▼▼▼▼▼▼▼▼▼▼▼▼

明　日

中央電視臺

●中央電視臺—1
6:00 走近科學
9:24 連續劇：西游記（縮編版）
（22-24）
12:38 今日說法
●中央電視臺—新聞頻道
6:30 媒體廣場
11:00 整點新聞
12:00 新聞 30 分
●中央電視臺—2
9:00 中國證券
9:48 健康之路
10:43 廣告經濟信息中心特別節目
12:00 全球資訊榜
●中央電視臺—3
7:45 文化訪談錄
8:20 中國音樂電視
9:05 劇場：東北一家人（38-40）
11:55 曲苑雜壇
12:30 快樂驛站
12:45 曲苑雜壇
●中央電視臺—4
7:10 探索 · 發現
8:00 新聞 60 分
9:00 連續劇：表演系的故事（8）
10:15 動畫城
11:10 走遍中國
●中央電視臺—5
6:00 健身房
9:00 早安中國
10:00 實況錄像：2005 年焦作 U17 乒乓球挑戰賽
●中央電視臺—6
6:51 故事片：東歸英雄傳
8:36 故事片：神女峰的迷霧
12:59 紀錄片長廊：飲食文化：世界蛋糕縱覽：澳門
●中央電視臺—7
7:30 科技博覽
8:30 動畫城
9:19 智慧樹
11:30 人與自然
12:30 致富經

●中央電視臺—8
6:00 每日佳藝（佳藝劇場）：隱秘的激情（第二部）（20）（哥倫比亞）
7:46 連續劇：再見阿郎（55-58）
11:38 連續劇：閑人馬大姐（133、134)
12:51 魅力 100 分：武裝特警（5、6）
●中央電視臺—10
7:55 教科文行動之科學發現篇
9:35 走近科學
10:05 教科文行動
11:05 科技之光
12:05 地圖上的故事
12:15 希望 · 英語雜志
●中央電視臺—11
6:00 九州大戲臺
7:35 名段欣賞
8:45 九州大戲臺（地方版）：越劇：灰闌記（周燕萍、鄭曼麗、李寶嬴主演）
12:05 跟我學
12:40 名段欣賞
●中央電視臺 -12
8:15 大家看法
8:35 道德觀察
9:00 第一綫
10:25 法治視界
12:00 中國法治報道
12:30 大家看法
●中央電視臺 -少兒頻道
6:00 中國動畫
8:00 中國動畫
9:20 （首播）中國動畫
10:00 動漫世界
10:30 快樂體驗
11:00 中國動畫
12:00 中國動畫
12:30 新聞袋袋褲
●中央電視臺 -（音樂頻道）
10:21 CCTV · 音樂廳（214）
12:40 影視留聲機（214）

北京電視臺

●北京電視臺—1
8:02 世界報道（早間版）
8:40 今日話題
10:50 紀錄

11:30 身邊
11:58 世界報道
●北京電視臺— 2
7:40 連續劇：楊門虎將（24、25）
9:45 天天影視圈）
10:55 每日文化播報
11:35 留聲機
12:10 電影直通車一小人國
●北京電視臺— 3
7:43 世紀之約
8:41 連續劇：仙劍奇俠傳（22-24）
11:22 科技全方位（1249）
12:00 法治進行時（1782）
12:37 印象
●北京電視臺— 4
6:07 連續劇：大馬幫（21、22）
8:00 連續劇：谷穗黃了（28-30）
11:00 連續劇：浴血男兒（16、17）
●北京電視臺 -5
8:20 首都經濟報道
9:57 連續劇：巡城御史鬼難纏（14、15）
12:30 首都經濟報道
●北京電視臺— 6
6:02 棋道經緯
7:35　BTV 賽　場
2004/2005WNBA
11:15 京城健身潮
12:20 足球報道
●北京電視臺— 7
9:10 時尚裝苑
10:07 快樂生活一點通
11:30 生活廣角
12:40 健康生活
●北京電視臺 -8
7:27 七色光
11:00 黃金五分鐘
12:00 開心一刻
12:35 連續劇：苦菜花（13-15）
●北京電視臺 -9
9:05 連續劇：少年包青天（二）（37-39）
12:00 系列片
12:30 都市陽光
●北京電視臺 -10

Page 173

▼▼▼▼▼▼▼▼▼▼▼▼▼▼▼▼▼▼▼▼▼▼▼▼▼▼▼▼▼▼▼▼▼▼▼▼▼

明日好節目

6:02	京城健身潮	BTV-1
7:40	健康生活	BTV-7
7:51	連 續 劇：小丈夫（11-14）	
	江蘇電視臺	
8:35	劇場：軍人機密（32、33）	
	河北電視臺	
9:00	連續劇：醉拳（22-24）	
	福建電視臺	
9:00	動畫片：迷你寵物星	
		BTV-10
9:30	連續劇：說出你的愛（15、16）	
	山西電視臺	
11:55	體育新聞	BTV-6

Page 155

全國主要城市今日天氣

哈爾濱	晴	20-26℃	濟南	雷陣雨	22-30℃
長春	多雲	20-27℃	鄭州	雷陣雨	24-30℃
沈陽	多雲	21-29℃	合肥	中雨	25-32℃
天津	雷陣雨	22-30℃	南京	雷陣雨	25-33℃
呼和浩特	多雲	18-28℃	上海	多雲	30-37℃
烏魯木齊	多雲	20-31℃	武漢	大雨	26-31℃
西寧	晴	13-31℃	長沙	雷陣雨	26-35℃
銀川	晴	21-32℃	南昌	多雲	28-36℃
蘭州	晴	20-31℃	杭州	多雲	28-37℃
西安	多雲	26-34℃	福州	多雲	27-37℃
拉薩	陰	15-24℃	南寧	陣雨	27-34℃
成都	多雲	23-31℃	海口	多雲	27-35℃
重慶	多雲	25-33℃	廣州	晴	27-36℃
貴陽	雷陣雨	20-28℃	臺北	多雲	24-36℃
昆明	小雨	18-26℃	香港	晴	28-32℃
太原	雷陣雨	20-28℃	澳門	晴	28-34℃
石家莊	中雨	22-29℃			

Page 177

Page 178

香	港	5300/ 5600	马尼拉		9600
		6600/ 7500	吉隆坡		9200
澳	门	5900/ 6400	槟	城	9200
深	圳	9300	汉	城	9000/10000
上	海	13300/13000	东	京	11000/11300
		14200/14600	大	阪	9100/11400
厦	门	10600/11800	美	西	23000
		11900	洛杉矶		20000/21000
福	州	11800/12400			25700
杭	州	13400/14700	旧金山		20000
宁	波	14700	纽	约	20000
北	京	16900/18200	温哥华		22000
曼	谷	5800/ 7300	欧	洲	24500/25500
新加坡		9200/11000	澳	洲	22000

▲以上报价均为现金价(不含 各地机场税、兵险费、安检费、燃料费)
★代办出国手续、各国签证、各国订房、各航空公司自由行、半自助旅游，专业人员为您作最精致的安排!

Page 179

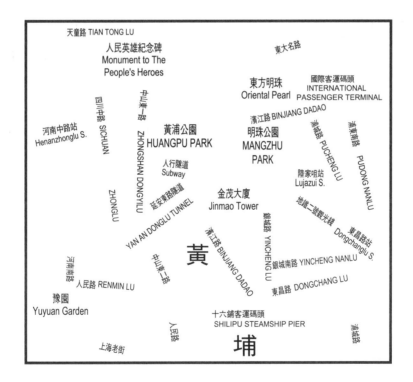

Page 218

民生东路
捷运双连站
重庆北路
中山北路
松江路
建国北路
长春路
台北捷运站
火车站
南京东路
新光三越
忠孝西路
中山南路
重庆南路
介寿路
信义路

Page 220

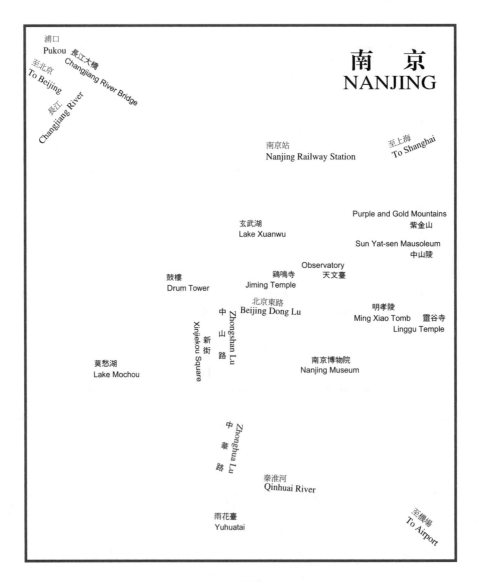

浦口
Pukou
至北京
To Beijing
长江大橋
Changjiang River Bridge
長江
Changjiang River

南 京
NANJING

南京站
Nanjing Railway Station
至上海
To Shanghai

Purple and Gold Mountains
紫金山
玄武湖
Lake Xuanwu
Sun Yat-sen Mausoleum
中山陵
Observatory
天文臺
鼓樓
Drum Tower
鷄鳴寺
Jiming Temple
北京東路
Beijing Dong Lu
明孝陵
Ming Xiao Tomb
靈谷寺
Linggu Temple
中山路
Zhongshan Lu
新街
Xinjiekou Square
莫愁湖
Lake Mochou
南京博物院
Nanjing Museum
中華路
Zhonghua Lu
秦淮河
Qinhuai River
雨花臺
Yuhuatai
至機場
To Airport

Page 235

（美东时间）

31日（周四）战绩

亚特兰大胜犹他 105:98
华府胜波士顿 114:69
沙加缅度胜波特兰 100:72

Page 284

卫视体育

02-273430✱✱

0700 2004美国网球公开赛
1030 FIM世界摩托车锦标赛
1200 SAMSUNG国家杯马术赛
1300 2004年雅典奥运会
2300 2004美国网球公开赛
0500 FIM世界摩托车锦标赛

Page 289

Page 419